# DARK RENAISSANCE

Also by Stephen Greenblatt

*Second Chances: Shakespeare and Freud* (with Adam Phillips)
*Tyrant: Shakespeare on Politics*
*The Rise and Fall of Adam and Eve: The Story that Created Us*
*The Swerve: How the World Became Modern*
*Shakespeare's Freedom*
*Will in the World: How Shakespeare Became Shakespeare*
*Hamlet in Purgatory*
*Practicing New Historicism* (with Catherine Gallagher)
*Marvelous Possessions: The Wonder of the New World*
*Learning to Curse: Essays in Early Modern Culture*
*Shakespearean Negotiations: The Circulation of Social Energy in Renaissance England*
*Renaissance Self-Fashioning: From More to Shakespeare*
*Sir Walter Ralegh: The Renaissance Man and His Roles*
*Three Modern Satirists: Waugh, Orwell, and Huxley*

Edited by Stephen Greenblatt

*Shakespeare's Montaigne: The Florio Translation of Essays* (with Peter G. Platt)
*Religio Medici and Urne-Buriall* (with Ramie Targoff)
*Cultural Mobility: A Manifesto*
*The Norton Anthology of English Literature* (general editor)
*The Norton Shakespeare* (general editor)
*New World Encounters*
*Redrawing the Boundaries: The Transformation of English and American Literary Studies* (with Giles Gunn)
*Representing the English Renaissance*
*Allegory and Representation*

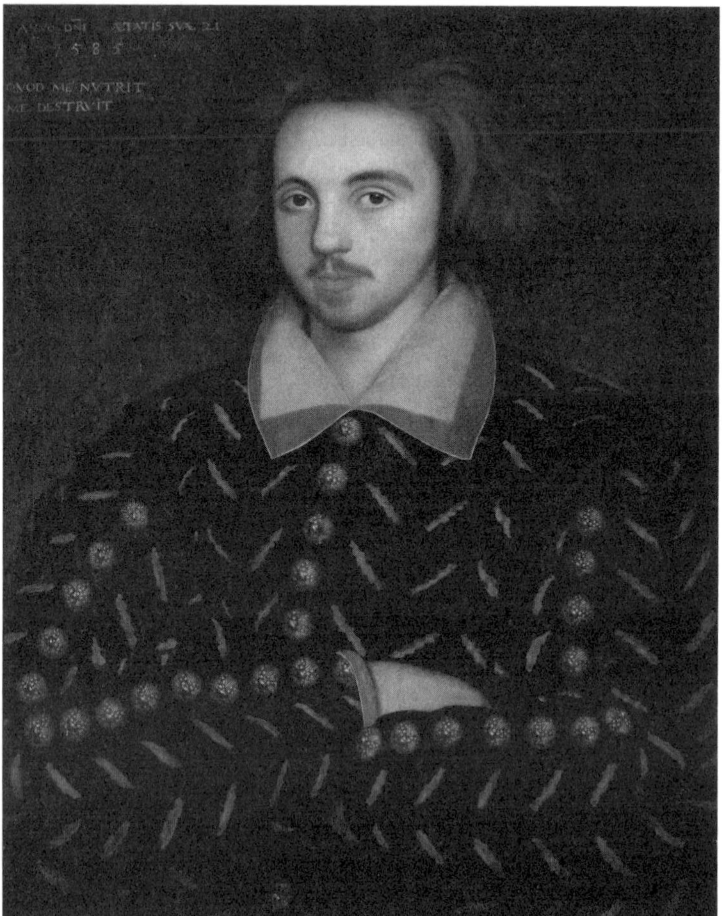
ÆTATIS SVÆ 21
1585
QVOD ME NVTRIT
ME DESTRVIT

# DARK RENAISSANCE

## THE DANGEROUS TIMES AND FATAL GENIUS OF SHAKESPEARE'S GREATEST RIVAL

### STEPHEN GREENBLATT

W. W. NORTON & COMPANY

*Independent Publishers Since 1923*

Copyright © 2025 by Stephen Greenblatt

All rights reserved
Printed in the United States of America
First Edition

For information about permission to reproduce selections from this book, write to Permissions,
W. W. Norton & Company, Inc., 500 Fifth Avenue, New York, NY 10110

For information about special discounts for bulk purchases, please contact
W. W. Norton Special Sales at specialsales@wwnorton.com or 800-233-4830

Manufacturing by Lakeside Book Company
Book design by Marysarah Quinn
Production manager: Lauren Abbate

ISBN 978-0-393-88227-8

W. W. Norton & Company, Inc., 500 Fifth Avenue, New York, NY 10110
www.wwnorton.com

W. W. Norton & Company Ltd., 15 Carlisle Street, London W1D 3BS

10 9 8 7 6 5 4 3 2 1

To Horst Bredekamp

# Contents

1. A World Apart ......................................................... 1
2. Handwriting on the Wall ........................................ 8
3. The Great Separation ............................................. 22
4. The Master's Books ................................................ 38
5. Bright College Years .............................................. 53
6. Gold Buttons ......................................................... 76
7. Recruitment .......................................................... 88
8. In the Liberties ..................................................... 113
9. The Conquest of London ..................................... 127
10. Secret Sharers ..................................................... 141
11. Hog Lane ............................................................ 158
12. The Counterfeiters ............................................. 170
13. Strange Company ............................................... 176
14. Dangerous Acquaintances .................................. 193
15. Wizardry ............................................................ 208
16. The Faustian Bargain ......................................... 226
17. Neptune's Smile ................................................. 253
18. Into the Light .................................................... 268

Acknowledgments ◆ 287

Notes ◆ 291

Index ◆ 319

# DARK RENAISSANCE

*Elizabeth I, "The Rainbow Portrait," c. 1600 (attributed to Marcus Gheeraerts the Younger or Isaac Oliver). Marquess of Salisbury, Hatfield House. The portrait celebrates the elderly queen, with dyed red hair and low-cut gown, as an ageless beauty, while the eyes and ears that decorate her dress suggest her omniscience.*

CHAPTER 1

# A World Apart

To a sophisticated Italian who traveled to England in the late sixteenth century, the island might not have appeared, as it had to the ancient Roman poet Virgil, "wholly separated from all the world." But it would certainly have seemed bleak. To be sure, in London the visitor would have seen many signs of wealth and power: the sprawling royal residence of Whitehall; grand dwellings along the Thames for the leading aristocrats and their entourages; the magnificent abbey at Westminster housing the royal tombs; in the busy commercial center paved streets, some of them graced with beautiful fountains; a brooding fortress, said to have been built by Julius Caesar and used in the sixteenth century as a prison, a mint, an armory, and the site of a royal menagerie. But there was much else that would have given a foreign visitor pause.

The weather was a trial. England, along with much of northern Europe, found itself in the midst of what is now termed the Little Ice Age, with bitter cold winters and fierce storms that destroyed crops and caused periodic famine. The roads were terrible, and after dark they were the haunts of robbers. In London the most popular entertainments were animal fights. Large crowds paid to see a horse with a monkey on its back attacked by fierce dogs. The poor beleaguered horse would gallop and kick; the monkey would scream; the audience would roar. When the exhausted horse collapsed and was killed, it would be time to bring out the bears and bulls, tie them to stakes, unleash the dogs, and repeat the fun. "This sport," remarked a visitor from the Continent, "is *not* very pleasant to watch." In the churches psalms were sung and Mass was celebrated not in the time-honored Latin but in plain English. The Reformation had left other, more tangible marks as well. "It is a pitiful sight," wrote an Italian merchant who kept a journal of his visit to London in 1562, "to see the beautiful marble statues of saints and other decorations there, broken and ruined because of their heresy." In the streets, foreigners were advised to keep a low profile, since the crowds could be suspicious or hostile.

Even hospitable encounters could cause considerable bafflement. If you were invited to dinner, you had to brace yourself. "It is almost impossible to believe," remarked the merchant, "that they could eat so much meat." To wash it down, the English "make a drink from barley and the seeds of hops which they call beer, healthy but sickening to taste." Compared to Italian women, English women seemed unnervingly free: they could go out of the house by themselves, unaccompanied by their menfolk; bustle about in the markets and serve in shops; even go by themselves to public entertainments. "They kiss each other a lot," observed the merchant of the men and women he was observing; "If a stranger enters a house and does not first of all kiss the mistress on the lips, they think him badly brought up." And yet at the same time women deemed to be scolds could be literally muzzled by a horrible device called a brank, and anyone suspected of sexual immorality could be publicly whipped and shamed.

It was disorienting. The mansions along the Strand and the handsome Royal Exchange in the city center gave way almost at once to a vast warren of tenements and hovels. Half-timbered buildings with dormers and gables extended out over the streets, blocking the light and forming malodorous tunnels for the carriages and pack animals and pedestrians to pass through. The narrow lanes were filled with excrement and offal. On London Bridge, alongside shops for luxury goods, the severed heads of convicted traitors were stuck up on spikes for passersby to contemplate.

On the gallows near Tyburn there were public mutilations and hangings almost every day.

The people spoke a language largely unknown to the rest of the civilized world. Virtually nothing written in English had aroused sufficient interest to merit translation into one of the dominant continental languages or into Latin, the shared language of learning. Early in the century an Englishman, Thomas More, had published a brilliant short work in Latin, *Utopia*, that quickly earned him Europe-wide acclaim, but More had been beheaded by the merciless king Henry VIII. Two gifted poets in Henry's court, Thomas Wyatt and Henry Howard, Earl of Surrey, had some success importing and adapting Italian and French poetic models—Wyatt introduced the sonnet form into English—but they too were both snuffed out. Accused of treason, Surrey was executed in the Tower at the age of thirty, and Wyatt, who had been imprisoned on suspicion of having had an affair with Henry's second wife, Anne Boleyn, died at thirty-nine in the wake of a second imprisonment. Their deaths seemed to have had a chilling effect on cultural life.

In sixteenth-century Italy the major universities were all sites of extraordinary achievements: the founding of the first botanical gardens for the scientific study of plants; epochal advances in anatomy and embryology; the positing of germ theory and the creation of epidemiology; a revolution in physics and astronomy. The two English universities by comparison were scientific backwaters. Learned scholars lectured on the ancients Aristotle, Ptolemy, and Galen, but new frontiers of inquiry were kept shut, and the attention of teachers and their students was focused elsewhere. Both Oxford and Cambridge were riven by bitter conflicts, as the ascendant Protestant authorities tried to eradicate any residual loyalty to Roman Catholicism and as more radical Protestants complained that the Reformation in England had not gone nearly far enough.

The religious conflicts had been going on for more than a half-century, ever since Henry VIII's break with Rome, and in their murderous tangles they caught up the lives and fates of virtually everyone in the kingdom. Officially at least, the ruler's religion was the religion of the entire country; no other faiths were tolerated, neither Judaism nor Islam, of course, but also not any version of Christianity other than the ruler's own. In making himself the Supreme Head of the Church in England, Henry's interests lay principally in getting his hands on a divorce and on the wealth of the monasteries. The six-year reign of his son Edward VI, who came to the throne at the age of ten, inaugurated a sharper turn in doctrine and church organization toward Protestantism. Then, after Edward's death from tuberculosis and after an abortive nine-day reign by his seventeen-year-old Protestant cousin Lady Jane Grey that ended in her execution, his sister Mary returned the country to the Roman Catholic Church. Five tumultuous years later Mary died, and with the accession of her younger sister Elizabeth, England once again officially became Protestant. Each of these changes of regime was accompanied by dark waves of conspiracies, suspicions, arrests, and executions, all on top of the ordinary punishments meted out in a brutally punitive society.

It is difficult to take in how nightmarish the situation was, for we have little or nothing comparable in our world. Perhaps the fate of a German family that experienced, in fewer than sixty years, the Weimar Republic, National Socialism, the Communist government of East Germany, the fall of the Iron Curtain and German reunification conjures up something of its unbearable stress and danger. A window into daily life in Tudor England is provided by a rare diary that survives from the mid-sixteenth century. The diary was kept by a merchant, Henry Machyn, who lived in London and took it upon himself to record events around him. On April 21, 1556, to open the pages at random, he wrote that two men, Master Frogmorton and Master Woodall, were taken from the Tower to a courtroom to be tried on charges of "conspiracy against the queen and other matters." On April 24 he noted that six men were "carried to Smithfield to be burned"—Smithfield was a preferred site for executing heretics—along with other men "carried into the country to be burned." Later that same afternoon he observed three men put into the pillory in Cheapside, near London Bridge, one for perjury and the other two for subornation of perjury. On April 28 Frogmorton and Woodall, Machyn noted, were hanged, drawn, and quartered, and their heads stuck on pikes on London Bridge. The next week he recorded more men hauled off to the Tower on charges of treason, more heretics ("one a painter, the other a clothworker") burned, and more malefactors put in the pillory, this time with their ears nailed to the wood. So, interspersed with notations about the outbreak of plague, the diary goes on, page after page, all more or less the same whether the regime was Catholic or Protestant, though of course the faith of those accused of treason or heresy would have been reversed. In such circumstances, in order to keep one's head on, it made sense to keep one's head down.

Henry VIII had separated his realm, already geographically isolated, from the old faith that united most of the rest of Europe, and in 1580 his heretic daughter, nearing fifty years old, sat on the throne unmarried and without an heir. Elizabeth I was not the monster that her father was, but the torturers and the executioners were kept extremely busy. To someone from the Continent, the queen must have looked exotic or perhaps simply outlandish. Her face painted white tinged with pink, her hair dyed bright red, and her teeth turning black, she was periodically paraded, like a weird religious icon covered with precious jewels, before her adoring people. At court richly clad favorites and even sober senior advisers had to address her on their knees and to couch their appeals in the language of romantic love, as if she were an alluring young maiden being wooed by smitten suitors.

Even in her sixties the queen was still at it. Upon being ushered into the Privy Chamber, the French ambassador André Hurault, Sieur de Maisse, was unnerved to find Elizabeth "strangely attired" in what seemed to him a dress of gauze. "She kept the front of her dress open," he wrote in his diary, "and one could see the whole of her bosom, and passing low, and often she would open the front of this robe with her hands as if she was too hot." The following week she received him again, this time in a black taffeta gown similarly slit in front. "She has a trick of putting both hands on her gown and opening it," the startled ambassador noted, "insomuch that all her belly can be seen."

The queen's gambit was quite deliberate; her interlocutors, thrown off-balance, felt they were entering into an unsettling, fantastical world. Her father's court had boasted the presence of the great German painter

Hans Holbein the Younger; Elizabeth would not tolerate any artist so committed to the nuanced depiction of reality. Instead, she patronized as her official painter a goldsmith by training whom she ordered never to use shadows in any portraits of her. She was to remain untouched by time.

It was as if a thick, hardened, protective coating, akin to the heavy white lead-based makeup applied to smallpox-scarred faces, had been spread over all of English cultural life. By 1580, though Elizabeth had been on the throne for more than twenty years, her reign had largely managed to produce among her own subjects only artistic mediocrities. Native English culture seemed as backward in poetry as it was in painting, sculpture, and the life of the mind. An Italian visitor—justifiably proud of Botticelli, Leonardo da Vinci, Michelangelo, Raphael, and others—would have been puzzled to see the miniaturist Nicholas Hilliard trotted out as the leading English painter. What then (if he could read English) would he have made of the leaden versifiers Barnabe Googe, Nicholas Grimald, and Thomas Tusser? Where, he might have asked, were the equivalents in England to Ariosto, Tasso, or Vittoria Colonna? The answer would have been that they did not exist, and there seemed little prospect that they ever would.

An alert observer in search of signs of cultural life in this wasteland might have noticed—alongside the bearbaiting pits and other venues for blood sports—a novel round structure that had been erected only a few years earlier in the rough area east of the city called Shoreditch. Called simply The Theatre, it was the first freestanding playhouse that had been built in England since ancient Roman times, and it was successful enough to have led to the construction of a second playhouse, The Curtain, a few hundred yards away. But to a visitor accustomed to such sophisticated entertainments of the Italian courts as Ariosto's comedy *Cassaria* or Tasso's pastoral romance *Aminta*, nothing that went on within the walls of these wooden theaters would have seemed worth the risk of exposure to pickpockets or worse. The plays were incredibly crude, and besides, the playhouses had been built in the suburbs because the authorities had expelled the playing companies from the city center in order to reduce the spread of deadly bubonic plague.

Then, not instantly but with startling rapidity, it all changed. The coating that had hardened over the realm's culture cracked. If four hundred years later we look back on this period as an astonishing time, it is because of what burst forth in the decades after 1580: a constellation of brilliant poets, the greatest dramatists in the English language, extraordinary advances in navigation, astronomy, and mathematics, the first attempts to establish English colonies in the New World, and in intellectual life, the speculative and experimental daring that led Francis Bacon to declare that "knowledge itself is power." There is no single explanation for an explosion of creative energy of this magnitude, yet one remarkable figure embodies the ferocious energy and daring that brought England, belatedly, into the creative cultural turmoil that had been transforming the Continent for more than a century.

Christopher Marlowe was an unlikely person to have played a major role in breaking open the rigid carapace that had constricted the English creative spirit. Born to a poor provincial cobbler, he was murdered at the age of twenty-nine. In those brief, tumultuous years he was a remarkably productive writer—no fewer than seven plays, along with extraordinary poems—but nothing bearing his name was published during his lifetime. No letters, diaries, or drafts in his hand are known to have survived; nor are there any surviving letters addressed to him. He wrote in a society in which the notions of freedom of thought, freedom of expression, and freedom of religion were unknown. Much of what we know about his life and opinions comes from the reports of spies and informants or from testimony extracted by torture. But Marlowe serves as the thread that leads us through a labyrinth of corridors, many of them dimly lit, dangerous, and shrouded with secrets, and finally into the light. In the course of his restless, doomed, brief life, in his spirit and his stupendous achievements, Marlowe awakened the genius of the English Renaissance.

CHAPTER 2

# Handwriting on the Wall

It had been a particularly miserable English spring. The rains refused to let up. The euphoria that had buoyed up the country five years earlier, with the defeat of the Spanish Armada, had long since evaporated; many believed that a new invasion was imminent. The sixty-year-old unmarried queen Elizabeth had no heir and steadfastly refused to settle the issue of succession. There were rumors that terrorist cells—fanatics determined to reestablish Roman Catholicism as the faith of England—would attempt to assassinate her. At the same time radical Protestant agitators were issuing vehement broadsides against the established church. As if this weren't enough, unemployment in London was high, the bad weather portended rising prices and possible food shortages, and landlords were demanding higher rents.

To make this season of discontent still worse, the dread bubonic plague, briefly in remission, had returned with a vengeance. The disease was terrifyingly contagious. Victims would awaken with fever and chills. A feeling of extreme weakness or exhaustion would give way to diarrhea, vomiting, bleeding from the mouth, nose, or rectum, and telltale buboes, or swollen lymph nodes, in the groin or armpit. Death, often in great agony, would almost inevitably follow.

Innumerable preventive measures were proposed, most of which were useless—or, in the case of the killing of dogs and cats, worse than useless, since as we now understand, the disease was spread by rat-borne fleas. In the absence of predators, rats proliferated. The smoke of dried rosemary, frankincense, or bay leaves burning in a chafing dish was thought to help clear the air of infection, and if those ingredients were not readily available, physicians recommended burning old shoes. In the streets people walked about sniffing oranges stuffed with cloves. Pressed firmly enough against the nose, perhaps these functioned as a kind of mask.

Civic officials, realizing that crowds heightened contagion, took steps to institute what we now call social distancing. Collecting data from parish registers, they carefully tracked plague-related deaths. When those deaths surpassed thirty per week, they initiated protective measures. In January 1593, they shut the playhouses and banned public spectacles, collective entertainments, and sporting events. Worship services were the only exceptions, since it was assumed that God would not visit the plague on anyone who was in church praying.

One entirely predictable outcome of the rising tension that afflicted everyone was a search for scapegoats. There were few or no Jews around to blame; the entire Jewish population of England had been expelled in 1290, in the first mass ethnic cleansing in Europe. In the absence of the traditional objects of religious hatred, Catholics were the obvious choice—after all, the state routinely hunted down and killed English priests, trained in overseas seminaries, who had returned to England in order to conduct clandestine masses. The established church also directed anger at Puritans who, agitating for what they saw as a "purer" faith, mocked the bishops and condemned as pagan such popular observances as Christmas and Maypoles. On April 6, 1593, two Cambridge-educated radical ministers were taken from Newgate prison to the gallows at Tyburn and hanged "for devising and circulating seditious books."

But the majority of ordinary Londoners did not seem drawn to interdenominational bloodbaths. Many Protestants had a residual loyalty to the old faith, and in most conforming families, there would have been at least one aunt or brother or cousin who was secretly an ardent Catholic. So too, almost certainly, other family members would have felt that the Protestant Reformation had not gone nearly far enough in England.

The populace in general was more amused than alarmed by the irreverent attacks on the establishment from Puritan separatists that circulated illegally under the pseudonym Martin Marprelate; they did not hold these religious activists responsible for economic hardship or social misery.

The most common target of antipathy was London's small community of resident aliens—"strangers." They were for the most part Protestant refugees, some from France in the wake of the Wars of Religion and the St. Bartholomew's Day Massacre, and others from what is now Belgium and the Netherlands after the Spanish army invaded and set up the Inquisition. The refugees were in general peaceful and hardworking people who dutifully paid the special tax imposed on foreigners and largely kept to themselves. Forbidden to compete in retail trade, they prospered in enterprises like brewing, engraving, and cloth weaving. But though they amounted to only a tiny percentage of the city's population of almost two hundred thousand, they were repeatedly charged with taking away the jobs of native-born Englishmen.

In the unhappy spring of 1593, an anonymous flyer circulated, angrily demanding that the foreigners all be expelled; members of Parliament made speeches about their alleged threat to the economy; drunken louts in taverns muttered about taking action. On May 5 Londoners awoke to see a particularly menacing placard nailed to the wall of the so-called Dutch Church, the church where the Protestant refugees from Roman Catholic persecution prayed.

For almost fifty years this church had been assigned by royal charter to London's community of "Germans and other strangers." But the fifty-three-line poem on the placard, addressed to the "strangers that do inhabit in this land," was a litany of accusations. "Your Machiavellian merchant spoils the state." "Your usury doth leave us all for dead... And like the Jews, you eat us up as bread." "Cutthroat-like in selling you undo us all." *You have caused our rents to rise. Your cheap, gawdy goods drive ours out of the market. You live far better here than you did back where you came from. Our soldiers are sent abroad to fight in your wars. You have forced us out onto the streets. You will make us all starve and die.* As the complaints reached a crescendo, they turned into a chilling warning:

> Since words nor threats nor any other thing
> Can make you to avoid this certain ill,
> We'll cut your throats, in your temples praying.
> Not Paris' massacre so much blood did spill
> As we will do just vengeance on you all.

Our swords are whetted, the placard ended; therefore, "Fly, fly, and never return." It was signed "Tamburlaine."

The Elizabethan state did not take such threats lightly. Apart from whatever sympathy the queen and her advisers may have felt for the plight of Protestant refugees from the Continent, they hated any popular disorder. In 1570, when collective discontent in Norwich, about one hundred miles northeast of London, led to a planned uprising to force the expulsion of the foreign weavers, the agitation's ringleaders were quickly identified and apprehended. They were then made examples of, in the way the authorities most favored to impress on the crowd the consequence of disobedience: they were hanged, cut down while still alive, castrated, disemboweled, and sliced in quarters.

Confronted in 1593 with comparable agitation, the authorities acted quickly. On May 10, the City of London offered a reward of one hundred crowns—roughly five times the average Elizabethan workman's annual income—for the identity of the person who wrote the words on the Dutch Church wall. At their weekly meeting, the Privy Council issued instructions to their officers "to make search and apprehend every person" who might be suspected of having written the libelous placard. The officers were authorized to "search in any of the chambers, studies, chests, or other like places for all manner of writings or papers that may give you light for the discovery of the libelers." And upon finding likely suspects, the order continued, if "they shall refuse to confess the truth, you shall by authority hereof put them to the torture in Bridewell, and by the extremity thereof... draw them to discover their knowledge concerning the said libels." The order was issued on May 11 and was set in motion immediately. The very next day there was an ominous hammering on the door of the writer Thomas Kyd.

The officers who barged into Kyd's rooms were not ordinary constables, the kind in buff-colored jerkins that might seize you for not paying your debts or for disturbing the peace. From their insignia, Kyd would have grasped at once that the business, whatever it turned out to be, was altogether more menacing. These were agents of the Privy Council, the queen's closest advisers, and they were clearly looking for someone or something.

It is possible that the first questions that they asked had to do with the whereabouts of Christoper Marlowe, for the name on the placard, Tamburlaine, was the hero of Marlowe's spectacularly successful two-part play, and its playwright had earned a dangerous reputation for blasphemy and provocation. But though, as poor, struggling young writers, they had once known each other reasonably well, Kyd might have had no idea. Over the past years Marlowe had begun to move in exalted social circles, to which Kyd had no access. As the officers could see for themselves, he was merely a humble scribbler, trying to eke out a living by writing plays and by translating contemporary works from French and Latin.

Kyd was arrested in his workspace. On his table, therefore, there would have been quills for pens, a knife to sharpen them, inkpots, notebooks, manuscripts, correspondence, and possibly a small number of bound and unbound books. (Books were relatively expensive, and Kyd, in his early thirties, was not a wealthy man.) The officers began immediately to gather up the papers on the table, and they proceeded unceremoniously to rifle through the cabinets, open the chests, and sweep up every piece of paper they could find. Attempting to show that he had nothing to hide, Kyd, his ink-stained hands no doubt trembling, obligingly brought them even more. Then and there they set about to read what they had seized.

Kyd was not one of those writers whose manuscripts were indecipherable. He had excellent penmanship and with good reason. He was the son of a scrivener, a professional scribe paid to draw up and copy official documents. To judge from the surviving specimens of his own handwriting, he had mastered his father's craft and probably practiced it himself during slack times. The profession was a reasonably remunerative one—Kyd's father had saved enough money to send him to London's celebrated

Merchant Taylor's School, located near Cannon Street in the commercial heart of the city—but copying was regarded as a mechanical trade and lacked social prestige. Scriveners were mockingly called *noverints*, after the Latin phrase ("Be it known to all present") with which most of their painstakingly inscribed legal documents would begin.

Real gentlemen were not expected to have good penmanship, to write "fair," as it was called; on the contrary, even if they had learned how to do so, they may have deliberately affected a certain casual untidiness. "I once did hold it," Prince Hamlet tells his friend Horatio,

> A baseness to write fair, and labored much
> How to forget that learning, but, sir, now
> It did me yeoman's service. (5.2.34–37)

The yeoman's service in question was the prince's ability to forge the commission that sent his school chums Rosencrantz and Guildenstern to their deaths.

Kyd had no comparable status-consciousness to induce him to hide his manual skills. Though he went to a fine secondary school, he lacked the ambition, or more likely the money, to follow in the path of many of his more privileged classmates and go on to Oxford or Cambridge. Had he done so, he could upon graduation have proudly styled himself a gentleman. Instead, after learning his father's trade, he took steps that any person anxious about rank and reputation would have regarded as rash: he embarked on the precarious path of writing for the professional stage.

An odor of shame hung over London's burgeoning entertainment industry. Religious moralists called the newly built playhouses satanic dens of iniquity; clergymen warned that God reserved a place in hell for those seduced by their sinister charms; civic authorities complained that they were public nuisances, promoting idleness, spreading disease, and causing traffic problems. Unpatronized actors were legally classified as vagabonds, liable to be branded and whipped out of town. At least in the early years, writers for the commercial stage rarely broadcast their names; most plays, when they were published at all, appeared anonymously.

Notwithstanding all the disapproving voices, the public flocked to the theaters by the thousands.

Repertory companies, in fierce competition with one another, had an insatiable appetite for new material, and they were willing to pay for it. The renumeration was sufficient to attract not only socially marginal people like Kyd but also university graduates, at least those who had failed to go on to more respectable careers or had chosen to walk on the wild side. The latter, even when they brazenly flaunted a bohemian lifestyle, shored up their shaky social standing by touting their own higher education and mocking anyone who lacked it. In 1589 the Cambridge-educated playwright Thomas Nashe, in a letter addressed "To the Gentlemen Students of Both Universities," ridiculed upstarts who "leave the trade of *Noverint*" and busy themselves "with the endeavors of art." If on a frosty morning you encountered one of these ignoramuses, "he will afford you whole Hamlets, I should say handfuls of Tragical speeches." In case Nashe's readers failed to identity the specific target of his mockery, he dropped another hint. These scribblers, he wrote, "imitate the Kid in Aesop" who, allured by the wily fox's tricks, tried "to leap into a new occupation." The foolish kid—Kyd—would get just what he deserved. He would be eaten alive.

Why was Nashe so annoyed? Perhaps because the scrivener's son had written a commercially successful tragedy about the Danish prince. Kyd's classmate at the Merchant Taylor's School, Thomas Lodge, also went out of his way to make fun of the white-faced "ghost which cried so miserably at the Theatre, like an oyster-wife, 'Hamlet, revenge!'" (Book hunters for centuries have avidly searched for this precursor of Shakespeare's great tragedy but thus far without any luck.) And much to the annoyance of his better-born and university-educated rivals, Kyd had scored an even greater success with another lurid revenge play, *The Spanish Tragedy*.

Kyd had always been very careful. He wasn't one of those reckless souls who loved to live on the edge: the heavy-drinking Robert Greene, whose mistress was the sister of a notorious London criminal; the sharp-tongued Nashe, who was imprisoned for one of his scurrilous pamphlets; the restless Lodge, who shipped out on a voyage to Brazil and the Strait of Magellan; and above all Christopher Marlowe, who said out loud what no one who wanted to live a long life would venture even to whisper. The scrivener's son showed no such signs of wildness. He was content to stay in the shadows and go about his work. Among the very few contemporary references to him, one simply called him "industrious Kyd."

But there was more to Kyd than met the eye. *The Spanish Tragedy* aroused popular excitement by its sly implication that since the wellborn and privileged are beyond the reach of the law, the less privileged can obtain justice only by taking matters into their own hands. Kyd contrived to convey this radical message safely by locating his tragedy in Spain, England's principal national enemy. The hero, Hieronimo, is an upright judge whose son is treacherously murdered by two men who are so well-connected that there is no hope for the crime to be punished. In the play's mad climax, the father enlists his son's grieving lover to help him kill the two aristocratic murderers before the eyes of the whole royal court. When the deed is done and he is asked to reveal his confederates, he refuses to speak. "Fetch forth the tortures," orders the king; "Traitor as thou art, I'll make thee tell." "Never," Hieronimo replies and then proceeds to bite off his tongue. The tongue, spat out onstage, must have made the audience scream.

The box office receipts for this piece of blood-soaked entertainment were spectacular and remained so for decades. Though the play's author would not have directly profited from the success—the theatrical entrepreneur who had bought the script and owned the rights would reap the benefit—his triumph made him well-known and aroused the jealousy of his fellow playwrights. In 1593, when the officers of the Privy Council arrested him, Kyd was at the top of his game.

His arrest must have taken him by surprise, for Kyd was by no means the most obvious suspect for the officers who were looking for the author of the incendiary verses. The placard's mentions of Machiavelli, of the Jews, and of the Paris massacre would immediately have conjured up someone else: the author of two popular, indeed notorious plays, *The Jew of Malta* and *The Massacre at Paris*. Before the plague forced the closing of the theaters, these plays had been seen by thousands of Londoners. And as was well-known, they were written not by Kyd but by Kyd's famous contemporary Christopher Marlowe. As if the heavy hints were not enough, the placard's signature, Tamburlaine, seemed to give the game away.

The officers could have immediately suspected Marlowe, but they might not have known where to find him. They could have gone to the neighborhood of the Rose Theater, where *Tamburlaine* and other of his plays had been performed, and made inquiries among those—actors, bookkeepers, producers, and the like—who had a professional relationship with playwrights. Marlowe's actual whereabouts may not have been forthcoming—in fact, as surviving records show, he was not in London at the time—but someone could have mentioned that a few years earlier he had shared rooms with Kyd. Hence the unwelcome visit Kyd received.

✦ ✦ ✦

THE SEARCH FAILED to turn up any evidence linking Kyd or anyone else to the Dutch Church libel. But the officers did not come away empty-handed. Somewhere in the pile of "waste and idle papers" that Kyd had handed over to them was a three-page document in which they spotted what they termed "vile heretical conceits denying the deity of Jesus Christ." It was as if they had come to investigate burglary and found evidence of something far worse.

Though the document was written in a fine professional hand, such as that of a trained scrivener, Kyd denied any knowledge of it and had many samples to show that in fact his handwriting was different. But heresy in Elizabethan England was a serious charge, one that carried a death sentence, and ultimately it did not matter whose handwriting it was. The officers arrested Kyd in order to have him explain the presence of the offending pages in his rooms.

The heretical text argued that there was a fundamental contradiction between the Bible's affirmation that God is "Everlasting, Invisible, Immutable, Incomprehensible, Immortal" and the claim that Jesus, who was certainly visible, comprehensible, and mortal, was God. Jesus may have been an inspired moral teacher, the greatest who ever lived, but he was a human being, not the incarnate deity. This argument, the familiar starting point for what would become Unitarianism, was regarded as tantamount to atheism. England in the sixteenth century had repeatedly changed its official religious orthodoxy—veering queasily from Catholic to Protestant to Catholic again and back to Protestant—but the changes never produced a genial spirit of tolerance. On the contrary, each religious regime furiously attacked its perceived enemies, sharpening axes and building terrible pyres in the name of the God of Love. And all the warring parties joined together to persecute anyone who had the temerity to question Jesus's divinity. Though the doubt must have arisen frequently—it springs naturally from the Gospels' moving depiction of Jesus's humanity—it was far too dangerous to express openly, let alone to be written down in documents of the kind found in Kyd's rooms.

Elizabethan plays often featured scenes in which a character, secure, comfortable, and confident, suddenly finds himself in a terrifying situation, without friends and without hope. Kyd had written just such a scene in *The Spanish Tragedy*, and now in real life he found himself in the midst of one. He was hauled off to Bridewell prison to be interrogated. The Elizabethans were technologically backward, by our standards, but they had developed a sophisticated array of techniques for causing pain. Simulated drowning (still favored by the CIA) was much in use, as was hanging prisoners in manacles with their feet not quite touching the ground. Even more feared were the demonic machines: thumbscrews, the rack, which slowly dislocated the limbs, and the scavenger's daughter, which bent the body in upon itself until it formed a circle of agony.

One or more of these methods was likely to have been Kyd's fate, for in a letter written a few weeks later he complained of the "pains and undeserved tortures" that had been inflicted on him. The ordeal caused mental as well as physical injuries. The next year he referred to his "afflictions of the mind," his "bitter times," and his "privy broken passions."

How much Kyd knew about the document that had caused him to be arrested is not clear. A copy of it, made at the time of the arrest, would sit unread in the state archives until a scholar in the twentieth century found it and identified its source. It turns out to have been an excerpt from a perfectly orthodox book published with the government's permission in 1549, more than forty years before the arrest. The book was *The Fall of the Late Arrian* by an English schoolmaster and academic named John Proctor. It had been written not to promote the heretical arguments that alarmed the arresting officers but to refute them. Even the most restrained Renaissance works of theology routinely excerpted or provided long summaries of the positions they intended to demolish. The incriminating document in Kyd's room was simply a handwritten copy of several of the printed pages.

Had Kyd explained the origin of the pages, he would still have had some further explaining to do: Why were those passages copied out? And where was the rest of the book, with its defense of orthodoxy? But the accused man could at least have begun by pointing out that the source was impeccably legitimate, and that fact would have been duly noted on the transcript. There is no such note, so it is possible that Kyd was completely in the dark.

Kyd was living the nightmare he had staged in *The Spanish Tragedy*. Refusing to reveal his accomplices, his hero Hieronimo bites off his tongue and stabs himself to death. Stretched on the rack, the poor playwright could hardly have been expected to follow his own script. To get the pain to stop, he claimed that the heretical pages belonged to his former roommate, who must have left them behind when he moved out.

Who was this roommate? Christopher Marlowe.

On May 30, 1593, less than a month after the placard was nailed to the wall of Dutch Church and only weeks after Kyd's arrest and torture, Christopher Marlowe was killed. He was twenty-nine years old. An official inquest was conducted and ruled that death came about as a result of an argument over the bill ("ye reckoning") for supper. No charges were brought against the killer.

The surviving records do not indicate what Kyd told the interrogators about Marlowe on those fateful days in the middle of May, but it was enough to win his release from Bridewell. We can be certain that they demanded more than just a name. The clearest indication of what he disclosed or at least hinted at during his detention comes in two desperate letters that he sent in June, a few weeks after Marlowe's death. The letters were addressed to Sir John Puckering, Lord Keeper of the Great Seal. Puckering was one of the principal figures on the Privy Council that had initiated the whole investigation into the placard on the Dutch Church wall.

Kyd had not been formally charged with a crime. Released from custody, he must have stumbled back to the room where he had been arrested. But he was facing ruin. Like almost all writers in the period, he depended on the approval and the financial support of a powerful patron. In Kyd's case, the patron was Ferdinando Stanley, Lord Strange, who supported an important theater company. The discovery in the playwright's possession of a document questioning Jesus's divinity had led him to be suspected of heresy, he wrote to Puckering, and now his patron—the man he simply calls his "Lord"—refused to have anything further to do with him unless he could exonerate himself. Kyd does not refer to this patron by name; he assumed, no doubt correctly, that Puckering already knew to whom he was referring.

In his anguished attempt to regain his patron's favor, Kyd struggled to distance himself from the person he had accused of atheism. "My first acquaintance with this Marlowe," he wrote to Puckering, "rose upon his bearing name to serve my Lord, although his Lordship never knew his service but in writing for his players." The two young playwrights then came to know each other, Kyd claims, because they were both working for the same patron's repertory company—hence "our writing in one chamber two years since." They were roommates, but Kyd managed to make it sound like they found themselves sitting by chance at adjacent desks in a writing studio.

Kyd knew at this point that he had to be extremely careful. The authorities' suspicions had been aroused by what they had stumbled across in his rooms, but if Kyd linked Lord Strange to heresy, it would lead to further investigations and would, whatever the outcome, destroy any chance of recovering his patron's favor. Did Kyd's excuse—that he and "this Marlowe" knew each other only because they were both writing for the same patron—implicate the patron in Marlowe's alleged wickedness? Not at all, Kyd claimed, for the patron, his Lordship, did not have any personal acquaintance with Marlowe and did not know his "conditions," as the letter termed them, that is, the opinions that revealed Marlowe to be an atheist. "Never could my Lord endure his name or sight," Kyd wrote, "when he had heard of his conditions." These conditions, he added prudently, would not have squared with "the form of divine prayer used duly in his Lordship's house."

Even if this excuse were accepted, where did it leave Kyd? If he were as innocent as he claimed, how was it possible that he "should love or be familiar friend with one so irreligious"? Here Kyd's writhings, accompanied by a flurry of Latin maxims, become ever more like those of Dickens's Uriah Heep. Neither "for person, qualities, nor honesty," he declares, was Marlowe ever worthy of friendship. Besides, Kyd adds of his erstwhile roommate, "he was intemperate and of a cruel heart."

Ask people who knew them both, Kyd pleaded with Puckering, to verify that he, innocent Kyd, had nothing to do with Marlowe's wickedness. In exchange for favorable treatment and a good word to his patron, he hinted that he might have further information to impart: "If I knew any whom I could justly accuse of that damnable offense to the awful majesty of God or of that other mutinous sedition toward the state, I would as willingly reveal them as I would request your Lordship's better thoughts of me that have never offended you."

Puckering was a tough, wealthy, well-connected lawyer with considerable experience in cases of sedition, conspiracy, and treason. He had been heavily involved in the complex maneuvers that led to the execution of Mary, Queen of Scots. He had interrogated men and sent them to their deaths. He demanded details about Marlowe's opinions and about his associates. Kyd knew that if he gave too many details, he would implicate himself as a willing sharer in those opinions. It would not do for anyone to think that the two were actually intimate or that Kyd had sat by willingly while Marlowe expounded criminal ideas. But having fingered Marlowe, he felt he had to give his interrogator more.

In a second letter sent the same month to Puckering, Kyd wrote that he knew only a few of Marlowe's "monstrous opinions." But even in casual talk it was Marlowe's custom, he said, to jest at the divine scriptures, to mock prayers, and to confute the sayings of the prophets and other holy men. He would "suddenly take occasion to slip out" his wicked notions, Kyd wrote, so that even the most pious person could not escape hearing him disparage Saint Paul as a confidence man or ridicule the parable of the prodigal son or argue that supposed miracles might as well have been done by ordinary mortals. The most startling of Marlowe's alleged opinions was one that Kyd could bring himself to pen only "with reverence and trembling." Marlowe, he reported, had said that "St. John [was] our Savior Christ's Alexis."

The literary allusion is now lost to most of us, but any educated person in the Renaissance would have understood it immediately. In a celebrated poem by Virgil, read in Latin by all students in the period, a shepherd falls madly in love with a beautiful boy. "The shepherd Corydon," the poem begins, "burned for the handsome Alexis." To claim that John was the Savior's Alexis and that he loved him "with an extraordinary love" was to claim that Jesus was a sodomite.

If Kyd was duly rewarded for his report on Marlowe by being restored, on Puckering's recommendation, to the good graces of his patron, it would not have been for very long. By the end of the next year, poor, broken thirty-five-year-old Thomas Kyd was dead.

CHAPTER 3

# The Great Separation

According to Kyd, Marlowe's signature quality—apart from atheism—was suddenness. He would "so suddenly" slip out his wicked opinions that no one could stop him; his "rashness" enabled him to get away with what otherwise would have been severely reprehended; his attempts at "sudden privy [i.e., stealthy] injuries to men" succeeded because they were so quick and unanticipated. The characterization obviously serves as an excuse: how else could Kyd explain why he ever associated with such a terrible person? Marlowe's viciousness must have burst out and taken poor, innocent bystanders by surprise. But it was not only a defensive strategy. There really was something unanticipated, unforeseen, and sudden about Marlowe.

Centuries later, the philosopher Friedrich Nietzsche, reflecting on his own experience, would write, "the young soul is devastated, torn loose, torn out—it itself does not know what is happening. An urge, a pressure governs it, mastering the soul like a command: the will and wish awaken to go away, anywhere, at any cost: a violent, dangerous curiosity for an undiscovered world flames up and thickens to all the senses." Nietzsche called this a "great separation," and something similar lay at the heart of Christopher Marlowe's young life. It drew Marlowe away from his family, his peers, his social class, his religion—the whole inherited set of accommodations to the world that makes life bearable to most people most of the time. It hurtled him toward his destruction. But it also made it possible for him to think and to do extraordinary things.

Driven by some such overwhelming urge, Marlowe found—or in many ways created—what he needed, helping to bring forth key features of the English Renaissance to which he gave supremely eloquent expression. Many of these features—the theater of cruelty, an obsession with otherness, an aesthetic fascination with criminality and violence, and an unconstrained freedom of thought—have become familiar. That familiarity makes them seem like inevitable parts of the landscape of modernity. Yet when they first appeared, they were uncanny, surging up with a suddenness that was the hallmark of Marlowe's brief existence.

The suddenness manifested itself almost from the beginning. Born in Canterbury in February 1564, he was the son of a shoemaker of very modest means. His parents had little or no formal education, and they had no family connections to anyone of higher social standing, wealth, or educational level. Access to education was hardly something to be taken for granted in Renaissance England, a hierarchical society that had no notion of universal public schooling and that was intensely allergic to social mobility. The female half of the population was, with a tiny number of exceptions, excluded from education altogether. Some minimal acquaintance with the ABCs was at least encouraged for boys who could attend (for a fee) what was called a petty school between the ages of five and seven. But then, for most boys, manual labor was expected to begin.

In the ordinary course of things, young Christopher Marlowe—Kit, as he was called—should have settled down to learn his father's trade and then stuck to his last. Though far from successful, Kit's father John had done for himself and his family what a man of his class could reasonably hope to do: mastered a skill and established himself in business. This had not been an easy task. Once a bustling, wealthy city, with enormous numbers of pilgrims annually visiting the shrine of St. Thomas à Becket in the great cathedral, Canterbury had fallen on hard times. Such economic vitality as it possessed was concentrated among the large numbers of Huguenots, French-speaking Protestant refugees, who crowded into narrow lanes near the city center and set up workshops for silk weaving.

From the perspective of provincial Canterbury, John Marlowe too was an "immigrant." Born in the village of Ospringe, about ten miles away, he was counted as an outsider, someone with no claims on any of the conservative city's social networks. Yet in 1564, the year of Kit's birth, he was admitted as a "freeman," that is, a citizen of Canterbury with the right to join a craft guild—in his case, the Shoemakers' Company—and to set up a workshop of his own. He had completed his apprenticeship and could now say with some confidence that he belonged.

Three years before John was made a freeman of the city, he married Katherine Arthur, who hailed from a family of menial laborers in Dover and was therefore also a poor immigrant to Canterbury. Katherine gave birth to a steady succession of children, of whom Christopher was the second. Five of these nine children lived beyond the age of fourteen; Kit was the only surviving son.

The Marlowes were quite a crew. Apart from Kit, there is no evidence of any upward mobility. Margaret married a tailor, Jane (who became pregnant at twelve) married a shoemaker like their father, Anne did the same. Dorothy, the youngest daughter, married an innkeeper, Thomas Graddell, but her husband hardly raised the family's standing in the community. In constant trouble with the law on charges ranging from assault to black-marketeering to the receipt of stolen goods, Graddell was described by a neighbor as a "knave" who "lived only by cozening, shifting, and coney-catching."

Perhaps the Marlowes didn't care. Dorothy was accused of theft and repeatedly charged with failing to attend the obligatory church services. Her sister Anne fared no better in reputation. The churchwardens in her parish denounced her as "a malicious, contentious, uncharitable person." She was, they added, "a scold, common swearer, [and] a blasphemer of the name of God." When already well along in her life, she was accused by one William Prowde of attacking him with a knife and a sword. Even in a culture that had a hypertrophied taste for lawsuits, few comparable charges were leveled against middle-aged women.

This then is the range of social expectations into which Kit Marlowe was born. His shoemaker father rented a house near Canterbury's eastern gate, in St. George's Parish, not far from the cattle market and the slaughterhouses. The gutter that ran down the middle of the street was frequently choked with garbage, privies and cesspits often overflowed, tubs filled with blood and offal from the shambles were wheeled along the lanes. There were recurrent outbreaks of epidemic disease, compounding the already high risks in a world with very few defenses against serious illnesses. In one terrible summer, over the course of a few weeks, plague took the lives of Kit's maternal uncle and aunt, Thomas and Ursula Arthur, along with four of his cousins. A single young child from the family survived and was taken in by the Marlowes.

Since most of the dying in this period was done at home, Kit, like everyone else, must from a very early age have been familiar with death. When he was four, his six-year-old sister Mary, with whom he had no doubt played constantly, died, and some two months later his mother gave birth—also no doubt at home—to an infant brother who did not live long enough to be christened. Two years later his infant brother Thomas died. And this is not to mention all the deaths in the houses of his neighbors and friends and relatives. The bells of nearby St. George's must have tolled constantly, echoing the bells of the other churches, including the great cathedral. This melancholy symphony surely registered somewhere on the child's psyche.

An appraiser's detailed inventory, drawn up after John Marlowe's death, provides a glimpse of the modest circumstances in which Kit grew up. A little table with a set of joint stools (extremely uncomfortable seats much used by Elizabethans), a wicker chair, a plate cupboard, a chest of drawers to hold the sheets and tablecloths, a plain bedstead with a mattress stuffed with coarse wool, trundle beds for the children, blankets, pillows, cushions, rugs, curtains, and the usual array of fireplace tools, chamber pots, and kitchenware ("Item 6 ketles, 2 brasse pots, 2 stupnets [saucepans], 2 iron pots, one chafinge dishe, 6 brasse candlestickes, and a morter with a pestle, one chafer of brasse, a skimmer and a bastinge ladle, and a warminge panne"). Among the very few items that were of more than strictly practical use were ten silver spoons and a "painted cloth" to hang on the wall. In the adjacent workshop, the shoemaker would have kept his most valuable possessions, the tools of his trade.

That trade, practiced well, required fine skills, but they were not the kind of skills that you learned in school. There is no sign that book learning was part of the Marlowes' plan for any of their children, any more than it had been for themselves. Katherine Marlowe signed her will with a mark; John Marlowe managed to scrawl his name on some documents, though on others he simply made a mark. John is likely to have been able to read—and since reading and writing are separate skills, it is possible even Katherine could read as well—but nothing indicates any real facility or interest in letters. Their poet son was an outlier, a mystery.

✦ ✦ ✦

THE FIRST AND in many ways the crucial sign of the great separation came in December 1578, when fourteen-year-old Christopher Marlowe enrolled in the King's School, Canterbury. It was his last possible moment: he was two months shy of his fifteenth birthday, which was the statutory cutoff point for admission. (Students could and often did enroll in the school at the age of nine.) He received a full scholarship—£4 per annum, paid quarterly—which was more than many artisans like his father earned. Admission was a coup. It changed Marlowe's life decisively and forever.

The King's School was a very ancient one in its origins, having been founded in conjunction with the great cathedral and its monastery, but when Henry VIII dissolved all the monasteries and seized their wealth, it had been reconstituted and renamed. Earlier in the century the wealthy citizens of Canterbury had pressed for admission to be reserved only for the children of the gentry. The lower classes, they argued, were more fit "for the plow and to be artificers than to occupy the place of the learned sort." But the Protestant archbishop Thomas Cranmer resisted. "Poor men's children," he replied, "are many times endued with more singular gifts of nature, which are also the gifts of God, as with eloquence, memory, apt pronunciation, sobriety, and such like," than gentlemen's sons, some of whom are "very dolts."

By the founding statutes, the fifty places were meant to go to "poor boys, both destitute of the help of friends and endowed with minds apt for learning." In reality, few truly destitute children were ever granted a place. Support generally went to families with means enough to prepare their sons to meet the high admissions standard and to forgo the money these sons could begin to earn as soon as they left primary school. How the shoemaker's son could have acquired the skills required to pass the rigorous entrance exam and be awarded such a handsome scholarship is a mystery.

Even had John Marlowe been inclined to send his son to school beyond the first few years, he is unlikely to have been able to afford to do so, let alone to hire a tutor to instruct him at home. The shoemaker's family was steadily growing in size, and there were many signs that he was in financial difficulties. In July 1573, he sued one Leonard Browne for debt. In September of that same year, he sued Hugh Jones for debt. The next month he sued Thomas Ovington for damages, and a few days later he told Michael Shaw, a basket maker, "Thou art a thief, and so I will prove thee to be." (Shaw duly filed a suit for slander.) So it continued, month after month, lawsuit after lawsuit.

Under the circumstances, it is difficult to understand how the son of this financially stressed, uneducated man reached the educational level that he would have needed to win the prestigious scholarship at the King's School. He had no social connections to enhance his competitive advantage. The fourteen-year-old Kit must have demonstrated through examination that he could compete with boys who had continued their education after petty school and in many cases had already been in the King's School, hard at their studies, for four years.

Kit must have caught the attention of an educated person who perceived the talented boy's hunger to learn and who generously undertook to teach him. The immediate neighborhood was not promising: the rector of nearby St. George's Church, William Sweeting, was barely literate; he is mentioned in a church report as unable to write a sermon. But the Marlowes lived less than half a mile from the magnificent cathedral that had for centuries been a magnet for the learned.

The cathedral was the center of Canterbury and the site of frequent spectacles, ceremonies, rituals, and popular festivities. As early as he could remember, Kit would have walked, first with his parents and then by himself, up the lane and away from the stink of the cattle market. A stroll down busy Burgate Street would have taken him to the gate that led into the cathedral precincts, which had been the site of Christian worship since the year 597. A visitor now can share what must have been his experience of looking up in awe at the two massive Gothic towers that dominate the west front and, then passing through the portal, entering into the soaring nave that had been built in the late fourteenth century to replace the earlier Norman nave that had in turn been built in the eleventh century to replace the still older structure.

The ancient Benedictine monastery associated with the cathedral had been dissolved by royal command in 1540, but in Marlowe's time, only a generation later, the precincts would still have featured many of the structures—the offices, dormitory, infirmary, herbarium, bakehouse, laundries, stables, and the like—that had served the monks. Farther back in the grounds were the beautiful buildings and lawns of the King's School, where the boy from the filthy lanes near the cattle market would have glimpsed for the first time the gowned students and where he may have suddenly thought to himself, against all likelihood, "This could be me!"

There were many learned priests associated with the great cathedral. It is possible that one of them took notice of Kit and thought that so promising a child might be a candidate for the ministry and therefore should be tutored in order to stand a chance for admission to the King's School. In the 1570s Protestant authorities recognized that for the Reformation to flourish, they needed a much larger cohort of educated clergy. To succeed, they grasped, they would have to draw not only from the younger sons of the gentry—those who could not expect to inherit the bulk of the family property and might therefore be open to a career in the church—but also from the most gifted children of the poor.

Though reading the Bible in the vernacular lay at the heart of Protestantism, training for the priesthood, as for virtually every other profession in the period, demanded the acquisition of Latin. At the King's School, that was the language of instruction and of much of the curriculum. Then as now, acquiring very good Latin is a difficult and often dull task. It requires careful instruction and sustained discipline, whether imposed from within or without. Mistakes were not tolerated; the long Elizabethan school day was punctuated with severe beatings. Learning Latin is not easily compatible with Marlowe's trademark suddenness.

Yet he evidently made his way. Almost certainly he'd have got his hands on a copy of William Lily's 1540 textbook, *An Introduction of the Eight Parts of Speech*, the first officially authorized and by far the most widely used Latin grammar in English schools. Virtually all Elizabethan schoolboys sweated over Lily's book—it is parodied by Shakespeare, among others—and its use extended well into the nineteenth century. It would have been Kit's entry into the language that reshaped his life.

Lily's introduction to the parts of speech—"A NOUN the name of a thing that may be seen, felt, heard or understand [sic]. As the name of my hand in Latin is *Manus*. The name of an house is *Domus*. The name of goodness is *Bonitas*," etc.—was prefaced by a stirring letter of encouragement to young readers who were facing the daunting challenge of memorizing word lists and learning conjugations and declensions. "You tender babes of England," Lily wrote, "shake off slothfulness, set wantonness apart, apply your wits wholly to learning and virtue, whereby you may do your duty to God and your king, make glad your parents, profit yourselves, and much advance the commonweal of your country."

The high-mindedness—Latin as the armor of a stalwart Christian knight of England—extends throughout the textbook, whose motto is "Learn diligently. Love God entirely." Lily conjoined to his grammar lessons a set of "Godly Lessons for Children," quotations and proverbs both in English and Latin designed to fashion a pious, dutiful student, one who understands that learning proper Latin—"As often as you speak, remember that you speak in Latin, and avoid barbarous words as rocks"—is bound up with an ethos of moral discipline:

> Keep away from noise, contention, scoffings, lies, thefts, scornful laughter, and avoid fights.
> Do not say anything filthy or dishonest,
> the tongue is the gate to life and also to death.

The young Marlowe, encountering these lessons, would have grasped that he was enjoined not only to behave himself in school but also to distance himself from the rough-and-tumble games of the children on the muddy lanes of his neighborhood. He would have known as well that he was meant to stay away from boozing houses like the one on High Street called the Vernicle, where his father exchanged dirty gossip with his mates. But already early on Marlowe may have begun to doubt the perfect coincidence of good Latin and good behavior. And so too he may have noticed that though the precepts in his textbook urged him to honor his mother and father, his education was drawing him ever further away from them.

Such separation has been the impact of higher education on working-class families over centuries, but it was particularly acute in an age when schooling beyond its earliest point ceased to be in English. Latin was an impenetrable barrier between the schooled and the unschooled. Since Elizabethan schoolmasters knew perfectly well that most of their charges were not going to spend the rest of their lives delivering orations and improvising Latin poems, their insistence on building the entire curriculum around exhaustive literary training in the ancient language seems strange. To be sure, some of the training would prove useful for those who entered the church or who studied law. But the core texts were neither theological nor legal. Instead of Aquinas, there was Ovid; instead of Justinian, the comic playwrights Plautus and Terence. Distance from direct and immediate utility—what has come to be called relevance—characterized the whole project. That distance heightened the emphasis on submission, unquestioning obedience, and the ability to comprehend an alien world. The system served as an arbitrary, narrow-gauge mesh with which to sift through the entire cohort and identify unusually gifted children, gifted first and foremost in enduring grueling discipline.

For a child born into a poor family, mastering Latin was the key to entering into a new and entirely different sphere of life. Without it, most professions were closed. Law, theology, medicine, government, and international relations all demanded a thorough knowledge of Latin; so too did scholarship of any kind, from physics to philosophy, along with the serious pursuit of poetry and the fine arts. Latin was a bridge on which no one in the Marlowe family had ever set foot. By the age of fourteen, when he entered the King's School, Kit was crossing it.

✦ ✦ ✦

Neither Kit's parents nor his siblings nor virtually anyone he had grown up with would have had much conception of the life he would go on to lead or the literary traces he would leave behind. In 1594, the year after he was murdered, his works began to appear in print with his name on them. The title page of *Edward II* announced that it was "Written by Chri. Marlow Gent." *The Jew of Malta* was printed in that same year, as was *The Tragedy of Dido, Queen of Carthage*, advertised as "Written by Christopher Marlowe, and Thomas Nash. Gent." In 1598, the publisher Edward Blount brought out Marlowe's long, unfinished poem *Hero and Leander*. "We think not ourselves discharged of the duty we owe to our friend, when we have brought the breathless body to the earth," Blount wrote in his prefatory letter. The further duty that the publisher had in mind was the printing of his work, since it would contribute to what he called the deceased author's "living credit." All the posthumously published works that appeared in quick succession were at once commercial enterprises and memorials, ways of honoring the poet and keeping him alive even after the stroke of death.

Over the years someone Marlowe's parents knew might have seen and acquired these books, for such small-format editions of plays and poems, unlike luxury productions affordable only to the wealthy, were usually modestly priced. It is conceivable then that John and Katherine could have held in their hands one or more of their dead son Kit's works. Though Marlowe's mother was not literate, his father might have been able to make his way through what their son had written. In any case, they could certainly have found a neighbor to read them out loud and to tell them that on the title pages their son was described as a "gentleman." But when John Marlowe died in 1605—twelve years after the death of his famous son—the inventory of his belongings, bequeathed entirely to his wife, listed only a single book, the Bible. And when, not quite two months later, Katherine in turn died, her will carefully parceled out every last item of value—each ring and silver spoon and tablecloth—among her three daughters, but the detailed list of her possessions mentions no scrap of writing, in print or in manuscript, by the genius she had brought into the world.

By 1605, when the inventory was drawn up, Christopher Marlowe had achieved both notoriety and fame. Lurid stories circulated about his life, his opinions, and the circumstances of his death. But there were also extravagant tributes. "That pure Elemental wit, Christopher Marlowe," effused one admiring contemporary; "the Muses' darling for thy verse," said another. He had gone "To live with Beauty in Elysium," wrote the poet Henry Petowe, where he would sing "Hymns all divine to make heaven harmony." Michael Drayton, himself a first-rate poet, recognized in Marlowe qualities possessed by "the first poets," that is, the greatest poets of antiquity. "His raptures were / All air and fire," Drayton wrote, adding perhaps a subtle defense of Marlowe's notorious wildness: "For that fine madness still he did retain, / Which rightly should possess a Poet's brain."

But if—as seems unlikely—any of this high-flown praise reached the Canterbury shoemaker and his wife, it might only have confirmed in them the sense that they had lost their son, had lost him well before the knife-thrust that finished him off. The gifts for which their son was celebrated marked an unbridgeable distance from their lives. What had they to do with Elysium or the Muses or the raptures of the first poets? This was the language of a different world, the world of the gentry from which they were excluded and into which their son was initiated when he entered the King's School.

❖ ❖ ❖

IF ENROLLING IN the King's School offered the teenaged Marlowe a thrilling prospect of enfranchisement—a world of possibility beyond the confines of the shoemaker's shop—his thrill must have been qualified by both anxiety and tedium. The school's principal goal was to teach the boys not merely to read Latin but to speak Latin and to write in Latin. Failure to master the language led to expulsion; someone else would be waiting in the wings to lay claim to the scholarship. No matter how quick a student was, the rote memorization and repetition that were the staples of Renaissance education must have seemed endless.

Someone who began, as Kit did, midway through what was called the fifth form (that is, what we in the United States today would call his junior year in high school) was expected, according to the school statutes, to "commit to memory the Figures of Latin Oratory and the rules for making verses." For the best students, this task entailed not merely reciting a vast number of dutifully memorized rules but using them in speeches and poems that were meant to have the ring of the ancient classics. The goal of the education, as one Elizabethan teacher put it, was "to make those purest Authors our own." If the boys could not quite sound like Cicero or Virgil, they could at least try to give the impression that their native tongue was the one spoken fifteen hundred years earlier in Rome. To that end, the school statutes stipulated that during the entire day, students had to speak only Latin or Greek, even at meals and during recess.

The school day was long, but it was not all uninterrupted study. At noon there was a break for meals prepared by the school cook (James Felle, a dubious character accused in 1580 of stealing a ring from a woman in the sex trade). On saints' days and festivals as well as Sundays, there were frequent outings to attend services and to sing in the great cathedral. At Christmastime and other holidays, the students performed plays. In the decade before Marlowe entered the school, these performances included raucous, vehemently anti-Catholic plays by the notoriously quarrelsome ex-monk John Bale ("Foulmouthed Bale," as he was called).

Canterbury, whose archbishop was the leader of the Church of England, was at the heart of the realm's ongoing battle against Catholicism. When Henry VIII broke with Rome, he shut down the city's priory, nunnery, and three friaries, along with St. Augustine's, the rich and ancient Benedictine abbey located just outside the walls. Living very nearby, Marlowe and his family would have witnessed for themselves the fate of the former abbey's buildings, some of them pillaged and then left slowly to decay, others repurposed to become the residence of newly wealthy followers of the king.

There was a still more resonant emblem of the radical assault on the old religion. In 1538, Henry VIII ordered the pillaging of the country's most celebrated devotional site, the shrine of St. Thomas à Becket. The shrine, in the cathedral where Becket had served as archbishop and where he had been murdered in 1170, drew some hundred thousand pilgrims a year. As attested by Chaucer's Canterbury pilgrims, the relics of "the holy, blessed martyr" were believed to possess miraculous powers of healing. When Kit was a schoolboy, there would have been many older people who still remembered when the king's agents marched in with chisels and crowbars to pry out the jewels that encrusted the tomb and to haul off the valuable marble paneling, along with the gold and silver vessels, *ex voto* offerings, and precious ornaments. The hallowed bones were taken out and burned to ashes that were scattered to the wind. The space that the magnificent shrine had occupied was still there, but now, when Kit and his schoolfellows marched through the cathedral, it was conspicuous for its eloquent emptiness.

But none of this was enough for the most ardent reformers. In their view, the struggle had only begun: that was the point of the anti-Catholic plays that the young scholars at the King's School were assigned to perform not long before Kit came on the scene. In Canterbury, Bale thundered, there were far too many popular festivities—bonfires, maypoles, wandering minstrels, Morris dances, parades with piping and drumming, carnivals, May ales, Whitson ales, hobby horses, pageants of Robin Hood and Maid Marion, Hocktide pastimes, St. George's Day celebrations— all stinking of what he called "the old, frantic superstitions of papistry." They needed to be stopped once and for all.

It took time, for these customs and rituals were deeply rooted in the life of the community, but the city authorities, increasingly dominated by a Puritan-leaning faction, came around to the position of Bale. Public dancing in taverns and inns was prohibited; maypoles were pulled down; minstrels were silenced. Some of the festivities lingered in the face of the assault. As late as 1570, when Kit was six years old, "certain Morris dancers of the country" were paid to perform by the mayor of Canterbury. But barely twenty years later, when Kit had become a celebrated London playwright, Morris dancers "with Maid Marion being a boy in woman's apparel" were arrested when they danced in front of the mayor's house.

Though they banned maypoles, public dancing, and gender-bending rituals, the city fathers left disciplinary spectacles in place. Public executions, a feature of every English city of any size, were frequent events. The popular taste for the blood sport of bull baiting—setting fierce dogs to attack and bite a bull tied to a stake—continued to be served by market regulations that prohibited butchers from slaughtering and selling beef until the bulls were baited. Next to the bull stake, a short walk from the Marlowes' house, was the pillory, and next to the pillory was a cage erected to punish women deemed to be too talkative. Women accused of public brawling—and Kit's sisters were prime candidates—could be hoisted onto carts and led through the streets, escorted by the "waits" or town watchmen banging cymbals or beating metal basins. (At the end of the spectacle the shamed women were themselves required to pay the waits for their rough music.) Similar humiliation, sometimes accompanied by public whipping, was meted out to those accused of sexual immorality, seditious speech, or witchcraft. The town records for 1576—when Kit was twelve years old, still living in Canterbury—include a payment "to him that was in the devil's clothes that whipped the man and the woman." One of the Marlowe family's neighbors, John Johnson, made his living by painting paper labels to stick on those carted through the streets.

Apart from punitive carting, basin ringing, whipping, and hanging, public spectacles were strictly curtailed. The annual Feast of Fools, with its mock election of a boy bishop, was abolished, as was the crowning of those who found a bean and a pea in their slices of Twelfth Night cake as festival king and queen. Banned too was what was called wassailing the apple trees, a custom that involved so-called "hood boys" singing and hitting the trees with sticks in order to increase the apple crop. When he was a small child, Kit could have witnessed or even participated in such amusements. But by the time he was at the King's School, many of the festive rituals that had enlivened everyday life in sixteenth-century Catholic Canterbury had been extinguished. Besides, even if they had still been going on, it is difficult to see where he would have found the time to join in. He was busy studying Latin (and soon Greek) from early in the morning until late in the evening, six days a week, with required attendance at Sunday services.

By statute, the headmaster was required to examine all the students every week, "once, twice, or three times and . . . ascertain their progress in learning." Though they had always to beware of the ferule used to beat those deemed lazy or dense, students with money or social position or friends in high places could afford to be somewhat relaxed; upon graduation, assuming that they wanted to continue their education (which many did not), they still had relatively easy access to Oxford or Cambridge. Not so the children of the poor. Those who did not prove their worth risked losing their scholarship to someone else, as a boy named John Elmley, stricken from the rolls in 1578, had evidently lost his to Kit. The only way to stay afloat was to work hard in order to master the complex and demanding Latin skills in versification and rhetorical improvisation.

The school day began at six a.m. with prayers for the queen—in Latin, of course. Classes met six days a week, and apart from early recess on Thursdays and Saturdays, they continued until seven in the evening. "Learning Latin," one of Marlowe's best biographers has written, "was the labour-intensive alternative to indigenous youth culture." Kit, in this account, must have suffered under the coercive educational regime. While he "conjugated irregular verbs, his old playfellows gathered at the Vernicle where they whiled away the hours drinking ale, talking, playing at cards, dice, and shove-groat, or just 'being merry.'" To compound the occasion for unhappiness and barely suppressed rage, there was the daily spectacle of his pampered, privileged schoolmates, children of Canterbury's elite, who could take their tasks less seriously. No doubt they found ways to register the difference between themselves and the son of an impoverished shoemaker.

With all this in mind, it is easy enough to picture the student Marlowe as an older version of Shakespeare's "whining schoolboy . . . creeping like snail / Unwillingly to school." But I think that the evidence points in a very different direction. Marlowe may not have spent any time at all lamenting what he had lost by immersing himself in his studies or wishing that he was playing cards in the ale house. It was not only a matter of the £4-per-year scholarship—a hefty sum for someone of his class—or of the social advancement that he could glimpse on the other side of his education. While the Elizabethan school day seems unbearably long and the pedagogical method cruel, the core of the experience meant something liberating to at least a small number of unusually gifted students. For someone like Marlowe, immersion in Latin—and shortly thereafter in Greek—was the very opposite of constraint. The tasks, to be sure, were demanding, with the absorption of complex grammatical rules, the feats of memorization, and the repetitive exercises. But once they were mastered, a whole world opened up.

CHAPTER 4

# The Master's Books

AN OPEN SECRET lay at the heart of the educational system meant to fashion an educated class to govern the country. The works that were the principal focus of study in Tudor grammar schools, such as the one Christopher Marlowe attended, were often wildly far from reflecting either the everyday practices or the dominant values of English society. Not only were they written in ancient languages that were not used in ordinary affairs and that most of the populace could not understand, but many of the key texts were untouched by faith in Jesus Christ. Therefore they were untouched by the radical transformation of values that Christianity and Christianity's Hebraic roots had brought about: they did not inculcate belief in the universal sinfulness of mankind, the value of suffering, the wickedness of adultery and sodomy, the providential justice of the One True God, and the whole suite of values and prohibitions that underlay the political and social order of medieval and Renaissance Europe.

Instead, Kit and his classmates immersed themselves in works that chronicled the extravagant sexual adventures and internecine struggles of multiple gods, celebrated the lies of Odysseus and the rage of Achilles, held up for skeptical questioning all prevailing notions of virtue and vice, explored a range of competing political and social arrangements, endorsed scientific rationality, and posited the possibility that the universe consisted only of atoms and emptiness. Very little that Kit studied in school during the week could be easily reconciled with what he heard from the pulpit on Sundays and holidays.

Christians had long recognized the problem. The most radically inclined—those who thought of themselves as most fully awakened to the truth—wanted to cancel the whole of pagan culture. In order to be cleansed and to feel safe, they had to discard the inherited works of art, literature, and philosophy. Those works were indelibly stained, and they corrupted those who came under their spell. To teach them to the young and impressionable was unconscionable. It was time, in the name of the redemption paid for by the blood of the Savior, to smash the idols once and for all. "What has Athens to do with Jerusalem?" one of the most radical asked.

But not all the fully awakened felt this way. Many early Christians, especially those whose tastes had been fully formed by gentile culture, wished to continue to use the inherited texts, just as they wished to continue to use the inherited buildings. They intended only to repurpose them. Theologians had a phrase for what they were doing: "despoiling the Egyptians." The phrase refers to the account in the Bible of the exodus from Egypt and particularly of the fact that God tells the Hebrews to "borrow" from the Egyptians whatever treasures they could carry and not return them: "Ye shall spoil the Egyptians" (3:21–23).

The strategy sounds morally dubious—all the more so in the light of the injunction "Thou shalt not steal"—but both Jewish and Christian commentators concluded that God would never have encouraged such actions by his own Chosen People, had they not been entirely appropriate. Some commentators suggested that the word *borrow* must somehow be a misunderstanding. Others claimed that the "borrowed" treasures were morally justified reparation for the enslavement of the Hebrews and their suffering under harsh Egyptian taskmasters. Still others, following Saint Augustine, argued that "borrowing" was actually returning the treasures to the use for which they had originally been created by God. It was not theft but restoration.

Augustine's clever argument won the day. The triumph of Christianity in western Europe brought no officially sanctioned, systematic, large-scale destruction of the kind whose emblem in our own time is the Taliban's dynamiting of the Bamiyan buddhas. Instead of the cancellation demanded by the radicals, there was adaptation and reuse.

In the case of buildings, Christians could use the existing structures (as they did notably with the Doric temple to Athena in Siracusa and with the Pantheon in Rome). They could haul off the statues of the pagan gods and replace them with statues of Jesus and Mary. They could even adjust the image of Venus to make it look like the Mother of God or turn a figure of Hermes into the figure of Christ.

It was more difficult to make such adjustments with texts. In philosophy, an enormous effort over many centuries was made to accommodate Plato and, still more, Aristotle to the fundamental principles of Christian doctrine. In literature, the task was if anything more difficult, since with a great poem, it is extremely awkward to choose one line and discard another or to alter a time-honored myth. But Christian interpreters could always use the intellectual resources of allegory to reinterpret myths as pious parables. It was often a stretch—Jupiter's abduction of the beautiful boy Ganymede was turned into an allegory of divine love—but even the most recalcitrant materials could be refashioned as Christian stories. And if this usually left some residual discomfort, the content of poetry at least could be set aside or excused as mere fantasy, the product of an overheated imagination.

By the sixteenth century, the notion of "despoiling the Egyptians" had become fully absorbed and domesticated in England and on the Continent under the impact of Renaissance humanism. The recovery of any work that had survived from the distant past was celebrated as a cultural triumph for the present. Ancient authors were praised for the purity of their diction, the elegance of their expression, the coherence of their vision. Schoolmasters no longer felt obliged to struggle quite so heroically to make Christian sense out of pagan texts; nor did they often argue, as Augustine did, that they were reclaiming for the true religion what the devil had stolen. They rarely had to ask themselves, "What on earth do we think are we doing? Why are we teaching these things?" The ancient works were simply held up as supreme models of style, and students were encouraged to steep themselves in them, absorb their every nuance, and imitate them as accurately as possible.

Such then was the justification of the Elizabethan grammar school curriculum in which Marlowe was educated. Schoolboys who had endured the rigors of Latin grammar and had worked their way through Cicero and Caesar were rewarded with Virgil's dark epic on the foundation of Rome and a hefty dose of Ovid's *Metamorphoses*, replete with its stories of seduction, adultery, rape, abduction, pederasty, and the infinitely perverse will of the gods.

Is it possible that the schoolmasters did not notice? One of the most famous of them certainly did. In his great educational treatise, *The Scholemaster*, Cambridge-educated Roger Ascham, who tutored Princess Elizabeth in Greek and Latin and continued to read the classics with her after she became queen, advised that beginning students of Latin be taught the Roman playwrights Plautus and Terence. But he acknowledged a problem. Those ancient comedies, he noted, feature only "hard fathers, foolish mothers, unthrifty young men, crafty servants, subtle bawds and wily harlots." And their plots, full of lying, cheating, and sexual assault, are "base stuff for that scholar that should become hereafter either a good minister in religion or a civil gentleman in service of his prince and country." The two playwrights were like painters who depicted "a naked person from the navel downward, but nothing else." And yet earnest, pious Protestant though he was, Ascham was simply overwhelmed by their artistic skill. "As oft as I read those comedies," he writes, "so oft doth sound in mine ear the pure fine talk of Rome, which was used by the flower of the worthiest nobility that ever Rome bred."

Ascham had no solution. However anxious he may have felt, he was too intensely drawn to the masterpieces of Greek and Latin literature ever to give them up or to urge that they be taken out of the hands of schoolchildren. What he did instead was largely to displace his anxiety from ancient Rome onto the Rome of his own time. *The Scholemaster* embarks on a rant against young Englishmen who travel to Italy and return "Italianated." Given the period's violent struggle between Protestants and Catholics, one would expect that the great fear would be that English travelers could be seduced into converting to the Roman faith. But it was cultural more than religious conversion that gave Ascham nightmares. The Italianated Englishman, he wrote, preferred the poetry of Petrarch to the Genesis of Moses, valued Cicero's dialogues over Saint Paul's epistles, and took more delight in a racy tale by Boccaccio than in a story from the Bible.

The problem was not that there was something necessarily wrong with Cicero, Petrarch, or even Boccaccio. It was rather that the pleasure that they offered threatened to unsettle the proper scale of values and even to call into question the Bible's absolute authority. The fallen reader began to "count as fables the holy mysteries of Christian religion." There was a further consequence, something that for Ascham clearly followed from this collapse of the distinction between fiction and sacred truth: those who regarded biblical stories as fantasies made "Christ and his gospel only serve civil policy." That is, the function of religion came to seem entirely social and political.

All this supposedly followed from an Englishman's vacation in Italy. Ascham wanted his readers to know that he had managed to escape the infection. "I was once in Italy myself," he confessed, "but I thank God my abode there was but nine days." "And yet," he added, "I saw in that little time, in one city, more liberty to sin, than ever I heard tell of in our noble city of London in nine year."

This was an impressive tribute either to the wickedness of Italy or to the provinciality of England or both. But the urgency of the declaration seems to reflect the fact that Ascham, born in 1515, made it through the perilous years in which England veered back and forth between Catholicism and Protestantism by signaling his adherence to one or the other side as the circumstances demanded. He had served not only as Elizabeth's tutor but also as Latin secretary to the Catholic Queen Mary. Writing in the 1560s, when the Protestants were securely in power, he gave the impression that he was always an ardent and outspoken reformer, but the reality was that he managed to accommodate himself in the manner of the Italianate Englishmen he so vehemently attacked.

Ascham knew perfectly well that the vast majority of his contemporaries managed to make it through the perilous midcentury changes in regime as he had done, by shifting religious allegiance as the wind blew. But what if it was not only a matter of prudential accommodation? What if the unsettling of values resulted in a more radical response? "Where they dare," he wrote of Italianated Englishmen who had come to regard the Bible as merely a fiction, "they boldly laugh to scorn both protestant and papist."

Ascham tried to come up with a word to describe figures who had been thus perverted. Failing to find the right English term, he turned to the Greek language that he taught and loved. They were, he wrote, "ἄθεοι in doctrine." *Atheoi*, "those without god": the word, taken from Saint Paul's Epistle to Ephesians, did not yet have its familiar English form. The phenomenon itself, Ascham claims, was unknown in England, "until some Englishman took pains to fetch that devilish opinion out of Italy." Italy was a place where a man "shall never be compelled to be of any religion." Such freedom from compulsion was Ascham's worst nightmare. "In Italy in some free city, as all cities be there," he wrote, a person "shall have free liberty to embrace all religions, and become if he lust, at once, without any let or punishment, Jewish, Turkish, papish, and devilish."

The Italy that Ascham conjured up did not exist, not even in Venice, which was famous for its religious tolerance. But it did exist where Ascham himself spent much of his life and where he bore considerable responsibility: in the grammar school curriculum he did so much to shape. There Ovid, Lucretius, and Lucian rubbed shoulders with Thomas More, Erasmus, and Lorenzo Valla, there a young Englishman could experience "free liberty to embrace all religions," and there Christopher Marlowe first encountered the "devilish opinion" that changed his life, the Italy of the mind.

The praises heaped upon Marlowe after his death—he had gone "to live with Beauty in Elysium"; "his raptures were all air and fire"—were not only conventional. His contemporaries saw qualities in Marlowe that reached all the way back to his adolescent studies, when he sat day after day construing verses of Greek and Latin poetry.

Ancient poetry, with its meter based on a complex system of imputed long and short syllables and its challenging word order, posed particular problems for native English speakers. But for a child with a fascination with the way language works, a steep learning curve, and a vivid imagination, the training was anything but tedious. At the point when Marlowe launched himself into the King's School curriculum, the lessons were already focused on Virgil and Ovid. Their electrifying effect on him can be gauged by the fact that those two great poets obsessed him for the rest of his life.

For centuries, sensitive readers had been deeply moved by Virgil's account in the *Aeneid* of the suicide of Dido, after she was cruelly abandoned by Aeneas. Romans used the mythical story to explain the bitter enmity between Rome and Carthage, but Virgil managed to confer on it an enormous pathos. In the fifth century CE, Augustine looked back at the emotion he had once felt (or, as he now thought, had been compelled to feel) for the Carthaginian queen:

> I was forced to memorize the wanderings of Aeneas—whoever *he* was—while forgetting my own wanderings; and to weep for the death of Dido who killed herself for love, while bearing dry-eyed my own pitiful state, in that among these studies I was becoming dead to You, O God, my Life. (*Confessions* iv)

The adult Augustine had some regret for the misdirection of his emotional investment—but still he remembered his tears.

More than a thousand years later, the schoolboy Marlowe experienced only deep delight. The lessons he learned in the King's School taught him to be sensitive to the desire, love, rage, and grief of characters in distant worlds and sensitive too to the poetic resources—the rich sound effects, the deft word choices, the repetitions, the rhythms, the metaphors—that Virgil and others deployed to produce their amazing effects.

In the typical Tudor classroom, the headmaster, or perhaps the students in unison, would have intoned Dido's bitter prayer that perpetual war would befall the perfidious Romans who have abandoned her: *Litora litoribus contraria, fluctibus undas / imprecor; arma armis; pungent ipsique nepotesque*. The teacher would point at someone and ask for a translation: "May shore with shore clash, I pray, waters with waters, arms with arms; may they have war, they and their children's children!" And then the classroom would have rung with Dido's final words, as she throws herself onto the fatal sword: *Sic, sic iuvat ire sub umbras*; "Thus, thus I go gladly into the dark."

Some of his schoolmates no doubt yawned their way through this kind of thing and longed to be anywhere but in school. Not Marlowe. When, a few years after he left the King's School, he decided to try his hand at writing a play, he chose for its subject *The Tragedy of Dido, Queen of Carthage*. The play, possibly written with help from his Cambridge university friend Thomas Nashe and performed by a company of school-age boy actors, has the awkwardness of an early effort, but it also has glimpses of passion and eloquence whose literary origins unmistakably lie in grammar school training.

"Grant, though the traitors land in Italy," the play's seduced and abandoned Dido prays to the gods,

> They may be still tormented with unrest,
> And from mine ashes let a conqueror rise,
> That may revenge this treason to a queen
> By ploughing up his countries with the sword!
> Betwixt this land and that be never league;
> *Litora litoribus contraria, fluctibus undas*
> *Imprecor; arma armis; pugnent ipsique nepotes:*
> Live false Æneas! Truest Dido dies,
> *Sic, sic iuvat ire sub umbras*.

In Marlowe's ears the words from the classroom clearly still echoed, so present to him and so powerful that he chose not to translate them, as if he were sure that his audience would remember them as he did, or as if he feared that in English he could only betray them.

But the central lesson Marlowe learned in the Elizabethan classroom was not that the classics were untranslatable or that the English language could never aspire to their grandeur. On the contrary, a core exercise in the King's School and elsewhere was the challenging task of double translation—from Latin to English and then (after waiting at least an hour) from the English back to Latin. To succeed in doing so—to create passable English verse out of the Latin hexameters and then back to metrically correct Latin—required a firm understanding of the ancient tongue, including many of its most arcane rules, but it also entailed intensive training in the composition of English verse. Why did so many members of the Elizabethan elite—judges, pastors, diplomats, members of Parliament, civic officials, soldiers, merchants, and the like—write poetry (often strikingly good poetry) all their lives? The answer lies in their years of such schoolboy exercises.

The ultimate goal of an Elizabethan grammar school education was the ability to speak with the dead. It underlay all its tedious exercises, its heavy demands, its deliberate self-enclosure within the ancient languages. It justified the central place assigned to literature, since it was preeminently in literature that the spirits of the dead were conjured up into renewed existence. For the majority of students, the whole pedagogical enterprise probably worked as often to crush as to awaken; it left in many only unpleasant memories of beatings at the hands of sadistic schoolmasters. But for Christopher Marlowe, it succeeded brilliantly.

❖ ❖ ❖

IN A SYSTEM in which the students were constantly examined, Marlowe's unusual skills and the intensity of his imaginative engagement would likely soon have come to the attention of the school's headmaster, John Gresshop. Oxford-educated Gresshop had been at the King's School for more than a decade. Unmarried, he lived alone in rooms attached to the school building, a proximity that was highly convenient since his day began early.

As far as is known, Gresshop never published anything—no works of scholarship and no reflections on his pedagogical methods—and neither letters nor other papers of his have survived. In addition to Marlowe, he had during his tenure at the school at least two other students who went on to become writers of some note—the playwright John Lyly and the satirist Stephen Gosson—but none of them left an account of their teacher. In 1580, when Marlowe was in his fifth term, Gresshop died—the cause is unknown—and a detailed inventory of all his possessions was duly drawn up. Along with such items as his "olde spanishe leather Jerkin" (a jerkin was a sleeveless jacket) and his "olde mockadowe cassok" (this particular cassock, a close-fitting tunic, was made from mockado, an inferior type of velvet and old at that), there is a remarkable list of more than 350 books, a personal library larger than those of all but the country's wealthiest bibliophiles. This is clearly where the Oxford-educated Gresshop's passion lay and where most of his income must have gone.

The makers of the inventory systematically went through the headmaster's rooms, keeping count of what was in each one: "In the upper study by the schoole doore (*In primis* in the windowe bookes-xxxvi; Item upon the east shelve bookes-Cxiiii; Item upon a hie shelve westward bookes-xxviii; Item upon a shelfe under that bookes-xxxvi)." They then proceeded to take the books off the shelves, write down the titles, and assign to each a cash value (the *d* stands for *denarii*, Latin for pennies):

> Cicero, *Tusculan Disputations* (English), with the *Offices*—vi d.
> Ovid, *Metamorphoses* (Latin) with the pictures—viii d.
> *Syntax of the Greek Language* (Greek and Latin)—iv d.
> Linacre, *Grammar* (Latin)—viii d.
> Sophocles, *Tragedies* (Greek)—viii d.
> Solinus, *Polyhistor* (Latin)—viii d.
> *A Precious Pearl* (English)—iii d.
> Elyot, *Governor* (English)—vi d.
> Erasmus, *Enchiridion* (English)—iii d.
> Castellio, *Sacred Dialogues* (Latin)—xii d.
> Chytraeus, *Catechism* (Latin)—iii d.
> Sadoleto, *On Teaching the Young* (Latin)—iv d.
> *The New Testament* (English)—xii d.

Erasmus, *On Copia in Things and Words* (Latin)—vi d.
Frisius Gemma, *Arithmetic* (Latin)—iv d.
Nicolò de' Tudeschi (Panormitanus), *Judicial Process* (Latin)—ii d.
Aesop's *Fables* (Latin)—ii d.
More, *Utopia* (Latin)—ii d.
Bede, *Sermons* (Latin)—viii d.
Cranmer, *On Transubstantiation* (Latin)—iv d.

A brief glance at this small excerpt from a single shelf takes us into the world of reading that shaped the culture of the English Renaissance: the New Testament rubbing shoulders with Aesop's *Fables*, Archbishop Cranmer's reflections on transubstantiation sharing a place with Ovid's *Metamorphoses* ("with the pictures"), Sophocles' tragedies together with More's *Utopia*. On nearby shelves were copies of Aristophanes, Chaucer, Petrarch, Erasmus's *Praise of Folly*, and along with other guides to humanist education, Ascham's *Scholemaster*.

This was not the King's School library; this was Gresshop's personal collection. Students in the school are unlikely to have ordinarily been granted access to it. Marlowe's biographers are united in doubting that their subject, only recently admitted to the school, got anywhere close.

And yet. Contemporary accounts suggest, for example, that Thomas More's *Utopia*—in its original Latin—occasionally figured in the Elizabethan curriculum. The children would not have owned a copy, and there was no school library. But this work was on a shelf in Gresshop's personal collection between the *Orations* of the ancient Greek rhetorician Isocrates and the defense of the Christianity by the second-century theologian Theophilus of Antioch. The headmaster may well have taken it down one day and read out to his students a sample of More's elegant Latin prose. *Itaque omnes has quae hodie usquam florent respublicas animo intuenti ac uersanti mihi, nihil sic me amet deus, occurrit aliud quam quaedam conspiratio diuitum, de suis commodis reipublicae nomine.* ("When I run over in my mind the various commonwealths flourishing today, so help me God, I can see in them nothing but a conspiracy of the rich, who are fattening up their own interests.") The only solution, Marlowe and his fellow students would have heard, was to overturn the social order, abolish private property, and create a communist society.

Much of Gresshop's daily work, endlessly drilling recalcitrant teenagers in Latin grammar and composition, must have been unspeakably tedious. But from time to time he almost certainly encountered students who made the whole enterprise seem worthwhile. After innumerable times reading and teaching the *Aeneid*, even Virgil's magic inevitably fades, leaving only the annoyance of what comes to seem almost deliberate dullness on the part of first-time readers. Then someone actually gets it, and the electric current of response passes from the pupil back to the teacher. It is reasonable to imagine that the shoemaker's son was one such pupil, that his quickness and excitement made the teacher's long day somehow feel short.

And what then? If Gresshop was impressed, he could have taken a special interest in his gifted student and guided him beyond the texts that formed the school's standard curriculum. What the headmaster could offer was access to a rare and precious commodity: books.

This may all be a fantasy. But what is not a fantasy is the peculiar intensity of Marlowe's response to his reading, an intensity that, as we have seen, left its vivid trace in *Dido, Queen of Carthage*. His response in that play was not only intense but also strikingly original. There were many moral lessons that Elizabethan teachers claimed could be derived from the *Aeneid*: the triumph of virtue over pleasure; the translation of empire from the East to the West; the supreme obligation that a son owes to his father; and above all perhaps, steadfast religious piety manifested in obedience to divine will. But Marlowe seems to have registered little or nothing of those lessons. Instead he focused almost entirely on Dido's plight in the face of Aeneas' fraud and betrayal.

Marlowe's play did something even more surprising. It opened with a bizarre and deliberately provocative scene, one calculated to exploit the fact, as the title page attests, that it was performed by "the children of Her Majesty's Chapel," a company of adolescent actors. As the play begins, Ganymede, the beautiful shepherd boy abducted by Jupiter in a shape of an eagle and carried into heaven, is sitting on the god's lap and making a request:

> Sweet Jupiter, if e'er I pleased thine eye,
> Or seemed fair, wallèd in with eagle's wings,
> Grace my immortal beauty with this boon,
> And I will spend my time in thy bright arms. (1.1.19–22)

The enamored Jupiter offers the boy whatever he wants. Would he like Vulcan to dance for his amusement, or to be entertained by the Muses, or to have a fan made from Juno's peacock or a featherbed made from down taken from Venus' swans? Ganymede has something else in mind:

> I would have a jewel for mine ear,
> And a fine brooch to put in my hat,
> And then I'll hug with you a hundred times.

Marlowe's delight in shocking his audience is clear. *This* was what the ancient world was about; *this* was the form of desire most treasured by the supreme god; *this*, though we might deny it, was what boys actually learned in grammar school. And perhaps, just perhaps, buried beneath this provocation was the memory of a negotiation from the author's own not-very-distant past. The headmaster possessed something that the young boy wanted, something more precious than a jewel or a brooch.

Even without direct access to the master's books, Marlowe would have encountered at least some of them: pedagogy at the time involved student performances of selected plays and dialogues. Several of the texts on Gresshop's shelves certainly figured in these performances. He owned two copies of Lucian's dialogues, one in Greek and the other in Latin translation, and they were routinely used in grammar school language lessons. Gresshop may even have followed a common pedagogical practice and had the boys perform the parts in the dialogues. Marlowe himself could conceivably have been assigned to read out the words of the cynic philosopher Menippus, conversing in the Underworld with Hermes in one of the best-known of Lucian's *Dialogues of the Dead*, and eager to see the great celebrities of the past. "Look over there to your right," Hermes tells him, "where you'll see ... all the beauties of old." "I can only see bones and bare skulls," Menippus replies, "most of them looking the same." He asks to be shown Helen; "I can't pick her out myself," he complains. When Hermes points to the skull of Helen, Menippus exclaims, "Was it for this that the thousand ships were manned from all Greece, for this that so many Greeks and barbarians fell, and so many cities were devastated?"

Years later, writing his great play *Doctor Faustus*, Marlowe would recall these words but transform them from an expression of dismay to one of ecstasy:

> Was this the face that launched a thousand ships,
> And burnt the topless towers of Ilium?
> Sweet Helen, make me immortal with a kiss.

The influence of Lucian in Marlowe's work is not itself proof that he read him at the King's School, let alone that he would have been allowed into the headmaster's private library. But at least one further tantalizing clue appears in the few handwritten pages that argued against the divinity of Christ, copied from John Proctor's book *The Fall of the Late Arrian*, found in Thomas Kyd's rooms in 1593. Kyd said under torture that they must have been left by Marlowe. Yet this book was not easily available: it had been published in 1549, during the reign of Mary Tudor, and was never reprinted. *The Fall of the Late Arrian* does not even figure among the books in Marlowe's college library at Cambridge. Yet during his time at the King's School, it was on a shelf in Gresshop's rooms.

Since classes were conducted in Latin and Proctor's work was written in English, Gresshop is unlikely to have brought it into the classroom, any more than he would have read to his students poems by Wyatt and Surrey from his copy of *Tottel's Miscellany*. If Marlowe encountered these books during his time at school, it would only have been by the headmaster's special permission. But is it so difficult to imagine the solitary schoolmaster drawn to a remarkable fifteen-year-old? Or the fifteen-year-old avid reader using his seductive powers to gain access to books?

The books, most of them in Latin and Greek with a heavy dose of theology, would hardly seem to be the stuff of adolescent dreams. But to grasp the desire aroused by this library—to take in what it meant, in a heavily repressive culture, to have access to such a range of reading—is to begin to understand the powerful hidden forces at work both in Christopher Marlowe and in his world.

Never mind the pious adjurations of Lily's grammar; the homilies endlessly reiterated in the schoolroom and in church; the blows of the ferule. Possessing Latin and Greek was the key to liberation. The books to which Marlowe was introduced in school, along with the books hidden behind the headmaster's door, offered an escape from the confining orthodoxies with which he and virtually everyone else was hemmed in.

Dangerous things could be said in the ancient tongues that, had they been said in English, would have been severely, even fatally, punished. To possess Latin and Greek was to possess access to a world in which power was revealed in its naked form, without the dress of divine right, in which the social order was examined coolly and objectively, in which the reader was at liberty to choose what to believe and what to laugh at, and in which many religious faiths coexisted and gods could be seen, as one poet gleefully put it, "in sundry shapes, / Committing heady riot, incest, rapes."

The poet who wrote these words was Christopher Marlowe.

CHAPTER 5

# Bright College Years

In December 1580, a few months shy of his seventeenth birthday, Marlowe left Canterbury and headed off to Cambridge to enroll in a university of some eighteen hundred students and faculty, all male, in a town of just under five thousand. In his last year at the King's School, he had applied for and won a prestigious full scholarship, one of several established some years earlier by Matthew Parker, Canterbury's extremely wealthy, powerful, and learned archbishop. The scholarships were for enrollment in Cambridge's College of Corpus Christi and the Blessed Virgin Mary, a small, walled residential college that had been founded in the mid-fourteenth century. This would be Marlowe's new home.

Matthew Parker, who had been a student at Corpus and later became its master, was one of the college's most generous benefactors. Not only did he endow scholarships such as the one Marlowe received, but he also bestowed on the college a mass of valuable silver plate (which still adorns the high table where the masters and fellows dine). He donated something else of still more significance. He gave the college a remarkable collection of books and manuscripts. Parker was a passionate collector, and as one of the principal leaders and enforcers of the Reformation, he was in a position to satisfy his most extravagant bibliophilic cravings. His agents traveled throughout the realm visiting the monasteries that were being dissolved and compiling detailed inventories of their possessions.

Parker therefore knew just where the most precious books, many of them centuries old, were to be found. Some of these he purchased; others he simply took.

After more than 450 years, this collection, one of England's greatest bibliographic treasures, remains completely intact in the college's library, and for a very good reason. The archbishop, who had long made a habit of taking books from monastic libraries and failing to return them, stipulated in his bequest an annual audit. If Corpus Christi were ever found to have lost six large items, or twelve small ones, the entire collection, along with the silver, was to be forfeited and sent to a different college. The audit (which is still observed today) seems to have concentrated the mind wonderfully; to date, no books have been lost. They sit there today on the shelves of the Parker Library, their handsome leather spines stamped in gold with the donor's insignia, an archbishop's mitre.

Christopher Marlowe himself was in effect one among the many gifts—books, silver, and students—that the munificent archbishop bequeathed to his beloved college.

Then as now, the whole concept of universities centered on assembling a cohort of young people who were not fully fixed in their beliefs and then keeping them for years at a significant remove from the surrounding world. A small number of the students at Oxford or Cambridge came from the vicinity, but most found themselves far away from their families and from their familiar social environments. They had to travel what were, given the conditions of the times, substantial distances. In 1549 the roughly 106-mile trip from Canterbury to Cambridge took the Protestant reformer Martin Bucer seven days. Bucer, in his late fifties, may have moved particularly slowly, or he could have been delayed in crossing the Thames between Gravesend and Tilbury. But even an energetic teenager with little money in his pocket to pay for food and lodging along the way would not have been able to make the trip in fewer than three days.

Our current regime of constant communication makes it easy to forget the full force of the separation that was the founding principle of universities. A pile of blue folded air letters that I sent in the mid-1960s from England back to my parents in Boston—long-distance phone calls being far too expensive for my family to indulge in except on the rarest of occasions—bears witness to how recently the whole system has changed. The young man who went to university in the late sixteenth century had well and truly left home. He was cut off from the people who had raised him, knew him intimately, and made plans for his future, and they in turn had no clear idea what he was doing. He had entered a new domain where it was possible to entertain unfamiliar ideas and fashion a new identity. Marlowe was ready.

Oxford and Cambridge consisted of separate colleges, some quite ancient, others of more recent founding, all with high walls and massive gates. What went on outside the walls—*extra muros*, or extramurally— was not the same as what went on inside, around the courtyards, in the dining halls and common rooms, and in the dormitories. Within the college precincts, an all-male society of students and faculty resided together in a world organized on principles quite unlike those in place elsewhere. Marlowe, the son of a cobbler, was there on a scholarship, but he took the same classes, shared the same jokes, and debated the same highly sensitive topics as the sons of earls.

Social distinctions were not entirely expunged. In Corpus Christi and the other colleges, there were marked differences between those known as fellow commoners, wealthy young men who attended college for a few years but did not take degrees; pensioners, who took degrees and paid for their tuition and other expenses; scholars like Marlowe, who held scholarships of various kinds; and sizars, who earned their keep (their "sizes," as they were called) by waiting on tables in the dining hall and running errands for their tutors. Each group generally sat in a different place in the dining hall, and the wealthiest enjoyed some special privileges. Still, in a society that ordinarily insisted on hierarchical distinctions as if they were God-given and indelible signs of identity, student life was relatively egalitarian. The authorities took steps to keep it that way.

In 1585 the chancellor of the university, Lord Burghley, issued an edict spelling out the university's dress regulations. All students were to wear gowns reaching to their heels, and no student was permitted to "wear any stuff in the outwards part of his gown, but woolen cloth of black, puke, London brown, or other sad color." (*Puke*, its current meaning notwithstanding, meant dark purple.) This insistence on relative uniformity of dress had considerable symbolic significance. When in 1517 Thomas More conceived of a radically transformed society in *Utopia*, he began by eliminating all distinctions in clothing: "As for clothes, these are of one and the same pattern throughout the island and down the centuries."

Political radicalism could not have been further from Burghley's intentions, but the regulations at Cambridge and Oxford marked out the university communities as special cases. In the walled courtyards, lecture halls, and rooms for conducting tutorials, debates, and examinations, something counted other than the distinction conferred by high birth. The sons of noblemen and knights could wear round caps made of velvet, while everyone else had to wear square caps of cloth. And yet the drab gowns—"black, puke, London brown, or other sad color"—that everyone had to wear temporarily effaced the differences on which, elsewhere, the peacock splendor of the elite insisted.

College life was a world without marriages, families, or children. Faculty members were required to be unmarried; this restriction, which derived from the monastic origins of universities, would be lifted only in the late nineteenth century. Those who wished to marry and start families had to leave and find positions elsewhere. Throughout their service at the university, they were expected to reside in the colleges, where they served as tutors to the undergraduates. Marlowe's tutor, Thomas Harris, had recently received his MA degree and was probably only a few years older than his charge. Tutors, as the statutes put it, "shall teach their pupils diligently, shall correct them in proportion to their faults, and shall not allow them to wander idly in the town." The students and the tutors to whom they were assigned often lived in the same rooms, sometimes even sharing the same beds. The cohabitation could lead to unusually close and nurturing relations or, on occasion, as in bad marriages, to seething hostility. In seventeenth-century Cambridge, the young John Milton would be whipped by his tutor, William Chappell, and had to be assigned to a different tutor.

Among the people Marlowe would have met when he arrived at Corpus in December 1580 was the college steward Francis Kett. It might have been Kett who led the new arrival, probably half-starved after his long days of travel from Canterbury, to the communal eating place known as the buttery to show him how to draw on his stipend for food and drink. Then he'd have taken Marlowe to the room—a recently converted storeroom on the north side of the old quadrangle—that he was to share with his roommates, Robert Thexton, Thomas Lewgar, and Christopher Pashley. They were all from comparably modest and provincial social backgrounds. Marlowe almost certainly already knew Pashley, the son of a Canterbury weaver; Lewgar and Thexton were from villages in Norfolk, north of Cambridge.

Kett too had come from a small Norfolk village, worked his way through Cambridge by waiting on tables, and been duly awarded both his BA and MA degrees. Settling into the university community, he was elected a fellow at Corpus and ordained as a minister in the Church of England. But at some point in his climb up the academic ladder, he must have begun to chafe against the reigning religious orthodoxy. A year after Marlowe enrolled as a student, he resigned his fellowship and went off to pursue his personal vision of the Christian faith.

This vision was a dangerous one. Kett let it be known that he believed that "Christ is not God, but a good man as others be." These beliefs were similar to those attacked in *The Fall of the Late Arrian*, the book that would lead to Kyd's torture. Denounced by a local clergyman and convicted of heresy, Kett would be taken to a ditch outside Norwich Castle and burned to death. The clergyman who brought the accusation was a witness to Kett's end: "When he went to the fire he was clothed in sackcloth, he went leaping and dancing. Being in the fire, above twenty times together clapping his hands, he cried nothing but blessed be God . . . and so continued until the fire had consumed all his nether parts, and until he was stifled with the smoke."

It is not at all clear that Kett would have shared his views with anyone during his time at Corpus, but all universities are peculiar places, and Renaissance Cambridge and Oxford were more peculiar than most. On the one hand, they were narrowly bounded and constrained. Fully half the population was excluded: this was a strictly all-male world. Excluded too was anyone who was not a Christian. Then anyone who professed Roman Catholicism. Then anyone who was openly at odds with the Thirty-Nine Articles of the Anglican Church. But on the other hand, they were spaces of hidden ferment, of quirky individuals quietly thinking through the meaning of their lives, of unexpected encounters with new ideas.

Around the time when Marlowe arrived at Corpus, fresh from Canterbury, there was a stir that had to have reached him. Robert Browne, a Corpus graduate who had been invited back to preach at the college's own St. Bene't's Church, had a crisis of conscience and abruptly quit his post, arguing that the whole ecclesiastical system was corrupt and that church authorities should be elected by their congregants, not appointed from above. Browne may have already left Corpus by the time Marlowe arrived and began to look around, but in the college and elsewhere, his passionate arguments for radical reform attracted many followers—called Brownists before they acquired the more familiar name Puritans. (The term remained well-enough known in the late 1590s to get a laugh: in Shakespeare's *Twelfth Night*, the ridiculous Sir Andrew Aguecheek declares that he would as soon "be a Brownist as a politician" [3.2.29].)

According to the college's so-called Buttery Books, in which the students' daily food and drink expenses were recorded, one of the best-known Brownists, John Greenwood, was still in residence at Corpus during Marlowe's first year. By the spring of that year, Marlowe had become friendly enough with Greenwood to share his food stipend with him. If Greenwood returned the favor, he may have introduced Marlowe to John Penry, a Welsh-born student in nearby Peterhouse College, and Henry Barrow, an older man formerly at Corpus but now studying law in London. The three friends were highly critical of the official religious settlement. They complained that English churches remained full of statues and paintings and stained-glass windows, all remnants of idolatrous practices that should have been destroyed as soon as the English broke away from Rome. Still worse, the old clerical hierarchy was in effect unchanged: the English bishops, in all their wealth and arrogance and power, were no different from the princes of the Catholic Church. The whole corrupt order needed to be toppled.

The English bishops were no more tolerant of Protestant radicalism than they were of Roman Catholicism. After several years of agitating in clandestinely published pamphlets, all three friends, Greenwood, Penry, and Barrow, were charged with violating a statute that made it illegal to "devise and write, print, or set forth any manner of book . . . , letter, or writing containing any false, seditious, and slanderous matter to the defamation of the Queen's Majesty." The foregone conclusion: they were found guilty and sentenced to death. The day after they were sentenced, Barrow and Greenwood were thrown into a cart, carried to the hanging ground at Tyburn, and marched to the scaffold. They were then told that they had been reprieved and were taken back to prison. A week later they were taken to Tyburn again. The noose was placed around their necks, and they

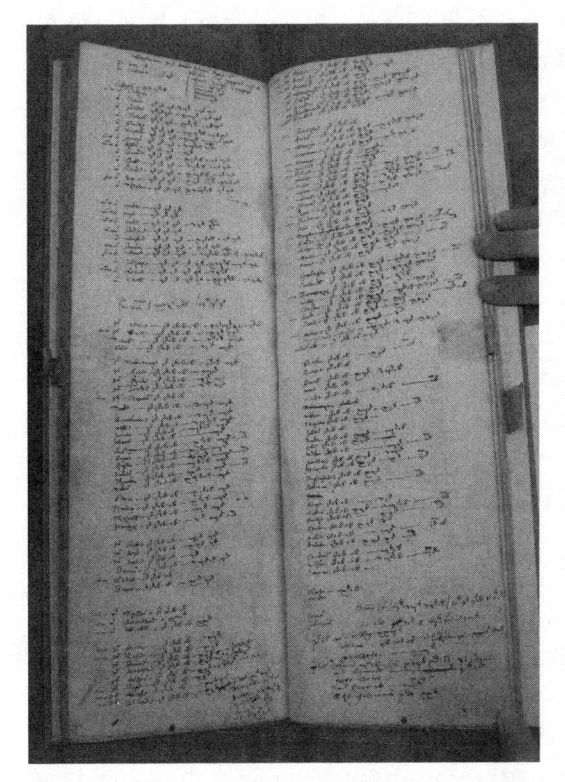

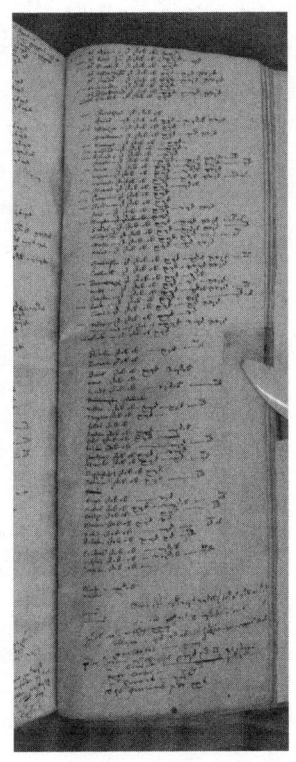

*The Buttery Book at Corpus Christi Cambridge recorded purchases of food and drink, especially beer and ale, by students and staff.*

uttered what they believed were their last words. Once again they were reprieved. A week later they were hauled off to Tyburn, as if to continue the charade, but this time the death sentence was carried out. A few weeks later Penry too was hanged. Their Separatist followers, understanding the fate that was in store for them, began to make plans to escape to more tolerant Holland. In 1620 some of them sailed to America on the *Mayflower*.

Greenwood's tragic end did not occur until years after Marlowe's dinner with him at Corpus, but the issues were already on the table back then in that liminal space where a company of late adolescents were engaged in sorting out their beliefs. The long hours of study in the library and in the lecture hall, the evenings in the dormitory room with Thexton, Lewgar, and Pashley, the times spent drinking with his friends and the whispered conversations with secret Catholics and dissident Protestants all played a part in Marlowe's effort to decide what to do with himself, where his loyalties lay, and what he believed.

In 1583, when Marlowe was already in his third year at Cambridge, the Italian philosopher, poet, and scientist Giordano Bruno, a refugee in England from the unwelcome attention of the Roman Inquisition, received an invitation to deliver lectures at Oxford. The two universities were far enough apart that the news would not have traveled between them instantly, but after a suitable interval Marlowe and his classmates would have heard that Bruno had decided to lecture on cosmology. He not only championed the Copernican theory that the earth rotated around the sun—a theory that almost all senior English theologians and scientists had rejected—but he also made matters worse by proposing that the universe was infinitely large and therefore must contain innumerable other suns and planets, some of which almost certainly hosted rational creatures like us.

To espouse such ideas openly on a university lecture platform struck some listeners as a deliberate provocation. Didn't the Bible clearly say that God stopped the sun from moving—the sun, mind you, not the earth—to enable Joshua to complete his victory over the Amorites? How was it possible that the earth was not the center of the cosmos? Doesn't everything revolve around us? If the universe was infinite, how could you ever hope to locate the right standpoint? Where was up and where was down, or more to the point, where were heaven and hell? And what would the existence on other planets of creatures like us mean for the story of salvation brought to us by the incarnation, suffering, and resurrection of Jesus Christ? Was our savior only an earth-bound hero, one messiah among many?

The reaction from the Oxford scholar assigned to respond to Bruno's argument was so hostile that the lecture series was abruptly halted. "Have them tell you with what uncouthness and discourtesy that pig acted," Bruno complained. On his return to London, he wrote several important philosophical works in which he reiterated his harsh view of English intellectual life. "In this country," he wrote, "there reigns a constellation of the most obstinate pedantry, ignorance, and conceit, mingled with rustic rudeness." Religious dogmas, at war with science, were fables used to intimidate and manipulate the ignorant. As for the reformed faith that had seemed to offer an escape from persecution, Bruno concluded after his experience in England, Protestants were just as bad as Catholics or perhaps worse. However cynical they were, Catholics at least had a compelling set of ceremonies. The more extreme Protestants, by contrast, wanted to strip away whatever was beautiful in the worship service. They celebrated a cruel, vindictive God, one even more detached from the world than that of the Catholics, and they congratulated themselves for their supposed purity. Protestants, in Bruno's view, were hypocritical asses.

It would, for his sake, have been better had Bruno modified his views or learned to keep quiet about them. Abandoning England in 1585, he would return to the Continent, where he would eventually be arrested for heresy, delivered into the hands of the Inquisition, and after years of interrogation in prison, burned at the stake. But his views did not disappear; they were quietly passed along, disputed, absorbed, and expanded. Several of them were distinctly echoed in the "monstrous opinions" that Kyd attributed to Christopher Marlowe. All revealed religions, Marlowe was accused of saying, were devices used to control and exploit the ignorant masses by making them believe in fables. The biblical fables propounded by Christians were refuted by science, but at least Roman Catholics had the benefit of compelling ceremonies, while the Protestants were hypocritical asses. Some of these notions probably first reached Marlowe in unlicensed reading and whispered conversations snatched in moments of unsupervised free time among his fellow undergraduates at Cambridge.

❖ ❖ ❖

THE COURSE OF STUDY to which Marlowe was introduced was designed to keep these moments of free time to the barest minimum. Shortly before his arrival at Corpus, the master of his college, Robert Norgate, drew up a detailed daily schedule, of which this is a small sample:

> On Mondaye after morning prayers, be red in the hall at vi of the clock, these thre Lecturs 1. Aristotles Naturall Philosophy. 2. Aristotells organon. 3. Seton w(hi)ch continewe for the space of one whole houre.
> At xii of the clock be red two greke lectures, one of construction. as Homere or Demosthenes. or Hesiod. or Isocrates. etc. The other. of the gra(m)mer
> At iii of the clock ys red a rhetorick lecture, of some p(ar)t of Tully. for the space of an houre.
> At iiii of the clock beginneth the schollers sophisme, w(hi)ch continueth untill 5

So it continued, from morning to evening, six days a week.

Earlier in the sixteenth century, in a rare burst of innovative zeal, the curriculum had been revised. A major role in the revision was played by the great Dutch scholar Erasmus, who had spent several years at Cambridge as a professor of divinity until the miserable weather and a craving for decent wine helped drive him back to the Continent. Along with other Catholic Humanists, including his close friend Thomas More, Erasmus was eager to emancipate education from what he regarded as the lifeless analytical abstractions of Scholasticism. He was confident that to shape the intellect and even to enhance the Christian piety of contemporary students, it would be more effective to use brilliant works by pagan authors rather than dull, often impenetrable treatises by perfectly orthodox theologians. This reform is why Norgate's scheme prominently features Homer, Aristotle, and Cicero ("Tully") and not Thomas Aquinas or Duns Scotus.

The lectures on logic and philosophy, followed by tutorials on such subjects as Greek grammar, geography, and rhetoric, took much of the day. After the formal instruction was over, students were expected to spend their time learning how to conduct the highly ritualized disputations that served as the formal capstone of undergraduate education. Four such disputations were required of every candidate for the BA degree, two in the role of Answerer and two in the role of Questioner. Preparation for these contests involved training in how to formulate, defend, and attack a thesis, in marshaling evidence and thinking quickly on one's feet, and in making points (ideally, devastating points) in logic. *Sic probo*—"Thus I prove": the triumphant words ringing out at the climax of a clever speech were meant to leave one's opponent crushed.

The disputations, intense and demanding, were held between one and five in the afternoon, with a break between three and four. They were public events, drawing spectators and, on occasion, hecklers. At Marlowe's college in February 1582, Thomas Evaunce, an undergraduate from another college, was beaten up "because he proposed offensive, stupid, and insulting questions [*scandalosas, ineptas, et opprobriosas questiones*] during the disputation." Most of the grainy day-to-day details of university life in this period are lost to us; this one survives because it was registered in the administration's so-called Buckle Book, the register where egregious disturbances were noted down for disciplinary action.

Very little recreational time was built into the undergraduates' days. An early supper was served, after which the students were expected to devote themselves to a few more hours of study by candlelight before praying and retiring to bed in anticipation of another five a.m. wake-up call. On Sunday, much of the day was given over to extremely long sermons at which attendance was required and monitored. As for the few free hours after Sunday sermons, students were officially prohibited from swimming in the river and from playing football beyond the college walls, for fear of clashes with the town rowdies. Some spaces for exercise could be found within the colleges, in the enclosed courtyards and in the Elizabethan version of indoor tennis courts. (One of these courts, from 1595, survives in Merton College, Oxford, and provides a glimpse of the way the game was played; it was rather like squash, with sloping walls and galleries.) But apart from these extremely limited opportunities for fun, one of Marlowe's biographers has written, "the Scholar's life was all work and no play."

Such, in any case, was the plan. How much this plan corresponded to reality is another matter. The authorities kept track of the students' presence or absence at the college—there was a residence requirement for graduation, but daily attendance in lectures and classes was not closely monitored. A speaker at the Cambridge commencement ceremony in 1547 complained that the professors often delivered their lectures to virtually empty halls. (On one occasion in the mid-1960s, I looked through the window of one of these halls at Cambridge and saw an elderly professor, dressed in full academic robes and standing formally at the podium, lecturing to a single student.)

Then as now, college students, living with one another away from home, created their own culture and found ways to fashion lives that did not entirely match the sober expectations of their teachers. The constant issuing and reissuing of regulations prohibiting students from frequenting taverns, gambling parlors, dogfights, dancing schools, and brothels suggests that they were on occasion doing just that. (So, for that matter, must have been some of their teachers.) Itinerant entertainers—acrobats, ballad mongers, fortune tellers, magicians, and the like—regularly passed through English towns, and though the university authorities disapproved, they drew audiences from among the college students. In April 1581 the Cambridge proctor tried to stop a bearbaiting in nearby Chesterton. Cruelty to animals was not the issue. Such an event was an outrage, the proctor wrote in his official complaint, not only because it was held on Sunday but also because "it is very likely there will be resort of scholars."

If the guardians of student life were unable to prohibit all amusements, they could at least do their best to keep the most alluring of them from being brought into Cambridge from outside. When, shortly before Marlowe arrived, a troupe of professional actors, patronized by a powerful aristocrat, showed up and proposed to spend four or five days performing "plays and interludes," the vice-chancellor of the university politely demurred. Another troupe, he explained, with a comparably powerful patron, had already been refused permission to perform, and it would not do to favor one over the other. The official excuse was fear of plague, heightened in any large assembly and particularly in "this hot time of the year." Besides, he added, with commencement fast approaching, the students had more need of "diligence in study than dissoluteness in plays." Then, to soften the blow of refusal, the university paid the players twenty shillings to get out of town.

University authorities were not uniformly hostile to all forms of theatrical entertainment, but they wanted them to be kept in-house and under their control. Students in many of the colleges, including Marlowe's, regularly wrote and acted in plays. Except in times of plague, the plays were generally meant to draw large audiences, and the organizers—known as stage-keepers—put on masks, carried torches, and went around the university advertising them. According to surviving university records, the crowded, often rowdy performances resulted in many broken windows, damaged walls, and scratched furniture, along with occasional brawls. In 1582 Thomas Mudd, a student in Pembroke Hall, was arrested for writing a play that depicted the mayor of Cambridge in an unflattering light. After being held in the town prison for three days, Mudd was released on condition that he acknowledge his fault and beg the mayor's pardon. At this same unfortunate performance, another student, Miles Moses from Gonville and Caius College, was imprisoned and fined "because he broke the head of Master Thexton"—none other than Marlowe's roomate in Corpus—"and shed blood while the stage production was being put on in Pembroke Hall."

Notwithstanding such disturbances, the authorities not merely tolerated the productions but even subsidized them, paying for sets, candles for lighting, stage props, and costumes and repairing the halls when the shows were over. After all, they were vivid displays to the whole Cambridge community of the splendid facilities of individual colleges—the surviving Renaissance dining halls are indeed magnificent—and equally, of the wit, intelligence, and Latin skills of their students. Several of the colleges, notably King's, St. John's, and Trinity, took particular pride in the quality of their theatrical offerings.

Not everyone in the university, however, agreed with the policy of encouraging student plays. A few of the colleges banned theatricals altogether (though they could not keep their eager students from strolling over to another college to see them). And not all the students were enthusiastic. In 1579 an obstreperous undergraduate from St. John's named Punter went on an antitheatrical rampage. At a performance in Caius, he rushed up and pulled the mask off a stage-keeper's face; at Trinity, he fought the stage-keepers who were trying to keep him out of the audience; at Corpus, disguised as one of the players, he secretly crept into the hall and "to the great disturbance of the whole assembly, did assault one of Trinity College whom also he afterward challenged"; and, still not finished, he returned to Trinity and staged yet another assault.

Perhaps Punter had a personal vendetta or was simply unhinged, but his actions reflected the vehement theater-hatred that was increasingly rampant in the circles of the pious. The more spiritually awakened— those who became known as Puritans—were convinced that Satan lurked behind the scenes. They thought it was sinful to allow, let alone encourage, the young to assume identities that were not their own. They dwelt on the fact that the word *hypocrite* derived from the Greek word *hupokritēs*, meaning actor. And they were particularly exercised by the cross-dressing—boys dressing up as girls and enacting scenes of flirtation and love—that was a frequent feature of many of the plays in these all-male communities.

When he was at university in the 1560s, the theologian John Rainolds recalled, he had taken the woman's part in a play that was performed before Queen Elizabeth herself, and the queen had showered him with gold coins. It was one of the proudest moments in his young life. Yet later, as a distinguished professor at Oxford responsible for the moral education of the young, he looked back with horror. He had come to understand that what he had been rewarded for was shameful and wicked. Such theatrical performances should be canceled, he thought, for they were not merely embarrassing but dangerous. "As certain spiders," he wrote, "if they do but touch men only with their mouth, they put them to wonderful pain and make them mad, so beautiful boys by kissing do sting and pour secretly in a kind of poison, the poison of incontinency."

Spiritual awakenings like Rainolds's were happening throughout the realm, and they worried traditionalists who feared that they were the harbingers of a more general attack on time-honored customs and established authority. Anxieties about the kiss of the spider boy spread and intensified. What was once scarcely noticed or cheerfully accepted came under vehement attack as immoral, irreligious, or evil. The attackers began to include not only a few marginal cranks with an ax to grind but also influential members of the establishment who spoke out against the very system that produced them.

There was some truth to the Puritans' criticism. Undergraduate plays were meant to hone and demonstrate advanced Latin skills, but they often fostered a sense of the exploratory and the transgressive. The student performers were encouraged to try out identities that were not their own, identities that in many cases were radically at odds with their fundamental beliefs and values. For the space of a few hours, everything was different, and what was cultivated and rewarded was the ability to assume any part and to articulate it with conviction.

This ability was bound up with the core of the undergraduate curriculum at Cambridge and Oxford, the *argumentum in utramque partem*, that is, learning to argue on both sides of a question. A topic was propounded, and the student was expected to speak eloquently and persuasively—in Latin, of course—first on one side and then on the other. A manuscript list of topics that survives from Cambridge in 1580, as noted by Marlowe's biographer David Riggs, includes such propositions as "The style of sacred Scripture is not barbarous," "There is a place of hell," and "Nothing is done without God's prior consent and volition." This means that the same students, turn and turn about, had also to argue that "The style of sacred Scripture is barbarous," "There is no place of hell," and "Things are done without God's prior consent and volition." The educational exercise, endlessly repeated, was intended only to sharpen the student's rhetorical skills. But it could also foster a frame of mind that was able, for a moment at least, to entertain virtually any position. When the doomed hero of Marlowe's tragedy *Doctor Faustus* flatly declares, "I think hell's a fable," he might well have been echoing a proposition that Marlowe or his classmates had formally defended.

University authorities would have been horrified at the suggestion that there was any possible connection between their standard academic exercises and such blasphemous remarks. The full scholarship that Marlowe held at Corpus was intended to recruit gifted young students from poor families for lifelong service in the church. Such scholarships initially covered only three years toward the BA degree. But there was a strong incentive for anyone without means to discover that he had a clerical vocation. Should the student, upon receiving his BA, decide to continue to the MA in preparation for ordination as a priest, the scholarship would be extended for another three years.

As Archbishop Parker and other donors at Cambridge and Oxford were anxiously aware, hundreds of pulpits all over the land sorely needed well-educated, suitably trained priests to minister to congregants, conduct services, and deliver doctrinally correct sermons. Though regarded as essential to keep the country from lapsing back into Roman Catholicism or lurching toward the almost equally feared and hated Puritanism, many of these positions were miserably remunerated and could not be reasonably expected to be filled primarily from the ranks of the gentry. Even a country squire's second or third son, with few expectations of a substantial inheritance, would think twice about a career scraping by in a rural parish. The educated son of a cobbler, however, might welcome the opportunity or at least have no better choice.

When Parker died in 1575, the administration of the bequest became the responsibility of his son John, who specified that the scholarships his father endowed were to go to "the best and aptest scholars well instructed in their grammar and if it may be such as can make a verse." The small additional specification may have had a special consequence for at least one applicant: "making a verse" was something we can be sure the young Marlowe was very well able to do. For those who weighed the candidates' qualifications, a mastery of the complexities of Latin versification was not meant to indicate a vocation to be a poet; it was meant to serve as a sign of diligence and potential eloquence in someone who would study divinity and ultimately take holy orders in the Church of England. But education, as Marlowe's whole career demonstrates, often has the opposite effect from the one that is intended.

Marlowe had always loved to explore the world through books, and now, thanks to Archbishop Parker's largesse, he had access to riches far greater than Headmaster Gressop's library. He could not simply take out whatever he wanted to read, but he could be granted permission to sit in the college library and consult the heavy reference volumes that were chained to the shelves. And as he came to know and be known to the faculty, he could ask them what they might possibly have in their rooms that he could look at. In any given year, in a process called the *electio*, many of the books in the college's collection were lent out to the fellows.

Some individual faculty members would have owned their own books, and these too they might have been willing to share with their favorite students. But the sheer value of books acted as a restraint on all but the closest relationships of trust. In Corpus Christi College, it is still possible to see something called the Billingford Hutch, a huge oak chest, almost six feet long, strengthened with iron bands and heavy riveted plates, shut up with three built-in locks and an iron bar padlocked at each end. The treasures that this heavily secured strongbox was meant to guard were for the most part books. These were books that fellows were allowed to use as collateral for loans from a special fund. The standard term was a year and a month; if the loan was not repaid, the pledge could be sold. The surviving register is a valuable record of the books that needy faculty members pawned.

There is no comparable record of Marlowe's own personal reading at Cambridge, but there is at least one striking clue. In the midst of his heavy schedule of reading and study—Greek lessons, Cicero's *Orations*, Quintilian's *Institutes of Oratory*, Aristotle's *Ethics*, various textbooks on logic, dialectic, natural history, and mathematics, plus frequent Bible study and constant exercises in debating—Marlowe undertook on his own initiative to translate the *Amores*, Ovid's three books of elegies. (*Elegy* is a technical term referring to the meter used in that type of Latin poem.) The headmaster Gresshop had a copy of these poems in his personal library, so Marlowe may have first heard of them when he was a student at the King's School. But Ovid's notoriously frank treatment of sex would not have been regarded as a suitable exercise for boys, and the poems were not part of anyone's curriculum even at university. Marlowe must have found them in the Corpus Christi library.

To translate even a modest sampling of the *Amores* would have been ambitious enough; to translate the complete work—forty-eight poems, some four thousand lines—in one's spare time is a startling achievement. When Marlowe set out to do so, there was no translation available; that may have been part of the allure for him. By the late sixteenth century, writers had been translating increasing numbers of works, both ancient and modern, into English. These translations could occasionally bring in some income, and as important, they provided an opportunity to test and expand the expressive power of the vernacular. The English language was finding a new range of voices.

A generation earlier Ovid's greatest work, the *Metamorphoses*, had appeared in English, but the translator, Arthur Golding, was a Calvinist whose values were profoundly at odds with those of the pagan poet and whose versification tended to fall flat. Before Marlowe, all translations of Ovid into English verse were either in "fourteeners," lines of fourteen syllables in length, or in "poulter's measure," alternating lines of twelve and fourteen syllables. (A poultry dealer traditionally gave two extra eggs when selling by the dozen—hence the term.) The long lines gave the translators room to expand the tight Latin syntax, but they generally played havoc with the tone and spirit of the original, making it sound plodding and ham-fisted:

> With peevish doors: she knocked thereat, and out there comes a trot.
> The goddess asked her some drink, and she denied it not:
> (*Metamorphoses* 5:409)

Marlowe's literary challenge with the *Amores* was to capture the racy, urbane Ovid of the original. The solution that he came up with, seemingly out of nowhere, was to keep the rhymes but cut back the syllables in each line from fourteen to ten. The resulting pentameter couplets capture much more of Ovid's quickness:

> Thus I complained, but Love unlocked his quiver,
> Took out the shaft, ordained my heart to shiver.

The undergraduate Marlowe's stylistic solution became the standard meter for classical translations in English, and it remained so well into the eighteenth century.

The *Amores* were exciting because they were unexpurgated and untamed. Since their content and tone made it almost impossible to dress them in pious robes, they had been left out of the school curriculum but also spared the moralizing commentaries that had long been attached to the *Metamorphoses* and Ovid's other major works. The language was often difficult, and modern scholars have noted mistakes in translation. But Marlowe's command of Latin was impressive enough, and it was not as a scholar that he approached the project he had hit upon. He sought to be truthful to the ancient poet and to the risky issues he explored.

The poems, probably written by Ovid in his early twenties and translated by Marlowe at an even younger age, are the poems of a very self-conscious young man brooding about his sex life, his vocation, and the meaning of it all. Why, he asked, am I drawn to writing little poems about love in the afternoon and not a great national epic about war? What should I say to someone who tells me that I am wasting my time? What is life all about anyway? The poems depict casual affairs, adultery, rivalry, bad faith, and betrayal, in tones ranging from exaltation to irony to abject misery. The poet's misery is particularly intense if his penis refuses to cooperate: "Like one dead it lay, / Drooping more than a rose pulled yesterday." But then there are hours of delicious pleasure. "In summer's heat, and mid-time of the day," one poem begins, "To rest my limbs upon a bed I lay." The speaker's mistress Corinna enters, wearing "a long loose gown."

He snatches at the gown, she coyly resists, and they have a playful struggle, at the end of which she is naked. "Judge you the rest: being tired she bad me kiss," he slyly says, closing with a final line that Marlowe renders perfectly: "Jove, send me more such afternoons as this."

Translating the *Amores*, during time carved out from the more sober pursuits that were meant to fill his waking hours, gave Marlowe the opportunity to experience afresh the transgressive thrill that made the study of the ancient past an adventure rather than a burden. "What, are there gods?" one of the most startling of Ovid's poems begins. It is important to imagine what it must have felt like in the early 1580s to put such words down on paper, when to say them in one's own voice would call down the most ferocious punishment:

> God is a name, no substance, feared in vain,
> And doth the world in fond belief detain.

In Augustan Rome, Ovid was exiled to the Black Sea and never allowed to return. Marlowe certainly knew of Ovid's fate, and he knew that in Elizabethan England his punishment would have been far worse than exile.

Like most poems in this period, Marlowe's translations of the *Amores* originally circulated in manuscript. They passed from hand to hand, with new copies made along the way. Marlowe earned no money from them. It was only in 1599, six years after his death, that a selection appeared in print. Under the title "*Certain of Ovids Elegies* by C. Marlow," they were published together with some scabrous epigrams by the poet and lawyer Sir John Davies. Officially, all books printed in England had to be approved and licensed by the authorities, but this one was unlicensed. The imprint on the title page claimed, probably spuriously, that it was printed abroad, in Middleburgh, a city in Holland. Later in the same year the book was ordered to be publicly burned by order of the Archbishop of Canterbury and the Bishop of London. The book burning, which took place on June 1, 1599, seems to have served, as censorship often does, as good publicity. In the years that followed, at least six further unlicensed editions were printed and sold, now expanded to include all the elegies Marlowe translated.

This yoking together of pleasure and condemnation, permission and punishment marked Marlowe's experience at university. Latin lessons were peppered with strict moral injunctions, but the ancient works assigned to students gleefully violated every one of those injunctions. Students were required to dress as if they were all equals, but some were more equal than others. Student theatrical performances were condemned as sinful, but they were also subsidized and widely enjoyed. Sunday sermons preached obedience to authority, but the English church was founded on a spectacular act of disobedience to papal authority. Protestants proclaimed the priesthood of all believers, but Protestant church authorities punished anyone whose beliefs did not match those officially sanctioned. Domineering women were condemned as scolds and muzzled, but the realm was ruled by a queen to whose will everyone was expected to bend.

All cultures issue mixed signals and harbor contradictions—perfect consistency is a fantasy that would make everyone miserable if it actually came to pass. Elizabethan culture carried its doubleness to an extreme, in part because its legal system routinely threatened ghastly punishments that it could not possibly inflict without bringing society to a halt. By an act of Parliament passed in 1533 during the reign of Henry VIII, the "detestable and abominable Vice of Buggery committed with Mankind" was declared a felony punishable by death. Parliament went out of its way to declare that no one charged with this offense could "be admitted to his Clergy." The phrase alluded to a legal device whereby the accused could, by reading aloud a passage from the Bible, have his case remanded to the ecclesiastical courts, where there was no death penalty. The law against buggery clearly intended to close the loophole for literate offenders, including university students like Marlowe.

But what exactly was buggery, so much worse even than murder for which the accused could claim "Clergy"? The act of 1533 did not provide a precise definition nor, for that matter, an account of why the vice was so detestable as to deserve death. Since the Buggery Act was not repealed until 1828, there was ample time over the centuries for English case law to settle whether the offense was limited to anal intercourse or included such acts as fellatio, whether it required emission of seed, whether it included heterosexual sodomy, and so on. None of these crucial details, however, was worked out during the course of the sixteenth century, for the simple reason that almost no cases were brought to court.

In their college dormitory rooms, the students generally shared beds, often sleeping with their tutors as well. It is as if there were a perennial bed shortage in Elizabethan England, a shortage that can be explained only by the fact that most people preferred to sleep with someone else. The preference no doubt helped with the pervasive cold and damp, and it was also a widely accepted and approved sign of same-sex friendship and intimacy. Men held hands, embraced, and kissed one another without fear of stigma. Such behavior did not signal that they belonged to a particular subgroup of men, let alone a subgroup whose identity was condemned. On the contrary, close male friendship was cultivated and celebrated.

Bed sharing in these all-male communities also, of course, facilitated sexual pleasure. But here the vocal celebrations of intimacy fall silent, and a heavy curtain drops. It drops not because people were afraid to be stigmatized as queer or gay—the terms, along with the category "homosexual," did not exist at the time—and certainly not because all bed partners were perfectly chaste, but because same-sex sexual acts were so vehemently condemned by law. Indeed, the extremity of the threatened punishment probably inhibited the filing of such complaints as there might well have been. It was better for everyone to keep it all quiet. What went on in the dark stayed in the dark.

Getting into bed with each other every night in the pitch-black room, Marlowe and his fellow students were aware that the practice of sodomy, whether consensual or not, was punishable by death. In theory, it is possible that in such circumstances bedfellows enjoyed no sexual arousal and no pleasure at all; in theory, anything is possible. But it is overwhelmingly likely that a very large number of them must have experienced for themselves various forms of what was called "forbidden and unlawful fleshliness."

The more religiously inclined could tell themselves that their moments of illicit pleasure were proof of the sinfulness of fallen mankind. Others could view these moments more indulgently as youthful escapades on the way to the lawful pleasures of the marriage bed. But for Marlowe, who never married, they were evidently the fulfillment of a desire he was inclined not to hide but to celebrate. Over the years that followed, he was drawn repeatedly to violate the code of silence that reigned over male homosexuality and to challenge his culture's duplicity.

In speaking out, Marlowe was not alone. Shakespeare in his sonnets to an effeminate young man explores the love aroused in him by the one he calls the "master-mistress" of his passion. But Shakespeare explicitly claims that the fulfillment of his desires was "defeated":

> And for a woman wert thou first created,
> Till Nature as she wrought thee fell a-doting,
> And by addition me of thee defeated
> By adding one thing to my purpose nothing.
>   But since she pricked thee out for women's pleasure,
>   Mine be thy love and thy love's use their treasure.

Marlowe offers no such disavowals.

Claiming that he could barely write the words, Kyd informed privy councilor Puckering that Marlowe had said that Saint John was Christ's Alexis and that Christ loved John "with an extraordinary love"—a gauntlet thrown down to the authors of the Buggery Act and to the moralists preaching hellfire and damnation from the pulpit. If these or some such words were in fact Marlowe's, perhaps they were laying claim to the essential worth of the desires that he felt. Perhaps Marlowe was using the highest terms his culture possessed to honor a love he himself had experienced.

CHAPTER 6

# Gold Buttons

He "who abideth in the university," wrote the clergyman William Harrison, "shall be reputed for a gentleman ever after." Harrison's 1577 *Description of England* laid out the crucial class distinctions: "We, in England, divide our people commonly into four sorts, as gentlemen, citizens or burgesses, yeomen, and artificers or labourers." The first "sort" ranged from the ruler at the very top through the dukes, earls, and others who bore aristocratic titles, then to the knights, and finally to all those who were entitled to be called gentlemen. Belonging to this elite group, roughly 2 percent of the population, was largely a function of birth, but Harrison added another way to make it: gaining admission to Oxford or Cambridge.

Once they obtained a degree, university students, whether they were the sons of cobblers, blacksmiths, carpenters, or yeomen farmers, had crossed a critically important line in the class system. In Marlowe's lowborn cohort, some had long been certain that they wanted to spend their lives in service of the Church of England; others were far from such certainty. Marlowe seems naturally to have gravitated toward those who shared his doubts. One was Thomas Nashe, the son of a poor parish curate. Another was Robert Greene, the son of a poor sadler. Greene had a knack for collecting undergraduates from poor backgrounds and bringing them together in his rooms in Clare Hall for long drinking bouts that mingled together mockery, obscene jests, and conversations about the latest literary trends.

Going to university, displaying literary talent, and being able to style themselves gentlemen after graduation did not give these gifted students the prospect of an income. They knew that if they did not want to slide back into the world from which they had been plucked, they had strong reasons to study theology and take holy orders. Though the scholarship system for children without means conferred status, it was not meant to foster social mobility. It was simply meant to recruit potential priests from families without means. That they may not have had a religious vocation did not greatly matter. There were very few alternative careers. Lord Burghley, the queen's chief adviser and chancellor of Cambridge, even contemplated legislation that would have closed off one of the most obvious of these alternatives; no one, the order stipulated, could "study the laws, temporal or civil, except he be immediately descended from a nobleman or gentleman."

Earlier in the sixteenth century, ambitious students from poor families had a greater chance to find careers outside the church. After he dissolved the monasteries and seized their vast wealth, Henry VIII recruited "new men"—ambitious, university-educated men drawn from outside the tight circle of the aristocratic elite—who were handsomely rewarded for zealously serving the crown's interests. Dazzling rags-to-riches careers, though they were always exceptional, were enough to lure bright children from poor families to clamber for admission to Oxford and Cambridge. But social advancement became ever less frequent during the reign of Henry VIII's daughter, Elizabeth. The need for new men had waned.

Once hopes are raised, however, they take on a life of their own. Poor students who had little or no intention to become clergymen continued to flock to the university. The old theology-based curriculum had centered on the search for ultimate truths; the new classics-based curriculum offered training instead in skills, such as logical reasoning and rhetoric, that seemed to promise advancement in the secular world. The changes in the curriculum had significant, often unintended consequences—among them, a heightened sense of undergraduate education as a tool in the service of ambition.

Marlowe would have sat on one of the hard benches in the lecture hall, squeezed perhaps between Robert Greene and Thomas Nashe, to listen to one of the star professors of the day, Gabriel Harvey. Learned, grandiloquent, and self-promoting, Harvey was a phenomenon to wonder at: a daring outsider from a background as modest as Marlowe's own who was shouldering aside the doddering figures of the old establishment by championing the work of another upstart, the fashionable French philosopher Pierre de la Ramée (known in England as Petrus or Peter Ramus). Ramus had caused a huge stir in French academic circles by defending such propositions as "Everything that Aristotle has said is false." At Cambridge, Harvey was achieving fame by importing from Paris ideas that predictably enraged his senior colleagues and thrilled his students.

But Harvey also made clear to the undergraduates who listened to him that academic ambition was only the first step. It was not enough simply to make it as an intellectual; what mattered, he insisted, was to succeed in the world beyond the university. He had already demonstrated, at least in his own estimation, that he was the master of multiple disciplines, and he imagined putting his learning and his great oratorical skills to triumphant use in the practice of law. And beyond the law court, there were still more fields to conquer. That was, after all, the open secret of the new arts-based curriculum, the hidden agenda of the revolution in thought championed by Peter Ramus and his ardent followers. Education was not an end in itself; all of it, including training in the arts, was meant to be put to use.

In the year Marlowe came to Cambridge, Harvey published a series of letters that he had exchanged with a spectacularly gifted former student, Edmund Spenser, on subjects ranging from a recent earthquake to "our English reformed versifying." The little book, *Three Proper and Witty Familiar Letters Lately Passed between Two University Men*, made its way through the Cambridge colleges and must have quickly reached Marlowe's hands. Anyone with poetic ambitions would have been interested in these reflections on meter and rhyme, but that was not all. Near the end of one of the letters, Harvey voiced a view of the current state of education at Cambridge. Things at the university, he wrote, were terrible: superficiality and ignorance reigned throughout the colleges. Almost no one—apart from Harvey himself, of course—could be trusted intellectually or morally. Harvey was burning his bridges; he clearly did not plan to spend the rest of his career at Cambridge.

But where did the upstart son of a poor ropemaker from the Essex village of Saffron Walden imagine that his academic achievements could possibly take him? What fantasies was he harboring or trying to awaken in students like Marlowe? A marginal note in one of his books provides a small clue. "Some good fellows amongst us," he jotted down, "begin now to be pretty well acquainted with a certain parlous book called, as I remember me, *Il principe di Niccolo Machiavelli*." Machiavelli's *Prince* was officially banned—it had been off-limits ever since its publication back in 1517—but copies were evidently circulating and being eagerly read. It offered a vision of the world stripped of the moral injunctions spouted by both secular and religious authorities. In its place was a world in which tough analytical intelligence, conjoined with boldness, courage, and ruthlessness, stood a chance of mastering fortune and seizing the reins of power.

Power fascinated Harvey; he longed to get close to it and to profit from the proximity. For a moment at least, it seemed tantalizingly possible. When the queen visited Cambridge in 1578, Harvey was chosen to deliver a Latin oration before her and was permitted to kiss her hand. (She remarked that he looked like an Italian.) The experience went to his head.

Harvey was convinced that he was not destined to remain in the confined setting of the academy. He presented manuscript copies of his verses to the queen and her courtiers, advertised his talents and achievements in print, cultivated important noblemen, and embarked on the study of law. He reminded everyone of his accomplishments and skills and reached out to every contact that he had made. But the glittering prize always eluded him. He would die in straitened circumstances in the small village in which he was born.

Even at the time of his greatest university acclaim, when his lectures on the latest intellectual theories from Paris were arousing the ire of his senior colleagues, the signs of Harvey's probable failure may have been glimpsed by a few undergraduate skeptics. One of these skeptics was Thomas Nashe. Like Marlowe, Nashe did not come from a moneyed or titled family, and like Marlowe, he early on showed signs of fantastic verbal adroitness and a streak of wildness. The two might have bonded over any number of things, including a taste for risk-taking college plays, an intense dislike of moralizing killjoys, and an ironic view of the vain, grandiloquent professor strutting before them on the lecture platform. Mocking Harvey became an obsession for Nashe, who would continue the game in print long after he left Cambridge.

Marlowe and Nashe exchanged cruel jokes about Harvey, toyed with possible writing projects together, and forged a friendship that would extend well beyond their student years. But their sensibilities were very different. Nashe was a born satirist. He loved to make things smaller, meaner, and more grotesque than they first appeared. Marlowe's imagination could certainly include the grotesque, but it tended to expand, not to belittle, whatever it touched. For Nashe, Gabriel Harvey's intellectual discontent and his fantasies of power were the foibles of a ridiculous little man always "ruffling it out, huffty tuffty, in his suit of velvet"; for Marlowe, they were the symptoms of an education that aroused intense desires and then cruelly and systematically thwarted them in anyone who lacked the requisite pedigree and privilege.

There were a few exceptions to the general history of frustrated ambition. For students from poorer families hoping to find a career outside the church, Edmund Spenser served as a model. A decade older than Marlowe, Spenser had worked his way as a sizar through Pembroke College, Cambridge, and, upon graduating, secured the post of secretary to a former master of Pembroke who had been named Bishop of Rochester. He then went on to be appointed secretary to Arthur Gray, Lord Deputy of Ireland. The position of secretary was a more important one than the word suggests: it was a principal aide, someone involved in key communications and decisions. As secretary, Spenser now stood a chance to reap rich rewards from the military occupation Gray was directing.

The son of a journeyman clothmaker, Spenser had succeeded in obtaining a valuable post, but in addition to his truly exceptional talents, he had a claim to be a poor relation of a noble family, the Spencers of Althorp. The cobber's son from Canterbury could make no comparable claim. Class divisions were being reinforced. The brief period of some limited social movement, when the increasingly powerful state and the court looked for educated functionaries wherever it could find them, was coming to an end.

Elizabethan Oxford and Cambridge were witnessing an influx of the wealthy. The change was noticed and lamented by contemporaries. Colleges, an Elizabethan observer wrote in 1577, "were erected ... at the first, only for poor men's sons ... : but now they have the least benefit of them, by reason the rich do so encroach upon them." A visitor to Oxford and Cambridge colleges today sees some surviving medieval quadrangles but also many far more magnificent Renaissance courtyards, dining halls, and chapels, built in the sixteenth and early seventeenth centuries to accommodate the steadily increasing number of the well-to-do.

This shift meant, among other things, ever fewer opportunities for university graduates from poorer families to find positions other than serving as parish priests, local clerks, schoolmasters, or college tutors. The tantalizing fantasy of secular advancement was still there—the dream of emerging from nowhere to become an imposing figure in the state—but it functioned largely to produce a lingering sense of disappointment and bitterness among those whose imaginations it had seized. A class of alienated intellectuals was in the making.

Marlowe took it all in. Years later he made the killing of the upstart Ramus a central event in his last play, *The Massacre at Paris*. The play's Machiavellian villain, the Duke of Guise, appears in person in Professor Ramus's modest study. The aristocratic leader of the Catholic League and instigator of the Bartholomew's Day Massacre stops the action and sounds for a moment exactly like one of the irate scholars Marlowe must have observed at Cambridge disputing with Ramus's champion Harvey. Ramus, the duke says, is a hopeless simplifier, a superficial thinker who "having a smack in all ... yet did'st never sound anything to the depth." Yet this intellectual lightweight has had the temerity to criticize

Aristotle's compilation of logical treatises, the *Organon*: "Was it not thou that scoff'dst the *Organon*, / And said it was a heap of vanities?" Ramus tries to defend himself, but Guise cuts him short and brings the disputation to a close. "Why suffer you that peasant to declaim?" he asks his ally the Duke of Anjoy; "Stab him, I say, and send him to his friends in hell." *That peasant*—there was, as always, a class dimension to these arguments. How dare someone whose father tilled the soil set himself up as a critic of Aristotle or bandy words with aristocrats? "Never was there collier's son so full of pride," exclaims Anjoy as he sinks his knife into the plebeian professor.

How quickly Marlowe would have grasped the full reality of the situation he was in is impossible to know. Later in his life, with Cambridge well behind him, he wrote *Doctor Faustus*, the single greatest tragedy ever written about an alienated intellectual. Faustus, "his parents base of stock," is a celebrated professor who has mastered every discipline to which he has turned his quick, capacious mind. But left profoundly unsatisfied by mere academic success, he turns to magic, confident that he will cut a grand figure in the world through the power of the devils he has learned to conjure. He pictures himself as the liberator and ruler of his land. In the event, he does nothing of the kind, becoming instead a kind of glorified court entertainer for the rich and powerful.

In creating Faustus, Marlowe drew on the bitterness of those many ambitious, eager, bright students, "born of parents base of stock," who dreamed of careers outside the academy or the church but found themselves blocked in every direction they turned. Each year the numbers of these frustrated career seekers grew, along with their anger and resentment. The authorities had no interest in addressing the underlying causes of alienation, even if they had perceived them better. On the contrary—they simply wanted the scholarship students to settle down and study theology. Most of those students did. Marlowe was hardly alone in being plucked from the poor and launched toward a career in the church. The outgoing holder of the scholarship that he was awarded, Christopher Pashley, was the son of a Canterbury weaver. William Potter, the son a butcher who lived across the street from the Marlowes, also managed to get funding to attend Cambridge. Just after he left Corpus, Christopher Pashley was duly ordained as a priest; William Potter likewise. So too after his graduation Robert Thexton, another of Marlowe's Corpus classmates, succeeded his father as rector of Trunch, a Norfolk village about eighty-five miles away.

The scholarships, then, often worked as they were intended to work, but there was a wrinkle. They put the recipients for six or seven long years in a zone of indeterminacy, an environment where they were encouraged to debate the most fundamental propositions and to imagine life as arranged other than it was. For the gentry, this experience might broaden their awareness before they settled into the roles for which they were destined. But for the lowborn, it could encourage precisely the hopes that gripped Harvey. And when those hopes were dashed, as they almost always were, it was not at all clear where the long immersion in the humanities could lead except to frustration, rage, or the fantasy of escape.

◆ ◆ ◆

MARLOWE CLEARLY TOOK his studies seriously, but the result, far from piety, was awakened curiosity and heightened skepticism. He plumbed the resources of the library to explore whatever lay outside the boundaries of his familiar world. To judge from the use he subsequently made of it, one book that he avidly consulted was *The Theater of the World*, by a celebrated geographer from Antwerp, Abraham Ortelius. After four hundred years, this large, expensively illustrated volume, the first modern atlas, remains startling to look at. Its elaborate allegorical frontispiece depicts the four known continents as four beautiful women. Sitting at the top, in pride of place, is Europe; below her on either side stand silk-clad Asia, holding a jar of spices, and half-naked Africa, with sunbeams radiating around her head and a leafy branch in her hand. Stretched out on the shelf below, a bow and arrows under her legs, is naked America, holding the severed head of a bearded European male. A sculpted female bust next to America represents Magellanica, a hypothetical fifth continent somewhere below South America.

When he first opened the pages of Ortelius, Marlowe's own travels may not have extended beyond Kent and Cambridgeshire. Here laid out before his enraptured eyes were vast realms outside the orbit of Christianity and of the classical civilization that lay at the center of his education. As he pored over the pages of the atlas, Marlowe evidently lingered with particular fascination on one of the most exotic of them, a detailed map of the lands that extended from the Crimea to Central Asia, depicting camel caravans, military encampments, and colorful religious rites. In the upper left-hand corner of the page, there was a drawing of a tent, its flaps tied back to reveal a throne on which a large turbaned and bearded figure sat holding a massive sword in one hand and pointing upward with the other. In the lower right-hand corner there was a tiny image of a city labeled "Shamarcandia," with a note in Latin that explained that this was "once the capital of all of Tartary, but now it has decayed to ruins, with many remnants from antiquity."

The note below Samarkand added something that seems to have caught Marlowe's eye:

> Here Tamburlaine lies buried, once the captor of the ruler
> of the Turks, Bajazeth. He took him as a prisoner and
> carried him off, bound in gold chains. The inhabitants
> are Muslims.

The detail seems to have gripped him, for he went on to look for further information. At some point he discovered that the great conqueror had come from a background poorer than his own. A mere shepherd had subdued much of the known world.

There is a moment early in *Tamburlaine*, the play Marlowe may have already begun to write in Cambridge and that made his reputation shortly after he left, in which the baseborn hero first reveals the titanic scope of his ambition. He does so with a symbolic gesture that resonated with the restrictive university dress regulations on which Marlowe seems to have brooded. He throws off the coarse cloak—a garment he declares "I disdain to wear"—and discloses beneath it the full battle armor of the military hero he intends to make himself. Comparable fantasies of transformation through dress recur elsewhere in Marlowe's plays. In *Doctor Faustus*, the magician intends not only to drive the Prince of Parma from the land and to reign as king but also to "fill the Public Schools"—the lecture halls—"with silk, / Wherewith the students shall be bravely clad." In *Edward II*, the ambitious young Oxford scholar Baldock, who has been serving as a private tutor to an aristocratic lady, is advised, if he wants to get on in life, to change the way he dresses. "You must cast the scholar off," says his friend, urging him to get rid of his sober black coat, "And learn to court it like a gentleman."

The obsession with dress as a key marker of social ambition and advancement may help to explain an intriguing object that dates from Marlowe's time at Cambridge. In 1953, in the course of construction work in Corpus Christi College, someone noticed that several boards that had been thrown into a dumpster appeared to be painted. The boards—retrieved, examined, and restored—turned out to be the portrait of a pale-skinned young man with flowing auburn hair, a thin beard, and a cool, skeptical expression. The sitter is not identified by name, but an inscription in the upper left corner reads, "Aetatis suae 21 1585" (Aged 21, 1585). That happens to be the year in which Marlowe, aged twenty-one, completed his BA degree and began his studies for the MA. Almost immediately the painting was taken to be a portrait—the only known portrait—of Marlowe.

Still, there were other twenty-one-year-olds at Corpus in 1585. There is a suggestive Latin motto inscribed just below the date: *Quod me nutrit me destruit* ("That which nourishes me destroys me"). The words, whether they refer to the simultaneously nurturing and destructive effects of time or of desire, are certainly compatible with Marlowe's sensibility, but they do not secure the identification. The idea was a familiar and widespread one.

Yet the painting of the young man in a black doublet fashionably slashed to reveal a salmon-colored lining is interesting not as an accurate representation of the way in which the sitter—whoever he was—is likely to have dressed and paraded through the streets of sober-suited Cambridge.

Portrait of a Young Gentleman (said to be Christopher Marlowe). Corpus Christi College, University of Cambridge. The date on the portrait corresponds to Marlowe's age, but the clothes, with their conspicuous gold buttons, hardly correspond to the dress mandated for university students. (National Portrait Gallery)

(Such attire was, after all, strictly against university rules.) It is interesting as a fantasy, akin to Faustus's fantasy of dressing the debaters in the lecture halls in silk. If the students—and to judge from the example of Harvey, at least some of their teachers—dreamed of careers in the great world, if they longed, like Marlowe's Baldock, to "learn to court it like a gentleman," isn't this precisely how they would have wanted to imagine themselves? What would the daydreams of students who wanted to cut a figure in the world look like, if not this? The subject of the painting looks slightly uncomfortable in his fancy dress, as if he has borrowed it (as so many sitters did) for the occasion, or as if he has thrust his head through a hole conveniently cut in a prefabricated image a shade too big for him.

Baldock, eager to cast off the scholar and leave Oxford behind, says that he actually hates the curate-like way he has been dressing, but the lord who hired him is so finicky "that he would take exceptions at my buttons, / And being like pins' heads, blame me for the bigness." One extremely prominent element in the Corpus Christi portrait stands out: the big gold buttons, thirty-two of them. It is as if a student, seething under the thumb of the authorities, here takes his imaginary revenge.

CHAPTER 7

# Recruitment

IN MARLOWE'S CAMBRIDGE, as in the same university today, the undergraduates did not receive grades in individual courses at the end of each term. Instead, earning the Bachelor of Arts degree depended entirely on the students' successful performance in a series of challenging final examinations based on what they had studied and learned to do over the preceding years. In the Lent term of his fourth year, in 1584, Marlowe jumped through the hoops. In front of an audience of his fellow students, he debated in Latin three propositions with three other undergraduates from other colleges. Having succeeded in this exercise, he underwent examinations from the faculty, and then he appeared in public again to answer questions taken from Aristotle's work on logical reasoning, the *Prior Analytics*. On Palm Sunday 1584 he formally completed all the requirements and was awarded the degree. In the university's ranked list of degree recipients, Marlowe's name appears toward the middle, but the ranking was deliberately skewed to favor the sons of the gentry and aristocracy, as if to mark the end of the institution's conscious efforts at leveling. The son of a poor nobody had in fact distinguished himself.

Marlowe told the authorities at Cambridge that he intended, as his scholarship allowed, to go on to the MA degree. The three-year degree program continued the study of philosophy begun during the undergraduate years and added the advanced study of Greek language, mathematics, geometry, geography, and cosmography. The overarching purpose of these wide-ranging inquiries was to understand God's creation in its full complexity and glory and to read the New Testament in its original tongue. Marlowe was in effect declaring his intention to become a priest in the Church of England.

No one was forcing Marlowe to head in this direction, and many students at Oxford and Cambridge, including some from families of modest means who were there on scholarships comparable to his, decided on their own volition to leave after the BA degree. That he decided to go on was a choice, however much it was constrained by his limited opportunities. Nothing in Marlowe's subsequent life suggests that he ever felt a religious vocation or imagined himself standing before a congregation to celebrate the Lord's Supper. But he opted to continue as if this were his goal.

Choosing to embark on the MA degree gave the twenty-year-old Marlowe more time to study, to think, to weigh his options. He was thoroughly at home at Corpus and familiar with all its routines. To continue to receive the funds for tuition and housing and to sign for his meals at the college buttery, he was not required by the terms of the Parker scholarship to make a formal commitment to enter the church and never turn back. The three additional full years of support were a boon, and they must have stretched out before him as toward a far-distant horizon. But he also knew that this privileged time was limited. Part of him must constantly have been looking around for what would come next. That looking was not limited to the precincts of Cambridge.

Marlowe's presence or absence from the university may be tracked by following the entries in the Buttery Books, where his food and drink expenses were recorded. The records are not easy to decipher. The spelling of proper names would not be regularized until the next century, so in these and other documents, Marlowe's name was spelled in a baffling number of different ways: Marlowe, Marlow, Marloe, Marlo, Marlen, Marlin, Marlyne, Marlinge, Merlin, Marley, Marlye, Morley, Morle. Nevertheless, starting from his arrival at Corpus in early December 1580, when he spent a penny for refreshment, and continuing throughout his

BA and MA years, it is possible to gauge when he was residing in college and when he was somewhere else.

On at least one of these absences, he returned home to Canterbury, for his name appears on a legal document as one of the witnesses to the signing of a new last will and testament by the widow Benchkin at her house on Stour Street. According to the document, Mrs. Benchkin, in very good health, threw her old will into the fire, then handed her new will to Christopher Marlowe. As befitted an accomplished young scholar and recently minted BA from Cambridge University, Marlowe read the document "plainly and distinctly," whereupon Mrs. Benchkin signed it with her mark. Along with the other witnesses, Marlowe signed it, writing "Cristofer Marley."

Many other long absences of his are completely unaccounted for. The university had a residence requirement for graduation: students were allowed to leave Cambridge for one month per year, and then only with official permission. During his undergraduate years, Marlowe for the most part observed the rules and duly received his weekly allowance for food and drink, but in the course of his MA years, something happened that led him to be away for prolonged periods. Altogether he missed almost half the year in 1584–85, and though not all the college's records have survived, there seem in the subsequent years to have been comparable unexplained and unexcused disappearances. Whenever he returned to Corpus from wherever it was that he had gone, he appeared to have money in his pocket, for he spent more in the buttery at those times than his scholarship would have covered.

Notwithstanding his mysterious absences, Marlowe continued his MA studies. In March 1587 he submitted a formal petition declaring that he had fulfilled all the requirements and requesting that he therefore be granted the degree. The petition was rejected by the master of Corpus Christi, Robert Norgate.

Marlowe's absences, in flagrant violation of the rules, had been noted. He would have nothing to show for his three years of work. When his scholarship came to an end, he would leave Cambridge without the advanced degree. His university career, according to the authorities, had ended in failure.

◆ ◆ ◆

WEEKS PASSED, stretching into months. Finally at the end of June an extraordinary letter regarding the obscure twenty-three-year-old cobbler's son whose unauthorized absences seemed to disqualify him from receiving his MA degree arrived in Cambridge from the Queen's Privy Council in London:

> Whereas it was reported that Christopher Marlowe ["Morley"] was determined to have gone beyond the seas to Rheims and there to remain, their Lordships thought good to certify that he had no such intent, but that in all his actions he had behaved himself orderly and discreetly, whereby he had done her Majesty good service and deserved to be rewarded for faithful dealing. Their Lordships' request was that the rumor therefore should be allayed by all possible means and that he should be furthered in the degree he was to take this next commencement. Because it was not her Majesty's pleasure that anyone employed as he had been in matters touching the benefit of his country should be defamed by those that are ignorant in the affairs he went about.

The five names, or rather five official titles, that were attached to this letter made it crystal clear that the instructions came from some of the most powerful people, next to the queen herself, in the land: Lord Archbishop, Lord Chancellor, Lord Treasurer, Lord Chamberlain, Master Comptroller.

Three days later Marlowe was granted his MA.

The privy councilors' letter included an important certification:

"*Whereas it was reported that Christopher Marlowe was determined to have gone beyond the seas to Rheims and there to remain, their Lordships thought good to certify that he had no such intent.*" The French cathedral city of Rheims was the site of the English College, a seminary to train English Catholics for the priesthood. There young English exiles from Cambridge and Oxford could discard the terms of the Anglican settlement that they found abhorrent and embrace what they regarded as the only true and universal religion. The certification does not make clear whether the rumor that Marlowe had gone—or more precisely, that he "was determined to have gone"—to Rheims and intended to remain there was true or false. It leaves in the dark whether he did in fact travel to France for a limited time, or whether he planned a trip that did not occur, or whether he never intended to go there. The words are a small masterpiece of studied ambiguity attached to an unambiguous command: *Give him the degree.*

England's small ruling elite was anxious that it had an insufficient hold on the hearts and minds of a large population that clung tenaciously to the old forms of belief and that would welcome the country's return to Roman Catholicism. Intolerance pervaded the realm's so-called religious settlement, as it had pervaded all earlier attempts to settle the proper form of Christian belief and practice. In Luke's Gospel, Jesus tells the story of a rich man whose guests decline his invitation to a feast. The man commands his servants to "go out into the highways and hedges, and compel them to come in." That last fateful phrase attributed to Jesus—in the Vulgate, *compelle intrare*—was used in every regime to encourage what the historian Alexandra Walsham calls "charitable hatred" and to justify persecution and murder in the name of faith. Queen Elizabeth professed an interest in ending the nightmare. She had no eagerness, she said, to open windows into men's souls. But she and, still more, her principal advisers feared that Catholics were conspiring to assassinate her and restore England's allegiance to the pope.

Much of the concern was overblown. By and large the population, including those who most longed for the way things had been under the Catholic queen Mary, was nonetheless loyal to the Protestant queen Elizabeth and obedient to authority. Even the exiles at Rheims who were studying for the priesthood and willing to risk their lives by returning to England intended for the most part to minister to their oppressed Roman Catholic brethren without involving themselves in treasonous conspiracies.

Still, the Privy Council was not merely suffering from groundless paranoia. The founder and head of the English College in Rheims (and of its earlier incarnation in Douai) was a Catholic priest, William Allen. Educated at Oxford before he went into exile in France, Allen was described by an English government spy as "tall of stature and slender; his beard cut short and somewhat red in color; his face full of wrinkles; under his right eye a mole, not very big; longhanded, the nails of his fingers long and growing up." Charismatic, tireless, and ardent in his faith, he was convinced that Protestantism had shallow roots in English soil and that the people would, given the slightest opportunity, rise up and depose the painted Jezebel who occupied the throne. To this end, all through the late 1570s and '80s he was in regular contact both with papal authorities in Rome and with high government officials in Spain and France who were prepared to offer military assistance to kill Elizabeth and her whole inner circle of heretics. Allen was actively trolling for English Catholics willing to participate in this wildly risky, treasonous enterprise. And he knew just where to look: behind the high walls that enclosed the handsomely endowed colleges of Oxford and Cambridge universities.

Just beneath the surface, those colleges were riven by the dangerous divisions that afflicted the whole kingdom. In 1572 the rooms of Dr. John Caius—a learned physician and the master of a college that bore his name—were raided. The men who broke into his lodging on the orders of high-ranking authorities searched through the cabinets, drawers, and bookshelves. Physicians had always been objects of suspicion. As a medieval Latin proverb put it, *Ubi tres medici, duo athei,* "two out of three doctors are atheists," and sure enough, back in the 1560s, Caius had been accused of atheism by fellows in his college. But evidence of atheism was not what the searchers in his rooms were looking for. A report to the queen's principal adviser Lord Burghley from Cambridge's vice-chancellor Andrew Byng reveals what they seized and hauled away:

> I received an inventory of much popish trumpery, as vestments, albs, tunicles, stoles, manicles, corporax cloths, with the pyx and sindon and canopy . . . with other such stuff as might have furnished diverse masses at one instant. It was thought good by the whole consent of the heads of houses, to burn the books and such other things as served most for idolatrous abuses, and to cause the rest to be defaced; which was accomplished yesterday with willing hearts, as appeared, of the whole company of that house.

The items bearing the technical names were vestments, cloths, specialized containers, and the like used to conduct the ritual of the eucharist in the Roman Catholic mass.

Notwithstanding the old charges of atheism, Caius had long been suspected of being a Catholic; it was even rumored that he was a priest who was secretly conducting masses in the nominally Protestant college. The cache of Catholic items of worship found in his rooms did not definitively confirm these rumors, but they showed that he had at least been attempting to keep the precious relics of the outlawed church from destruction. The bonfire and smashing that were celebrated, if the letter is to be believed, by the "whole company" of the college, and that were approved by the heads of the other colleges, were meant to put an end to the old faith. But that faith persisted, and its adherents were fertile ground for William Allen and others.

In 1570 the pope in Rome had excommunicated Queen Elizabeth. Declaring that she was no longer a legitimate sovereign, Pius V ordered her subjects, on their faith as good Catholics, not to obey her laws or commandments. This put pious English Catholics in an exceedingly difficult position. If they followed the injunctions of the supreme leader of their faith and denied the queen's sovereignty, they were subject to heavy fines, imprisonment, and potential accusations of treason. If they obeyed the laws of the land and went to Anglican services, as those laws required, they risked excommunication and the eternal damnation of their souls. Small wonder then that a significant number of young men—many of whom had come to university to study theology and presumably took matters of faith seriously—experienced a crisis of conscience that led them into exile. By 1583 the English College at Rheims was apparently receiving disaffected students from Oxford and Cambridge at the rate of about twelve a month.

Theology was not the only topic of conversation at the English College. The students and their teachers talked a great deal about their fondest hope: returning England to the Catholic fold. If only the heretic queen were dead; if only her wicked Protestant counselors and bishops were toppled; if only the loyal Catholics everywhere in the land, inspired by the glorious martyrs and aided by their foreign allies, rose up as a mighty force; if only a strong Catholic claimant to the throne emerged from the shadows; if only Henry VIII's great-niece, the Catholic Mary, Queen of Scots, could be crowned Queen of England...

In September 1581 the Jesuit priest Robert Persons, who like Allen was in exile in France, wrote to the general of his order in Rome that he had succeeded in insinuating a priest into Cambridge University "in the guise of a scholar or a gentleman commoner." Within only a few months, Persons wrote to his superior, his agent "sent over to Rheims... seven very fit youth." The identity of this secret agent is unknown, as is the college where he resided. But during the years he was at Cambridge, from his matriculation in 1580 to his MA degree in 1587, Marlowe would have been intensely aware of these efforts to recruit Catholic dissidents, just as he would have been aware of the radical Protestant dissidents who were drawn in the opposite direction.

In the chapel of Corpus, the impossibility of healing the kingdom's divisions was visible in miniature. As befitted a setting where everyone was required to speak Latin all the time, the universities had received special permission to conduct their chapel services in Latin, forgoing the English Book of Common Prayer that had been officially instituted throughout the realm by the Church of England. But to the more ardent Protestants, to pray in Latin was to pray in the language of the pope in Rome. Eight faculty members staged a protest: they went "contemptuously out of the chapel whilst the Master was reading, saying 'Latin service is the Pope's dregs.'" At the same time, another Corpus faculty member named Marmaduke Pickering, representing a faction still inclining to Catholic tradition, loudly condemned Calvin as a heretic and called priests' wives whores and their children bastards. This is the community that Christopher Marlowe entered to begin his studies.

❖ ❖ ❖

EVERYONE WHO ATTENDED university in the 1580s knew that members of hidden cabals there were making fateful and potentially fatal choices. These cabals were of the highest concern to the queen's principal advisers, several of whom recruited secret agents to try to infiltrate them and find out their precise aims, along with the identity of their members. As the Lord High Treasurer and the queen's most trusted counselor, William Cecil, Lord Burghley had a substantial team of personal informants, both in the two universities and in the country at large. So too did the queen's favorite, the immensely ambitious Robert Devereux, Earl of Essex. And above all, the queen's principal secretary, Francis Walsingham, put together a powerful intelligence network throughout the realm and abroad.

Walsingham had been the English ambassador to France in the early 1570s. In August 1572, on the eve of St. Bartholomew's Day, he had witnessed the massacre of Huguenots that began in Paris in the wake of the shooting of their leader, Admiral Coligny. The killings by Catholic mobs, incited by priests and their political allies, quickly spread throughout the country and took the lives of thousands. The memory of that terrible event remained etched in Walsingham for the rest of his days. He was determined to stamp out whatever sparks might ignite a comparable conflagration in his own country. He was the right person for the task: a contemporary and friend, the historian William Camden, described him as "a most subtle searcher of hidden secrets." Dark complexioned, with a pointed Italianate beard and habitually somber black clothing, contemporaries found him distinctly alarming, even spiderlike.

He worked out of his house on Seething Lane, very close to the Tower of London. There, in a modest office, he pored over information sent by

*Sir Francis Walsingham, 1589 (attributed to John De Critz the Elder). National Portrait Gallery. Walsingham's official title was the queen's principal secretary, but he is best known as the regime's spymaster. From his office in Seething Lane, he recruited young agents like Marlowe.*

agents from all over the country and abroad. He read descriptions of foreign spies, of subversive pamphlets produced by hidden printing presses, of Catholic priests disguised as merchants or soldiers, of plots to poison or stab or shoot the queen. He received reports of English Catholics in exile who were urging the Spanish king Philip II to organize an army of invasion that would sail to England in a vast fleet and do whatever it would take to free the island from the heretic Jezebel. These invaders, it was said, would be warmly greeted by a Catholic populace that was quietly longing for their aid.

Seething Lane also received regular accounts of the Oxford and Cambridge students who were leaving the country and going to the English

College at Rheims. Since a principal funder of that college was Spain's Philip II, it would stand to reason that at least some of these students would be recruited by William Allen to participate in the proposed invasion. Walsingham therefore made a special effort to infiltrate spies into the English College. One of his successes in the late 1570s was recruiting a Cambridge-educated student who in his mid-twenties arrived in Rheims and applied to the English College to train to be a Catholic priest. The applicant's name was Richard Baines.

From William Allen's perspective, Baines had highly plausible credentials, since his Cambridge college was the one whose master, John Caius, had been suspected of harboring secret Catholic loyalties. Admitted to the program, Baines immersed himself in his clerical training, studied Scholastic theology, took solemn oaths, officiated at mass, and vowed that he would, on the command of his superiors, risk his life and return to England to minister to the Catholic faithful. In September 1581, he was ordained as a Catholic priest. But all along, he was watching, listening, gathering information, and sending clandestine messages to Seething Lane. Baines's motives, whether hatred of Catholics, desire to serve his queen and country, greed, or all of these at once, are not clear. His behavior in the end suggests a streak of wildness, not altogether safe for doing this kind of work. Or perhaps the pressure of doing this kind of work finally made him crack.

Baines took the risk of revealing himself, or at least a significant part of himself, to an inner circle of friends. It was evidently an attempt at seduction, which may have begun with secretly sharing meat pies on meatless Fridays and then extended, no doubt tentatively at first, to more disturbing transgressions. He confessed to his fellow seminarians that he was disgusted with the theological works that they were constantly forced to read. He told them that he much preferred pagan literature. He amused his intimates with cynical jokes about the religious rituals that they were learning to conduct, remarking that they were nothing more than elaborate theatrical gestures. Most of what they were taught to believe, he said, including the requirement of clerical celibacy, was utterly worthless.

To say all this even in jest was dangerous enough, but with one friend in particular—someone Baines must have thought he had completely won over—he took a further step. He whispered that he knew that William Allen and others in the seminary were secretly plotting against the queen, and if his friend would accompany him, they could slip away to London, where he was confident that the queen's secretary would pay them 3,000 crowns to disclose all they knew. Baines then even went further. He floated the idea—how seriously is not clear—that before they left Rheims, he could add poison to the communal well or the soup and finish the whole seminary off.

The friend had heard enough. He went to Allen and revealed that they had a spy and a potential mass murderer in their midst. In May 1582 Baines was seized, imprisoned in chains, and repeatedly stretched on the rack in order to make him confess everything. The records of his confessions, both oral and written, have survived and reveal a man willing to say whatever was required to get the pain to stop. Yes, he had been puffed up with satanic pride and with an uncontrolled desire for rich food, illicit pleasures, and personal advancement; yes, he had failed to see what he now understood, that the plain, pious lives of those in the seminary were supremely blessed; yes, he had been dragged by his sins into the Protestant heresy and its inevitable consequence, atheism. Baines professed himself to be infinitely grateful to the friend who had denounced him, thus saving him from the power of the devil and returning him to the one true faith. He swore on that faith and on the salvation of his immortal soul that he would cling now in all things to the holy, Catholic, apostolic, and Roman Church.

Did the tough-minded Allen believe any of this? It seems highly unlikely, but he let Baines go. The spy's cover had been blown, he had been kept in prison for almost a year, and whatever secret plans he once knew of, if any, had long changed. He was now a known quantity and would be unable to do any further harm. Keeping him locked up cost the seminary money—the college was perennially short of funds—and, to give Allen credit, he chose not to poison the prisoner's soup. All he did was have the broken wretch write and sign a confession.

During his years in the seminary, Baines confessed, he had cultivated "jocular expressions and bon mots, partly of my own making and partly from the profane authors to whom I was addicted." The "mystical ceremonies" of the Catholic Church, he had told his confidants, were "no more than pretty gestures, performing which even a Turk would look holy." The doctrine of Purgatory, he had said, was rubbish; "there was no fire by which souls may be tortured but it was the worm of conscience." Most of the liturgy, he had pronounced, was worthless; "I could teach a more useful method of prayer—reciting the twenty-four letters of the alphabet." For these wicked blasphemies, he now sincerely repented. The confession was printed and smuggled back into England for the gratification of the faithful and the instruction of the faithless. Baines made his way back to London and tried once again to make himself useful to Walsingham. The one place where he could never again be useful was the English College at Rheims.

♦ ♦ ♦

RHEIMS WAS THE place to which the Cambridge authorities believed that Marlowe had gone or was intending to go. Though the letter from the Privy Council in 1587 clearly implies that he had been recruited for some confidential work for the state, it leaves discreetly unclear the nature of the good service he was doing "in matters touching the benefit of his country" or where he was doing this service. There were many destinations to which he could have been sent to collect confidential information and get it safely back to London, including the Netherlands, where wars were being waged, or Scotland, where both Calvinists and Catholics posed a threat to the Elizabethan regime. But the likeliest place, especially given the rumors that the university authorities themselves reported, was the English College in Rheims. And the likeliest person to whom the reports would have been delivered was Sir Francis Walsingham.

The initial contact between Marlowe and Seething Lane may have been made by Nicholas Faunt, some ten years older than Marlowe and linked to him in several different ways. Faunt came from Canterbury, had like Marlowe been one of Gressop's students at the King's School, and had, also like Marlowe, gone as a Parker scholar to Cambridge, where he received his BA from Corpus Christi College. In 1580, after spending several years in France, he was appointed Walsingham's secretary. Faunt may have kept track of other Parker scholars at Corpus. And even if their paths had not already crossed in Canterbury or Cambridge, Marlowe would certainly have heard of Faunt's success. As he pursued his MA degree and pondered what to do with himself, Marlowe could have reached out to his well-situated townsman or been approached by him.

Walsingham was looking for people like Marlowe. Seething Lane had lost Baines's service at Rheims, but other informants were still quietly collecting whatever hints of conspiracy they could gather from conversations overheard in the corridors of the English College or wherever else English Catholic exiles gathered. Whoever was now spying for Walsingham at the English College in the wake of Baines's expulsion would have been waiting to hand his report over to a courier, a stranger who could give him a prearranged signal. The challenge was to find a reliable courier to collect the report.

The secure delivery of letters and other secret documents was not an incidental part of Walsingham's spy service. It was, as it remains, a critical and vexingly difficult part of intelligence gathering. Messengers were stopped on roads and searched. Policemen ferreted through saddlebags, broke open strongboxes, and looked for hidden compartments in trunks. Ports were heavily watched and guarded. Then as now, spies used elaborate techniques to try to secure the confidentiality of their communications or at least to reveal to the recipients any attempts at tampering. Agents used an array of ciphers, along with invisible ink, decoys, seals, and other devices. But their first line of defense was the courier, someone who could blend in and not call attention to himself, pick up any alarming signs of danger, quickly alter plans when circumstances changed, protect his contacts, and lie effectively to whomever tried to intercept or interrogate him. Walsingham was constantly on the lookout for gifted couriers and was willing to pay handsomely for their services.

Marlowe was precisely at the right age and educational level not to arouse suspicion if he were assigned to pay a brief visit to the seminary under the pretense of an interest in someday continuing his studies there and in possibly converting to Catholicism. He could converse in Latin with the priest assigned to receive visitors and could talk plausibly about the theological issues that were troubling him. Having grown up surrounded by Huguenot refugees in Canterbury, he probably understood and might well have spoken French, so that he would have been able to negotiate encounters with customs officials at the border and in inns. And most important, he was a perfect nobody. No descriptions of him would have been in the hands of the watchers at the French port. No warnings about him would have been sent ahead to the college by Catholic spies who tried to identify possible agents in Walsingham's employ. He did not trail family connections that would have been of interest to anyone beyond his immediate neighborhood in Canterbury. And if by chance some former Cambridge student who had gone into exile at the college recognized him, it would have made perfect sense that here was another soul drawn to the Roman faith.

Marlowe's employment "in matters touching the benefit of his country" could have involved more than the collection or delivery of secret documents. The fact that the Cambridge University authorities believed that the theology student was about to flee to Rheims almost certainly means that Marlowe had cast himself in the role of a Catholic dissident, someone who was not merely quietly sympathetic to the old religion but was poised to participate in treasonable efforts to bring it back. This reputation would have given him access to a diverse clandestine community at Cambridge, a secret sodality of pious young men who longed for the Roman rites and feared for the damnation of their immortal souls: nostalgic dreamers, would-be saints and martyrs, drunken adventurers, scholarly intellectuals, fervent believers stubbornly clinging to the faith of their ancestors, and muddleheaded romantics who idealized Mary, Queen of Scots.

The Elizabethan spy's business was not only a matter of observing carefully, remembering, and passing along compromising details to the authorities; the task also typically involved provocation. The successful double agent would draw his targets out, encourage them in their schemes, shore up their shaky confidence, and urge them on to the most violent courses. Then the trap would be sprung, and the gullible intriguer would find himself in the capable hands of the queen's torturer Richard Topcliffe and on the way to a hideous death on the scaffold.

Whatever his assignment, Marlowe would have needed some training. If his destination were Rheims, it is possible that Richard Baines, who wound up playing a well-documented and fateful role in Marlowe's life, might have been called in to instruct him about the English College where he had spent four years under cover. Baines could have described Allen and the other characters to be glimpsed or avoided and could even have gleefully recounted his lurid plot to poison the whole seminary. Perhaps it was with a sly nod toward what he had been told that, a few years later, in his play *The Jew of Malta*, Marlowe had his antihero Barabas poison a nunnery's porridge and kill all the nuns, his own daughter included.

Pope Pius V's excommunication of Queen Elizabeth in 1570 had licensed and in effect encouraged attempts on her life by desperate Catholic plotters. Walsingham strongly suspected that some of the plotters would come from the English College in Rheims. He feared that assassination attempts originating there and elsewhere might be coordinated with a planned invasion of the country by a Spanish fleet with the goal of placing a Catholic on the throne. The principal Catholic claimant was Elizabeth's younger cousin, Mary, Queen of Scots. In 1568, in the wake of a rebellion in Scotland, Mary had fled across the border to England, where she had been held in so-called protective custody. Walsingham and other close advisers to Elizabeth had urged that Mary be killed, but Elizabeth refused to give the order to do so, choosing instead to keep her locked away. Rumors of conspiracies to free her abounded.

Abroad, Walsingham planted his agents in embassies, as well as in Catholic institutions like the English College. At home, he recruited informants in the houses of noblemen suspected of Catholic sympathies, stationed what he called "watchers" in taverns and inns near all the port cities, and placed double agents—spies who claimed to be Catholic conspirators but who were actually in the employ of Seething Lane—in places where he thought treasonous plots were particularly likely to be hatched.

The most promising of these places were the prisons that held Catholics who had been arrested on suspicion of harboring priests, attending illegal masses, or distributing illegal books sympathetic to Rome.

Any Catholic seriously drawn toward a potentially treasonous conspiracy would have had to be insane to confide in a stranger or casual acquaintance. The spymaster needed agents who inspired trust in those who had every reason not to trust, agents whose bonafides would seem impeccable even on the closest inspection. He had therefore to find people with utterly convincing credentials of steadfast loyalty to the interests of Rome who yet would be willing to betray those whose hard-won confidence they had earned.

Walsingham looked to recruit Roman Catholics who, though they adhered to their faith, were horrified by talk of assassination and foreign invasion. He was also good at giving Catholics who had been caught in illegal actions the choice of death or espionage. And he could employ recently lapsed Catholics who professed a newfound hatred of the pope. The challenge was how far to trust them. Some of them could be concealing Catholic loyalties; some could be bought by the highest bidder; some could be sociopaths. The unstable, treacherous Baines—solemnly ordained as a Catholic priest, gleefully sharing his fantasies of poisoning the entire seminary—was a perfect example of the problem.

Walsingham had the virtue of patience as well as cunning. He was playing a long game and could test and test again those whom he thought he might be able to use. A Catholic turncoat named Robert Poley offered his services to Seething Lane. Poley had been a student at Cambridge when Faunt and Baines were enrolled there. They were in different colleges but may well have known each other. Faunt, the most fortunate of the three, wound up in the head office in Seething Lane. Where Baines, after being assessed by Walsingham, was planted at the English College at Rheims, Poley was given a more disagreeable assignment: in 1583 he was sent to the Marshalsea prison, a sinister half-decayed hulk of a building in London's Southwark, on the south bank of the Thames. Like Bridewell, where Kyd would be racked, the Marshalsea was a scene of misery. Setting aside the torture chambers from which bloodcurdling groans and screams periodically issued, the whole place reeked with filth and disease. One of the common fates of those incarcerated for any length of time in the sixteenth century was to die of "prison fever."

Nonetheless it suited Walsingham to park Poley there for a while. It would give the agent-in-training a kind of certificate of suffering for the Catholic cause and allow him to demonstrate his usefulness as an informer. Initially he was held in close confinement, as if to demonstrate the seriousness of his alleged crime, but then the strictness of his imprisonment was relaxed, giving him access to a wider circle of inmates. At the same time, money from an unidentified source began to come into his hands, no doubt further easing access and loosening tongues. Always good at looking out for himself, Poley spent some of this money to make his confinement less disagreeable. Though he was married "to one Watson's daughter" and had a young daughter, he refused to see them. Instead, in his cell he entertained a woman named Joan Yeomans, evidently his mistress and perhaps another of Walsingham's employees.

Poley turned out to have perfect gifts for the trade: he somehow made people instinctively trust him; he was a fantastic liar; and he had no conscience at all. Walsingham clearly valued these skills, but he remained wary. Perhaps Poley seemed to him too good to be true; perhaps he suspected that Poley was secretly reporting to the Catholics while only pretending that he was secretly working for the Protestants. After months of imprisonment in the Marshalsea, he was released, but Walsingham, while keeping an eye on him, did not immediately give him a new assignment.

Then in 1585 Poley was caught in his lodging in possession of forbidden books, foremost among them *Leicester's Commonwealth*, a scabrous piece of Catholic propaganda. Possessing this tract was a criminal offense. Poley was interrogated by Walsingham himself, a notoriously subtle and relentless inquisitor. But as Poley subsequently bragged—to the husband of his mistress Mrs. Yeomans, no less!—he came out of the interrogation unscathed. How could he have denied being in possession of the book, Mr. Yeoman's asked, when the spymaster knew perfectly well that he had it? "It is no matter," Poley answered, "for I will swear and forswear myself, rather than I will accuse myself to do me any harm." As Poley told the story, his flat denials put the spymaster into such a "heat" that "he looked out of his window and grinned like a dog."

If he had wished, Walsingham could have crushed Poley like a bug. But the agent had evidently passed some kind of test. Walsingham would never trust him, but he had now taken the measure of the man and knew that he could make use of him. The first task he was assigned was to deliver certain secret letters to Mary Queen of Scots' principal friend in Paris. Much more would soon follow.

✦ ✦ ✦

By 1586 Mary had been under house arrest for eighteen years and held virtually incommunicado for the past two. Walsingham set a new trap by infiltrating her inner circle with one of his agents who pretended to be her loyal follower and proposed a secret means by which she could correspond with her friends and supporters. The beer for the large household where she was being held was delivered once a week in a large barrel. Her sealed letters, written in cipher, could be concealed in the barrel's bunghole, the agent said, and he would undertake to get them to their intended recipients. He did just as he promised, but before he delivered them, he first handed them over to Walsingham, whose assistants were able to open letters without breaking the seals. One of these assistants, Thomas Phelippes, was particularly valuable. Unprepossessing in appearance—"of low stature, slender every way, dark yellow haired on the head, and clear yellow bearded, eaten in the face with smallpox [and] of short sight"— Phelippes was a genius at deciphering codes of any complexity.

Into this trap stepped the wealthy, idealistic young Anthony Babington, hopelessly besotted with Mary, whom he had briefly served as a page, and with the cause of the old faith to which he passionately adhered. Sometime in 1585 Babington was introduced to a tall, gallant-looking soldier named Captain Fortescue. Fortescue, described on one occasion as wearing "a fine cape laced with gold, a cut satin doublet and silver buttons on his hat," looked every inch a gentleman home from the wars, but he revealed to Babington that his real name was John Ballard and that he was a Catholic priest in disguise. Like Baines, Ballard had been educated at Catholic-leaning Caius College, Cambridge—the college whose master's rooms had been raided—and then at the English College in Rheims.

The two men took the risk of revealing to each other their passionate desire to rid England of the heretic queen and put Mary on the throne. Then in early 1586 Ballard met and introduced to Babington another man, John Savage, who shared their goal and had sworn a solemn oath to carry out the assassination of Elizabeth. The conspiracy began to take on a plausible form. Others were sworn to secrecy and added to their group.

There was a problem, however. Babington's conscience troubled him. Could he in good faith, he asked himself, kill the queen? The other conspirators were not comparably troubled; they believed that the murder of the wicked heretic, excommunicated by the pope, was a lawful and meritorious act. But Babington was focused less on Elizabeth or on the pope than on his beloved queen of Scots. Was this a course of action that Mary, whose life had after all thus far been spared by Elizabeth, would consent to? Babington would want to do only something that the lodestar of his life actively wanted. He shared his concerns with a person he had met and come to trust. That person was Robert Poley.

This was a moment for which Walsingham, who had been quietly tracking Ballard and the others, was hoping and waiting. Poley had wormed his way into Babington's confidence and, having established his eagerness to return England to the one true faith, had been introduced to the key conspirators. He had managed to persuade them that by a fantastic stroke of luck, he had found a position as the servant of Frances, Walsingham's daughter. The Catholics congratulated themselves on having their own man inside Walsingham's actual headquarters on Seething Lane.

Poley seems to have been composed of some strange icy substance. A parenthetical word in a letter he once wrote to Seething Lane reveals something about his mentality. He would gladly accept any task either abroad or at home, he explained, but he would particularly like to spy on Thomas Morgan—Mary's chief friend and agent in Paris—"my plat being laid that way." A *plat* is the term playwrights used to describe the outline of the script they intended to write. They would show the outline ahead of time to a producer or a company of players in hopes of being hired to do the work. Poley wrote that he had worked it all out—"the grounds being secretly laid and so kept"—and just needed the go-ahead. It is as if the lives he was manipulating, including his own, were characters in a play.

Over the months that the conspiracy to assassinate Elizabeth took shape, Poley and Babington spent more and more time together. Babington unpacked his heart to Robin, as he called the friend with whom he had become inseparable. Warmly sympathizing with Babington's ethical dilemma, Poley suggested to his trusting confidant a way that he could salve his conscience: he could secretly contact Mary and ask her permission to proceed. Babington took the advice and did so. His letter was smuggled into the bunghole of the beer barrel and duly delivered to the imprisoned queen—but not, of course, before Walsingham had read it. In due course, Mary sent her reply, and when it was deciphered, it gave Walsingham what he had so long been trying to provoke. Mary had given her consent to the assassination plot.

Mary's letter was resealed and sent on to Babington. But Walsingham made an uncharacteristic blunder. He instructed his people to imitate the handwriting in the reply and to forge a postscript from Mary asking Babington to give her the names of the principal conspirators who would carry out the deed. Immediately after the letter had been sent, he regretted the addition—"you will not believe how much I am grieved with" this mistake, he wrote to an associate—since he thought it would arouse Babington's suspicions. It may well have done so. But whenever Babington expressed uneasiness, his beloved Robin reassured him and urged him on, all the while duly sending the names of the principal conspirators and copies of their secret correspondence to the spymaster. The copying was risky—he was caught in the act once, though he quickly ripped up the paper and, with his signature effrontery, denied that he was doing anything of the kind. Toward the end, even the naïve Babington began to have doubts about his best friend. "Farewell, sweet Robin," he wrote, "if as I take thee, true to me. If not, adieu, *omnium bipedium nequissimus* [the worst of all two-legged creatures]."

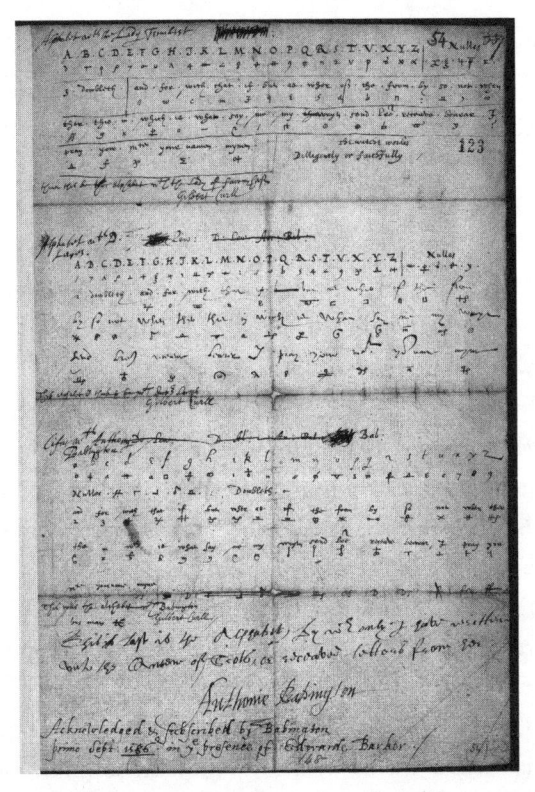

*This cipher was used by Mary, Queen of Scots, for clandestine communication with Anthony Babington in 1586. The letters, deciphered by Walsingham's spy service, helped to bring Mary, Babington, and others to their deaths.*

Walsingham sprang his trap and sent Babington, Ballard, Savage, and the others, fourteen of them in all, to be hanged, drawn, and quartered. Poley may well have been there among the witnesses to admire his handiwork. The executions were meant to be an exemplary spectacle, and they were. The first seven to be hanged were cut down while they were still breathing and castrated before they were sliced into pieces. The rope hanging John Savage had broken almost immediately, leaving him to be dismembered fully alive and conscious. The crowd of spectators, ordinarily inured to such scenes, were so horrified by his screams that the second batch of victims were allowed to die prior to dismemberment. But the spymaster's real coup—and the ultimate goal for which he was working—was the entrapment of Mary, Queen of Scots, whose communication with the conspirators led directly to her beheading on July 24, 1587.

❖ ❖ ❖

RICHARD BAINES AND Sweet Robin Poley. They were experienced players in the game in which Christopher Marlowe, in his early twenties, had somehow become involved. The game was inherently destabilizing. Many of the spies in Walsingham's employ give the impression of inhabiting a strangely ambiguous space, one in which they themselves were not always absolutely certain where their deepest loyalties lay. In order to be convincing, they had fully to inhabit the role they were playing: not merely to recite scripted lines but, entering the whole lifeworld of their intended victims, to share their grief, anxiety, and pious exultation.

To the extent that Marlowe was initiated into this enterprise—and this is presumably what was meant by the Privy Council's certification of his service to the state—he entered a world in which virtually everyone was in disguise and it was fantastically difficult to know whom to trust. These professional role-players, operatives supremely gifted at inspiring confidence, whispered what one most hoped to hear and made one want to relax, open up, and reveal the truth. For a newcomer, everything depended on an ability to distinguish between friends and enemies, but nothing was as it seemed to be. The person who appeared the most trustworthy could easily be the most treacherous. The true believer who swore by the fate of his own immortal soul could be lying through his teeth. The lover who seemed to disclose intimate secrets might be searching for hidden points of extreme vulnerability. It was impossible to act alone, yet all the signals by which one ordinarily assessed safety and danger were corrupted and ambiguous. And anyone who participated necessarily contributed to the corruption and was tainted by it. The whole enterprise centered on betraying your friends, revealing to merciless authorities what those who most trusted you whispered in your ear. Why would Marlowe become involved in such a horrible business?

The most obvious answer is money. Lowly couriers, picking up and delivering the intelligence that others had gathered, were reasonably well compensated, so that when they were at leisure, even experienced spies were not above performing such errands. For a trip carrying letters back and forth to the Hague in 1593, Poley received the substantial sum of £30. And there were other less formal sources of income as well, such as blackmail and small-scale pillaging. A reptile named David Jones, who was trolling for information about priests in London prisons, reported to Walsingham's secretary in August 1574 that he had been saved from starvation by the charity of one Mrs. Cawkin. Mrs. Cawkin, Jones wrote, was a "notorious papist" who should obviously be prosecuted. "I pray you desire my master that I may have the benefit of what she doth lose by statute even if it be but the chain she doth wear." In general, this was not a trade that drew people of exquisite moral sensitivity.

After several of his unexplained absences, the Corpus Buttery Books indicate that on his return to Cambridge, Marlowe spent much more on food and drink than he had done earlier. He clearly had happened upon a source of income beyond the modest regular allotment that the Parker scholarship provided. But risky decisions of the kind Marlowe had evidently made are not always motivated solely by the desire for a significantly larger portion of mutton and ale.

A person could become involved out of a desire to serve queen and country. "Though I profess myself a spy (which is a profession odious though necessary)," declared one of Walsingham's agents, Nicholas Berden, "I prosecute the same not for gain but for the safety of my native country." Berden, alias Thomas Rogers, went to France, where he posed as a Catholic so successfully that, on his return to England, he was hunted down by Justice Young, among the realm's most determined and ferocious persecutors of clandestine priests. Marlowe too could have wished to serve his country by striking a blow against the pope and his allies. He had, after all, grown up in Canterbury among Huguenot refugees who had horror stories of St. Bartholomew's Day. Yet nothing in Marlowe's subsequent career provides grounds for concluding with any confidence that in becoming involved in intelligence work, he was principally motivated by either patriotism or piety, any more than by money.

All were possible motives, but none of them seems quite adequate in the light of Marlowe's abundant irony and skepticism. As he neared the end of his Parker scholarship, he had to decide whether to be ordained as a minister in the English church, as his roommates were doing, and find a parish somewhere. If when you are young, you conclude that the whole thing is a tissue of delusions or frauds imposed on vulgar minds, if you fear that all your dreams for yourself are about to be dashed, if you feel that the world is closing in on you, what career choices do you make? How do you conduct your life? What do you do, in your early twenties, with the time that you have left?

CHAPTER 8

# In the Liberties

IN 1587 TWENTY-THREE-YEAR-OLD Marlowe packed his belongings, left Cambridge, and moved to London. The neighborhood in which he found rooms, Norton Folgate, was close to two purpose-built playhouses, the Theatre and the Curtain, and to the Bull, an inn in whose courtyard plays were performed. But he may have had a reason, beyond proximity to the theaters, for choosing this particular area on the northern edge of the City of London (near today's Liverpool Street Station). The people for whom he had done important work "in matters touching the benefit of his country" may have strongly suggested that he take lodgings there. Of course, in principle he was free to live wherever he chose, but in practice it is not clear whether someone who had become involved in whatever it was that Marlowe had done was ever completely free.

Norton Folgate may have been of special interest to Marlowe's government contacts because of the person who owned most of it, Stephen Vaughan. Before the Reformation, the area had been a priory, St. Mary Spital, dedicated to the care of the poor; after the dissolution of the monasteries, when the canons and lay brothers and sisters were expelled, the real estate was sold to Stephen Vaughan's merchant father, who bequeathed it to his son. Vaughan, who lived in a mansion carved out of the former priory and rented out the rest, had a typically complex family situation. One of his sisters, Anne Locke (or Lok), was a staunch Protestant. An exile during the reign of the Catholic Mary Tudor, Anne translated Calvin and published what may be the first English sonnet sequence, *A Meditation of a Penitent Sinner*. Their sister Jane was an equally staunch Catholic who attended illegal masses and managed to send four of her daughters abroad to become nuns. She was eventually arrested and charged with harboring Catholic priests. When she refused to enter a plea, she was sentenced to the *peine forte et dure*, that is, being pressed to death under increasingly heavy weights. (She was spared this cruel death when Elizabeth died and James, ascending the throne, issued a partial amnesty.)

In the tense atmosphere of 1587, with rumors swirling about an impending Spanish invasion, the English authorities may have had a considerable interest in knowing who was coming and going in Norton Folgate. In addition to Vaughan's sister Jane, they would have wanted to keep an eye on his tenant Robert Hare and his neighbor Sir Edmund Hudleston, both known Catholic sympathizers. If Marlowe was good at persuading some people that he was a secret Catholic—as he had evidently done at Cambridge, when the authorities believed that he had gone or was intending to go to Rheims—then this was a good place for him to be. Renting rooms from Vaughan, he would have been perfectly situated to observe and report anything suspicious and to be paid for it.

Norton Folgate was a decidedly mixed neighborhood, though by no means as mixed as the adjacent parish of St. Botolph, Bishopsgate, with its high crime rate and heightened susceptibility to plague. Still, it was insalubrious and crowded enough, and it undoubtedly saw its share of the dubious characters who trolled many of the streets of London. These characters in Marlowe's time had an array of colorful names: "Anglers," thieves who carried hooked staffs with which they could snare linen hanging from upstairs windows; "Abraham Men," beggars who pretended to be mad, along with "Counterfeit Cranks," who feigned falling sickness; "Cony-Catchers," con men on the lookout for easy marks; "Priggers of Prancers," horse thieves; "Rufflers," former soldiers who showed their real or pretended wounds in order to compel charity; "Bawdy Baskets," "Walking Morts," "Kichin Morts," and other names for women who worked the sex trade. The likes of these, together with cutpurses, pickpockets, and all the rest of London's lower depths, rubbed elbows with the street hawkers, fortune tellers, tinkers, tradesmen, maids, apprentices, porters, bailiffs, sailors, perfumed courtiers, idle gentlemen, fashionable ladies, and on occasion, as in the case of Marlowe, poets and playwrights. On any given afternoon, they all converged on the nearby playhouses, those large wooden O's that had room for all of them.

Marlowe arrived in London with more than his newly minted, government-ordered MA and whatever experience he had acquired abroad. He had at least the idea for a play about Tamburlaine. It is not clear whether he carried a draft with him from Cambridge, but its seeds must have been planted from the moment as a student he turned the pages of Ortelius's great world atlas and glimpsed the images of the turbaned ruler in the tent and the ruins of Samarkand.

The Turco-Mongol ruler Timur the Lame (1336–1405) was one of those charismatic leaders—Alexander the Great, Julius Caesar, Genghis Khan, and Napoleon all come to mind—who inspire and organize vast numbers of followers to embark on enterprises of murderous conquest. It is estimated that his military campaigns across much of Asia caused the deaths of 17 million people, some 5 percent of the world's population at the time. Since he was the last great conqueror to have defeated the powerful Ottoman Empire, the fascination he aroused from the beginning grew throughout the sixteenth century, as the West looked toward Istanbul with increasing preoccupation and dread. The library at Cambridge would have provided an array of sources for Marlowe to plunder.

At some point, Marlowe must have said to himself that it should be possible to turn the abundant traces of this astonishing life into a spectacle. He had already tried his hand at playwriting, aided perhaps by his Cambridge friend Thomas Nashe, and the results were promising. In the year he came to London, their play, *Dido, Queen of Carthage*, was performed at Norwich and Ipswich by a children's company. The play featured another celebrated empire founder, but Aeneas' story was about piety, the renunciation of sexual pleasure, and submission to the will of the gods. Tamburlaine's story was exactly the opposite: it was about the impious breaking of every rule, the ruthless satisfaction of desire, and the triumph of the will. And while Aeneas was a prince by birth, Tamburlaine was a person who started from nothing—a poor shepherd in an obscure corner of what is now Uzbekistan.

Marlowe's imagination was on fire. Tamburlaine's rise must have resonated with all that had been pulling Marlowe away from his studies for the MA degree, with its predictable outcome of a vicar's life in a small parish. Here, in the pages of the histories he found in the college library, was an extreme version of the worldly power he had begun to glimpse in the course of whatever clandestine work he was doing. He jotted down exotic-sounding names and contemplated the long list of those whom the mere nobody had conquered: the emperor of the Turks, the king of Persia, the king of Arabia, and on and on across much of Central Asia and North Africa. He could hear the conqueror's speech, as he imagined it, echoing in his ears. Before he left Corpus, his play may already have begun to take shape.

But once he arrived in London, how could Marlowe, whose life experience had centered on Canterbury and Cambridge, have made contact with the right people in the professional theater and gotten his play produced? No legends surround him comparable to the ones that circulated about another young provincial who probably arrived in the city at about the same time. According to Samuel Johnson, writing in the mid-eighteenth century, William Shakespeare first made his name known by standing at the playhouse door and attending to the horses of those theatergoers who had no servants. "In this office he became so conspicuous for his care and readiness," Johnson writes, "that in a short time every man as he alighted called for *Will. Shakespear*, and scarcely any other waiter was trusted with a horse while *Will. Shakespear* could be had." Such a Horatio Alger beginning, implausible enough for the newcomer from Stratford-upon-Avon, is even less likely to have been true for a Cambridge graduate whose name had already come to the attention of the Privy Council.

Marlowe's associates from the spy service are unlikely to have been much help breaking into the literary scene or launching a career in the commercial theater. Still, he had avenues other than holding horses at the playhouse door. One obvious contact was John Lyly, who had graduated from the King's School in Canterbury in the 1560s and whose younger brothers had been Marlowe's schoolmates. Lyly moved to London in the 1570s after studying at Oxford and quickly made a name for himself with the publication of a flowery literary romance called *Euphues: The Anatomy of Wit*. The story concerns a young man who leaves the university, moves to the big city, succumbs to various temptations, receives his comeuppance, and finally returns home, sadder but wiser. The tale of the repentant prodigal was nothing new, but the plot was distinctly secondary to Lyly's elaborate prose style, replete with patterned antitheses, fanciful similes, and classical allusions. "The freshest colors soonest fade, the teenest [sharpest] razor soonest turneth his edge, the finest cloth is soonest eaten with moths, and the cambric sooner stained than the coarse canvas: which appeared well in this Euphues," etc., etc.

*Euphues* is one of those literary works that arrives with splash, strikes the reigning tastemakers as irresistibly elegant, and is widely read and imitated before succumbing first to parody and then to oblivion. It was still in vogue when Marlowe reached London, though as far as we can tell, he had no interest in Lyly's rococo prose style. But he would have heard that his distinguished townsman had moved on from prose romance to playwriting. Lyly had found a place in the household of an important nobleman, the Earl of Oxford, under whose patronage he was writing and directing a succession of stylish plays for performance by children at court and in small private playhouses. The actors—current and former choirboys organized into a troupe called "the Children of her Majesty's Chapel and the Boys of [St] Paul's [Cathedral]"—were highly accomplished, and Lyly's signature blend of classical allusion, witty repartee, and titillating cross-dressing was a hit with the sophisticated audiences in the earl's orbit and at the royal court. The playwright had been paid handsomely for his elegant confections, and the texts had aroused enough interest among the reading public to be printed and sold at the booksellers' stalls.

Whether Marlowe simply encountered Lyly's plays in print or somehow was able to see one of them rehearsed or performed, he would have grasped that these sophisticated entertainments were a way for a gifted university graduate to monetize his elite education. Given his own *Dido, Queen of Carthage*, that way might have seemed within his reach. But productions in two provincial towns were a far cry from the critical and commercial success in London that the sly, cultivated Lyly had achieved. Lyly managed to toy with delicate matters—gender ambiguity, infidelity, even such sensitive affairs of state as the queen's marriage negotiations—but he had an unerring sense of just when he should turn any potential discomfort into gracious compliment. Marlowe may have grasped that urbane courtly divertissement would never be his métier. He could not resist his transgressive impulse.

That impulse was already clear in the outrageous opening scene of *Dido* with Ganymede sitting on Jupiter's lap. And what he had brought with him from Cambridge, his play about the ferocious Scythian conqueror, could not possibly be tamed to resemble Lyly's subtle allegories of sexual accommodation and renunciation. Imitating Lyly, in the hope of breaking into his exquisitely refined theater circle, would not work. He would have to find his way into a very different scene.

One plausible alternative route was through a far less reputable contact.

◆ ◆ ◆

ROBERT GREENE, WHOM Marlowe may have known at Cambridge, had moved to London upon graduating a few years earlier, and by the time Marlowe arrived, he was earning his keep by selling whatever he wrote to commercial publishers. The publishers—known in this period as stationers, after the guild to which they belonged—sold their books wholesale to booksellers who peddled them (usually unbound) from stalls set up in the churchyard of St. Paul's Cathedral and other locations in the city. They served an amorphous market, ranging from university-educated gentlemen, preachers, lawyers, courtiers, and the like to a much broader spectrum of readers, including artisans, apprentices, and women. Though literacy rates—extremely difficult to gauge—were still probably no higher in London than 20 percent, a book-buying public was emerging that scarcely existed before the Protestant Reformation.

Greene had begun his writing career by shamelessly imitating the mannered style of *Euphues*. His output was rapid and prodigious. A contemporary wrote that "in a night & a day" he would rapidly scribble a whole work, "and glad was that printer that might be so blest to pay him dear for the very dregs of his wit." In quick succession, he churned out three flowery prose romances—*Gwydonius: The Card of Fancy*; *Arbasto: The Anatomy of Fortune*; and *Morando: The Tritameron of Love*—that succeeded in finding eager buyers. The printers kept asking for more.

This popular success was enhanced by Greene's marketing himself as a celebrity. He played the role of the prodigal. Having graduated with a degree from Cambridge (to which he added an honorary degree from Oxford), he could rightly call himself a gentleman, and yet as he was the first to point out in a succession of cheap, autobiographical pamphlets, he was living a wild, disorderly, thoroughly disreputable life in London. He dressed flamboyantly, let his hair grow long, and cultivated a pointed red beard ("like the spire of a steeple," in Nashe's description). He married a wealthy gentlewoman from Lincolnshire, rapidly spent all her money, and then, sending her and the child she had borne him back to the country, took up with a mistress, Em Ball, whose brother, Cutting Ball, was the leader of a gang of thieves. (Cutting Ball was eventually hanged at Tyburn.) Greene and Em had an illegitimate son, whom he grandly named Fortunatus. All along, he noisily advertised his transgressions, his fits of repentance, and his inevitable backsliding, proudly branding his pamphlets with his name: *Greene's Farewell to Folly*; *Greene's Metamorphosis*; *Greene's Never Too Late*; etc. He made himself a fixture in London life.

Let us imagine a scenario in which, soon after his arrival, Marlowe reached out to Greene. Marlowe might have contrived to meet him at one of the haunts where the red-bearded celebrity typically swept in with assorted admirers, hangers-on, and down-at-heels printers vying for the next pamphlet. There was raucous laughter, calls for bottles of Rhine wine and plates of pickled herring, and the lighting of clay pipes filled with the strangely addictive weed that Sir Walter Ralegh had brought back just in the previous year from his colony in Virginia. (No one spoke of smoking tobacco; the word used at this time was "drinking" it.) And in the midst of it all, there was a jumble of the underworld jargon that Greene transcribed and popularized in some of his pamphlets: *We will filch some duds off the ruffmans, or mill the ken for a lag of duds. So may we happen on the harmans, and cly the jerk, or to the queer-ken and scour queer cramp-rings, and so to trining on the chats.* ("We will steal some clothes from the hedges or rob a house for a basket of clothes. But we could be set in the stocks and be whipped or taken to prison, there to be shackled with fetters, and then hanged on the gallows.")

Fresh from university, Marlowe did not understand any of this—it was far more obscure to him than Greek. But he listened with interest, especially when Greene spouted off about the state of literature, attacked his rival writers, and boasted about his own latest masterpiece. And then (or in some comparable scenario) Marlowe caught the attention of a well-dressed man in his early thirties, with the look more of a prosperous businessman than a celebrity-seeker or scrounger. This was Philip Henslowe, an entrepreneur with interests in the starch trade, pawnbrokering, real estate, cloth dyeing, timbering, and the purchase and dressing of goatskins.

By 1587, when Marlowe moved to London and was scouting the literary scene, Henslowe had conceived an ambitious enterprise. Together with a well-to-do grocer named John Cholmeley, he had leased a plot of land with several buildings and an attractive rose garden on the south bank of the Thames. The parcel, near Southwark Cathedral, was in an area known as the Clink, after the name of a notorious prison in the neighborhood (whence our phrase to be thrown "in the clink"). The Clink was, from an administrative point of view, what was called a "Liberty"; that meant that it was not under the authority of the local sheriff or of the city authorities across the river, but under the much looser authority of the bishop, in this case the Bishop of Winchester. That particular bishopric had long been relaxed about all forms of popular recreation. (A common term for a prostitute in the period was "a Winchester goose.") Henslowe had a vision: he wanted to erect a theater there. The grocer Cholmeley agreed to underwrite a significant portion of the cost in return for the right to sell food and drink to the crowds they expected to draw.

During the previous decade on the other side of the river, near the commercial and political center of the city, the two large, freestanding public playhouses, the Theatre and the Curtain, were doing extremely well. Plays were performed in the afternoon—the theaters were unlit—most days of the week, and each of the playhouses could accommodate several thousand people. Large numbers of Londoners of all social classes crowded in to see whatever was on offer. The wealthy paid for a place to sit in one of the covered galleries, where they were protected from the sun and rain; the cheapest admissions were for standing room in the large open-air space around the bare stage that thrust into the center of the roughly circular theater. The key to commercial success was entertainment for everyone—not like the esoteric plays John Lyly proffered to the favored few. It was about sheer popular pleasure.

The enterprise—one of the world's first mass entertainment industries—was raw, expansive, and unstable. London's civic authorities and sober-suited moralists hated the new phenomenon. They worried about traffic problems—an unwelcome concentration of carriages and horses in the narrow streets. Still more they worried about the threat of infectious disease, the prime opportunity given to pickpockets, and the encouragement of idleness. The whole business seemed to them an incitement to vice. Performances took place during hours when responsible people should all have been at work; the women's parts were played by lascivious boys who pranced around the stage in wigs and dresses; and the plots aroused fantasies at odds with the moral lessons intoned in Sunday sermons. The audiences were full of apprentices, workmen, soldiers returned from the war, sailors on shore leave, whores, confidence men, city women enjoying an afternoon away from their husbands, tradesmen, and foreigners—a volatile mix. The public theaters, officials urged, should all be torn down.

The officials could complain all they wanted, but they didn't have the legal right to padlock buildings constructed in the Liberties, except in a public health emergency or by order of the crown. And the crown was not on their side. The queen took pleasure in theatrical entertainments and favored them for "the recreation of our loving subjects." In 1574 she had issued a special license on behalf of the Earl of Leicester's troupe "to use, exercise, and occupy the art and faculty of playing comedies, tragedies, interludes, stage plays, and other such like" throughout the realm.

The way had thus been paved for the construction in 1576 of the first freestanding public theater in England since the time of the ancient Romans. Another theater soon followed, and their ability to turn a profit aroused Henslowe's entrepreneurial interest. There were certain conditions: the plays had to be approved in advance by an official called the master of the revels; they could not be performed during the time of church services; and all performances were prohibited when London was experiencing outbreaks of the dread bubonic plague.

Even among civic leaders who felt obliged to condemn the theater, there were defectors who enjoyed an afternoon's entertainment. Well-to-do merchants and their wives—goldsmiths, haberdashers, vintners, armorers, scriveners, apothecaries, clockmakers, and the like—sat in the galleries alongside gentlemen and ladies. And the companies that performed had friends in high places. Powerful aristocrats had long patronized troupes of actors for private performances in their castles and city mansions. Now some of them, surrounded by their armed retinues, came to the public theaters, where they bought the best seats, showed off their flamboyantly expensive clothes, "drank" tobacco, and applauded performers who wore their liveries or the liveries of their friends.

The queen herself lent her supreme prestige to one of these companies—the Queen's Men—and welcomed performances at court by this and other companies at Christmastime and other holidays. She professed to regard the staging of plays in the public theaters—which she never personally attended—as a species of rehearsal for these court appearances. The notion that the playhouses were venues for perfecting royal entertainments gave the commercial theaters an extra measure of protection against those who wished to close them.

The queen's interest in keeping the playhouses open in her capital city may have extended beyond her desire for personal pleasure and the entertainment of her royal court. City authorities and puritanical moralists railed against the theater as a sink of vice, but the playhouses could have seemed to her a boon. For several hours every afternoon, thousands of London's citizens—including large numbers of potentially unruly young men—stood or sat quietly in an enclosed place and watched plays that had been vetted by the government censor. What else might they have been doing during those idle hours?

Prominently present among the mass of playgoers were men who had returned home from one of the overseas wars in which England had become involved. These were not wars of short duration or with clear end points; they were more like the interminable wars in which America and its allies became entangled post 9/11. From the mid-1580s onward, there were constant levies of troops, initially for the bloody ongoing struggles in the Netherlands, then for the feared Spanish invasion, and then for battles in Portugal, France, and above all, Ireland. The soldiers, thousands of them, were recruited, cursorily trained, and shipped abroad to fight. At the end of their service, they returned to England, where they were most often given a small sum and sent packing. On occasion they were obliged to hand over their weapons, but more often they just kept them as part of their very modest wages. The military historian C. G. Cruickshank has estimated that in the last two decades of Queen Elizabeth's reign, there were more than one hundred thousand such troops, to which one should add large numbers of men serving in the trained bands and militia that were organized for home defense, as well as the comparably large numbers impressed to serve in the navy.

"There is a certain waste of the people for whom there is no use but war," Marlowe's friend Nashe wrote; "if they have no service abroad, they will make mutinies at home." The last thing that Elizabeth and her advisers wanted in London was a mass of underemployed, heavily armed young men inured to violence, feeling bored and looking for trouble. "It is expedient," Nashe wrote of such people, that "they have some light toys to busy their heads withal, cast before them as bones to gnaw upon, which may keep them from having leisure to intermeddle with higher matters." The "light toys" that Nashe had in mind to offer them were plays, performed in "the afternoon being the idlest time of the day, wherein men that are their own masters (as gentlemen of the court, the Inns of the Court, and the number of captains and soldiers about London) do wholly bestow themselves upon pleasure." To expect such men to sit around reading stories of their forefathers' military triumphs in worm-eaten old chronicles was absurd, but those stories were exactly what they could see thrillingly reenacted on stage. Such, Nashe wrote, was "the policy of plays."

No wonder the queen and her principal advisers protected the playhouses from excessive interference. They saw in them a hedge against popular disorder. The Elizabethan state became alarmed and sprang into action whenever a handful of drunken louts got together and grumbled that England was going to the dogs. "We can get no work," a wool-weaver named White complained, "nor have we no money and if we should steal we should be hanged, and if we should ask, no man would give us, but we will have a remedy one of these days, or else we will lose all, for the commons will rise, we not know how soon, for we look for it every hour." White's words were reported. He was arrested, tried, and hanged along with three of his mates. But the same easily panicked authorities watched complacently while private citizens erected large wooden buildings in the capital city with the intention of bringing together masses of people in broad daylight to watch spectacles that included mutinies and regicides. Whatever happened within those wooden walls must have seemed far safer than the alternative.

The playhouses were all designed roughly on the same circular model. The platform stages in these open-air buildings had no curtains, no scenery, and no lighting. The effectiveness of the performances depended on the force and conviction that the costumed players managed to bring to their words. Audiences in the period talked about going "to hear" a play, not "to see" one. The trained actors had extraordinary powers of projection, as well as prodigious memories: in any given week, they could be performing up to six different plays.

The all-male companies of professional players that performed in the new theaters, each competing fiercely for audience share, were in constant need of new material. The old repertoire was of no use. The Protestant authorities had banned the grand Catholic religious pageants that were traditionally staged on holidays in towns and cities across England, and the moral fables that had suited audiences earlier in the century, such late-medieval plays as *Everyman* and *Mankind*, now seemed hopelessly outdated. Writers hurried to supply what was desired. But the early results, to judge from what little has survived in print (and what was printed must have been thought the best of the lot), were often dismal.

Elizabethan listeners counted on the language of the plays to do what spectacular scenic effects and lighting do in the modern theater: enhance illusion, heighten emotion, and excite the imagination. That is why Elizabethan drama from its inception was written largely in verse. But the verse that was initially ground out was almost comically inept. Typical is this attempt, in a play called *A Lamentable Tragedy, Mixed Full of Pleasant Mirth, Containing the Life of Cambyses, King of Persia*, to conjure up an exotic world of power politics and war:

> I am the King of Persia, a large and fertile soil:
> The Egyptians against us repugn, as varlets slave and vile;
> Therefore I mean with Mars' heart, with wars them
>     to frequent,
> Them to subdue as captive mine, this is my heart's intent.

The unwieldy fourteen-syllable lines almost inevitably give the impression of bouncing along a bumpy road. Still, audiences kept coming.

Henslowe gambled that a large theater erected on the south bank property that he had leased could be just as successful as the venues on the other side of the river. It was a risky idea. To come to his new theater, the paying public could not simply slip away from work and walk around the corner; they would have to cross London Bridge or take a boat across the Thames for the afternoon's entertainment. The compensatory advantage was the fact that the Rose, as he would call his playhouse, would be situated in the midst of an already popular entertainment zone, with nearby gambling dens, archery grounds, and venues for blood sports like bullbaiting and bearbaiting. The Rose would attract a young crowd, less likely to share the sour prejudices of the puritanical moralists. Henslowe reserved one of the existing buildings on his site for a brothel.

To turn a suitable profit, the Rose Theater would need to attract many hundreds of spectators on each day that its doors were open. The entrepreneur set about putting together a stable of writers who could steadily churn out plays. This was an enterprise that needed production in bulk: different plays were performed on consecutive days, and though a new play might return to the stage more often, the runs were generally quite short. A few plays outlasted a year or two, but most disappeared quickly. Writing for the new public theaters was generally regarded as hack work, but if it lacked cultural capital, Henslowe and his competitors were willing to pay reasonably well to fuel the rapid turnover. For a new play, a writer could get up to £6—about half the average annual income of a skilled worker—or share that sum with others if they individually contributed a few scenes or sat together in a room and hammered something out.

Ever since he arrived in London, Marlowe had probably gone frequently to the theater. What he had seen and, more important, heard had not impressed him. He was confident that he could do better and offered to show Henslowe a play he had begun at Cambridge and had just completed. He called the play *Tamburlaine the Great*.

What happened next changed both Marlowe's life and theater history.

CHAPTER 9

# The Conquest of London

Henslowe, alert for a way to challenge the existing playhouses on the other side of the river, seems to have grasped at once that *Tamburlaine* would be ideal for his new theater. No doubt with his encouragement, Marlowe began his play by deliberately insulting the competition. He made clear that he was launching a frontal attack on the reigning style of contemporary writing for the public theaters, a style he likened to the spectacle of novices awkwardly dancing a jig:

> From jigging veins of rhyming mother wits,
> And such conceits as clownage keeps in pay,
> We'll lead you to the stately tent of War,
> Where you shall hear the Scythian Tamburlaine
> Threat'ning the world with high astounding terms
> And scourging kingdoms with his conquering sword.
>      (Prologue 1–6)

The words set the stage for the martial hero to emerge dressed in crimson velvet and copper lace and to begin to threaten the world he intended to conquer.

But Marlowe knew that it was he the writer who was threatening the world—at least the world of the theater—with "high astounding terms."

If he succeeded in conquering the stage, everything before him would look like clownage. It would not be up to the academic authorities, the moral censors, or the elder statesmen of high culture to decide the outcome. Men and women of all social classes, the educated and the illiterate, silk-clad courtiers and rowdy apprentices, highborn ladies and sex workers from the nearby brothels: this crowd of random spectators who all paid their pennies for admission would watch and decide. "View but his picture in this tragic glass," the prologue to *Tamburlaine* insouciantly ends, "And then applaud his fortunes as you please."

The spectacular applause that followed vindicated Marlowe's boldness. Virtually everything in the Elizabethan theater is pre- and post-*Tamburlaine*.

Most literary innovation is incremental; it is rare for a work of art to change everything so quickly and decisively. But *Tamburlaine* is one of those rare instances. No one in English poetry had ever spoken with the grandeur and magnificent self-confidence of Marlowe's Scythian hero:

> Nature, that framed us of four elements
> Warring within our breasts for regiment,
> Doth teach us all to have aspiring minds:
> Our souls, whose faculties can comprehend
> The wondrous architecture of the world
> And measure every wandering planet's course,
> Still climbing after knowledge infinite
> And always moving as the restless spheres,
> Wills us to wear ourselves and never rest
> Until we reach the ripest fruit of all,
> That perfect bliss and sole felicity,
> The sweet fruition of an earthly crown. (2.7.18–29)

The lust for power—secular ambition at its most naked, with no end other than its own realization—is here given its supreme expression. From the "wondrous architecture" of Marlowe's unrhymed iambic pentameter—elegant, musical, and forward-thrusting—it became clear virtually overnight that there was a new, far more powerful way of writing for the stage. Drawn by what Ben Jonson would later call "Marlowe's mighty line," paying crowds flocked to the theater.

Nothing in Marlowe's play remotely conforms to the moral lessons taught in schools or preached from the pulpits of Elizabethan churches. Tamburlaine begins as the leader of a robber band. Through eloquence, boldness, and limitless self-confidence, he turns this "troop of thieves and vagabonds," as they are called, into an invincible fighting force. He defeats a succession of formidable enemies, all of whom have long-established hereditary claims to power and authority. He routs the Persian army and topples the emperor from his throne. He captures the Turkish emperor Bajazeth and his wife and throws them into a cage on whose iron bars they finally brain themselves. He seizes the beautiful Zenocrate, no less than the daughter of the sultan of Egypt and the intended bride of the king of Arabia.

The play reaches its climax with Tamburlaine's siege of Damascus. The sultan of Egypt and the king of Arabia are both assembling huge armies to come to the aid of the threatened city and to rescue the captive Zenocrate. Marlowe, greatly struck by a story repeated in several of his sources, has a messenger explain the procedure Tamburlaine always observes in conducting sieges. On the first day he pitches white tents and wears a white feather on his crest "To signify the mildness of his mind / That, satiate with spoil, refuseth blood." Then on the second day, if the city has not submitted and opened its gates, the color changes to scarlet to indicate that his kindled wrath must be quenched with the blood of all able-bodied men. But if this threat still does not produce submission, on the third day "His spear, his shield, his horse, his armor, plumes," and all else turn to black, signifying that "Without respect of sex, degree, or age, / He razeth all his foes with fire and sword."

Expecting that the sultan's army will arrive in time and compel Tamburlaine to lift the siege, the governor of Damascus has refused the first two menaces and now faces the nightmare of the black banners. Zenocrate pleads on behalf of the city—the city of her birth—but her captor is adamant. The desperate governor knows it is too late to negotiate a surrender or appeal for clemency; Tamburlaine is unlikely to suspend his custom "which he observes as parcel to his fame / Intending so to terrify the world." The only measure that the desperate citizens can come up with is to send out their virgin daughters as supplicants, in the hope that "their unspotted prayers, / Their blubbered cheeks, and hearty humble moans" will soften Tamburlaine's fury. But to no avail. "Behold my sword," Tamburlaine says to the trembling delegation; "What see you at the point?" "Nothing but fear and fatal steel," one of them timidly replies. "Your fearful minds are thick and misty, then," he says, "For there sits Death: there sits imperious Death, / Keeping his circuit by the slicing edge." And with that he orders his troops to "show them Death" and to hoist their "slaughtered carcasses" up on Damascus's walls as a foretaste to the general massacre.

Marlowe weirdly heightens the sadistic pleasure of this scene by immediately following it with a long, ecstatic soliloquy in which Tamburlaine muses on the ineffable loveliness of Zenocrate's tears and their powerful impact on his sensibility: "What is beauty, saith my sufferings, then?" A heightened sensitivity to beauty was assumed to be part of the repertory of qualities in great rulers, even the cruelest of them. It was well known that Henry VIII wrote plangent love lyrics—"Alas, what shall I do for love? / For love, alas! What shall I do?"—expressing his vulnerable feelings toward some of the very women he axed. But what did Marlowe think he was doing by conjoining the killing of the virgins of Damascus to Tamburlaine's love song? Did he intend his audience to feel revulsion at the way the massacre of the innocents is somehow braided together in the conqueror's mind with his thoughts of love? Did he hope to awaken the spectators to the moral implications of what they were watching? Or was he offering them the pleasure of experiencing vicariously for their pennies what a victorious army would do when it had finally breached the defensive walls?

Marlowe certainly knew that his audience would have expected that, since pride comes before a fall, Tamburlaine would ultimately be defeated, the dying curses of the vanquished would finally be fulfilled, and the captive Zenocrate would be freed. But as the last act sweeps toward its conclusion, the expectations that innumerable sermons would have aroused in any sixteenth-century spectator are dashed. The armies that have come to raise the siege arrive too late and are crushed. Zenocrate's betrothed, the king of Arabia, is mortally wounded and lies dying before her. Tamburlaine is triumphant.

Though she laments that she has witnessed the streets of her birthplace "strewed with dissevered joints of men, / And wounded bodies gasping yet for life," Zenocrate has in fact fallen passionately in love with her murderous captor. Even with her city dying around her, it is the city's destroyer whom she adores. Tamburlaine loves her as well, but as always, he is most passionately in love with himself. "Jove, viewing me in arms, looks pale and wan," he boasts, "fearing my power should pull him from his throne." The corpses of emperors and kings lie at the victor's feet:

> All sights of power to grace my victory;
> And such are objects fit for Tamburlaine,
> Wherein as in a mirror may be seen
> His honor, that consists in shedding blood. (5.1.521–22)

Having conquered everything "from the bounds of Afric to the banks / Of Ganges," Tamburlaine declares a truce with the world and takes Zenocrate's hand in marriage. Notwithstanding all the blood and gore, the play turns out to have the happy ending of a comedy.

Nothing so outrageous had ever been staged before. Marlowe must have known that he had gotten away with something extraordinary. Henslowe knew it too and urged that Marlowe quickly write a sequel to take advantage of the phenomenon. Though he had used up most of the material he culled from his sources, Marlowe obliged. In *Tamburlaine the Great, Part 2*, he rehearsed the formulas that had worked so well already, pushing them still further into the sphere of the grotesque and the unsettling, as if to see how far he could go. He found that on stage there were virtually no limits.

Vast armies, Muslim and Christian, unite to stop Tamburlaine's relentless sweep across Central Asia and into Turkey. Their leaders negotiate a mutual defense treaty, the Christian emperor Sigismund solemnly swearing "By Him that made the world and saved my soul, / The son of God and issue of a maid, / Sweet Jesus Christ," and the Muslim king Orcanes swearing by Mohammed "Whose glorious body, when he left the world, / Closed in a coffin mounted up the air / And hung on stately Mecca's temple roof." But the Christian ruler soon breaks the treaty. The betrayal has the effect of putting on the same plane claims about the Virgin Birth and the legends about Mohammed's floating coffin. Jesus or Mohammed—there seems to be, as one character observes, no religious meaning to any of this, least of all to the oaths and devout professions of the ruler.

Sigismund is defeated and killed; Orcanes is captured by Tamburlaine and taken, along with other captive kings, to be harnessed like animals and forced to pull the conqueror's chariot. The slaughter continues with no apparent point other than the graphic manifestation of Tamburlaine's power and an exploration of its natural limits. He is powerless to prevent his beloved Zenocrate from falling ill and dying—such is simply the course of nature, which even the greatest conqueror cannot alter—but he burns down the town where she dies. So too he is unable to make one of his three sons share his taste for bloodshed—"I take no pleasure to be murderous," the boy admits, "Nor care for blood when wine will quench my thirst." For a moment in this son, Calyphas, we seem to glimpse an alternative to Tamburlaine's limitless appetite. "While my brothers follow arms, my lord," he tells his father,

> Let me accompany my gracious mother:
> They are enough to conquer all the world,
> And you have won enough for me to keep.
>    (Part 2 1.3.65–68)

But Tamburlaine deals with this disappointing child by killing him.

At the second play's climax, in the siege of Babylon, the citizens are shown pleading desperately with the governor to surrender before it is too late, only to have the governor stubbornly refuse. The results are by now grimly predictable: when the city is taken, the governor is chained, hoisted up on the walls, and shot to death by the troops. Tamburlaine, asked what should be done with everyone else, gives the fatal command: "drown them all, man, woman, and child; / Leave not a Babylonian in the town."

Though little is known about how these plays were first staged—theater reviews lay far in the future—the original production must have gone out of its way to bring the horror home with realistic sound effects. A letter written by a member of the audience to his father describes a ghastly accident. At the performance on November 16, 1587, one of the guns used to simulate the shooting at the governor was inadvertently loaded with a projectile (probably a broken piece of the rod used to scour the barrel). When it was fired, the shot missed its intended target but struck and killed a child and a pregnant woman. The bloodshed that the audience had come to see depicted suddenly became all too real.

The huge crowds that flocked to see these plays were drawn by the noise and smoke of simulated battles, along with the exotic setting and the larger-than-life characters. But for the tradesmen, artisans, mechanics, and apprentices who made up a significant portion of the crowd, the experience must also have had a radical dimension—one made acceptable to the government censors only because of the plays' historical and geographical distance. The baseborn Tamburlaine shuts up a great emperor in an iron cage and drags him out only to serve as his footstool, but because the emperor in question is the Muslim sultan of Turkey, the fantasy can be savored with impunity. A shepherd and his henchmen mock aristocrats, overthrow civic officials, topple monarchs, and get away with it all—hardly a spectacle the authorities would normally tolerate—but the kingdoms are in faraway Asia and Africa, and the audience could safely cheer. Tamburlaine gave them a voice.

The plays also included a dangerous element of religious skepticism. Tamburlaine calls himself the Scourge of God, but it is not clear what god he has in mind or indeed whether there is a god anywhere in the world that the plays depict. "If thou have any power," Tamburlaine shouts as he burns sacred scriptures,

> Come down thyself and work a miracle.
> Thou are not worthy to be worshipped
> That suffers flames of fire to burn the writ
> Wherein the sum of thy religion rests. (Part 2 5.1.185–89)

Without incurring the wrath of the government censors, such words could be spoken on the public stage before thousands of people only because the scriptures in question were copies of the Koran. Tamburlaine's blasphemous words are addressed to Mohammed, but it was easy enough to grasp that their implications extended beyond Islam. As if to play further games with the censor, Marlowe has Tamburlaine fall ill immediately after this moment. If there is a god, the play suggests, it might as well be the god of the Muslims. The displacement allows skeptics and heretics to constitute a subversive audience within the play's larger audience.

A further element in Marlowe's *Tamburlaine* plays helps to explain their extraordinary success and their enduring influence: they are written in richly sonorous, unrhymed iambic pentameter, known as blank verse. This brilliant technical innovation almost instantly displaced the reigning fourteeners and poulter's measure and became the dominant verse form on stage. It was a bit like the arrival of talkies in cinema: there were quite a few fascinating plays before Marlowe's came along, but all at once they seemed wooden and old-fashioned.

It is difficult for us to register the shock waves produced by Marlowe's blank verse; we no longer have the ear for it. Elizabethans of all social classes spent many hours every week listening to elaborately fashioned oral performances, ranging from epic adventures recited by professional storytellers in the town square and folktales told in the candlelit darkness to public proclamations recited by heralds and weekly sermons that the entire population was legally required to hear. Certain celebrity preachers with particularly dazzling rhetorical skills succeeded in attracting huge crowds. Having developed the ability to savor complex structures of syntax and metaphor, the London public flocked to see plays that were generally written in verse. But Marlowe gave them something new, a verbal music that they had never heard before.

Marlowe's blank verse carried a peculiar charge of energy that jolted audiences, as if they had been shocked. Here, to take a single tiny example, is Tamburlaine boasting of his power:

> I hold the Fates bound fast in iron chains,
> And with my hand turn Fortune's wheel about,
> And sooner shall the sun fall from his sphere
> Than Tamburlaine be slain or overcome.
> (Part 1 2.173–76)

There is nothing particularly fancy about these lines. Twenty-six of the thirty-two words are simple monosyllables. The effect does not depend, as Shakespeare's mature verse frequently does, on a surprising word or phrase—Othello's "speculative and officed instrument" or Macbeth's "the multitudinous seas incarnadine." Marlowe's imagery tends to be conventional and familiar. The turning of Fortune's wheel and the sun falling from his sphere are quite unlike such wild flights of fancy as Hamlet's "let the candied tongue lick absurd pomp / And crook the pregnant hinges of the knee." And yet the special energy in Marlowe's verse is unmistakable.

To capture something of the music and rhythm that pervade the play, it is worth reading the brief passage out loud to experience for oneself its succession of *f*'s and *s*'s and its recurrent light pauses. In the climactic line, the word "Tamburlaine"—the proud conqueror naming himself—bursts forth, as it if were a revelation. Throughout the play, Marlowe's blank verse functions like the cylinder of an internal combustion engine: a certain substance—here Tamburlaine's boundless self-confidence—is injected, compressed, sparked into explosion, and then vacated in order to make room for the next injection. And the play is propelled forward.

As Marlowe depicts it, this propulsion, fueled by the hero's stupendous egotism, takes the form of poetic speech that drives everyone and everything along with it. "And with our sun-bright armor as we march," Tamburlaine tells his followers, "We'll chase the stars from heaven and dim their eyes / That stand and muse at our admired arms." "What working words he hath!" one of these followers exclaims.

How was it possible, the play asks, for a mere nobody to gather a vast army and conquer the known world? The answer: working words. This is the solution to the riddle Marlowe must have pondered when he pored over the heavy tomes in the Corpus Christi College library. Perhaps it reached still further back in his life to the half-mad dream of a cobbler's son from Canterbury who secretly harbored fantasies of great power and had fallen in love with poetry. His is a poet's version of Archimedes' famous law: "If you give me a lever and a place to stand, I can move the world." For Marlowe, the lever was a perfect line of blank verse.

The play provides an explicit instance of this lever from a moment early in Tamburlaine's career. The hero is still not much more than a mercenary who has fought to help the leader of one of the warring factions in Persia win the throne. At the battle's end, someone congratulates the leader and says that he shall soon have his wish "And ride in triumph through Persepolis." Tamburlaine immediately picks up this line and repeats it to his trusted companions:

> "And ride in triumph through Persepolis"?
> Is it not brave to be a king, Techelles!?
> Usumcasane and Theridamas,
> Is it not passing brave to be a king,
> "And ride in triumph through Persepolis"?
> (Part 1 2.5.50–54)

A moment later he decides to topple the leader he has just assisted and to seize the throne for himself—inspired by the incantatory power of those ten syllables.

For the audience in the late 1580s, the blank verse of *Tamburlaine* had precisely the effect of suddenness that we have already identified as one of Marlowe's most striking characteristics. It is as if almost everyone in the theater spontaneously agreed that English at its most rhythmically beautiful and most natural was meant to sound like this.

There were a few dissenters: Greene called Marlowe's poetry "intolerable." But those who were not consumed with envy grasped its great power, as Shakespeare would almost immediately do. In *Tamburlaine*, Marlowe used that power principally for what his prologue called "high astounding terms," but he also showed that his blank verse was equally good for quiet moments of intimacy, for subtle inward reflections, and for simple exposition. One of his characters, among the play's few cowards, observes that those hit by cannon shot "Stand staggering like a quivering aspen-leaf," and Marlowe seems to make the verse itself quiver.

✦ ✦ ✦

THE PART OF Tamburlaine requires an actor of remarkable gifts, and Henslowe found the perfect person. London-born Edward Alleyn was only twenty-one years old—two years younger than Marlowe—but had already been performing professionally for three or four years. His innkeeper father died when he was only four, and his mother remarried an actor; hence no doubt the early start on the stage. Ned, as he was called, was tall, with a powerful build and a booming voice, and to these fine physical gifts he added the intelligence, extraordinary memory, and charisma that the part of Tamburlaine demanded.

Playing Tamburlaine was the making of Ned Alleyn. He became famous almost overnight, and with each new role, his fame grew. At the Rose as at the other theaters, the companies had multiple plays in repertory at the same time. The surviving records for the theatrical seasons are very uneven, but Henslowe's financial notations for 1592 show that in that year's first ten performances, the company in which Alleyn was the star performed ten different plays. Somehow he managed to handle what seems from this distance a humanly impossible feat of memory. The scope of his ability must have been equal to that of the larger-than-life Tamburlaine who had made him a celebrity.

In only a few years' time, he married Henslowe's stepdaughter, Joan, and entered into a partnership with his father-in-law. His marriage was a long and an apparently happy one; the actor who as Tamburlaine persuaded thousands of Londoners that he was the Scourge of God addressed his wife as "my good sweetheart and loving mouse" and signed off, "Thine

*Edward Alleyn (?). This illustration of Tamburlaine, from Richard Knolles's* General History of the Turks *(1603), may be based on Edward Alleyn's famous performance of the role in Marlowe's two-part play. (Houghton Library, Harvard)*

ever, and nobody else's by God of heaven." And Alleyn turned out to be as good in business affairs as he was on the stage. As the money accumulated, he gradually cut back on performing, though for some years he continued to act: always in great demand to play Tamburlaine-like roles, he appeared on stage in plays with names like *Godfrey of Boulogne, Constantine, Harry of Cornwall, Zenobia,* and *Cutlack the Dane.* And the play that had first made him a celebrity remained in repertory. More than a decade after its premiere, the costumes in the Rose's inventory included "Tamberlaine's breeches of crimson velvet" and "Tamberlaine's coat with copper lace." Meanwhile Alleyn focused increasingly on the financial side of the entertainment industry. He invested in bear- and bullbaiting and even, on one occasion, lionbaiting; he financed and built a new and highly successful theater; he bought and sold property. He became a rich man, ultimately buying a country estate. And he generously endowed a fine school, Dulwich College, that still exists. To this day the alumni are called "Old Alleynians."

His is the kind of career on which, in our own time, the highest social honors are bestowed, but he never received the knighthood for which he angled. In Renaissance England, a stigma was attached to the stage that even Alleyn's eventual wealth and his philanthropy could not erase. He did not try to hide his origins. When someone expressed reservations about selling a prestigious property to a former actor, Alleyn replied with quiet dignity: "That I was a player I cannot deny; and I am sure I will not. My means of living were honest, and with the poor abilities wherewith God blessed me I was able to do something for myself, my relatives, and my friends." "Therefore" he added, "I am not ashamed."

In a world replete with disasters of one kind and another, Alleyn's was a rare success story. His talents were recognized and rewarded, and though knighthood eluded him, his social standing nonetheless rose. When after Joan's death he remarried, Alleyn's second wife was the daughter of the distinguished dean of St. Paul's Cathedral, the poet John Donne. This remarkable career was built on the foundation laid by Christopher Marlowe's *Tamburlaine*.

Marlowe himself did not, as far as we know, reap any special financial reward from the play that brought crowds flocking to the Rose. He was presumably paid the going rate. It was Alleyn's name, not Marlowe's, that was in everyone's mouth. Authorship of plays in this period (rather like movies and television shows today) was rarely of interest to the general public. Even when the two parts were first printed in 1590, under the title *Tamburlaine the Great: Who, from the State of a Shepherd in Scythia, by His Rare and Wonderful Conquests, Became a Most Puissant and Mighty Monarch*, they appeared anonymously. Marlowe did not stand to make any money from the publication; both plays belonged to Henslowe.

Marlowe had conquered London, but his parents, if they even knew of the conquest, might still have wondered why their gifted son had not become a priest.

One spectator who clearly grasped why he had not become a priest was Robert Greene. Greene perceived the current of religious skepticism in *Tamburlaine* and was outraged that Marlowe was not only getting away with it but also achieving spectacular popular success. This success roused Greene to overcome his professed reluctance to write for the stage and to dash off a shameless imitation entitled *Alphonsus, King of Aragon*. But *Alphonsus* was a flop, and Greene returned to his familiar genre of prose tale. In a letter to the reader prefixed to his new work, he expressed his frustration: "I could not make my verses jet upon the stage in tragical buskins." But that failure, he piously declared, was because he refused to be an immoral writer, the kind of writer whose appeal depended on "daring God out of heaven with that atheist Tamburlaine or blaspheming with the mad priest the sun." Better to forgo popular success "than wantonly set out such impious instances of intolerable poetry, such mad and scoffing poets that have prophetical spirits as bred of Merlin's race."

"The mad priest of the sun" may refer to Giordano Bruno, whose heretical ideas Greene evidently detected in *Tamburlaine*. And anyone remotely interested in the quarrels of contemporary writers knew just who "Merlin" was. (For that matter, in Elizabethan pronunciation, the names might have sounded almost the same; in several Cambridge University records Marlowe's name is written as Merlin.) To have one's name associated with atheism in this period and for long afterward was extremely dangerous. Most people, even constitutionally irreverent ones, understood that it was wise to remain silent. As late as 1697 a twenty-year-old Scottish medical student, Thomas Aikenhead, was hanged for telling his friends that he thought the Bible was "stuffed with madness, nonsense, and contradictions." In the late 1580s, however, Londoners by the thousands went to the theater to hear "Merlin," as Greene put it, "daring God out of heaven with that atheist Tamburlaine."

CHAPTER 10

# Secret Sharers

WITH ABUNDANT PROOF of how gifted his new young playwright was, Henslowe had a strong incentive to draw Marlowe into his stable of writers. The two parts of *Tamburlaine* had been a spectacular commercial draw. Its religious skepticism may have aroused some hostility, but skating near the edge was good for box office receipts. If serious trouble lay in the future, it would likely befall the imprudent writer and not the businessman who had merely risked some of his money behind the scenes. It seems likely, then, that in the wake of *Tamburlaine*, the entrepreneur proposed a new project to Marlowe: one or more plays about the Wars of the Roses, those vicious dynastic struggles in England that had left a trail of blood across the preceding century.

Marlowe would not be working alone. A great many plays in this period were written collaboratively, as movies and television series often are today, and Henslowe was accustomed to putting teams together and working out the appropriate rate of compensation. The issue of authorial credit was less important than the money. Even if the plays eventually appeared in print—which happened infrequently—they most often appeared anonymously or on occasion with only the name of the writer who was responsible for the bulk of the writing. And there were no royalties.

Marlowe may have hesitated to join in the project: having been drawn

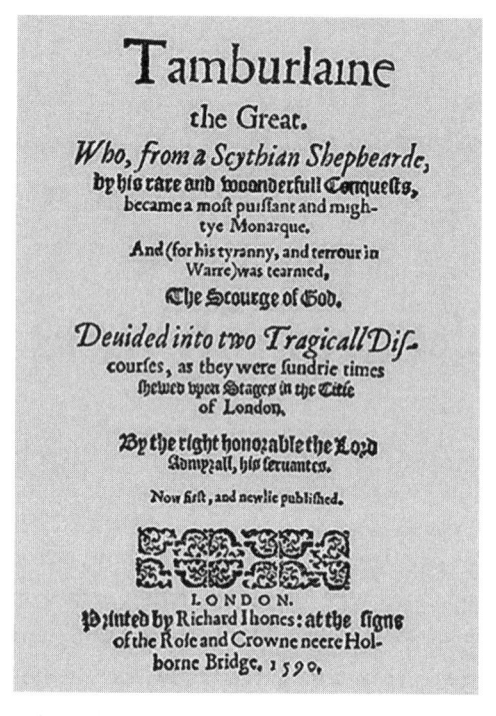

> Title page of Marlowe's Tamburlaine, *printed anonymously in 1590. (British Library)*

to the classics and to the exotic geography of Central Asia and the Middle East, he had thus far shown no interest in English history. Perhaps he spent a little time reading a chronicle history of the turbulent reign of the ill-fated Henry VI before he agreed that it could make for interesting theater. He would then have found himself in a room with one or probably two other playwrights. One of them remains unknown; it might have been Thomas Kyd, with whom he would eventually share a room. The other playwright in the room was William Shakespeare.

That Marlowe and Shakespeare were well aware of each other is clear enough from their work. A web of allusions and echoes and borrowings survives, evidence that has been recognized and pored over for several hundred years. Some literary scholars have written about this web as if the two contemporary playwrights never actually met in person, the one presumably going out the door just a moment before the other arrived. But recent studies, including a series of sophisticated computational analyses, have led to a growing scholarly consensus that the trilogy of history plays known as the three parts of *Henry VI*, plays printed in the First Folio of 1623 as written by Shakespeare, were in fact written collaboratively. In 2016–17 *The New Oxford Shakespeare: Authorship Companion* took the step of listing parts 2 and 3 (both written before part 1) as authored by William Shakespeare, Christopher Marlowe, and at least one other as yet unidentified playwright. (The prequel, known as *1 Henry VI*, is credited, in the *New Oxford* edition, to Shakespeare and Marlowe's Cambridge friend Thomas Nashe, along with one or more other playwrights.)

Only in their early twenties, Marlowe and Shakespeare had been born a few months apart—the former in February 1564 and the latter in April. They were both provincials, relative newcomers to London. And they were both the sons of artisans, a cobbler in one case, a glover in the other. But here the close parallels stopped. Marlowe's father was a nobody; Shakespeare's father, though he had fallen on hard times, had been bailiff—equivalent to mayor—of his town. Shakespeare had a wife and three children whom he had left back in Stratford-upon-Avon. His education had stopped at the end of grammar school; he was probably earning a bit as an actor; and though he was trying to make his way as a writer, he had as yet very little to show for himself. Marlowe, with his BA and MA from Cambridge, was entitled to call himself a gentleman. He was fluent in Latin and Greek. He had a network of talented friends and acquaintances from the university. He knew someone on the Privy Council who had looked out for him. And he was already the author of the celebrated *Tamburlaine*.

Marlowe might therefore have been surprised to discover that it was Shakespeare, not he, whom Henslowe had tapped to take charge of the writing project on the life of Henry VI and who had drawn up the "plat," the preliminary plot outline. The resulting plays have many Marlovian phrases and touches, but they are folded into a structure that Shakespeare clearly dominates. "Do but think / How sweet a thing it is to wear a crown," a character remarks in 3 *Henry VI*, "Within whose circuit is Elysium, / And all that poets feign of bliss and joy" (1.2.28–31). We are for a moment back in the heady world of *Tamburlaine*, where the aspiring soul cannot rest until it reaches "That perfect bliss and sole felicity / The sweet fruition of an earthly crown." But in *Henry VI*, as in all the plays that Shakespeare fashioned, the crown is far more nightmare than bliss.

The precise scope of Marlowe's involvement in the project is impossible to determine. He may have been pleased to be paid to do little more than to write a few bits of dialogue and to keep an eye on his less accomplished collaborator. Playing a secondary role in the writing may have surprised him, but there is no evidence, on his part, of resentment. If there was any anxiety or competitiveness in their relationship, either at the start or as it developed over the years, the signs point almost entirely to Shakespeare. Those signs would not have precluded admiration, though it is difficult to imagine that Shakespeare ever let down his guard.

Marlowe was evidently skilled at drawing out what others intended to keep in the dark. That is, after all, a spy's skill. He might have hinted first at Catholic sympathies to see how Shakespeare would respond. Then, failing to get an interesting response, he might have revealed to Shakespeare that he didn't believe any of it, Catholic or Protestant—the stories about the Virgin Birth and the Son of God, the raising of Lazarus, the miracle at Cana, and all the rest, stretching back to the primordial garden with the talking snake and the magical trees. Again, no revealing response. Given what Marlowe had already made manifest in *Tamburlaine*, he could also have conveyed his doubts about the alleged sacredness of authority and the sanctity of royal blood. Was it not after all a matter of sheer power? Could they not agree that, as Machiavelli had written, "All armed prophets have conquered, and the unarmed ones have been destroyed"? Once again Shakespeare is unlikely to have replied in a way that revealed very much. His beliefs, whether about religion or the state, remained elusive.

Then—to continue this imaginary conversation—Marlowe might

have looked quizzically at Shakespeare and ventured on the subject of love. True, Shakespeare had a wife and three children, but he had left them back in Stratford-upon-Avon and was free to explore other pleasures. What did he think, Marlowe may have slyly asked, of the alluring teenaged Henry Wriothesley, Earl of Southampton? At the theater the earl, with his beautiful long auburn curls, his delicately plucked eyebrows, and his expensive earrings, had been seen intently staring at Shakespeare, who was performing some part or other on stage. And Shakespeare, as Marlowe and others observed, had looked directly back at the earl and smiled.

Shakespeare is unlikely to have responded in kind to any of these provocations, had they come his way. He was far too careful and discreet, and he had no reason to trust Marlowe. The seventeenth-century biographer John Aubrey, who went about collecting gossipy anecdotes, was told that Shakespeare was not a "company keeper." If he was invited out for a "debauch," Aubrey's informants told him, Shakespeare would decline, writing that "he was in pain." Perhaps Marlowe received one of those polite refusals.

It is not that Shakespeare was sublimely indifferent to those with whom he lived and worked. Quite the contrary: throughout his life, he drew on virtually everything and everyone he encountered. How could the brilliant Marlowe, of all people, not be present in his works? His collaboration with Marlowe on the *Henry VI* plays occurred near the very beginning of Shakespeare's career, when as a writer he was only half-formed. Shakespeare was likely fascinated not only by his collaborator's immense poetic skill and originality but also by the reckless, rash, overreaching, and possibly doomed person he seemed to be. There may be glimpses of Marlowe—character sketches to which we have only partial or indirect access—in any number of Shakespeare's later plays: in the wild, extravagantly imaginative Mercutio in *Romeo and Juliet*, for example, or in Hotspur in *1 Henry IV*, or in the skeptic Thersites in *Troilus and Cressida*.

But a great gap lay between Shakespeare and the Cambridge-educated poet with whom he was collaborating and to whom he must inevitably have compared himself. Marlowe's years of higher education were enough to make Shakespeare feel, or at least claim to feel, what in one of his sonnets he called his own "rude ignorance." And to compound the difference between them, Shakespeare was not only writing for the stage, as Marlowe was; he was also performing on it.

Though Marlowe had chosen not to pursue a safe, respectable career in the church and had opted instead for a marginal life, the cachet conferred by his university degrees was important to him. That cachet—being known as a scholar and a gentleman—was compatible, if just barely, with writing plays, but it would certainly have been threatened by any more complete involvement in the public theater, even had he possessed the talent and the inclination for such involvement. Putting on greasepaint and getting up on stage to entertain a crowd that included servants, apprentices, porters, prostitutes, and assorted riffraff would have left a social stain that could not be scrubbed away.

Loathing for the stage and for anyone who performed on it was not limited to a few fanatical Puritans. Being a "common player" was not classified as a profession and therefore did not count legally as the labor of a true man. Only at the very top of the social order was it acceptable to have no officially sanctioned gainful employment. Up there, in the rarefied air of the elite, the very thing that counted as a disgrace for everyone else was a mark of privilege. To have no need to work for a living—to be able to "live idly," as a contemporary put it—was the key to being counted as a gentleman or lady. Those who did not belong to this very small, privileged group were expected to work in ways deemed legitimate or to face the consequences. It was not a mere matter of social disapproval. An act drawn up during the reign of Henry VIII, and renewed in still harsher terms under Edward, Mary, and Elizabeth, called for anyone identified as a vagabond or idle person to be apprehended and then "to be tied to the end of a cart naked and be beaten with whips ... until his body be bloody."

Professional actors were counted among the class of "idle persons" and hence subject to this brutal punishment. The fact that actors traveled about made the situation worse, since it confirmed that they were not merely idlers but vagabonds, that is, wanderers without a settled home.

According to the statutes, vagabonds who were caught begging—and what else were actors doing when they passed the hat?—were not only to be whipped until bloody but also to be "burned through the gristle of the right ear with a hot iron of the compass of an inch about." Alternatively, they were to be branded on the forehead with the letter *V* and then hauled off without delay "to labor, like as a true man ought to do."

Nonetheless, by the end of the sixteenth century, bands of full-time actors were crisscrossing the country, and some of them were performing in large public theaters in London under the nose of the civic and religious authorities. Already earlier in the century, in the time of Henry VIII, a certain number of intrepid performers had devised a means to get away with their forbidden occupation: they found positions as liveried servants in the royal court or in the household of wealthy aristocrats who wanted to have gifted entertainers at their beck and call. In the decades that followed, they organized themselves into small playing companies and used their powerful connections to obtain permission to perform before the public in innyards and halls and to collect money for these performances.

For the aristocrats, it was a good arrangement: they had the services of professional entertainers, usually gifted at music and dance as well as acting, for the modest cost of providing them with official liveries and a modicum of protection. Armed with a letter from their patron, the actors knew that they could perform almost anywhere they wished. Local officials and puritanical ministers might strenuously object, but they could do little to resist the pressure of great lords.

For those who performed on the public stage, the great lords provided protection from the law but not a steady income. Like Ned Alleyn, Shakespeare eventually made a great deal of money in the theater. He did so by becoming a shareholder in the playing company in which he acted and part-owner of the playhouse in which his company performed. These multiple roles meant, in effect, that he sold his playscripts to himself, helped to shape the productions of the plays he and others wrote, performed parts in them, and took a significant share of the box office receipts. His main income came not from the coffers of a handful of aristocrats but from the hard-earned pennies of the thousands of people who paid to see his plays.

This unprecedented feat of entrepreneurship, an avatar of the rise of capitalism, was a brilliant solution to the problem of a writing life in Elizabethan England. London's new commercial theaters held out the prospect of generating a viable income, but only, as Shakespeare grasped, for someone who utterly immersed himself—as actor, writer, and entrepreneur—in the medium. Ultimately, Shakespeare's spectacular success enabled him to acquire (in his father's name) the status of gentleman and to purchase for himself and his family a fine house in Stratford-upon-Avon.

But by virtue of his university degree, Marlowe had already achieved the status of gentleman, and he would not have been inclined to plunge any further into the theater, as Shakespeare was clearly doing. Such immersion, and the steady, long-term commitment that it entailed, was not for him. Writing plays and selling them to acute businessmen like Henslowe was one thing; collecting pennies from threadbare apprentices at the playhouse door quite another. Though he had enjoyed unprecedented success with *Tamburlaine*, he had no interest in the day-to-day operations of a playing company. Over the course of his brief career, he showed no sign of business acumen or an ability to plan for the future. Acquiring a share in a theatrical joint-stock company, as Shakespeare succeeded in doing, along with using the profits to buy real estate in the provincial town of his birth, seems utterly alien to Marlowe. He appears to have lived on whatever he received for the successive plays that he wrote, along perhaps with payment for occasional service as a courier or secret agent. He might have taken as his motto words he adapted from the Roman playwright Terence and used in *The Jew of Malta*: *Ego mihimet sum semper proximus*, "I am always closest to myself," or perhaps "I am always by and for myself."

◆ ◆ ◆

IN THIS PERIOD, as for centuries before and after, most writers who lacked an independent income scrambled to find wealthy, powerful people who, in exchange for receiving an effusive compliment in print, would offer some support. It was the socially acceptable alternative to the far more dubious career in the entertainment industry. "They who write to Lords, rewards to get," observed John Donne, "Are they not like singers at doors for meat?" Notwithstanding Donne's irony, there was nothing shameful about it: in Elizabethan society not writers alone but virtually everyone stood with outstretched hands at the doors of the wealthy few. Apart from a small urban middle class, almost all the country's riches were concentrated in the hands of the roughly 5 percent of the population that constituted the gentry and aristocracy, and within this group an even smaller number possessed the great bulk of the money, land, prestige, and power. At the top of the social hierarchy was the queen herself. Below her there were some fifty-five hereditary peers—dukes, marquesses, earls, viscounts, and barons—and below them, fewer than a thousand knights. Almost no one else counted.

Where else could a writer without means turn? Our capitalist system, with agents, copyrights, advances, royalties, and the like, lay far in the future. Elizabethan stationers would pay only a pittance for a manuscript, which then ceased to be the property of the author. More to the point, the institutions that today make careers in poetry and fiction possible for all but a handful of the most famous writers—university literature departments and grant-giving foundations—did not yet exist. A writer's best hope in the sixteenth century was to find a rich man or woman who took an interest both in literature and in being flattered and who would in return offer a monetary reward.

Among the elite, the exchange of gifts—beaded bags full of sweet-smelling herbs (to ward off plague), exquisitely painted tiny portraits called miniatures, illuminated manuscripts, cloth embroidered with gold and silver thread, boxes of sweets, haunches of venison, even, in one instance, eighteen larks in a cage—was widely understood to be obligatory. The recipient of the larks was none other than Queen Elizabeth, whose officials kept a detailed record on long vellum rolls of every gift she received on New Year's Day, together with the carefully calibrated gifts she gave in return. Cash value was significant—sometimes the gifts consisted of a pouch, or still better, a gilded cup filled with gold coins—but the givers often aimed for symbolic significance. For example, in the Metropolitan Museum in New York a pair of sixteenth-century English leather gloves, with delicate gauntlets made from satin worked with silk, metal threads, and tiny seed pearls, featured weeping eyes, with silken tears dripping down on elegantly stitched pansies. It is a perfect emblem of the lovesickness that courtiers typically claimed they felt toward their royal mistress. And she in turn would grace her favorite of the moment—Robert Dudley, Earl of Leicester, or Sir Walter Ralegh, or Robert Devereux, Earl of Essex—with tokens of her love. (She would also grace them with monopolies, such as Ralegh's lucrative one on playing cards, and grants of land.)

The ethos of gift-giving extended beyond the court and the circles of the nobility. In *The Merchant of Venice* Shakespeare depicts a rustic bringing a present—a dish of doves—to his son's employer, and there are many comparable instances, in life as well as literature, of offerings made from those below to those above, as a way of currying favor or soliciting other gifts. It is in this context that the patronage system for writers must be understood. Instead of a dish of doves, a sequence of sonnets; instead of a cageful of larks, a collection of recipes; instead of a jeweled crucifix, a sermon on predestination. Marlowe's Cambridge friend Tom Nashe could not afford to send a barrel of oysters, but he dedicated to the young Earl of Southampton a pornographic poem that quickly became known as "Nashe's Dildo."

The dedicatory letters and poems in the works of this period can be thought of as grant applications in the form of elaborate, often nauseating praise. A few writers of independent means were spared the tiresome exercise; almost everyone else had to submit. They had no guarantee of success. Often the compliment was simply ignored, or the aspirant received a pittance, while a rival's compliment was preferred. The hack Thomas Churchyard complained that he had dedicated sixteen books to "men of good and great credit, but to be plain not one among them all, from the first day of my labor and studies to this present year and hour, hath any way preferred my suits, amended my state, or given me any countenance." On occasion, however, the gift of a dedication could be handsomely rewarded. Richard Robinson, a writer of very modest talent who kept a record of his successes and failures, received nothing when he dedicated *King David's Harp* to the Earl of Warwick, but he fared much better from Sir Philip Sidney, who gave him a handsome £2 for a book of prayers.

The average reward for a dedication was £1, and as Churchyard bears witness, by no means everyone got that. More substantial support, enough to live on comfortably and that could be renewed over a long period, was rare, and it tended to go to important scientists, historians, and chroniclers, not to poets. The latter could expect to receive words of thanks, but as the poet Richard Barnfield wrote, "Who can live with words, in these hard times? . . . Words are but wind, and wind is all but vain."

Some writers tried to enhance their income by tacking multiple dedications onto a single book. Others tried threats. "If I be evil entreated or sent away with a flea in mine ear, let him look that I will rail on him soundly," Nashe warned anyone who stiffed him, "not for an hour or a day, whiles the injury is fresh in my memory, but in some elaborate, polished poem which I will leave to the world when I am dead, to be a living image to all ages of his beggarly parsimony and ignoble illiberality."

When in 1592 an epidemic of plague forced the temporary closing of the theaters, Shakespeare looked about for a patron to whom he could make a literary offering. He dedicated his long erotic poem *Venus and Adonis* to the immensely wealthy nineteen-year-old Earl of Southampton, Henry Wriothesley, to whom Nashe had offered his "Dildo." The poet did not, of course, set a sum in cash that he was hoping to get in exchange for the dedication, but he did suggest that if the earl showed himself "pleased," then a further work in his honor would soon follow. The recipient's expression of pleasure must have come promptly, since in the following year Shakespeare dedicated to him another long poem, *The Rape of Lucrece*. The overheated dedicatory letter this time suggests that the young earl's reward had far exceeded Shakespeare's expectations: "The love I dedicate to your lordship is without end. . . . What I have done is yours; what I have to do is yours; being part in all I have, devoted yours."

❖ ❖ ❖

OVER THE CENTURIES, there has been speculation that on at least one occasion Marlowe entered the competition for patronage. The speculation focuses not on any work by Marlowe that survives but on Shakespeare's sonnets. Several of these celebrated poems, written some years after the two of them met and worked together on the *Henry VI* plays, feature an "alien pen" that competes with Shakespeare's own for the favor of the beautiful, wealthy young man, possibly the same Henry Wriothesley. The rival poet is not named (any more than is the young man), but there are a few hints to his identity. He brings with him a "golden quill / And precious phrase by all the muses filed" (Sonnet 85). That is, he has the advantage of the elite education that the speaker of the sonnets—Will, as he calls himself—knows that he lacks. Will, in love with the young man, has through his poems established a relationship that is now threatened. The learned rival piles one beautiful phrase on another, "making his style admired everywhere" (Sonnet 84). The young man, fond of being immoderately praised, seems smitten with his new admirer.

With an anxious glance over at the eloquent competitor, Shakespeare acknowledges the disgrace brought upon him by his profession. "Alas, 'tis true I have gone here and there," he admits, "And made myself a motley to the view" (Sonnet 110). *Motley* was the multicolored costume of a jester; taken out of context, the line need mean only that the poet has made a fool of himself. But since the poet in question was a professional actor who went here and there as part of a company of players, it implies that he was earning a living by performing for a paying audience. The next sonnet in the sequence makes the social disgrace still more explicit, blaming fortune that "did not better for my life provide / Than public means which public manners breeds." "Thence comes it," Shakespeare adds, as if he has been apprehended as a vagabond, "that my name receives a brand, / And almost thence my nature is subdued / To what it works in, like the dyer's hand." The stigma of the stage cannot be easily removed.

In the face of the rival's celebrated rhetorical skills—"the proud full sail of his great verse" (Sonnet 86)—Will claims to feel tongue-tied and abashed. He cannot match such a pyrotechnical display. But perhaps, he slyly tells the youth whom both poets are courting, all the "strainèd touches rhetoric can lend" will ultimately prove of less worth than "true plain words by thy true-telling friend" (Sonnet 82). The real question is whose poetry will endure. In the midst of his expressions of insecurity, Will looks ahead with steely confidence to the time when he and the young man and, for that matter, the rival poet will all be gone:

> Your monument shall be my gentle verse,
> Which eyes not yet created shall o'er-read,
> And tongues to be your being shall rehearse
> When all the breathers of this world are dead.
> You still shall live—such virtue hath my pen—
> Where breath most breathes, even in the mouths of men.
> (Sonnet 81)

The proud claim—"such virtue hath my pen"—sweeps away any fear of being outdone.

It is remotely possible that Marlowe was the rival, competing for the love and the money of the seductive aristocrat whom Shakespeare calls "the master-mistress of my passion." If he did so, it appears that, notwithstanding his university degrees and all his skills, he lost out. After all, only Shakespeare's "sugared sonnets" to the young man survive.

There is, in any case, no hard evidence that Marlowe ever threw himself, as his friend Nashe did, into the penning of flattering words in the hope of gaining a reward. Perhaps he looked about, as he had earlier looked at the career choices of his roommates at Corpus Christi, and decided that singing at doors for meat alongside the other poets was not for him.

It is not that he was indifferent to important people. In the few incandescent years he lived after leaving Cambridge, Marlowe's name repeatedly emerges as someone in the orbit of several wealthy and powerful figures who took an interest in artistic and intellectual life. But it is not in dedications or other forms of flattery that Marlowe's name appears. His goal, it seems, was not to stand on the outside hoping for largesse but to be accepted in their intimate circles and to take part in the conversations, many of them highly sensitive, that went on in private behind closed doors. He wanted to be *known*.

Marlowe's preferred way to come to the attention of important people, and in the meantime to survive, was to continue to write plays. Several of the principal bands of performers had been legally organized as joint-stock companies. The companies were no longer mere vagabonds, endlessly packing up their ratty wigs and moth-eaten costumes and wandering from place to place. In the crowded capital of the realm, they now had beautiful purpose-built theaters. But the basic rule remained the same: if they were not to be regarded as vagrants, professional actors had to be nominally the servants of one or another wealthy patron or of the queen herself. Alongside the Earl of Leicester's Men, there sprang up the Queen's Men, the Earl of Sussex's Men, the Earl of Essex's Men, the Earl of Oxford's Men, the Lord Admiral's Men, Lord Strange's Men, and many others. The first recorded example of daily performances by a professional acting company at a London playhouse was the residence of Lord Strange's Men at the Rose Theater in 1592–93. Lord Strange's Men performed several of Marlowe's plays, and the lower-class playwright from Canterbury declared that he was very well known to Lord Strange himself.

✦ ✦ ✦

Marlowe and Shakespeare were what the novelist Joseph Conrad calls "secret sharers." Beyond their similar provincial origins and class backgrounds, the two of them shared immense poetic skill, an ability to please both high and low, an insatiable curiosity, and an imagination that seemed to have no limits. To judge from their surviving works, they seem also to have also shared what we would now call queer desires and experiences. And though Shakespeare was far more reticent about his views, there is ample, if subtle, indication that his skepticism about the reigning orthodoxies of his age approximated that of Marlowe's.

Even setting aside the competition that was built into their professional careers, however, their basic approaches to life could hardly have been more different. Shakespeare managed to get through a long, brilliantly successful career not merely with his limbs intact but without spending a day in prison, and he did so while prudently guiding an entire playing company along with him. He had left his family in Stratford-upon-Avon, but he remained in regular contact with them, and as he steadily accumulated capital, he invested much of it in local real estate, with an eye to his eventual retirement there. Several members of the playing company were clearly his good friends, including John Heminges and Henry Condell, to whom he left bequests in his will and who undertook after his death to edit his plays for the First Folio. Whether Shakespeare extended his trust far beyond this inner circle is unclear. In *Hamlet* the prince has the bantering company of two old school friends, Rosencrantz and Guildenstern, but he suspects them correctly of delivering reports about him to the king, and in the end he sends them without a qualm to their deaths. Hamlet has only a single friend—Horatio—to whom he can confide his most intimate secrets. We can be virtually certain that Marlowe was not Shakespeare's Horatio.

Shakespeare's nineteenth-century biographers liked to imagine him in the Mermaid Tavern, exchanging sallies of wit with Ben Jonson and other poets and playwrights, but there is no evidence for this. There is abundant evidence from early in Shakespeare's career, however, that he was closely tracking Marlowe's every move, learning from his daring stylistic inventions, and copying his thematic choices, while at the same time carefully avoiding the extreme risks to which Marlowe was clearly drawn. In Shakespeare's first tragedy, *Titus Andronicus*, the villain, Aaron the Moor, vaunts himself in a hyperbolic style lifted directly from *Tamburlaine*:

> Then, Aaron, arm thy heart and fit thy thoughts
> To mount aloft with thy imperial mistress,
> And mount her pitch whom thou in triumph long
> Hast prisoner held, fettered in amorous chains
> And faster bound to Aaron's charming eyes
> Than is Prometheus tied to Caucasus.
> Away with slavish weeds and idle thoughts!
> I will be bright and shine in pearl and gold. (2.1.12–19)

But Shakespeare would never have ended the play with Aaron triumphant, as Marlowe did with Tamburlaine. At the close of *Titus Andronicus*, the order is given to bury Aaron breast-deep in the earth and let him starve to death. So much for the dream of "mounting aloft."

Shakespeare worked hard to put some distance between himself and the achievements of his rival. In a celebrated moment of *Tamburlaine, Part 2*, the triumphant Tamburlaine harnesses the kings he has conquered to his chariot and cruelly whips them forward:

> Holla, ye pampered jades of Asia!
> What, can ye draw but twenty miles a day,
> And have so proud a chariot at your heels,
> And such a coachman as great Tamburlaine?
>     (Part 2 4.4.1–4)

In the second part of Shakespeare's *Henry IV*, Pistol, Falstaff's swaggering companion, drunkenly spouts a version of Tamburlaine's taunt to the whores in Mistress Quickly's tavern:

> Shall packhorses
> And hollow pampered jades of Asia,
> Which cannot go but thirty miles a day,
> Compare with Caesars, and with cannibals,
> And Trojan Greeks? (2.4.142–46)

The overheated rhetoric that so excited the crowds at Marlowe's play is parodied as incoherent noise coming from the mouth of a braggart soldier.

But that parody came late, when Marlowe was dead and Shakespeare reigned as England's leading dramatist. In Shakespeare's early career, Marlowe had clearly served as what one scholar called a "provocative agent." Marlowe's *The Jew of Malta* was answered by Shakespeare with *The Merchant of Venice*; *Edward II* with *Richard II*; *Hero and Leander* with *Venus and Adonis*. It would not be accurate to say that Shakespeare's responses were more conventional or cautious—his engagements with Marlowe's achievements are brilliant, broodingly complex, and radical—but they are in every instance more self-protective. They represent a deep ongoing conversation with Marlowe, one mingling together admiration and disagreement. But they never once signal trust.

CHAPTER 11

# Hog Lane

"If you press me to tell why I loved him," Montaigne wrote about his beloved friend Étienne de la Boétie, "I feel that this cannot be expressed, except by answering: Because it was he, because it was I." Marlowe may have longed to find such a perfect soulmate, but he lived in a competitive, duplicitous, dangerous world that made it extremely difficult to fashion a relationship of trust. The closest he seems to have come was with Thomas Watson, some eight years older than he. London born, Watson had been a student at Oxford, but he did not take a degree. After dropping out, he had gone abroad and spent some seven years traveling in France and Italy, in whose languages, music, and culture he became fluent. Much of the time he seems to have been reading, studying an eclectic range of subjects and honing his skills as a scholar and a writer. He was the sixteenth-century epitome of the cosmopolitan intellectual: he acquainted himself with leading contemporary poetic styles, interested himself in the word-sensitive songs known as madrigals (which he later helped to introduce into England), studied Roman law, science, and theology, took a deep dive into Greek and Latin classics, became skilled in the elaborate memory systems of the kind that Giordano Bruno made his living teaching. Watson was no Bruno—he lacked the Italian's half-mad daring, originality, and genius—but he shared something of the restlessness, the omnivorous interests, and the air of possessing knowledge hidden from most ordinary mortals.

It is not surprising that during his continental wanderings, Watson sooner or later made the acquaintance of Sir Francis Walsingham, who was serving as Queen Elizabeth's ambassador in Paris. Young English gentlemen abroad would almost inevitably present themselves to their ambassador, but in Watson's case there seems to have been something more than a pro forma introduction. With his unusual linguistic skills and his trained memory, Watson may have been of particular use to Walsingham, who was beginning to put together the spy network over which, upon his return to London, he would preside.

Twice during his peripatetic years abroad, Watson's name shows up in the register of visitors to the English College in Douai—the predecessor to the hotbed of Catholic piety and treason that Marlowe may have visited in Rheims. It is certainly possible that Watson's visits had nothing to do with the machinations of the English embassy in Paris. He may have wanted only a few months of studies in canon law, or perhaps he was drawn to the Roman Catholic faith into which his parents had certainly been born. Still, it is striking that when he finally brought his years of wanderlust to an end, he served as a clandestine courier on his return to London, carrying confidential letters from Walsingham to William Cecil, the queen's principal secretary. And it is striking too that in 1590, when Walsingham died, Watson put his rhetorical skills to use by publishing a poetic dialogue on the great spymaster, which he dedicated to Sir Francis's cousin, Thomas Walsingham. Though busy with affairs of state, the great man had taken a personal interest in him, the poet claims, and when he most needed it had offered him comfort of some unspecified kind. "Who should more lament his loss than I," one speaker of the elegy asks, "That oft hath tasted of his bounteous store / and knew his secret virtues perfectly?" What those secret virtues were remains discreetly unspecified.

Around the time Marlowe arrived in London in 1587, Watson moved to Norton Folgate. A surviving record links the two of them in 1589, but their friendship is likely to have been formed much earlier. They may have been neighbors or even roommates (especially if Francis Walsingham was somehow involved in making the connection). They were both struggling to make their way as writers. London was a huge city, but theirs was a relatively small community within it.

Watson wrote plays for the public theater, though none of them has survived. His principal source of income, it seems, was what he received from the patrons to whom he dedicated his writings. The first of these was an unusual gift that he presented in 1581 to the wealthy Catholic magnate Philip Howard, the 13th Earl of Arundel: a translation from Greek to Latin of Sophocles' *Antigone*. This particular bid for patronage, as Watson must have been well aware, was not without risks. A graduate of Cambridge, the twenty-four-year-old Howard had enough learning (or at least pretentions to learning) to appreciate what Watson had accomplished, but his name came with quite a bit of baggage. The 12th Earl of Arundel, Howard's father, was accused of plotting to marry Mary, Queen of Scots, and to join her in returning the realm to Roman Catholicism. He was executed for treason in 1572. Howard's grandfather, the poet Surrey, had likewise been executed for treason, back in 1547. With that sobering pedigree, Philip Howard, for all his wealth and power, was a marked man. Suspected of a secret adherence to Roman Catholicism, he was arrested in 1585 while attempting to flee the country. He was imprisoned for ten miserable years in the Tower of London, where he died of dysentery at the age of thirty-eight. In the twentieth century, he was made a saint by the Catholic Church.

When Watson dedicated *Antigone* to him, Howard still professed himself a Protestant. Though the dedicatory letter could hardly hint at any such thing, rumors of his Catholic sympathies may have been part of his allure, or Watson may even have been urged by Walsingham to try to insinuate himself into his circle. *Antigone* is a play about someone who defies the regime in power and dies for her unshakable principles. "I should be happy to be called your poet," Watson declared, and to become your servant, he added, "as Ganymede was to Jove." Ganymede was Jove's cupbearer and also his sex toy. It is difficult, probably deliberately difficult, to know exactly what Watson was offering here. Marlowe, who had staged the scene of Ganymede in Jove's lap, would have his own idea of its full implication.

In the year after his *Antigone*, Watson followed up by publishing an elaborate sequence of poems in English with the grandiose title *The Hekatompathia, or, Passionate Century of Love*. Hedging his bets, he dedicated this book to a bitter enemy of the Howards, Edward de Vere, the Earl of Oxford. Watson had now reached out in print both to a powerful Catholic (or suspected Catholic) nobleman and to a powerful Protestant (or at least ostensibly Protestant) nobleman. He had a chance to gain support from one or the other or both, and taken together, the two dedications would confer a potentially welcome ambiguity about his own position. He was a man for all factions.

The ornate title page declared that the *Hekatompathia* was "composed by Thomas Watson Gentleman, and published at the request of certain Gentlemen his very friends." The poems—which Watson terms "passions," though there is nothing very passionate about them—were largely elegant exercises in imitation, designed to convey the author's sophisticated grasp of the standard conventions of European love poetry. They enjoyed what is called a *succès d'estime*: the author was praised as "a man very well learned," but the work was not reprinted. Watson's next effort in 1585 was an exceedingly long Latin poem called *Amyntas* that, like the *Hekatompathia*, was no doubt destined for oblivion, but it received an unexpected second life when a poet named Abraham Fraunce rendered it into English. Fraunce's translation, *The Lamentations of Amyntas for the Death of Phyllis*, found a surprisingly significant readership.

In *Amyntas* Watson drew on both his classical learning and his familiarity with sophisticated French and Italian sources to write pastoral poetry—that is, poetry about the lives of shepherds. Anyone who lived in England had to be quite familiar with shepherds, since sheep-rearing was a major part of the economy, but in literature these figures generally have far less to do with backbreaking rural reality than with dreams of love in an idealized landscape. City dwellers in London, as in Paris and Rome, liked to fantasize about country folk who stretched out on the grass all day, listening to the warbling of the birds and the sound of the babbling brook, and singing songs of love and longing.

Watson's venture into pastoral poetry is likely to have been the occasion for a comparable venture by Marlowe—but with a world of difference. Instead of his friend's heavy classicizing in pursuit of literary reputation, Marlowe wrote the luminous lyric "The Passionate Shepherd to His Love":

> Come live with me, and be my love,
> And we will all the pleasures prove
> That valleys, groves, hills and fields,
> Woods, or steepy mountain yields.
>
> And we will sit upon the rocks,
> Seeing the shepherds feed their flocks
> By shallow rivers, to whose falls
> Melodious birds sing madrigals.
>
> And I will make thee beds of roses,
> And a thousand fragrant posies,
> A cap of flowers, and a kirtle
> Embroidered all with leaves of myrtle.
>
> A gown made of the finest wool
> Which from our pretty lambs we pull,
> Fair linèd slippers for the cold,
> With buckles of the purest gold.
>
> A belt of straw and ivy buds,
> With coral clasps and amber studs,
> And if these pleasures may thee move,
> Come live with me and be my love.
>
> The shepherd swains shall dance and sing
> For thy delight each May morning.
> If these delights thy mind may move,
> Then live with me, and be my love.

It all has the feeling of something tossed off quickly, the very opposite of Watson's laboriousness.

Perhaps the poem's air of simplicity really came about effortlessly, but it is a sly simplicity. The birds in Marlowe's poem do not merely sing; they sing madrigals, those part-songs that had been introduced by Watson and were all the rage in London's sophisticated musical circles. The gifts with which his shepherd hopes to seduce his beloved are a mixture of things that might be found in or around an actual sheepfold—wool, flowers, and straw—and things that belong to a decidedly different sphere: coral clasps and amber studs, along with "buckles of the purest gold." The slyness that insouciantly mingles such distinct worlds extends to leaving the sex of the desired one unspecified: both men and women in this period wore gowns and kirtles (a kind of tunic). This is a love song for all sexual tastes.

The freshness of Marlowe's verses, their frank appeal to pleasure, and their musicality quickly made them famous. People almost immediately began to sing the lines, to imitate them, and to write replies. In a poem called "The Bait," Marlowe's younger contemporary John Donne shifted the setting to a river:

> Come live with me and be my love,
> And we will some new pleasures prove,
> Of golden sands and crystal brooks,
> With silken lines and silver hooks.

A generation later Robert Herrick—most famous for the *carpe diem* poem that begins "Gather ye rosebuds while ye may"—adapted Marlowe's poem for one of his many attempts to woo his beloved: "Live, live with me. And thou shalt see / The pleasures I'll prepare for thee." Herrick expanded Marlowe's list of presents, though as befitted an Anglican clergyman, he claimed his interest was love, not lust:

> Thou shalt have ribbands, roses, rings,
> Gloves, garters, stockings, shoes, and strings
> Of winning colours, that shall move

Others to lust, but me to love.
—These, nay, and more, thine own shall be,
If thou wilt love, and live with me.

Over the centuries Marlowe's lyric has proved irresistible if not to lovers, at least to other poets. In the twentieth century, Dorothy Parker wryly wrote "The Passionate Freudian to His Love":

With your hand in mine, idly we'll recline
Amid bowers of neuroses,
While the sun seeks rest in the great red west
We will sit and match psychoses.

And *Mad* magazine offered a parody of its own:

Perhaps you'll dig companionship
With leather gear and boots and whip;
If so, my love, I'll serve you well
And let you chain me in a cell.

A recent online version opens with what the author, Daniel Ortberg, claims to be Marlowe's true voice: "Fuck this, let's just go live in the woods."

To almost anyone who read *Amyntas* and "The Passionate Shepherd to His Love" when they were first in circulation, Marlowe must have seemed the incomparably superior poet. But that fact does not seem to have caused a rift in their friendship. They had much in common. They had both attended universities and could style themselves gentlemen; they were alike immersed in Greek and Latin classics; they shared an ambition to achieve literary fame. And both had probably been associated in some way or other with the spy network.

The Renaissance was one of the greatest ages for the ardent celebration of friendship, especially male friendship. Writers like Montaigne insisted that true friends should share with each other their riskiest thoughts and their most vulnerable feelings. But it is impossible to understand the centrality of intimate friendship in this period without understanding the omnipresent threat of betrayal.

In late sixteenth-century England, the stakes could not have been higher, because the consequences could not have been more dire. Many, perhaps most, extended families harbored secrets, some of them potentially dangerous—Catholics inwardly unreconciled to the English state church, Puritans plotting the downfall of the bishops, closeted radicals regarding the whole belief system as a mass of superstition. As always, people felt the powerful need—like Midas's wife—to share their secrets with someone. But how could you do this safely? Whom could you trust? Who was not, unbeknownst to you, already quietly sending reports to Secretary Walsingham in Seething Lane? The doomed Babington's note to Poley sits on the table in the room to which he will never return: "Farewell, sweet Robin, if as I take thee, true to me." Perhaps the fact that Marlowe and Watson both understood this dark world from the inside served as the basis of their friendship.

❖ ❖ ❖

IN AUGUST 1587, around the time that both he and Marlowe moved to Norton Folgate, Watson was called in to be examined by an officer of the Privy Council who had been charged with getting to the bottom of a troubling rumor. The report by the officer, a Mr. Dalton, survives and provides a strange glimpse of the intense anxiety that was building up in the months before the Spanish Armada. It had come to the attention of the authorities that a married woman named Anne Burnell, the daughter of a London butcher, was telling people that she was the illegitimate daughter of King Philip II of Spain, who had been married in the 1550s to England's Queen Mary. In ordinary times, such a story would have been laughed at or dismissed as the delusion of a mentally unstable person. But these were not ordinary times, and when someone mentioned to Anne Burnell that Sir Francis Drake had captured a ship named *The Phillip of Spain*, she made the serious mistake of remarking, in the hearing of others, that "the king of Spain would not be long after." Those simple words, reported to the authorities, were enough to trigger an official investigation.

If Marlowe asked his friend what the brouhaha was about, Watson would have explained that when, some eight years past, he was staying in London in the house of an acquaintance of his, he had been introduced to the Burnells. Learning that Watson was a scholar, Mrs. Burnell turned to him with the naïve assumption that motivates the guards in *Hamlet* to believe that the university-educated Horatio will know the right way to address a ghost: "Thou art a scholar. Speak to it, Horatio." Mrs. Burnell's encounter with the supernatural had taken place a year earlier when, on a visit to her husband's family in the country, she had a conversation with an old woman known as "the witch of Norwell" who said to her that she "was a Spaniard's bird and that she had marks about her which would more appear hereafter." Unsurprisingly, these words had stayed with her, and she hoped that the learned Watson could elucidate them.

Watson rose to the occasion. Swearing Mrs. Burnell to secrecy, he told her with a straight face that "the best Spaniard that ever came in England was her father" and that certain marks on her body would appear to confirm her exalted origins. "She should have a lock of hair like gold wire in her head," along with other occult signs. Sure enough, when Mrs. Burnell examined herself carefully in a mirror, she saw, or thought she saw, a red spot on her back, over her kidneys. That spot, in her eyes, resembled the coat of arms of England. What more proof could she want? True, when she showed the telltale sign to others, they told her that she was deluded and that they saw only a great many veins, but her compliant young maidservant, Anne Digges, confirmed that she could make out something resembling a lion, a dragon, and a crown.

It all ended badly, of course, though not for Watson who, in his examination, denied that he had said anything of the kind to Mrs. Burnell or that she had ever told him that she was the king of Spain's daughter. He was dismissed without charges, and the maidservant too was let off lightly. But poor Mrs. Burnell remained under prolonged investigation. Eventually, at the order of the Privy Council, she was taken out on a market day, stripped to the waist, and tied to the back of a cart. Then, with a note attached at the back of her head explaining what she had done, she was whipped through the streets of the city.

Watson's cruel practical joke took advantage of the exaggerated respect that the uneducated had toward scholars, and it drew as well on a poet's imagination. His literary circle would certainly have recognized that the "lock of hair with gold wire" was taken directly from the familiar playbook of the Italian poet Petrarch. Marlowe may have simply laughed when Watson recounted this story, or he may have been sobered by the ugly consequences of what must have begun as a silly prank. As Marlowe certainly knew, Watson had a rather unsavory reputation. He could "devise twenty fictions and knaveries in a play," wrote someone who had been stung by one of his tricks, "which was his daily practice and his living."

The reservations that any prudent person might have had about trusting such a cruel trickster evidently did not keep Marlowe from spending time with Watson. And after all, Watson too would have had to set prudence aside to spend time with Marlowe. Each of them might have felt strangely safer to see certain of his most sinister qualities reflected in the cracked glass of the other.

The closeness of their relationship is indicated by an episode that occurred on the afternoon of September 18, 1589: a murder.

The victim's name was William Bradley. In his mid-twenties, Bradley, the son of a London innkeeper, evidently had had an ongoing feud with Watson, and over the summer it reached the boiling point. Bradley filed a petition in court requesting protection from Watson and two others *ob metum mortis*, "for fear of death." At this point Marlowe does not seem to have been directly involved: his name does not appear in the petition as any of the men whom Bradley said he feared.

Marlowe's neighborhood in Norton Folgate was bordered by lanes that led into grassy fields where horses grazed, laundry women laid out sheets to dry, and men set up targets to practice archery. On the afternoon in question, passersby on Hog Lane noticed two men fighting with swords. They were Bradley and Marlowe. Sword fighting would not have been an unfamiliar sight in these fields: men often met for exercise and practice, and actors from the nearby theaters may have come to rehearse their battle scenes. But the bystanders could see that this was not innocent practice: the sharp points of the swords were uncovered, and tempers were high. People in the crowd began to shout, and one of them ran for the constables. Meanwhile, Watson appeared on the scene, and Bradley, according to witnesses, said to him, "Art thou now come?" Watson drew his sword, Marlowe withdrew from the fray, and the two enemies continued the fight. Watson was backed up to the edge of a ditch and had nowhere to go. He thrust his sword into Bradley's chest, killing him instantly.

My friend's enemy is my enemy. The feud had not been Marlowe's, as the absence of his name from Bradley's petition suggests, but he was now directly involved in a killing. The fight had occurred in broad daylight, and the parties involved had been seen and identified by the gawking crowd. Marlowe waited with Watson by the bleeding body until the constables arrived. The two friends were both arrested for murder and taken to Newgate prison. In the charge, Watson is designated a gentleman; Marlowe—his origins still marking him as lower class, notwithstanding his Cambridge degrees—is described as a yeoman. By the beginning of October, Marlowe had managed to raise the substantial bail of £40; Watson remained in prison. Two months later the case was heard at the Old Bailey. All the witnesses testified that Marlowe had had nothing to do with the fatal thrust, and he was discharged. The following February, Watson, judged to have acted in self-defense, was also released.

The killing of Bradley could have either ended the friendship between Watson and Marlowe or bound them still closer together. That it did the latter is suggested by a final trace of their relationship. In September 1592 Watson died. He was only thirty-seven. There is no record of the cause of death, though in those years in London, plague was a constant menace. Later that same fall Watson's final collection of poems, *Amyntae Gaudia*, were published. By an ironic reversal, these were not poems of the shepherd's mourning and death but poems of joy. The book was dedicated to Mary Sidney, Countess of Pembroke, a generous patron and herself an extraordinary poet. For once the extravagant compliments in the dedicatory letter seem well deserved. The countess—"Muse of the poets of our time"—is asked to accept the protagonist of Watson's poems as her adoptive son, all the more so since "his dying father had most humbly bequeathed to thee his keeping." Whether the dying Watson had himself actually chosen to dedicate the poems to Mary Sidney is not clear, but on his deathbed he very likely gave them to his friend to publish. The letter of dedication is signed "C.M."

CHAPTER 12

# The Counterfeiters

IN 1589, WHILE he was being held in Newgate prison as an accessory to Watson's murder of William Bradley, Marlowe made the acquaintance of one of his cellmates, a Catholic named John Poole. Perhaps their conversation was entirely random, or perhaps Marlowe was fishing for secrets, as he had been trained to do. What Marlowe said has vanished into air, but it must have produced in Poole an unusual trust and sense of intimacy. In the course of their conversation, Poole explained to Marlowe how to counterfeit coins.

This introduction to the art of forgery turned out to have strange consequences. Some two years later Marlowe left England and traveled to the town in the Netherlands that the Dutch called Vlissingen and the English, Flushing. A strategically important harbor under English military control at the mouth of the river that controlled access to Antwerp, Flushing housed a garrison that was engaged in war against the occupying Spanish army. That army was attempting to secure the Low Countries for the Catholic faith; the English expeditionary force was fighting in support of the Dutch Protestants. The wars had been going on for years and had taken many lives, including that of Mary Sidney's celebrated brother, the poet Sir Philip Sidney. At the time when Marlowe arrived, Sidney's younger brother Robert was serving as Flushing's military governor.

What exactly Marlowe was doing in this garrison town in January

1592 has never been resolved. The armed conflict in the Netherlands was seconded, as wars always are, by networks of spies, double agents, counterfeiters, munitions makers, confidence men, and criminals. The lines of the struggle were blurred, for the Dutch, like the English, were bitterly divided between Catholics and Protestants. A few years earlier John Poole's brother-in-law, Sir William Stanley, who was one of the principal English commanders but harbored secret ties to the Jesuits, surrendered to the Spanish the city that he was meant to be defending for the Protestants. He took with him into the service of Spain many of the troops he commanded, and he quickly became involved in a succession of plots to launch an invasion of England and murder Elizabeth.

Stanley was not alone. At least some of those who professed to be actively engaged in the war effort against the Catholics were secret Catholic sympathizers, and so too the cells of secret Catholic sympathizers were penetrated by agents working for Walsingham. Marlowe, in his late twenties, was by this time a London playwright and poet. His student days, when, as the letter from the Privy Council discreetly put it, he had been employed "in matters touching the benefit of his country," were well behind him. But his presence in Flushing may suggest that this employment had never quite come to an end, whether through his own choice or the choice of others.

A small number of spies, couriers, and specialists in ciphering worked full time for one or another of the great magnates—Walsingham, Essex, and Cecil—each of whom had assembled his own secret service. The careers of most agents, however, were far more irregular. They picked up occasional tasks or were tapped for missions for which they seemed particularly suited, and they were paid on a piecemeal basis. The fact that they had regular occupations was useful since it provided a cover for clandestine activities. Even the most minor employee who collected a coded letter in Dover to be delivered to Walsingham in Seething Lane needed to pretend to be something other than he was, for he could be intercepted and searched by foreign spies or by agents of one of the other, competing services. There was little or no sharing of the information gathered, and no central office kept track of who was working for whom. The riskier enterprises required considerable ability to dissemble. Once a person displayed such ability and proved that he was serviceable, he might be called upon to do something for "the benefit of his country" at any time—and it is not at all clear that he could refuse.

Possibly Marlowe's presence in the Netherlands had nothing to do with government service. He might have had some other trick up his sleeve and gone to the English garrison camp entirely on his own initiative. But it is far more likely that in 1591 he was assigned to do something for Walsingham. Even had he been given the choice, Marlowe may not have wished to refuse the assignment. He would see a new part of the world; he had been long fascinated by the strategies of diplomacy and war; he would acquire knowledge and experience that he could make use of in his writing. Moreover, clandestine work was generally well compensated.

In Flushing he found lodgings with none other than Richard Baines—the ex-priest who almost a decade before had been outed as Walsingham's double agent at the English College in Rheims and had then been tortured and released only after he signed an abject public confession. It was Baines, as we have speculated, who on his return to England may have initiated Marlowe into the spy trade and instructed him on the organization, customs, and personnel of the English College. The two were likely, in any case, to have been acquainted, though whether they shared any fondness or trust is another matter. Anyone who read Baines's confession—as Marlowe almost certainly had, since it was printed and in circulation—would have been well advised to be on guard.

Baines had danger written all over him. By his own account, he had violated the sacred oaths he had sworn during the years he trained for ordination as a Catholic priest. He had not merely harbored doubts about the doctrines in which he solemnly professed his absolute belief; he had actively despised those doctrines, just as he hated the pope to whom he swore his utmost loyalty. In the classrooms, at the refectory, and in the dormitory, he looked around at the people who befriended him and whose lives he was plotting to destroy. He listened to their plans to smuggle themselves back into England to serve the flock of Catholic faithful, and he took careful note of their appearance so that, armed with his description, the watchers stationed at the ports could identify and arrest them. He knew the grim fate to which he was consigning them.

Why Marlowe would have chosen to room in Flushing with such a man is not clear. Perhaps, since they were already acquainted, he simply found it convenient. Perhaps, if his trip had something to do with espionage, he had been ordered to do so by his superiors. Or perhaps he was drawn to the qualities that would have made a more prudent person run the other way. Marlowe always courted danger. It seems to have excited him, as it excites all the main characters in his plays. To know that Baines was devious, treacherous, and even murderous could have been part of the attraction. He may have felt the thrill of a tightrope walker, aware that one slip would lead to a fatal fall but confident that he could keep his balance.

Then too they had a strangely intimate affinity, a meeting of minds and sensibilities suggested by the confession that Baines had been required to make as the price of his release from the Catholic prison in Rheims. That confession was a theatrical rehearsal of all the wicked actions and beliefs that the prisoner now repented, and Baines had known exactly what would most appall his pious audience. He enumerated in lurid detail the "jocular expressions and bon mots" that had emerged from his mouth during those years in which he had been proceeding along the "sure road to heresy, infidelity, and atheism."

Baines's account of himself in 1583 bears a striking resemblance to the "revolting and blasphemous remarks" attributed to Marlowe some ten years later in the letter Kyd sent to Justice Puckering. Perhaps in their lodgings abroad, Baines played the same game that he had played with the seminarians in Rheims, only to discover that Marlowe held views more radical than the ones he had dared to utter. What for Baines were only anti-Catholic jibes were in Marlowe the elements of a systematic, skeptical critique of religion. Both were gifted, in any case, at venturing out on a limb in order to dare others to venture out still further. All pretended, of course, to be acting in the spirit of play, intending no harm. How openly they would have danced this risky pas de deux is not clear, however, for there was a third lodger in their company in Flushing, and he is less likely to have joined in the dance.

The third man was an English goldsmith named Gilbert Gifford, and his presence takes us back to the Catholic prisoner named Poole whom Marlowe encountered in 1589, two years earlier, during his brief imprisonment in Newgate. As they sat together in the cell, Poole had explained to Marlowe how to make counterfeit currency, and it seems that Marlowe had waited until he was out of the country and in the company of his shady companions to put the explanation to a test. At the urging of Baines and Marlowe, the goldsmith began to produce a variety of counterfeit coins. Toward the end of January 1591, they put one of the coins, a Dutch shilling, into circulation, presumably as a trial run to see if it would pass as current.

The trial came to an abrupt end, for the very next morning Baines went to the headquarters of the military governor, Sir Robert Sidney, and denounced his confederates. Behind Gifford's fumbling attempt to forge a single shilling lay, according to Baines, a monstrous plot and an outrageous claim. The impudent Marlowe, Baines declared, asserted "that he had as good right to coin as the queen of England." The claim was tantamount to treason, and its menace was heightened by the ongoing war in which both armies were scrambling for funds. A large infusion of money could tip the balance to one side or the other. Baines told Sidney that Marlowe had boasted that he had "learned some things" from "one Poole, a prisoner in Newgate," and that he planned "through help of a cunning stamp maker to coin French crowns, [Spanish] pistoles, and English shillings."

The charge could not have been more serious: counterfeiting was a capital offense. Baines hoped to see Marlowe strung up from the nearest tree.

Sidney immediately ordered the arrest of Marlowe and Gifford and proceeded to examine them separately. Marlowe did not deny that there had been an experiment in counterfeiting coins, but he claimed that it was Baines and not he who had urged the attempt in order "to see the goldsmith's cunning." It seemed clear at least that Gilbert Gifford was not a professional criminal and had only been trying to humor his roommates. "The metal," Sidney observed, "is plain pewter, and with half an eye to be discovered." But if the experiment had been a success—what would they have done then? Marlowe said that if it worked, Baines intended to "go to the enemy"—that is, to the Catholic forces in the Netherlands—or, alternatively, to Rome. Baines made the identical charge against Marlowe, both, as Sidney noted, "of malice to one another."

Of the two accusers, Baines was given the benefit of the doubt; after all, it was he who had come forward initially. But though he was in charge of a garrison in the midst of a war, Sidney did not proceed summarily to punish Marlowe. Instead, he sent Marlowe and the goldsmith under guard back to England, along with a carefully phrased letter to Lord Chancellor Burghley. The letter disclosed the reason for this cautious procedure. "The scholar"—as Marlowe had identified himself—said that he was "very well known both to the Earl of Northumberland and my Lord Strange."

Henry Percy, the 9th Earl of Northumberland, was the head of one of the realm's great families and had inherited not only huge tracts of land in the north of England on the strategically vital border with Scotland but also enormous prestige, wealth, and power. Ferdinando Stanley, Lord Strange, was the heir to the Earldom of Derby, another vastly wealthy and influential family that had played an important role in the founding of the Tudor dynasty. These were two of the most important men in the kingdom.

Marlowe did not identify himself to Sidney as an agent working for Walsingham or another of the queen's councilors. Perhaps he was instructed not to do so, or perhaps he really was in Flushing for some purpose of his own. In describing himself as a "scholar," he no doubt invoked his BA and MA from Cambridge, and he could have proved it by rattling off some Latin to the Oxford-educated Sidney. Sidney prudently decided to suspend judgment and to check his prisoner's references. One or the other or both great aristocrats must have vouched for Marlowe, for upon his return to England, he was promptly released. The case against him vanished into thin air. Of this whole murky affair, only one thing is clear: Richard Baines wanted Marlowe dead.

CHAPTER 13

# Strange Company

"**M**Y LORD STRANGE.*" Lord Strange was not the nobleman's proper name; it was the title traditionally held by the eldest son of the hugely powerful Earl of Derby, who controlled much of the north and midlands of England. Since the mid-fifteenth century, the earldom had been in the possession of the Stanley family, avid patrons of the arts and especially of theatrical entertainments. In the late 1570s, Ferdinando Stanley, who as the current earl's heir bore the title Lord Strange, conferred his protection on a company of entertainers. The company, which originally included acrobats as well as actors, flourished and performed at the royal court and in many cities and towns throughout the kingdom.

In 1577 they arrived at Dover, Marlowe's mother's hometown, where, if he happened to be visiting his relatives at the right moment, the thirteen-year-old boy could have had his first glimpse of professional actors. In 1580 the company came to Canterbury, and Marlowe, just before he left home to begin his studies at Cambridge, could have joined the excited crowd following the performers as they paraded through the streets, to the sound of drums and trumpets, toward the stage erected in an innyard.

Such encounters made a powerful impression, enough to awaken in some provincial youths the dream of a career in the theater. On at least one occasion, Lord Strange's Men performed in Stratford-upon-Avon, where the young Shakespeare could easily have been in the audience. A popular, if unverifiable, speculation is that Shakespeare somehow caught their attention and went on the road with them.

The constant traveling must have been exhausting for the actors. The rise of the permanent, freestanding London theaters gave the principal troupes of players a chance for at least part of the year to lead a more settled life. In London, Lord Strange's Men seem to have performed principally at Henslowe's Rose. They had over the years acquired an impressive repertoire, and their performances drew large audiences that increased still further when they effected a merger in the 1580s with the Lord Admiral's Men. That merger brought them as their lead actor Edward Alleyn.

The spectacular success of *Tamburlaine* must have been what initially aroused Lord Strange's interest in Marlowe. In the years that followed, Marlowe wrote a series of plays with Alleyn and the company in mind, and it is probably through them that he became "very well known" to the wealthy patron. How closely the patron involved himself in the activities of the troupe that bore his name is unclear, but each company had a distinct identity, and it would have been folly for the key elements of that identity to run counter to his wishes. Even if the troupe derived most of their income from the admission fee charged at the theater door, it still depended on the protection conferred by the nobleman's name and the livery he allowed them to wear. In its range of plays, Lord Strange's Men almost certainly reflected its patron's family history and his political and aesthetic sensibility.

The wealthy lord himself may have interested himself in the choice of the playwrights who wrote for the actors who wore his livery. If so, he had an exceptional eye for talent. Along with works by more seasoned writers like Thomas Kyd, George Peele, and Thomas Lodge, his company acquired plays by two newcomers: Christopher Marlowe and William Shakespeare.

Lord Strange himself wrote poetry. Perhaps that pastime made him highly alert to the surpassing gifts of the new playwrights. The plays that they proceeded to write, beginning with the series of history plays about the Wars of the Roses, were calculated to catch his attention. The Stanley family had played a significant role in those wars and their aftermath, managing by strategic marriages and by deftly switching sides at the right moment to survive and flourish. The Earldom of Derby had come into the family's possession through Thomas Stanley (1435–1504). In the reign of Richard III, this powerful warlord had served as constable of England, but in a perilous gamble, he violated his oath of allegiance and threw his support to his stepson, the rebel Henry Tudor.

Ferdinando Stanley, Lord Strange had been raised with stories of the events that had led to his family's current greatness. Surviving archival documents show that among the treasures he grew up with and that he inherited when he became the Earl of Derby were actual hangings that had been in King Richard's tent at the battle of Bosworth Field. Sitting in the gallery of the Rose Theater for a performance of Shakespeare's *Richard III*, Ferdinando would have watched his own troupe of actors portraying Richard in his tent on the eve of the battle and highlighting the role his distinguished Stanley forebear played in toppling the tyrant. At the play's close, he would have joined the crowd applauding the spectacle of a Stanley crowning the first Tudor monarch and thus helping to shape the subsequent history of England from Henry VII to his son Henry VIII and on to his daughter, the reigning Queen Elizabeth.

Would the company's aristocratic patron have been interested in personally making the acquaintance of the glover's son from Stratford-upon-Avon who had penned such a remarkable tribute to his family or the cobbler's son who had written the unforgettable *Tamburlaine*? It may sound unlikely, given the social distance between lord and playwright, but it was at least imaginable. In Marlowe's play *Edward II*, the scholar Baldock—the character whom we already encountered complaining about the restriction on the size of his buttons—rises to intimate friendship with the king. "Tell me, where was thou born? What is thine arms?" the king asks the scholar. "My name is Baldock," comes the answer, "and my gentry I fetch from Oxford, not from heraldry." The upstart, a gentleman not by birth but by university degree, soon becomes the king's constant companion.

This is a dramatist's fantasy, but it is one based on historical reality: in the early fourteenth century, the actual Robert Baldock was Edward

II's trusted friend and adviser. So too, in the late sixteenth century, did Oxford-educated Henry Cuffe, the youngest son of a modest landowner, become a close and influential associate of the great Earl of Essex. These and similar stories suggest both the rewards and the risks of such relationships. You could prosper mightily when your master or mistress was on high, but woe betide you if fortune's wheel ever turned. After Edward's fall, Baldock was imprisoned and murdered; Cuffe was executed along with his disgraced superior. On the scaffold, before the hangman did his work, Cuffe declared that he had been condemned to death "for plotting a plot never acted [and] for acting an act never plotted." It did not really matter. The actual guilt of these lowborn intimates was beside the point; it was the proximity that brought them to grief. "Mingle not your interest with a great one's," an anxious father in this period warned his son.

But such cautionary tales would not have served as much of a deterrent. For anyone with ambition, the rewards of success were too great. Beyond the money he could bestow on the writer who caught his fancy, a patron like Lord Strange had immense glamour. Talented people vied for his attention and were proud to wear his livery. He had the magic of royal blood: his great-grandmother, on his mother's side, was Henry VIII's sister Mary. His family history and its rich network of associations excited the imagination of playwrights like Marlowe and Shakespeare. To be accepted by him, admitted to his circle, and known to him personally was an extraordinary boon.

In return for his patronage, Lord Strange received from the best writers in his orbit something more than casual delight or simple flattery (though there was plenty of that). The *Henry VI* trilogy and *Richard III* staged before thousands of spectators the central importance of the Stanley family in the history of England and hence undergirded the authority of the current earl. And for the young man who was poised to assume that exalted title, it offered a way to make sense of his family's tumultuous past and to understand his role in the present.

If, in Shakespeare's character of Lord Stanley in *Richard III*, Ferdinando Stanley could see himself as in a distant mirror, it is less immediately apparent what beyond entertainment he could have derived from

Marlowe's plays. In the wake of *Tamburlaine*, Marlowe gave Lord Strange's Men a new play, *The Jew of Malta*. The play was once again a great success, and Lord Strange would certainly have gone to the Rose Theater to see it. No character named Stanley strode across the stage, but Marlowe may have had a particular, urgent message for his discriminating patron.

The character who does stride across the stage in *The Jew of Malta* is Barabas, named after the convicted criminal Barabbas who, according to the New Testament, was chosen by the crowd to be pardoned instead of Jesus. Marlowe's hero makes his way through a perilous world by means of ruthlessness, cunning, and double-dealing. These were hardly qualities that any respectable member of society then or now could openly embrace, but as in *Tamburlaine*, displacement onto an exotic figure in a distant clime may have licensed thoughts that could not have been safely voiced closer to home. Not merely on a remote Mediterranean island but here, on this island of England, life is a snake pit, Marlowe implied, though anyone who ventures to say so openly is punished. *If you hope to survive, my thrice-honored Lord Strange, you need to watch and learn.*

The plot of *The Jew of Malta* is brilliant; no play like it had ever appeared on the English stage, and few since have matched it. To devise its fiendish twists and turns, Marlowe seems to have drawn on everything he had observed and experienced in the clandestine struggles into which he had been recruited. The play's hero has something of the jaunty viciousness of the spy Richard Baines, amusing his fellow seminarians with his cynical bon mots while all along planning to murder them by slipping poison into their soup. Marlowe's Malta is a world of ruthless trickery and danger, of oaths solemnly sworn and then broken, of intimate family bonds ruptured, secret alliances forged with bitter enemies, and murderous betrayals. The enraged Jew Barabas, his wealth seized by the antisemitic Christians, sets out to recoup his losses and to take his revenge. Aided by his enslaved Muslim sidekick Ithamore, he embarks on a series of homicidal schemes that he carries out with sadistic glee.

Along the way, using his beautiful daughter Abigail as bait, Barabas contrives to arrange the murder of the governor's son together with Abigail's betrothed Don Mathias. Horrified at what has been done, Abigail converts to Christianity and becomes a nun, whereupon her father determines to get rid of her as well. Taking a hint from Baines's confession, Marlowe has Barabas spike a vat of porridge and poison her and the entire convent. Pretending then that he wishes to convert and give away all his money—"What is wealth? / I am a Jew, and therefore am I lost"—he excites the greed of two friars from competing monasteries. He proceeds to strangle one of the friars and to trick the state into executing the other for the crime. Finally, he manages to open Malta's gates to the enemy Turks. Rewarded by the Turkish commander with the governorship of Malta, Barabas cannot resist one further act of betrayal, this time switching sides and setting in motion a plot to destroy the Turks. The plot succeeds, but Barabas has not counted on the superior duplicity of the Christians. He falls literally into the trap he has prepared, dropping through the trapdoor into a cauldron of boiling oil. At the play's end, the dying Jew curses all "Damned Christian dogs and Turkish infidels." The supremely cynical Christian governor lifts his eyes in triumph and gives thanks to heaven.

What Marlowe was offering to his patron and to the crowds that flocked to the theater can be summed up in a single word: Machiavelli.

✦ ✦ ✦

"HOW WE LIVE is so different from how we ought to live," wrote Machiavelli in *The Prince*, "that he who studies what ought to be done rather than what is done will learn the way to his downfall rather than to his preservation." Machiavelli's observations appalled his contemporaries and continued to alarm them long after his death in 1527. *The Prince* became one of the first books put on the Roman Catholic Index of Prohibited Books, and in 1559 the rest of Machiavelli's works were added. For their part, Protestants wrote that Machiavelli embodied all that was wicked about Catholicism. In England as elsewhere, his books were officially banned and thrown onto bonfires. In the polemical attacks on his ideas that were continually published throughout the sixteenth century, the subtlety of Machiavelli's political analysis, his nuanced account of religion, and his visionary longing for an Italy liberated from foreign bondage largely dropped from sight. In England, his name was invoked instead to conjure up everything that was most frightening and villainous—and everything that in the eyes of the provincial Protestant moralists of the time was most Italian. The supreme master of lies, deception, and murder, he was the implacable enemy of God.

Away from prying eyes, however, clandestine copies of Machiavelli were still being passed from hand to hand, and never more so, as Gabriel Harvey observed at Cambridge, than by students in the two English universities. *The Jew of Malta* is a fruit of this encounter.

As he did in *Tamburlaine*, Marlowe found a way to bring forbidden thoughts out of dark corners and onto the public stage. *The Jew of Malta* introduces the apostle of wickedness in person—his name probably pronounced something like "make-evil"—to deliver the play's prologue. "I am Machevill," he tells the audience. My soul has flown over the Alps and crossed the whole of France. I am now come to this land to frolic with my friends. These friends will not admit to having a close relationship with me; on the contrary, they will loudly profess their detestation. But do not be fooled, Machevill slyly confides: "Admired I am of those that hate me most."

Then as Marlowe's audience would have expected, he adds a nod toward one of his most faithful readers, the pope:

> Though some speak openly against my books,
> Yet will they read me, and thereby attain
> To Peter's chair, and when they cast me off,
> Are poisoned by my climbing followers. (Prologue, 10–13)

The lessons he has come to teach can be learned by anyone: that is at once their advantage and their danger. They can lead to a spectacular success, even to an ascent to St. Peter's Chair. But if a disciple of Machiavelli who has scrambled to the top casts him off—if he forgets to follow the rules—then he becomes prey to a fatal dram administered by another disciple.

Marlowe's contemporaries who could not get hold of one of the originals could acquire at least a limited sense of Machiavelli's work from the numerous published denunciations, many of which included long quotations that conveyed some of the core arguments, though in reduced and distorted form. Traces of them appear in the opening of *The Jew of Malta.* "I count religion but a childish toy," says the prologue, "And hold there is no sin but ignorance." Then, having dismissed the validity of religion, Machevill goes on to dismiss the validity of political entitlement: "Many will talk of title to a crown. / What right had Caesar to the empery?" If there is no truth to the claims of birth or divine right, what is there? The answer: "Might first made kings."

The author of *The Prince* did not in fact regard religion as a childish toy; he never underestimated its enormous power. But he did famously write, "All armed prophets have conquered and unarmed ones failed." So too he did not ridicule all claims to legitimate rule, but he did offer advice on the proper course of action for a ruler who seized power by force: "in taking a state the conqueror must arrange to commit all his cruelties at once." And he reflected darkly on what any ruler had to do in order to survive: "It is necessary for a prince, who wishes to maintain himself, to learn how not to be good."

Marlowe's Machevill, brought on stage to provide a pleasant shiver to the spectators, pulls aside a curtain and reveals Barabas in his counting house surrounded by chests of gold and jewels. It was Edward Alleyn who played Barabas in the original production and whom the crowd had come to see. There was probably a burst of laughter at the "Jewish nose"—the stereotypical caricature alluded to both in the play and by contemporaries—that Alleyn evidently wore.

*The Jew of Malta* traffics in the murderous calumnies spawned by centuries of antisemitic prejudice, superstition, and credulity. Barabas is a monster who brags about practicing usury, driving his poor debtors to suicide, poisoning wells, and betraying entire cities. He is the stuff of the most grotesque Christian slanders. Actual Jews had been expelled from England in 1290—the first mass ethnic cleansing in modern European history—and Marlowe's character is the self-conscious embodiment of a fantasy. His claims are so obviously absurd and his actions in the play so theatrically wicked that they are more likely to evoke laughter than fear.

In the opening scene, contemplating his "Bags of fiery opals, sapphires, / Jacynths, hard topaz, grass-green emeralds, / Beauteous rubies, sparkling diamonds," the rich Jew revels in possessing "Infinite riches in a little room." His delight immediately vanishes, however, when the governor of Malta arbitrarily appropriates his riches to pay for the island's defense against the Turks. Barabas complains at the injustice, but the hypocritical governor, using a time-honored Christian justification for the oppression of Jewish subjects, says that this seizure is what comes of the merchant being a Jew:

> If your first curse fall heavy on thy head,
> And make thee poor and scorned of all the world,
> 'Tis not our fault, but thy inherent sin. (1.2.110–12)

His daughter Abigail is in despair at the loss, but Barabas's spirit is unbroken: "Think me to be a senseless lump of clay / That will with every water wash to dirt?" No, he declares, "I will live." He instructs his daughter that they will need to lie and dissemble, but he explains, "A counterfeit profession / Is better than unseen hypocrisy." We will never know, of course, how Marlowe justified to himself the "counterfeit profession" that he had undertaken in Walsingham's service. But we can be certain that whatever it was, it involved pretending to be someone or something that he was not. Barabas's enigmatic little phrase—a falsely pretended belief is better than the self-serving lies that people like the governor tell themselves—is in effect a spy's self-justification.

"A savage farce," as T. S. Eliot called it, *The Jew of Malta* lacks Machiavelli's seriousness, realism, and undercurrent of republican idealism. Yet bringing Machevill on stage as the prologue was not altogether a send-up. Buried deep in Marlowe's play is an understanding of the human condition that was given its most eloquent and memorable expression in *The Prince*'s notorious aphorisms:

> Men must either be caressed or annihilated.
>
> Whoever is the cause of another becoming powerful is ruined himself.
>
> It is much safer to be feared than loved.
>
> Men will always be false to you unless they are compelled by necessity to be true.
>
> In the actions of men, and especially of princes, the end justifies the means.

No one quotes these aphorisms in *The Jew of Malta*, but they capture the essence of a character who, through plots and betrayals, rises to power, only to be in turn betrayed and murdered by someone more cunning than he.

Barabas has his own maxims to live by, beginning with a phrase borrowed from the Roman playwright Terence, whom Marlowe had studied at the King's School: I am always closest to myself. As the play progresses, he constantly sums up his philosophy:

> A reaching thought will search his deepest wits and cast with cunning for the time to come.
>
> He that liveth in authority, and neither gets him friends, nor fills his bags, lives like the ass that Aesop speaketh of.
>
> He from whom my most advantage comes, shall be my friend.
>
> For so I live, perish may all the world.

These egomaniacal formulations are far closer to Richard Baines than to Machiavelli. But Marlowe's understanding of Machiavelli was not superficial: the spirit of the actual Florentine informs the play's vision of life as a struggle to survive in a hostile world by any means necessary. Anyone who attended carefully to the implications of *The Jew of Malta* was receiving a deep immersion in Machiavelli's fascination with the way power is seized, held, and lost, in his contempt for the fatuous moralizing that passes for wisdom, and in his wry skepticism about all competing religious doctrines. This immersion was what the playwright was offering to his audience and above all to his patron, Lord Strange.

All the moral authorities of the young nobleman's time counseled obedience, submission, truthfulness, and unclouded honor. But toppling these lessons was precisely the thrill provided by Marlowe's play. Its overarching vision was a dark and cruel one, but there was something liberating, even gleeful about it. It promised the joy of sweeping away false pretenses and looking fearlessly at the way Lord Strange's family and others like it had prospered and at the way they could hope to survive.

Members of the powerful Stanley family would never, of course, have openly subscribed to religious skepticism or professed themselves to be followers of the notorious Florentine. But for generations, successive Earls of Derby had demonstrated their willingness to play one warring religious faction off against the other, to swear eternal allegiance and then to change sides, to plunge into the shark pool of murderous factions and somehow emerge wealthier and more powerful than before. During the Pilgrimage of Grace, a popular uprising in the north of England that opposed Henry VIII's break with Rome and the dissolution of the monasteries, Ferdinando's grandfather, the 3rd Earl of Derby, somehow retained the loyalty of the local Catholic populace, evidently persuading them that he was on their side, while at the same time persuading the king that he was tirelessly serving the crown. In the end, after the uprising was suppressed and its leaders had been hanged and disemboweled, the earl emerged with vast expropriated monastic lands in Staffordshire, Cheshire, Lancashire, and Shropshire.

Ferdinando's father, the 4th Earl of Derby, followed a course comparable to his father's. He had ostensibly been a Catholic under Queen Mary, devout enough to be appointed, upon her marriage, a gentleman of the privy chamber to her husband Philip II of Spain. Then under Elizabeth, he was a staunch Protestant. He patronized preachers and theologians who advocated reforms, in some cases more radical than the Church of England was willing to sanction. As was expected of someone in his position, he persecuted Catholics in his region, imposing fines and imprisonment on some of them. But the north of England, which he and his family ruled and largely owned, was notoriously sympathetic to the Catholic cause, and even as the earl professed his Protestant convictions, he quietly assisted family friends who adhered to the old faith and resisted the more energetic persecution called for by the law. Though his duplicity was noted at the time, he managed, like his father, to avoid the dangers that beset him, and he lived the life of a grandee, accruing huge debts, fathering children both in and out of wedlock, and patronizing heralds, actors, acrobats, wrestlers, musicians, poets, and a motley host of hangers-on.

This then was the earldom that Ferdinando was poised to inherit. Of all the writers who dedicated books to him or wrote plays performed by his troupe, Marlowe seems to have understood most completely the Machiavellian implications of the twisting path that his family had been following for decades. The playwright did not have to bring characters named Stanley onto the scene, as Shakespeare did, to manifest this understanding to his patron. It was better and safer to keep it discreetly buried beneath the exotic setting and outlandish plot of a play like *The Jew of Malta*. For the whole paradox of Machiavelli was that he articulated behavior that was meant to be unspoken and that was indeed unspeakable.

In *The Jew of Malta*, Marlowe signaled that he grasped the challenge the Stanleys faced, took in the risks that they ran, and admired their adroitness. Out of the dangerous game that they played with such consummate skill, he fashioned a fantastic piece of theater, one that entertained the masses and at the same time offered the protector of the theater troupe that bore his name a cunningly sympathetic reflection. *I know you, Lord Strange*, Marlowe managed to suggest, *though I will not presume to say so openly; I know that you walk on the edge of a precipice; I admire the strategy that you are following; I urge upon you, by the example of the fable I have staged, to be supremely alert and cunning. I know from everything I have observed and from own life that someone is always trying to outsmart and destroy you.*

Would Lord Strange have picked up on any of these signals or paid the slightest attention to the playwright who was sending them? As patron, he offered his protection to the theatrical company, but would he have extended that protection to one of his company's playwrights? The answer is unclear, but when Marlowe, faced with possible execution, claimed that he was "well known" to Lord Strange, it appears that Lord Strange vouched for him. It is highly unlikely that Lord Strange would have done so had he not actually known Marlowe and felt some interest in saving his life.

✦ ✦ ✦

THERE WERE LIMITS to the protection that Lord Strange could offer Marlowe or anyone else. The very thing that conferred glamour and power on him made him extremely vulnerable. By birth he had a place in the line of succession to the throne, and with Queen Elizabeth aging and childless, he was closely watched for any sign that he harbored political ambitions or unorthodox religious views. Government agents opened his letters and questioned anyone who was thought to be carrying messages to him. In 1587 they intercepted a sinister letter sent from abroad by Sir William Stanley, his renegade Catholic cousin. Sir William was known to have been involved in multiple assassination plots against the queen. If something should happen to the queen, he wrote, "he would be one that should stand [by] my Lord Strange, one day."

Further confirmation of an ominous interest in Lord Strange came from captured emissaries bearing instructions from the leader of the Catholic community in exile, Cardinal William Allen. Allen had been tirelessly working to return England to the faith of Rome. He had been actively engaged in the planning of the Spanish Armada, and he had his hands in numerous ongoing designs for toppling the queen or at least ensuring that her successor would be a Catholic. The emissaries were to ask the Jesuit priest John Gerard, who was in hiding in England under an assumed name, "to make trial of my Lord Strange, and see how he was affected to that pretence of the crown after her Majesty's death."

The authorities did not confront Lord Strange with these intercepted communications; after all, they had no evidence that he was part of any plot. He could not be held responsible for letters that he did not write or for conspiracies in which he had no part. To all appearances, he was an entirely trustworthy and loving subject of the queen. But the spy agencies redoubled their watch for anything that suggested that Lord Strange was not altogether loyal. This heightened suspicion would not have escaped the notice of anyone in his orbit. When, after his arrest and torture, Kyd reported on Marlowe's "vile heretical conceits," he knew that the officers in charge would be eager to link Marlowe to Lord Strange. That was why he quickly exculpated his patron from any taint: "Never could my Lord endure his name or sight," Kyd declared, "when he had heard of his conditions."

The scrutiny only intensified when, in September 1593, the Earl of Derby died, and Ferdinando Stanley, no longer Lord Strange, assumed the title. As the 5th Earl of Derby, he was now in effect the principal ruler of much of the north of England. The Jesuit Robert Persons, who from his headquarters abroad was plotting to restore England to the Roman Catholic fold, wrote that by virtue of his descent, Ferdinando was "nearer to King Henry the seventh by one degree, than any other competitor whatsoever." The problem from Persons's perspective was that it was difficult to determine where the nobleman's loyalties lay.

It was the old problem. Was the Earl of Derby a supporter of the Church of England or a more radical Protestant reformer or the secret agent of recusancy? No one quite knew. His actual religious convictions, Persons brooded, were enigmatic and doubtful. "Some do think him to be of all three religions [that is, Protestant, Puritan, and Catholic], and others of none." If the maddening ambiguity was strategic, it was not even clear whether it would help or harm him: "Some do imagine that this opinion of him, may do him good . . . but others do persuade themselves that it will do him hurt, for that no side indeed will esteem or trust him."

On the very day that his father died, Ferdinando received a visit from Richard Hesketh, a member of a well-known family in Lancashire.

Hesketh handed the new earl a sealed letter. He broke the seal and read that it was an offer from the exiled Catholics in Prague to support his claim to the throne in the event of the queen's death. He must have understood at once that he was in extreme danger. True, the queen was childless, old, and clearly near death, and she had steadfastly refused to name a successor. The Tudor dynasty by direct succession was at an end, and the Stanleys were closest by blood to the royal line. But it was treason to meddle in the succession to the throne. Who exactly was Hesketh, how much did he know, and whom did he actually represent? Was the letter authentic or a government trap? If it was authentic, had its seal already been tampered with by an agent of Walsingham or Cecil? And did he, Ferdinando Stanley, actually dream of being king?

He did not act at once—a delay that, in the event, aroused some suspicion. He evidently needed some days to think through the implications of the situation and decide what was best to do. He must have drawn on his life experience, his family history, and everything he had read and seen. Perhaps somewhere in the back of his mind there was a dim recollection of the scene that Marlowe had written a few years back in *The Jew of Malta*, the scene in which the Jew has to decide whether to hold on to the governorship of Malta or, in light of the risks involved, to be, as Barabas puts it, "more circumspect."

Some such calculation must have led the earl, after several days had passed, to bring the letter to the queen. The reaction by the state was immediate and brutal: Richard Hesketh was seized, and after a summary trial, he was hanged, disemboweled, and cut into pieces. Whether he knew the contents of the letter he had carried was almost beside the point—merely delivering it to the earl was treason enough. But though sharp questions were asked about the length of time that had elapsed before he reported the treasonous approach, the earl himself was allowed to return home. After all, he had on his own volition disclosed the attempt to draw him into a plot to claim the throne and return England to the Catholic faith.

Ferdinando must have given a sigh of relief as he once again headed north. Hesketh's grisly end was a reminder, if he needed one, of the fate that awaited anyone who meddled in the succession, all the more so at this moment when the queen was showing many signs of her age. Almost sixty years earlier the poet Thomas Wyatt, arrested on suspicion of having had an affair with Anne Boleyn, watched from his cell in the Tower while Anne, her brother, and several other of her supposed lovers were led out and beheaded. "These bloody days have broken my heart," Wyatt wrote, "My lust, my youth did then depart, / And blind desire of estate." Wyatt himself was spared the headman's ax—it is not entirely clear why he was released—but he could not free his mind of what he had witnessed:

> The Bell Tower showed me such a sight
> That in my head sticks day and night.
> There did I learn out of a grate,
> For all favor, glory, or might,
> That yet *circa regna tonat*.

*Circa regna tonat*: the phrase, borrowed from the Roman poet Seneca, means "It thunders around the throne." This ominous thunder must have rumbled in Ferdinando's ears too as he returned to the reassuring security of his home ground, far from London. He resumed the life of a great lord, assuring his dependents, including his players, musicians, and acrobats, of his continued support and throwing himself into familiar occupations of his rank.

At Easter 1594, a few months after his close call with treason, he was at Knowsley Hall, his grand estate in Lancashire (now a 2,500-acre safari park). In the vigorous good health befitting a man in his early thirties, he went hunting for four days. But then without warning, he fell violently ill. Vomiting repeatedly, he was moved to a nearby estate, and physicians were called in. According to the careful records that they kept, they tried a wide range of treatments—money being no object, these included a famously expensive unicorn's horn—but the earl's condition only worsened. He vomited again and again, bringing up evil-smelling liquid "of a dark color, like rusty iron." The doctors urged him to drink some of it, as a possible cure, but he refused. They purged him and bled him and chafed his flesh and did everything they could, but after seven days of excruciating suffering, Ferdinando Stanley died.

The doctors, confident that their medical treatment would have cured any natural illness, determined that the cause of death could only have been witchcraft. Conveniently, they found in his chamber a wax image, "the belly pierced through with hairs of the same color that his were." They had noticed "a homely woman, about the age of fifty years," who had been sitting in the sickroom straining herbs in a pot and mumbling something. They had chased the woman away, and she was now nowhere to be found.

Skeptical of the explanatory power of witchcraft, modern medical analysis of the surviving records has reached a different conclusion, one that was hinted at even at the time. The earl's symptoms are consistent with acute poisoning, most likely from arsenic. It is possible that the allies of Richard Hesketh, enraged by the betrayal of his secret mission, could have arranged the murder; after all, they had many allies in the north. But it seems more probable that someone in the queen's orbit—Robert Cecil is the likeliest suspect—decided that it was better that the earl, with his Tudor claim to the throne and his ambiguous religious beliefs, be removed permanently from the picture. Cecil was already secretly writing to James VI in Scotland and preparing the way for him to ascend to the throne upon the queen's death.

Marlowe had, of course, tried to warn his patron: *When you think you have outsmarted your enemies and feel the most secure, it is then that there is almost certainly someone plotting your downfall.* But by the time that Ferdinando Stanley ate his fatal meal, Marlowe himself was dead, mysteriously stabbed with his own knife four months earlier in a meaningless argument, or so it was claimed, about the bill for a dinner.

CHAPTER 14

# Dangerous Acquaintances

One day Marlowe read a poem entitled "The Nymph's Reply to the Shepherd." "If all the world and love were young," the opening verse ran, "And truth in every shepherd's tongue, / These pretty pleasures might me move / To live with thee and be thy love." Marlowe would have seen at once that he was reading a clever response to his poem "The Passionate Shepherd to His Love." The shepherd in his poem had conjured up a happy vision of May mornings, with fragrant flowers and singing birds. Sadly, the nymph replies, the world is not like that. The weather inevitably turns, and the nightingale stops singing:

> But Time drives flocks from field to fold,
> When rivers rage and rocks grow cold,
> And Philomel becometh dumb;
> The rest complains of cares to come.

As for the shepherd's array of seductive gifts—"Thy gowns, thy shoes, thy beds of roses, / Thy cap, thy kirtle, and thy posies"—these too will not last: "Soon break, soon wither, soon forgotten— / In folly ripe, in reason rotten." The nymph therefore decisively refuses the invitation:

> Thy belt of straw and ivy buds,
> Thy coral clasps and amber studs,
> All these in me no means can move
> To come to thee and be thy love.

The fifth stanza concludes with this decisive rejection. Then—or so I imagine it—Marlowe took up a pen and quickly added a final stanza of his own:

> But could youth last and love still breed,
> Had joys no date, nor age no need,
> Then these delights my mind might move
> To live with thee and be thy love.

That the last lines were Marlowe's addition is only my fantasy, though it is a fantasy based on the kind of game that Renaissance poets often played with one another. "The Nymph's Reply" first appeared in print anonymously in 1600. A half-century later Izaak Walton quoted it together with Marlowe's song in his celebrated book on fishing, *The Compleat Angler,* adding a note: "'Twas that smooth song which was made by Kit Marlowe, now at least fifty years ago; and the milkmaid's mother sung an answer to it, which was made by Sir Walter Ralegh in his younger days." This direct response reinforces other, more fugitive suggestions that Marlowe quickly found a place in Ralegh's circle of writers, intellectuals, explorers, and scientists.

When *Tamburlaine* was drawing crowds to the Rose Theater, Ralegh, still only in his mid-thirties, was at the height of his power and influence. The play almost certainly would have resonated with him, for he shared with its author an obsession with maps, an admiration for ruthless ambition, a fascination with military conquest, and a willingness to entertain dangerous thoughts. Its hero's combination of murderous violence and heightened sensitivity to beauty would have made perfect sense to him. These were, after all, notable features of his own personality. Moreover, as a gifted poet himself, Ralegh would have been highly alert to the

Sir Walter Ralegh, 1588, attributed to Federico Zuccaro. At the height of his favor at court, Ralegh goes out of his way to display his wealth and status. (National Portrait Gallery)

incantatory power of theatrical blank verse, and as a soldier, he had firsthand knowledge of siege warfare.

It would have been easy enough for him to find out who wrote the play and to send for its young author. Marlowe would have been ushered by a liveried servant into Ralegh's palatial dwelling on the Strand known as Durham House. So called because it had belonged to the Bishop of Durham, the mansion had been bestowed on her favorite by the queen, to dwell in as long as it pleased her to grant permission. During Ralegh's occupancy, even visitors accustomed to the Elizabethan taste for extravagant display were astonished by its magnificence. There would have been gorgeous tapestries on the walls, inlaid cabinets, walnut tables covered with precious carpets from Turkey and Iran, gold and silver-gilt goblets, and such exotic New World objects as necklaces, featherwork headdresses, longbows, and deerskin cloaks with elaborate designs made from cowrie shells.

Ralegh is said to have been particularly fond of one of the house's features: what in architecture is called a lantern, an openwork timber structure placed on top of the building. In that tower room, with the light pouring in from all sides, he created his study. There Marlowe might have first seen the great man standing at one of the windows, smoking the addictive American weed that he had introduced to England, and looking down at the barges on the river below. Six feet tall—unusual for that period—with curly brown hair, blue eyes, and a sharply pointed beard, he cut a glamorous figure. Notoriously arrogant in his bearing, he went about resplendent in silks, velvet, and furs. His shoes, tied with white ribbons, were studded with jewels. The twenty-three-year-old Marlowe would have encountered a man who must have seemed a character straight out of his own most extravagant theatrical imagination. Ralegh was the living embodiment of that "aspiring mind" by which the author of *Tamburlaine* was fascinated: "Of stature tall, and straightly fashioned / Like his desire, lift upwards and divine."

Born in the west of England to country gentry of modest means—a visitor to his birthplace at Hayes Barton in Devonshire sees a pleasant but unassuming farmhouse—Ralegh had not started off on any obvious path to greatness. In his teens, he seems to have gone for a year or two to France to serve as a volunteer with the Protestant forces fighting against the royalist Catholic army. He somehow kept up his studies enough to obtain admission to Oxford (which he left after a few years without a degree) and then to the law school in London known as the Middle Temple. In none of these arenas did he leave much of a trace—a contemporary of his at Oxford remarked sourly long after that Ralegh had borrowed a gown from him and never returned it.

After a few knockabout years marked by imprisonments for brawling and failed ventures at sea, he managed at the age of twenty-eight to get a captain's commission to serve in Ireland with the army that was attempting to secure Protestant England's colonial control over the Catholic population and to subdue yet another of a seemingly endless succession of rebellions. Ireland was the sink of military reputations, and there Ralegh might have disappeared from view forever had it not been for an expeditionary force of some six hundred Spanish and Italian troops that landed in 1580 at Smerwick, on the Dingle Peninsula. Their plan was to join up with the Catholic rebels, for whom they were bringing a boatload of military equipment, but they found their way blocked by the English army.

Lord Grey de Wilton, the lord deputy of Ireland under whom Ralegh served, succeeded in driving the expeditionary force into a fort and then mounted a siege. The fort lacked water, and after three days, Sebastiano di San Giuseppe, the troops' leader, surrendered and ordered his men to throw down their weapons. The terms of the surrender remain in dispute, but the resulting action does not. On the orders of Lord Grey, Ralegh and his band proceeded to massacre virtually all the prisoners, sparing only the leader and his gentleman officers. Killing so many men, not in the heat of battle but systematically and coolly, must have required organizational skill, along with a strong stomach. The beheadings took two days, and the place where the event occurred is still known in Irish as *Gort a Ghearradh* ("The Field of Cutting"). Di San Giuseppe and a handful of others were spared and allowed to return to Spain and Italy in order to bear witness to the fate of anyone rash enough to attempt the same. The rest of the officers were offered the choice to renounce their Catholic faith or suffer the consequences. Those who refused had their legs and arms broken in three places by an ironsmith, presumably on Ralegh's command, and then, after a day and night of agony, they were hanged.

In 1581, the year following these horrific events, Ralegh returned to London, made his appearance at court, and began his spectacular rise. The story, first told in the next century, of how he caught the Virgin Queen's attention by gallantly throwing his cloak down on a muddy place for her to walk across without soiling her shoes, has its charm, but Elizabeth is likely to have had an eye on him already because of his rather less gallant service at Smerwick. Questions had been raised at the time about the legality of this service—even by contemporary standards, the killing of defenseless prisoners seemed excessive to some—but evidently the queen herself was impressed. Far from objecting, she criticized Lord Grey for not ordering the killing of the captured officers along with the troops. Upon the handsome captain who carried out the massacre, she looked with favor.

Elizabeth began to shower gifts on her new favorite: precious jewels, powerful offices, and hugely lucrative monopolies on wine, tinned fish, and other commodities, as well as mansions and lands expropriated from enemies of the regime. In 1587—the year Marlowe arrived in London—Ralegh was granted forty-two thousand acres of cultivatable land in Ireland, which, on top of his already vast holdings, made him by far the largest colonial landlord there. This acquisition hardly satisfied his appetite for possessions, either for himself or for his queen. Fascinated by the exploits of Cortés and Pizarro, he tried to intercept and seize Spanish ships carrying treasure back from Mexico and Peru, organized an expedition to search for the fabled Northwest Passage to the Far East, sent a reconnaissance fleet to a part of the North American coast that, in honor of his royal mistress, he called Virginia, and attempted to establish a permanent colony there. His imagination may already have been drawn to the stories of El Dorado that would in 1595 take him on a voyage to Guiana in a quest "for gold, for praise, for glory."

Such then was the patron—soldier, murderer, pirate, monopolist, and colonial adventurer—into whose orbit Marlowe was drawn. The perpetrator of the Smerwick massacre must have eerily resembled the ruthless warrior who coolly orders his men to take the unarmed losers of the siege of Damascus and "show them Death." But Ralegh had other qualities as well. He read widely and assiduously in a range of ancient and modern languages—poetry and history, as might be expected, but also law, theology, philosophy, medicine, chemistry, geometry, and geography. He demonstrated remarkable gifts as a poet—not in public, for he was intensely averse to appearing in print, but in poems circulated in manuscript—and he was an energetic, effective prose stylist as well. He gathered interesting people around him not for show, though he no doubt welcomed the impression they made, but out of genuine interest in their knowledge and abilities and for the use he might make of them. A few of these people were fortunate enough to be, as it were, on the payroll; that is, they received annual pensions or were employed in various household offices. But most, like Marlowe, had less reliably remunerative connections.

Ralegh moved in a heady world of political intrigue, historical inquiry, geographical exploration, scientific investigation, and philosophical doubt. This conjunction was perhaps the most exciting of any that Marlowe had yet encountered. It bespoke a freedom of thought that, poring over the books in the Corpus Christi library and venturing occasional conversations with his friends, he had only dreamed of during his Cambridge years. Ralegh also asked bold, irreverent questions. To do so was risky, even for someone who enjoyed the queen's favor. Discretion was in order. In his circle, there was no equivalent to James Boswell who in the eighteenth century eagerly jotted down everything discussed in the coterie around Samuel Johnson. On the contrary, such a record would have been exceedingly unwelcome, and anyone who attempted to keep one would have been quickly shown the door. Nevertheless, there were always rumors. A government panel investigating charges of atheism against Ralegh was told that "one Harriot, of Sir Walter Ralegh's house, hath brought the godhead into question, and the whole course of the Scriptures." Another witness testified that this same Harriot denied the "resurrection of the body."

Oxford-educated Thomas Harriot, whom Marlowe encountered in Ralegh's circle, was the most brilliant mathematician, astronomer, and natural scientist in England and one of the greatest in Europe. He preceded Galileo in using the telescope to draw a detailed map of the moon, to discover sunspots, and to observe satellites orbiting around planets other than the earth. There is a reason Harriot did not receive credit for these or any of his other scientific achievements: he was afraid to publish. Instead, he merely recorded his experiments and discoveries, often in code, in voluminous notebooks, many of which have only been recently deciphered. He anxiously kept a list in his notebook of all the people who had called him an atheist. His rooms were broken into and searched for subversive materials, but the searchers could not make out what was in the papers they leafed through. Nonetheless he was arrested and spent a spell in prison on suspicion of atheism before he was released for lack of evidence. He swore that he was a perfectly faithful Christian and that all he wanted was the opportunity to study in peace and quiet.

"We are not safe here," he wrote to his frequent correspondent Johannes Kepler in Germany, "to think as we wish." But Harriot could not keep himself from at least sharing with the great astronomer one of his discoveries: the planets moved not in the perfect circles imagined by the theologians but rather in elliptical orbits. "I have now led you to the doors of nature's house," he told Kepler, "wherein lie its mysteries." Then he added a cryptic remark that gestures toward what he could not openly write: "If you cannot enter because [the doors] are too narrow, then abstract and contract yourself into an atom, and you will enter easily. And when you later come out again, tell me what wonders you saw."

Atomism—the theory that the universe consisted of atoms and emptiness and nothing else—seemed a key to solving a great many of the puzzles of the natural world, but it was scandalous because it left no room for spiritual beings like angels and demons, for the existence of miracles, and, ultimately, for God. Harriot therefore tried not to make his atomism and his skepticism too explicit. Though it cost him his fame, his caution at least allowed him to die in his bed. All the same, suspicion pursued him to the end. When in 1621 at the age of sixty he died of cancer of the nose, his enemies exulted that an "atomy," as they mockingly put it, had popped up and given him what he deserved.

Only once during his lifetime was Harriot, ordinarily eager to avoid the public eye, persuaded to appear in print. In 1588 he published *A Brief and True Report of the Newfound Land of Virginia*, on its surface a bland promotional pamphlet on behalf of one of his patron's projects. From this work, but only by reading between the lines, it is possible to get a sense of what dangerous topics were being discussed in the Ralegh circle and why Harriot felt he had to be extremely careful.

In 1584, four years before Harriot issued his report, Ralegh had funded an expedition to explore the Carolina coast. The explorers in charge brought home to London what were described as "two savage men of that country": Manteo, a *werowance*, or petty chief, from Croatan Island, and Wanchese, from nearby Roanoke Island. The natives were introduced to Queen Elizabeth and aroused widespread popular interest in London. But they were not there merely as exotic curiosities. Ralegh planned to use them to help establish a permanent settlement in the New World, and his plan involved Harriot.

Ralegh lodged the natives in his house. He assigned Harriot the task of both learning their language—a dialect of Algonkian—and teaching them to speak English. To facilitate the task, the brilliant scientist invented what he called a "universal alphabet" of thirty-six phonetic symbols to record the language of these and any other people. He compiled word lists, sample sentences, and as much preliminary information as he could glean about geography, customs, and beliefs.

In 1585 Harriot put what he had learned to test. Along with Manteo and Wanchese, he accompanied a fleet, again largely funded by Ralegh, that was charged with establishing an armed English outpost on Roanoke Island. The attempt turned out to be more difficult than anticipated. Manteo was extremely helpful, but Wanchese and his people, angered by the heavy-handed tactics of the English, proved recalcitrant and increasingly hostile. At the end of a year, anxious and tired of waiting for reinforcements and supplies, the entire English contingent accepted the offer of Sir Francis Drake, who had fortuitously sailed by, to take them back to England. Manteo joined them; Wanchese did not.

By late 1586 Manteo and Harriot were back in Durham House, Manteo only briefly. In May 1587 the bilingual chief, much in demand as a translator and a go-between, sailed back to Roanoke Island for a second attempt to establish a colony there. Something more than a military outpost was projected; this time the colonists included women as well as men. The attempt, which saw the birth of the first English child in the New World, a girl christened Virginia Dare, was even more ill-fated than the first. Ships sent in 1590 to resupply the colony encountered only an abandoned settlement with the cryptic word *Croatoan* carved on the palisade. The approximately 120 English colonists were nowhere to be found. No trace of them has ever been discovered.

Harriot had the good sense or the good fortune not to have joined them. He remained behind in London as one of the intimates in Ralegh's circle, where he wrote up his eyewitness observations. The published result, the *Brief and True Report*, was clearly meant to dispel the fears of skittish investors, but the terms in which it did so had potentially subversive implications for anyone who had ever read Machiavelli. On the surface, Harriot's report looked harmless enough, but Marlowe must have felt that it confirmed the Florentine's most dangerous thoughts.

Harriot's account opens with inventories of the valuable natural resources of the "newfound land of Virginia," commodities like flax, alum, cedar, iron, copper, pearls, and the like, all there for the taking, along with sources of food abundant enough to sustain large numbers of enterprising colonists. All this is clearly meant to counter what Harriot calls the "many envious, malicious, and slanderous" rumors circulating about the colony and to reassure potential investors or voyagers in any future enterprises that everything was immensely promising.

But the rumors that were causing concern were not principally about the environment; no one seriously questioned whether there was enough fish and game in Virginia. Worries were being voiced about the willingness of the indigenous population to tolerate, let alone welcome, the presence of English strangers who were thousands of miles from their homeland and who would have to depend for their survival on local cooperation. To allay this anxiety, Harriot drew on his knowledge of the Algonkian language and the relationship he had established first with Manteo and Wanchese and then on Roanoke Island with the chiefs and the priests. He had made careful observations about the beliefs and practices of the natives and, still more, about the effect that the English colonists had had upon them, and he wanted his readers to feel reassured.

It was the nature of this reassurance that would have caught Marlowe's attention. Harriot wrote that the "natural inhabitants," as he called them, were taught by their chiefs and priests to believe that their souls were immortal and that they would be rewarded and punished in the next life for whatever they did in this life. These beliefs, he noted, served a social function: "What subtlety soever be in the *Wiroances* and Priests, this opinion worketh so much in many of the common and simple sort of people that it maketh them have great respect to the Governors, and also maketh them have great care what they do, to avoid torment after death and to enjoy bliss." As Machiavelli had proposed, religion functioned as a clever device used by the governing class to control the behavior of the common and simple sort of people, a tool manipulated by and for the chiefs and the priests.

There was something still more subversive in Harriot's report. Though he admired certain of the inhabitants' skills, particularly their clever fishing weirs and their method for hollowing out trees to make canoes, he concluded that their technology was primitive compared to what he and his fellow Englishmen had brought with them. More important, he concluded that the natives were dazzled. "Most things they saw with us," he wrote, such as

> mathematical instruments, sea compasses, the virtue of the loadstone in drawing iron, a perspective glass whereby was showed many strange sights, burning glasses, wildfire works, guns, books, writing and reading, spring clocks that seem to go of themselves, and many other things that we had, were so strange unto them, and so far exceeded their capacities to comprehend the reason and means how they should be made and done, that they thought they were rather the works of gods than of men, or at the leastwise they had been given and taught us of the gods.

What Harriot observed—or more accurately, thought he had observed—in Virginia seemed to confirm the Machiavellian hypothesis about the origins of pagan religion in popular credulity. It therefore reinforced Marlowe's darkest suspicions about the origins of his own religion, suspicions at which he had hinted in *Tamburlaine* and *The Jew of Malta*. The supposed miracles in the Scriptures on which faith was based were in fact merely technological achievements—the ancient equivalent of magnets, magnifying glasses, fireworks, and the like—that simple people mistook for proofs of divine power.

Harriot's account gave every reason for optimism about the success of Ralegh's colonial enterprise. The natives, he wrote, saw us doing our tricks—shooting off a musket or using a magnifying glass to set fire to a dry leaf—and they mistook us for gods. This mistake not only made them tractable but also led them to call into question their own beliefs. For, Harriot wrote, they were "not so sure grounded" in their own religion, "nor gave such credit to their traditions and stories but through conversing with us they were brought into great doubts of their own, and no small admiration of ours." Deceived into thinking that we were gods or specially favored of the gods, they would be easy to convert, he told his readers, as soon as we had enough mastery of their language to explain our religion to them in sufficient detail.

Such was the reassurance that Harriot offered his English readers. But for someone already grappling with skeptical doubt, this reassurance could have served as a bomb that finally blew up any last traces of naïve faith. Had Harriot meant to call into question, at least for those who understood the hidden implications of his report, his own faith and the faith of his countrymen?

In 1592 the Jesuit Robert Persons published an attack claiming that Ralegh presided over a "school of atheism" in which, under Harriot's direction, "both Moses and our Savior, the Old, and the New Testament are jested at." Persons claimed that he derived his information about the Ralegh circle from "such as live with him and others that see their lives," but it would be rash to take his words on trust. The Catholic plotter was trying everything in his power to bring down the heretic queen. He wanted to depict her whole governing class as a sinister conspiracy of atheists.

The charge that Harriot—"the conjuror," as Persons called him—was the master of the alleged school of atheism seems particularly unlikely, especially in the light of the scientist's lifetime of caution. Yet the terms of the polemic are intriguing, as though Persons had gotten wind of something without knowing exactly whom to incriminate. If there really was a circle in which "both Moses and our Savior, the Old, and the New

Testament are jested at," the prime suspect for its central figure would not be Harriot. It would have to be Marlowe.

In the spring of 1593, a few months before Marlowe's murder, the authorities became alarmed at sinister rumblings that bore a striking resemblance to what Persons was claiming. Government officials assigned one of their agents to report on a shady character named Richard Cholmeley, a sometime provocateur and spy against the Catholics who was now rumored to be part of a desperate gang of atheists plotting "to make a king among themselves and live according to their own laws." On closer inspection, the gang disappeared like a will-o'-the-wisp, and after his arrest and examination, Cholmeley dropped from the records, presumably because he ceased to be a person of interest. But the agent's report is tantalizing.

Cholmeley, wrote the agent, "sayeth and verily believeth that one Marlowe is able to show more sound reasons for atheism than any divine in England is able to give to prove divinity." No address or occupation was given for "one Marlowe," the persuasive proselytizer of unbelief, but Cholmeley added a further detail that would clearly have enabled the authorities, if they wished, to track him down: "Marlowe told him that he hath read the atheist lecture to Sir Walter Ralegh and others."

A "lecture" sounds very much like something one would hear in such a school as the one Persons fulminated against. The authorities must have asked for more information, for in a follow-up report, the agent provided details of what Cholmeley had evidently taken away from Marlowe's lesson. These details read less like "sound reasons" for atheism than a set of blasphemies jotted down by a shocked or perhaps amused auditor:

- Jesus Christ was a bastard, St. Mary a whore, and the Angel Gabriel a bawd to the Holy Ghost.
- Christ was justly persecuted by the Jews for his own foolishness.
- Moses was a juggler and Aaron a cozener, the one for his miracles to Pharaoh to prove there was a god, and the other for taking the earrings of the children of Israel to make a golden calf.

There were, according to the agent, many other "fearful, horrible, and damnable speeches," but he was too scandalized to rehearse them.

Was there really a "school of atheism" associated with Marlowe, Harriot, and Ralegh? Did Marlowe actually deliver a lecture against faith, as Cholmeley claimed? It all sounds far more formal and organized than seems remotely likely for anything so dangerous. Cholmeley was one of that shadowy crowd—Shakespeare's Rosencrantz and Guildenstern come to mind—whom the government constantly ingested, absorbed, and evacuated. He is no more to be trusted, as Hamlet says of his treacherous school friends, than an adder fanged.

And yet. Among the blasphemous quips that Cholmeley repeated was the odd claim that "Moses was a juggler." *Juggler* here does not mean someone gifted at throwing multiple objects up into the air and adroitly catching them; it means an illusionist, a skilled performer of magic tricks. At their most spectacular, these tricks can persuade naïve viewers that some mysterious power beyond the natural order of things is at work. Turning a staff into a writhing serpent, transforming water into blood, and bringing frogs out of the earth, as Moses and Aaron did, were meant to convince Pharoah of the power of the Hebrew God. But according to Exodus, the Egyptian "magicians did the same by their secret arts," so Pharoah's heart remained hardened. It was only when Moses performed wonders beyond the repertoire of the local magicians and hence beyond anything seen before in Egypt that Pharaoh changed his mind. So too the technological devices—fireworks, magnifying glasses, and the like—that Harriot displayed seemed to the Algonkians like miracles.

Harriot then was a juggler, and by virtue of his success, he revealed that Moses too was a juggler. Such at least was a possible implication of Harriot's *Brief and True Report*. Marlowe might not have been the only person to have noticed this subversive suggestion. Whoever drew up or copied the report on Cholmeley scribbled several names on top of the page, including "Harriot" along with the word "dangerous." But if the claim that Marlowe delivered an "atheist lecture" is true, then he may have brought what had only been implicit out into the open. It seems entirely possible that the peculiar atmosphere of liberty among those who assembled in Ralegh's Durham House triggered in Marlowe his most transgressive and risk-taking impulses. He might well have suddenly stood up and, with his characteristic blend of sly intelligence and anarchic humor, made his listeners gasp and laugh and look nervously around.

CHAPTER 15

# Wizardry

AMONG THOSE IN the Ralegh circle who may have listened most attentively to Marlowe's words was a young man in a black cloak. He said very little, and when he spoke, he had a pronounced stutter. His name was Henry Percy, and he was the 9th Earl of Northumberland.

Percy and Ralegh were friends. They gambled, exchanged gifts, and pursued common intellectual questions. One day someone in Ralegh's circle or perhaps Ralegh himself introduced Marlowe to the earl, and implausible as it may seem, the nobleman registered the plebeian's existence. Unlike Lord Strange, Percy did not support a troupe of players or patronize playwrights. He may never have seen any of Marlowe's plays. But he and Marlowe were exact contemporaries, and they shared a deep interest in such subjects as geography, cosmography, and the conduct of war. Above all, they shared a fascination with books, which aroused in each of them an intensely personal, almost magical response.

An obsessive bibliophile, as Percy was, almost always needs someone who can appreciate the treasures he has accumulated. In Marlowe, the avid collector would have found a person whose whole life had been shaped by the thrill of reading. That he was a shoemaker's son would have mattered far less to Percy than that he was, as Marlowe described himself, a "scholar." Their acquaintance was more than casual. When several years later in January 1592 Marlowe found himself facing the possibility of being hanged as a counterfeiter, he invoked his relation to Percy. "The scholar," the English commanding officer Robert Sidney wrote to his superiors, says that he is "very well-known" to the Earl of Northumberland.

The social distance that they somehow bridged was vast. When Marlowe was an MA student at Cambridge, living on a scholarship of £2. 13s per annum, the twenty-one-year-old Percy came into his earldom. The newly minted earl plunged immediately into a wild life: his felicities, by his account, were "hawks, hounds, horses, dice, cards, apparel, mistresses." It was as if he possessed the magical power to conjure up all the pleasures of the world. He lived in a gaudy dream of seemingly limitless wealth. "I knew not where I was or what I did," he wrote, looking back on this time, until "out of my means of £3000 yearly, I had made shift in one year and a half to be £15000 in debt." The figures are staggering.

By the time Marlowe met Percy, in the late 1580s, the young earl would have begun to pull back from the brink of ruin. Hidden behind the relentless pleasure-seeking was a current of melancholy, shaped by a family history that was as grim as it was glamorous. His great-uncle had supported the Catholic uprising in the reign of Henry VIII known as the Pilgrimage of Grace. Tried and convicted of treason, he had been hanged, drawn, and quartered in 1537. The earldom had passed to his eldest son Thomas, who supported another Catholic uprising in the north, this time against Queen Elizabeth. He was convicted of treason and beheaded in 1572. The title then went to Henry Percy's father, the eighth earl, who once again was implicated in Catholic conspiracies, now on behalf of Mary, Queen of Scots. In his case there was no official show trial and execution: the earl had been more prudent than his predecessors. Instead, he was first placed under house arrest and then imprisoned in the Tower of London. Months passed, and then in June 1585, he was found dead of a gunshot wound to the heart. The inquest ruled that he had taken his own life, but rumors abounded that it was an assassination. The so-called suicide, it was widely whispered, had been shot at least three times.

Such was the family inheritance that passed at this point to Henry

Percy. The young spendthrift was prone to fits of anger and engaged frequently in bitter quarrels. In the wake of the initial burst of gambling and whoring, he seems to have begun to turn inward. He continued to amuse himself in his friend Ralegh's company, smoking, playing cards, and betting on horse races, but he also was drawn to Ralegh's less trivial pursuits. A portrait miniature from the period by Nicholas Hilliard depicts Percy reclining in a garden setting, staring out pensively, his head resting on his hand, an open book by his side.

Writers quickly picked up on the signal that the wealthy earl had artistic and intellectual inclinations and tried to calculate what might win his valuable patronage. Marlowe's friend Watson dedicated two books to him. One of these, *The Abduction of Helen*, a translation from an early sixth-century CE Greek poem, was an appeal to Percy's literary tastes; the other, *On Waters and Fountains*, translated from French, addressed his interest in gardens. Another writer, alert to the earl's dark family history, slyly dedicated to him an edition of a celebrated work on cryptography by the Italian philosopher Giovanni della Porta. Della Porta's book was intended to be of practical use to anyone who had dangerous secrets to keep. It not only offered a highly sophisticated system of substitution cipher (this letter means that one, etc.) but also included detailed guides to such cunning practices as writing messages on the inside of eggs. How was it done? A special ink was used that penetrated the shell. When the egg was boiled in hot water, the ink was washed away on the outside, but on the inside the message remained legible in the egg white. Perfect if you are trafficking in treason.

The ninth earl, however, had no intention of following in the fatal footsteps of the eighth and the seventh. From his teenage years, his every move was carefully watched by government agents who opened his letters, spied on even his most casual contacts, and tracked with growing alarm the frequent attempts by powerful Catholics to recruit him to their cause. Knowing that he was under close scrutiny, he repeatedly declared that "he troubled not much himself" over religion. Fascinated by a dizzying array of topics—architecture, gardens, astronomy, chemistry, physiology, medicine, mathematics, and cartography, to name a few—he pored

*Henry Percy, 9th Earl of Northumberland, c. 1595, miniature by Nicholas Hilliard. Reclining in a garden, the elegantly dressed "Wizard Earl" has put down his book and gazes out with a melancholy air. (National Portrait Gallery)*

over works by Bruno, Kepler, Tycho Brahe, and others. He began to buy books in ever greater numbers, until his personal library became one of the best in England.

Together with books, Percy purchased scientific instruments, maps, globes, models—anything that a fabulously rich man could acquire to further his restless pursuit of knowledge. When he became interested in fortification and arts of war, he not only collected books on the subject but also paid for four thousand carefully painted lead soldiers that he could deploy in mock sieges and battles. When his imagination was aroused by cosmography and exploration, he sent for sea captains to instruct him in their craft and bought the map of North America and the Arctic that the scholar John Dee had made as a navigator's guide for an ill-fated voyage to Newfoundland in 1583. When he was excited by the cosmos, he had Harriot, the greatest astronomer in the kingdom, teach him how to observe the stars and planets through a telescope and to make astronomical calculations.

In all these pursuits, his friendship with Ralegh served Percy extremely well. Among Ralegh's associates he encountered not only Harriot but other adventurous intellectuals as well, including the mathematician and geographer Robert Hues, who was busily observing compass variations and recalculating latitudes for the benefit of navigators, the experimental scientist Walter Warner, who was investigating animal locomotion and the circulation of the blood, and the mathematician Nathaniel Torporley, who was working on a spherical trigonometry for computing astronomical tables. Percy entered into extended speculative discussions with all of them. The discussions led to the further purchase of scientific equipment and the fitting out of rooms in his house to conduct experiments. As word of these occupations spread, Percy, with his dark cloak, became known as the Wizard Earl, and his companions—Harriot, Hues, and Torporley—as the Three Magi.

Unlike Ralegh, Henry Percy did not court controversy. But his restless curiosity and his wide-ranging scientific experiments, along with his friendship with Ralegh, brought him into the danger zone of heterodox thought in which Marlowe thrived. As he made clear first in *Tamburlaine* and then in *The Jew of Malta*, Marlowe could draw out into the open the most radical implications of the writings of Machiavelli and Bruno, two of the writers in whom Percy was interested and whose books he purchased. And though he was not a scientific genius like Harriot, Marlowe also grasped, perhaps more fully than anyone around him, the most radical implications—the far-reaching significance for religious doctrine and for humanistic thought—of the discoveries that were being made in the heavens and on the globe. Where others who might have sensed these implications were prudent enough to keep their reflections to themselves, Marlowe was willing to give them voice.

Sometime in the late 1580s, Marlowe came upon a book that jolted him, enabling him to pull together his various perceptions about the glittering courtier Ralegh and the brilliant, melancholy Wizard Earl. He could never write about them directly; as he knew, that would lead to immediate exclusion from their midst and quite possibly to still more unpleasant consequences. But it was always possible to write about them obliquely. The book that Marlowe found gave him the opportunity to exploit and embellish, in disguised form, some of the strange, risk-taking behavior he had been observing.

Entitled *The History of the Damnable Life and Deserved Death of Doctor John Faustus*, it was an English translation, done by someone who signed himself "P.F. Gent.," of a text originally published in German. (I will call this translation the *English Faust Book*.) It professed to be the true story of a notorious magician named Johann Faust. There seems to have been an actual person of this name in late fifteenth- and early sixteenth-century Germany, a Johann Georg Faust who traveled widely performing magic tricks, casting horoscopes, practicing alchemy, and claiming to possess mysterious powers. Various documents survive—records of payments, denunciations for fraud, accusations of blasphemy, charges of sodomy, notices of banishment, and the like—that have enabled researchers to track the career of this one (or perhaps more than one) historical figure on whom the narrative is based. But that career quickly became the stuff of wild legend, and the account that reached Marlowe was full of magical flights through the heavens, carriages drawn by fire-breathing dragons, and paramours conjured up from the spirits of the dead, all woven together with farcical episodes drawn from popular jest books.

None of this would have been of obvious appeal to Marlowe, given the plays and poems he had already written, but the tangle of fantastic adventures narrated in the *English Faust Book* was wrapped around a core of theological transgression in pursuit of power and hidden knowledge. It was this core that evidently seized the attention of the former theology student at Cambridge University. The itinerant magician, Marlowe read, was not a typical charlatan, coaxing pennies from the crowd with his shopworn bag of tricks. He claimed or was thought to be something far more alarming than a showman. In exchange for scientific enlightenment, forbidden experiences, and superhuman powers, he had sold his soul to the devil.

Born in a small town in central Germany, the story goes, Faustus attends university in Wittenberg, where he studies theology, earning the degree of Doctor of Divinity. He is well on his way to a brilliant academic career, but he is secretly drawn to the study of necromancy and conjuration. One night in a dark wood, he draws a mystic circle around himself, and making many special characters in the dust, he calls up a spirit named Mephistopheles. The spirit's initial apparition is terrifying: trees bow their tops to the ground, the whole forest shakes to the sound of innumerable lions roaring, lightning flashes, a dragon hovers in the air, a cry echoes as if of souls in torment, and a strange flame descends and turns into a fiery globe.

To continue the conjuration takes great courage, but Faustus persists, and out of the globe emerges a burning man who eventually takes on the appearance of a Franciscan friar—the first of the *English Faust Book's* many swipes at the Catholic Church. On the following day the spirit appears in the conjuror's chamber, where they negotiate an agreement. In return for giving himself, body and soul, to Lucifer, Faustus will be granted a period of twenty-four years during which he will receive whatever his heart desires. At the end of this period, he will be fetched away. Faustus confirms the agreement by opening a vein, writing out the terms in his own blood, and signing his name.

Having taken this fatal step, Faustus begins to ask Mephistopheles such questions as the precise nature and location of hell, the torments of the damned, the possibility of an ultimate reconciliation with God, and the like. The devil is compelled by the agreement to reply truthfully, but the answers bring the magician no comfort: Lucifer and his followers fell through pride; their only satisfaction is to lure souls to their damnation; God is their eternal enemy; there will be no forgiveness. Faustus has scientific questions as well—the cause of eclipses of the moon, the distance and height of the poles, etc.—but the answers to these leave him no happier.

Persuaded that he can do nothing to save himself, Faustus embraces whatever pleasures he can conceive to fill his allotted years. The bulk of the remaining narrative—several hundred pages—chronicles these pleasures, a confused jumble of erotic adventures, journeys through the air, encounters with the rich and powerful, shrewd tricks played on his enemies and on the gullible, all interleaved with periodic attacks of despair and failed attempts to repent. Along the way he converses pleasantly with the Holy Roman Emperor in Innsbruck, conjures up the spirits of Alexander the Great and Helen of Troy, sleeps with six of the sultan's concubines in Istanbul, and visits Rome, where he makes himself invisible and enters the innermost chambers of the Vatican. There, observing the pope and his cardinals—a pack of "gluttons, drunkards, whoremongers, breakers of wedlock"—all gorging themselves, he gives himself (and the Protestant readers) the satisfaction of striking the pope on the face.

In the end, having returned to Wittenberg, Faustus delivers a farewell oration to his students, urging them to be good Christians and to avoid his terrible fate. That same night, between midnight and one a.m., a violent storm arises; from inside Faustus's house, the frightened students hear a noise as of hissing snakes. In the morning, when they go to see what has happened, they find the great magician lying dead. "All the hall lay besprinkled with blood, his brains cleaving to the wall: for the Devil had beaten him from one wall against another, in one corner lay his eyes, in another his teeth, a pitiful and fearful sight to behold."

It is not immediately apparent that this rambling combination of moral parable, Protestant satire, and jokebook could have been made into a coherent play by anyone, let alone by the author of *Tamburlaine* and *The Jew of Malta*. Marlowe's works had gone out of their way to challenge conventional morality; the story of Faustus, aside from its farcical episodes, seemed designed to reinforce the most rigidly orthodox and punitive vision of the Christian faith. If there is any truth at all to Cholmeley's account of Marlowe—that he was "able to show more sound reasons for atheism than any divine in England is able to give to prove divinity," etc. —then he could not possibly have taken the Faustus story at face value. But he embraced the story all the same, not only the fatal pact with the devil but the whole jumble of adventures, from pummeling the pope and hobnobbing with the great all the way to indulging in sensual pleasures and tricking fools out of their money.

Marlowe set to work using theatrical skills he had perfected in *The Jew of Malta*. A succession of cruel, often grotesquely comical stories, culminating in the wicked protagonist's violent end: this is precisely what Marlowe might have been expected to make out of his source. The actor who had played the Jew, Edward Alleyn, would have a similar part in another savage farce, and the audience would laugh and shudder. But something strange happened, something Marlowe himself might not have anticipated. He created in Faustus a tragic hero unprecedented not merely in his own writing but in all of English drama.

◆ ◆ ◆

THE DEEPEST SOURCES of radical artistic creativity are probably impossible to fathom, but we can at least glimpse some of the encounters in Marlowe's life on which he was able to draw. Along with Ralegh's cruelty, ambition, and moral indifference, Marlowe might have observed in his powerful patron a diverse range of other traits that characterized the notorious German magician: a willingness to entertain skeptical ideas, arrogance, a vehement hatred of Catholicism, a refusal to suffer fools gladly, greed, sensuality, generosity, social climbing. In the crude succession of episodes that constitutes the *English Faust Book*, such traits seem baffling and incoherent, but in the remarkable figure in whose presence Marlowe likely sat in Durham House, they came alive. Ralegh was the demonic magician, or close enough to make the magician seem real.

It was not only in studying Ralegh that Marlowe could have found a way to confer upon Faustus a sense of reality. Henry Percy shared few or none of Ralegh's more flamboyant qualities, but he had other traits that appeared in heightened form in the German magician. Dressed in his somber robes and followed by his acolytes, he was, after all, the "Wizard Earl." And Marlowe had had occasion to observe his profound curiosity. The extravagance that had marked his first wild years as earl had been transformed into intellectual extravagance: Percy longed to know everything.

Percy's determination to have his questions answered and to discover the secrets of the universe was linked to an unappeasable restlessness. His mind could not settle but moved from one obsession to another. In an extraordinary autobiographical account of the origin of his fascination with optics, he recalled the way his thoughts kept "tumbling... from corner to corner of my brains." "Both I and my fancies walked in a circle," he wrote, "until I grew giddy with thinking, and thinking giddily made me giddy in walking." Anxious to escape from this "circular maze," as he called it, he looked about in the books scattered on his desk, hoping to lose himself in a literary romance like Sidney's *Arcadia*. Instead, he picked up a scientific "demonstration of the colors of the rainbow" and an explanation of its "arkedness." He found this inquiry into the natural world gripping, and with the help of his assistants, he began a wide-ranging series of experiments.

Marlowe would certainly have heard of these experiments, and he may even have witnessed some of them for himself. If, when he read the Faustus story, Marlowe recognized in Ralegh certain of the magician's characteristics—his aggression, his skepticism, his dream of power and wealth and social station—he would have recognized in Percy the magician's overarching dream of scientific knowledge. To Faustus's restless inquiries, Mephistopheles promises to teach him "the cause of winter and summer, the exaltation and declination of the sun, the eclipse of the moon, the distance and height of the poles and every fixed star, the nature and operation of the elements, fire, air, water, and earth, and all that is contained in them." Marlowe had witnessed in the Wizard Earl precisely this insatiable desire to know the answers to fundamental questions about the nature of the heavens and the earth.

In exchange for selling his soul to the devil, Faustus acquires the truths Percy was eagerly seeking through his scientific equipment. The magician is also able directly to have the perceptions that Percy's valuable collection of maps and atlases could only offer in symbolic form. Ascending high into the heavens on a wagon drawn by two dragons, Faustus looks down and sees the earth spread out as if on a map: "There saw I many kingdoms and provinces, likewise the whole world, Asia, Europa, and Africa.... There looked I on the Ocean Sea, and behold a great many of ships and galleys ready to the battle, one against another; and thus I spent my journey, now cast I my eyes here, now there, toward South, North, East, and West." This experience, Marlowe would have understood, was a fantasy that underlay much of the earl's expenditure of time and wealth.

Ralegh and Percy were not the only people in his world who enriched Marlowe's conception of the magician and helped him confer upon his character a touch of the real. Marlowe is likely to have known the strange figure of Simon Forman, a medical astrologer and occultist whose patients included Philip Henslowe and others in London's theatrical community. Forman set himself up as a doctor—though the College of Physicians repeatedly pursued him for practicing without a license—and advertised that he had skills "in the calling up of angels and spirits."

People came to Forman for a whole host of reasons: to seek cures for illnesses, of course, but also to ask a wide array of questions, documented in the detailed record books that he kept. The occult powers on which Forman claimed to draw seemed to have all the answers: Is this a good moment to buy rhubarb? Which rooms should I rent? Who has stolen the books from my study? Is this the right time to acquire property? Should I loan the money? Has my wife been faithful? Will I meet again the woman I encountered at Sturbridge Fair? (Yes, Forman replied, but she was a harlot and "she useth sodomy.") Some of the questions veered into still more dangerous territory: Will the Earl of Essex be successful in Ireland? Will there be peace with Spain?

Forman took a particular interest in his female patients, many of whom he seduced or at least attempted to seduce. (In his case notes, his shorthand for intercourse with his patients was "halek.") He frequented the theater—often to meet women—and jotted down an invaluable, surprisingly detailed record of some of the plays he had seen, including

*Richard II, Macbeth, Cymbeline,* and *The Winter's Tale.* He also jotted down some of his dreams, which provide a startling insight into the way the practice of magic was woven together, as it is in the Faustus story, with fantasies of sexual conquest and social triumph.

The most famous of these dreams brings the magician together with none other than the queen, "a little elderly woman in a coarse white petticoat":

> I led her by the arm still, and then we went through a dirty lane. She had a long white smock, very clean and fair, and it trailed in the dirt and her coat behind. I took her coat and did carry it up a good way, and then it hung too low before. I told her she should do me a favour to let me wait on her, and she said I should. Then, said I: "I mean to wait upon you, and not under you, that I might make this belly a little bigger to carry up this smock and coats out of the dirt."
> And so we talked merrily and then she began to lean upon me, when we were past the dirt, and to be very familiar with me, and methought she began to love me. And when we were alone, out of sight, methought she would have kissed me.

Given such dreams, it is hardly surprising that Forman was frequently in serious trouble and landed several times in prison. He traded in the fantasies of others and clearly indulged in transgressive fantasies himself. He lived on the edge, and though he vehemently denied the charge of necromancy, the popular belief that he was in league with the devil was probably good for business. A contemporary, Thomas Overbury, described Forman, "that fiend in human shape," sitting in his consulting room "poring over his blasphemous books" and "making strange characters in bloodred lines." It must have been an impressive show.

At moments at least, Forman seemed to believe in his own extravagant powers. He practiced what was called "skrying," that is, communicating with spirits. "This year," he wrote in 1579, "I did prophecy the truth of many things which afterwards came to pass, and the very spirits were subject unto me, what I spake was done." He conjured up a troubled spirit that appeared "like a great black dog" and spewed fire. He wore a magic ring on the little finger of his left hand that prevailed against witchcraft, offered protection from lightning, and made the wearer "famous in his profession." He claimed success at healing victims of the plague.

To fashion the character of Doctor Faustus, Marlowe could also have drawn on one other figure he may have glimpsed in person more than once. This was the Welsh mathematician and astrologer Dr. John Dee, who was in frequent contact with Harriot, Percy, and Ralegh. Dee was celebrated—and feared—not only for his deep knowledge of astronomical and navigational calculations and for his vast collection of books and scientific instruments but also for his skill in magic. When in 1577 an image of Queen Elizabeth was found with a pin stuck in its breast, Dee was called in to examine it and to reassure the queen that she was not in grave danger.

Like Forman, Dee had a particular interest in "skrying." (The crystal ball he used is now in the British Museum.) With the aid of an assistant, Edward Kelley, he achieved success in receiving supernatural messages that urged him to travel to central Europe and request audiences with the Holy Roman emperor Rudolf II in Prague and the king of Poland near Krakow. Implausibly enough, Dee actually managed to make the voyage and was received by both monarchs. But he returned to England to find that in his absence, his house in Mortlake, just outside London, had been attacked by an agitated mob that ransacked his precious library and smashed his scientific instruments. All this found obvious echoes in the story of Faustus who had, according to the German narrative, been welcomed at the court of Emperor Charles V. Even the angry mob was suggestive. The fear and fascination that someone like Dee aroused was a playwright's gift. Marlowe could use every bit of it.

Records do not survive that indicate reliably when *Doctor Faustus* was first performed or how it was initially received. Prevailing scholarly opinion points to 1592, though it could, as some have argued, have been earlier. Marlowe's success at tapping into the currents of popular fear is attested by a series of panics that performances evidently provoked. On one occasion a cracking sound when the devil was on stage, probably at the theater in Shoreditch, evidently terrified the audience. On another, the actors in a provincial production suddenly thought that there was an extra devil in their midst. A contemporary jotted down what then happened:

> As a certain number of devils kept every one his circle there, and as Faustus was busy in his magical invocations, on a sudden they were all dashed, every one harkening the other in the ear, for they were all persuaded, there was one devil too many amongst them; and so after a little pause desire the people to pardon them, they could go no further with this matter; the people also understanding the thing as it was, every man hastened to be first out of doors. The players (as I heard it) contrary to their custom spending the night in reading and in prayer got them out of the town the next morning.

Whether Marlowe believed any of it did not matter; he understood that he had struck theatrical gold. He had unearthed a deep vein of popular fear and fascination.

❖ ❖ ❖

IF IN *THE JEW OF MALTA* Marlowe delivered a sly message to the company's patron, Lord Strange—"Beware, my lord, you are surrounded by enemies, and it is almost impossible to stay one step ahead of them"—it is possible that in *Doctor Faustus* he was similarly attempting to issue an oblique warning to the great men in whose company he found himself and whom he was closely observing. Every time he walked past the Tower of London, Marlowe could easily have sensed the disaster threatening the lives of Ralegh and Percy. His play is a tragic vision of a looming catastrophe.

But though in fashioning Faustus, Marlowe almost certainly used what he had observed in Ralegh and Percy, it is unlikely that either of them would have recognized themselves in the doomed German magician. For the moment, both were at the top of fortune's wheel. Their favors were eagerly sought by multitudes. The Wizard Earl was an especially generous patron—Harriot in particular received from him a handsome pension of £80 a year for life, along with other lavish gifts. In later years, these associates would prove invaluable to the patron himself; indeed, they probably enabled him to remain sane. For though he was spared the horrible end of his father, uncle, and grandfather, Percy was unable to escape the dark fate that hung over his family.

In 1605 Percy was charged with complicity in the Gunpowder Plot, the attempt by a renegade band of Catholic terrorists to blow up Parliament and assassinate King James I, his family, and his principal advisers. On the night before the projected explosion, the earl had dined with his cousin Thomas Percy, who turned out to be one of the principal plotters and was subsequently killed resisting arrest. There was no corroborating evidence to suggest that the earl knew what was being planned, but that dinner was enough to incriminate him. He was not executed with the ringleaders—to that extent, his lifelong prudence in matters religious saved him—but he was arrested, stripped of all public offices, fined a staggering £30,000, and condemned to imprisonment in the Tower at the king's pleasure. That pleasure turned out to last sixteen years: the earl was not released until 1621, as part of an amnesty to mark the king's fifty-fifth birthday. After his release, he lived quietly in rural retirement until his death in 1632.

The long years in the Tower might have broken the spirit of anyone, and certainly that of a man accustomed to indulge his every whim, had it not been for the intellectual interests that Percy had cultivated in the company of his friend Ralegh. As it happened, the storm winds that brought Percy to ruin wrecked Ralegh's life as well. The particular charges and the secret machinations that brought them about were different, but Ralegh too found himself imprisoned in the Tower with no prospect of pardon. Because of their wealth and connections, their confinements were relatively lenient. They were allowed to spend time with each other, to surround themselves with books, and to be visited by family, friends, and associates. Ralegh embarked on writing a history of the world, from creation onward. (He eventually reached 130 BCE.) In this wildly ambitious project, he was aided by a host of learned friends who regularly visited him in prison, including the playwright Ben Jonson. The Wizard Earl for his part applied his energies to scientific inquiry. Together with his three magi, Harriot, Hues, and Torporley—whom he installed in rooms in the vicinity of the Tower, so that they could come and go easily—he set up a full-scale laboratory to conduct experiments in optics, physiology, physics, and chemistry.

Though these pursuits did not eradicate the sense of injustice and the constant fear of death that both prisoners acutely felt, they provided something more than distraction. They gave Ralegh and Percy a way to exist in what a contemporary, the Italian philosopher and monk Tommaso Campanella, called "a double world," that is, a world of radical confinement and a world of radical freedom. Campanella knew whereof he spoke. Tortured multiple times and imprisoned by the Inquisition for twenty-seven years, he kept reading, thinking, and writing. "According to the body," he wrote, a person may be "held fast in prison and in chains to the extent that he is not able to be in or to go to the place attained by his intellect and will, nor to occupy more space than defined by the shape of his body," But "according to the mind he is contained by no physical space and by no walls, but at the same time he is in heaven and on earth, in Italy, in France, in America, wherever the mind's thrust penetrates and extends by understanding, seeking, mastering." In just this way, through their projects in the Tower, Ralegh and Percy both managed to enter vast realms: Ralegh the temporal and spatial realm of migration, empire, and conquest; Percy the scientific realm of matter and the structures of the cosmos.

Christopher Marlowe died before his two most powerful patrons wound up in the Tower together. Had he lived, would he have been one of those intellectual associates invited to spend time with the grand prisoners? It seems doubtful. Percy was focused at that point on experiments and could draw on the remarkable talents of his scientific magi. As for Ralegh, he could no longer afford to court controversy through either his opinions or his companions. As he remarked in the preface to his *History of the World*, he would have been perfectly situated to write a candid history of his own times, but he knew the likely consequences: "Whosoever, in writing a modern history, shall follow truth too near the heels, it may haply strike out his teeth." Safer for him to stay back with the Greeks and the Romans. Neither prisoner could have risked the whiff of atheism and transgression that Marlowe always carried with him.

But Marlowe was closely associated with Ralegh and Percy well before the disasters that befell them. It is possible that the two illustrious prisoners, sitting together in their confinement in the Tower, recalled the dead poet and playwright whom they knew at a very different moment of their lives. The Ralegh whom Marlowe had encountered was not the cautious chronicler of ancient history but the arrogant freethinker, the "best-hated man in the world," as a contemporary described him, "in court, city, and country." He was the demonic figure—"that great Lucifer"—about whom a libelous couplet widely circulated: "Damnable fiend of hell / Mischievous Machiavel." As for Marlowe's Percy, he was at first the prince of limitless luxury, the commander of all the pleasures that the universe had to offer. And when those pleasures had begun to pall, he became the intellectual determined to unlock the hidden secrets of universe, the scientist whose experiments were the objects of whispered speculations and fears.

For Marlowe, these were two demigods, masters of power and pleasure and free thought. And what was Marlowe to them? Probably very little, given their vast resources and the crowds of retainers vying for their attention, but not nothing at all. The author of *Tamburlaine* was not a cipher, and Ralegh would not have bothered to write "The Nymph's Reply" to a poet whose words seemed to him worthless. Nor was Marlowe merely a poser when, in claiming that he was well-known to Percy, he characterized himself as a scholar: he had spent the better part of six long years poring over Aristotle and Augustine, disputing points of grammar and logic with his fellow students and mastering the subtleties of dialectic. Perhaps in the endless hours of their imprisonment, Ralegh and Percy recalled the celebrated play *Doctor Faustus*. But had they done so, they are not likely to have seen their own fate in the terrible end of its hero; nor would they have registered the play's dire warnings about the dreams of absolute empire or of limitless knowledge. In his prison laboratory, the Wizard Earl continued to probe the secrets of the universe, and in the midst of writing his history of the world, Ralegh was still insisting that in 1595 he had glimpsed a mountain of gold in Guiana and that he would gladly sail back to claim it for England. Eventually, in 1616 Ralegh got his wish, and the result was a catastrophe that led to the death of his only son and his own execution. But that tragic outcome lay in the future. If in the Tower the two grand prisoners had cast their minds back to the life of the playwright whom they had known many years before, when they were both still at the pinnacle of wealth and power, they might only have felt a twinge of pity that so gifted a writer had died so young.

CHAPTER 16

# The Faustian Bargain

MARLOWE'S PLAY BEGINS deep within Faustus's mind and follows his restless struggle to make a crucial life decision. Nothing in the *English Faust Book* anticipates this inwardness. There we read simply that Faustus, "being of a naughty mind," gave himself over to "Necromancy, Charms, Soothsaying, Witchcraft, Enchantment." A naughty man begins to do naughty things; that's all. It was not in his source book that Marlowe found what he needed to make the pasteboard magician into a figure worthy of great tragedy.

Today we are so familiar with the dramatic representation of a powerful, complex inner life, largely through the intimacy of the soliloquy, that we somehow assume that it was always an available artistic resource. But in *Doctor Faustus* it emerged on stage for the first time. Along with Marlowe's other contemporaries, Shakespeare was watching its astonishing emergence. It was from *Doctor Faustus* that the author of *Hamlet* and *Macbeth* learned how it could be done.

Ralegh, Percy, Forman, Dee—each of these figures seems, in distinct ways, to have helped Marlowe confer upon his character the stature and vividness altogether lacking in his literary source. But their probable influence cannot adequately account for the invention of inwardness that makes the play so remarkable. For that invention, Marlowe had to bring to his creation one further and all-important figure: himself. Of course,

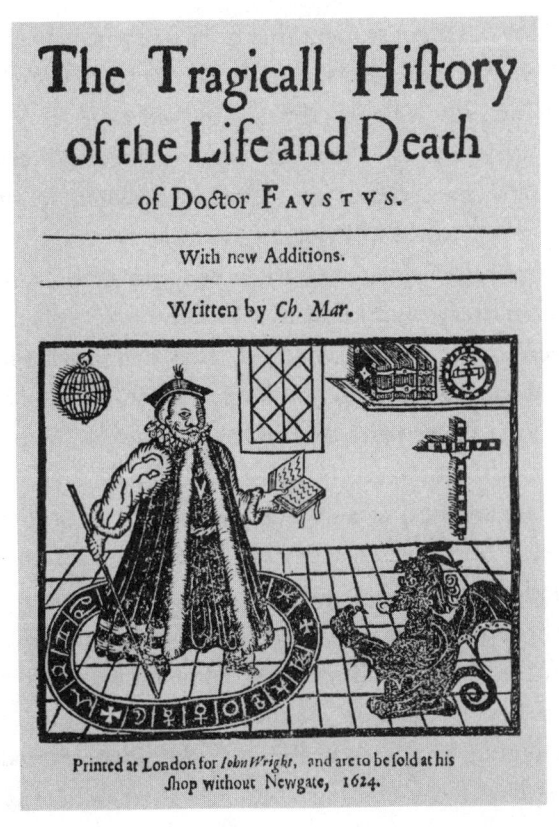

*The quarto of Marlowe's Doctor Faustus ("with new additions"), first printed in 1616, depicts the hero in a magic circle conjuring up Mephistopheles.*

he was present in his other works as well, but largely through leaps of imagination, leaps that took him out of himself. Tamburlaine, the Jew of Malta, Dido and Aeneas are all as far removed as possible from the provincial shoemaker's son who won a scholarship at Cambridge to study for the priesthood. The creation of those characters drew directly on Marlowe's wide reading but not on the life he had actually lived.

In writing *Doctor Faustus*, Marlowe tapped into the world he knew firsthand. The play's opening setting, as the prologue announces, is a scholar's study. Its action is driven forward not by the sword or by gold but by the dangerous allure of books. "Necromantic books are heavenly," the hero exclaims. Ardent student that he is, he enlists as his teachers two experienced German magicians who can guide him in his reading. "Faustus," they tell him, "these books, thy wit, and our experience / Shall make all nations to canonize us." He must master a daunting series of "Lines, circles, seals, letters and characters." Once he has done so, they are confident that the whole world will worship them.

The teachers acknowledge that they themselves cannot reach the necessary level of mastery; they know they lack the "wit"—the sheer intellectual firepower—that Faustus possesses. They can provide him access to the books and the basic instruction he needs, but he will have to take it from there. "First I'll instruct thee in the rudiments," one of them says, "And then wilt thou be perfecter than I." The play captures a teacher's excitement at encountering a spectacularly brilliant student, one who absorbs with uncanny quickness what the teacher grasps only laboriously and imperfectly. It captures a student's pride at being recognized for his brilliance. Above all, it captures the joy of serious study.

Buried in the background of these moments may be traces of Marlowe's own earliest instruction "in the rudiments": his still unexplained access to the literacy that no one else in his family possessed, the excitement he must have felt—that any child feels—when he was first able to sound out the marks made in black ink, the particular satisfaction that he must have derived from acquiring Latin. That acquisition brought with it the dream of extraordinary things, things far beyond the orbit of the father's workshop in Canterbury. And it was this dream that Marlowe's tragedy deftly turned into brilliant nightmare.

In a scene that terrified contemporary audiences (and that is depicted in a woodcut on the title page of the first printed edition), Faustus sets about putting his serious study into practice. He draws a magic circle on the ground, writes mystic characters and signs within it, and then recites a long Latin incantation. The incantation is left untranslated. If they listened very attentively, some of the better-educated members in the galleries might have understood it, but it is clearly meant to impress precisely by being opaque. It relies on the magic of strange words—*Acheron Beelzebub, Demogorgon*—and the special resonance of the Latin language.

Since the Act of Uniformity in 1559, the Mass throughout Queen Elizabeth's realm could legally be celebrated only in English, the Latin Mass having been banned. But many of those who crowded into the theater in Marlowe's time could have still heard in Faustus's incantation parodic echoes of the illegal Catholic ritual: *"Per Jehovam, Gehennam, et consecratam aquam quam nunc spargo, signumque crucis quod nunc facio."* ("By Jehovah, Gehenna, and the holy water I now sprinkle, and by the sign of the cross I now make.") Faustus is celebrating a Black Mass.

Marlowe spent years at Cambridge poring over books that were meant to prepare him for the priesthood. Now he was using the fruits of his scholarship to entertain London audiences with the spectacle of a character poring over books and using the fruits of his scholarship to conjure up the devil. From the perspective of the Puritans, who regarded the theater as Satan's playground, it was Marlowe who had betrayed the proper purpose of learning and turned his theological studies into devil worship. For neither the playwright nor his character does this enterprise signal a repudiation of learning. All of Marlowe's plays, including *Doctor Faustus*, entailed a deep dive into books.

And what does Faustus do as soon as he has mastered the books that his magician teachers have given him and signed away his soul? He asks Mephistopheles to bring him more books: "a book wherein I might behold all spells and incantations," "a book where I might see all characters and planets of the heavens," and "one book more ... wherein I might see all plants herbs, and trees that grow upon the earth." The play is nominally set in Wittenberg, but we are eerily close to the library at Corpus Christi College or to the headmaster's library at the King's School in Canterbury where Marlowe must have first encountered the seductive, subversive, magical power of books.

The prologue goes on to provide a crucial piece of information: Faustus's origins were lower-class. His parents, like Marlowe's own, were "base of stock," yet through sheer intelligence he managed to get from the town of his birth to a prestigious university. Once again, as he did in *Tamburlaine* and *The Jew of Malta*, Marlowe chose as his hero a class outsider like himself, someone who manages to surmount the obstacles erected to keep him in his place. But where Tamburlaine feels fully himself only in the war zone and Barabas in the counting house, Faustus is most at home surrounded by the books that have enabled him to rise and that hold out the promise of boundless knowledge.

Like Marlowe's MA course at Cambridge, Faustus's education at Wittenberg centered on training to be a Protestant minister, but in the play's long opening soliloquy, he flatly declares his intention to be only what he calls "a divine in show." Notwithstanding the years of preparation and the promising career that lies ahead, something inside him resists his ostensible vocation. Now, thinking about his future, he reviews the disciplines that he has studied, from philosophy to medicine to law to theology. In these studies, he has experienced the special thrill that comes with serious intellectual engagement, the feeling of blissful absorption that Marlowe must have known throughout his years at school. Ancient books that no doubt struck his fellow students as burdensome and boring filled him with pleasure that bordered on the erotic. "Sweet *Analytics*," Faustus says of Aristotle's treatise on logic, "thou hast ravished me."

Philosophy is not the only subject that has had this effect on him. *Ubi desinit philosophus, ibi incipit medicus.* "Where the philosopher leaves off," he says to himself, quoting Aristotle (in Latin translation), "the physician begins." In the study of medicine too, Faustus has known intellectual passion and success. He has already made important discoveries. Thanks to him, "whole cities have escaped the plague," and he has reaped both praise and profit. "Be a physician Faustus," he tells himself, "heap up gold, / And be eternized for some wondrous cure." His mind then turns to two further disciplines that he has mastered. One of these, law, now leaves him cold. He may have begun, like so many law students, thinking that its principal focus is the pursuit of justice, but it is, he has concluded, entirely dominated by questions of property. Faustus is not indifferent to money, but accumulating wealth cannot for him be the whole point of a career: "Too servile and illiberal for me." The fourth and final subject that he has studied, theology, seems to him the best of the lot.

The problem, however, is that with each of these disciplines, Faustus feels that he has reached the end. That is, he has grasped their core, or so he thinks, and has therefore exhausted whatever interest they once had for him. As he considers them in turn, rehearsing key tenets that he has committed to memory, he experiences a growing disillusionment bordering on disgust:

> *Bene dissesrere est finis logices.*
> Is to dispute well logic's chiefest end?
> Affords this art no greater miracle?
> Then read no more, thou hast attained that end.
>
> *Summum bonum medicinae sanitas:*
> The end of physic is our body's health.
> Why Faustus, has thou not attained that end?
>
> This study [the law] fits a mercenary drudge
> Who aims at nothing but external trash. (1.1.7ff)

Only theology continues to retain some interest for him, but then, as he contemplates the New Testament and broods about its basic propositions, this interest too begins to crumble. Employing the tried-and-true method of theologians, Faustus sets one passage in the Bible against another. He quotes a phrase (first in Latin and then in English) from Saint Paul's Epistle to Romans and then compares it to a phrase from the first epistle of John:

> "*Stipendium peccati mors est.*" Ha!
> "*Stipendium,*" etc.
> The reward of sin is death—that's hard.
> "*Si peccase negamus, fallimur,*
> *Et nulla est in nobis veritas.*"
> If we say that we have no sin
> We deceive ourselves, and there's no truth in
>   us. (1.1.39–45)

Scripturally alert audience members may have observed that in both these quotations Faustus has left out the corresponding hope that our sins will be forgiven through faith: "But the gift of God is eternal life through Jesus Christ our Lord" (Romans 6:23).

The omission is no mere oversight. Lacking faith, Faustus precisely does not have any such hope. The dominant theologians and ministers of Marlowe's time, the kind of men he studied under and whose long weekly sermons he listened to, did not generally traffic in reassurances. Deeply influenced by Calvin, they embraced the doctrine of predestination according to which God from the beginning of time had chosen those who would be saved and those who would be damned. The choice was not determined by anything that believers or unbelievers would or could actually do. Having absorbed Calvin's doctrine, Faustus knows that salvation exists only for those whom God has chosen, and he knows too that you cannot simply will yourself to have a faith that you do not possess. What he is left with then is the dual certainty that he will sin and that the reward of sin is death. "That's hard," he says to himself.

The Scriptures repeatedly urge sinners to repent and look to God, but there is no guarantee, as contemporary preachers stressed, that God will regard the repentance as adequate and look back with favor upon the sinner. At the play's climax, as his terrible end approaches, Faustus desperately tries to call upon Christ:

> O, I'll leap up to my God! Who pulls me down?
> See, see, where Christ's blood streams in the firmament!
> One drop would save my soul, half a drop. Ah, my
>   Christ! (5.2.78–80)

But as he all along feared, the half a drop is not forthcoming for him: "Where is it now? 'Tis gone!"

Several times in the play a character called the Good Angel appears and urges the magician to leave his wicked ways and rely on God's mercy, but there is, as Marlowe makes clear, something absurd about thinking that a timely reminder might return Faustus to the happy assurance of pious faith. The salvation of the elect, Calvin wrote, depends on God's "free mercy, without any respect of the worthiness of man." Conversely, the vast majority of humans, however well they behave, are fated to be excluded from eternal life. They will instead be forever tortured in hell, and there is absolutely nothing they can do about it.

At this distance, it is difficult to reconstruct how large numbers of people could have been persuaded to embrace principles so profoundly disturbing. As Calvin himself understood, predestination is a dangerous doctrine. To inquire into it too closely, he warned, was to "pierce into the secret closets of the wisdom of God: whereinto if any man too careless and boldly break in, he shall both not attain wherewith to satisfy his curiousness, and he shall enter into a maze whereof he shall find no way to get out again." Though they embraced the doctrine, the authorities of the Church of England in Marlowe's time were well aware of the risk. "For curious and carnal persons, lacking the spirit of Christ, to have continually before their eyes the sentence of God's predestination," declares one of the Thirty-Nine Articles that articulated the core beliefs of the Church of England, "is a most dangerous downfall, whereby the Devil doth thrust them either in desperation, or into wretchlessness [i.e., recklessness] of most unclean living." Most people were meant to rest content with the hope that they were among the elect and to leave any probing into God's secret closets to a tiny handful of spiritual experts.

But the Faustus of Christopher Marlowe is emphatically not one of those obedient souls disposed to keep his intellectual curiosity in check, any more than the reckless Marlowe himself was. And when he puts the two biblical passages together, he draws what seems to him an inescapable conclusion:

> Why then belike we must sin,
> And so consequently die.
> Ay, we must die, an everlasting death.
> What doctrine call you this? *Che sarà, sarà,*
> What will be, shall be? Divinity, adieu. (1.1.46–50)

*Che sarà, sarà.* What lies on the other side of this conclusion is his decision to cross the line into forbidden territory and practice the arts of magic.

The lure is akin to the dream of domination that inspired Tamburlaine, but Faustus promises himself something even greater than anything the Scythian conqueror achieved:

> Emperors and kings
> Are but obeyed in their several provinces,
> Nor can they raise the wind or rend the clouds;
> But his dominion that exceeds in this,
> Stretcheth as far as doth the mind of man. (1.1.59–63)

Faustus's goal is nothing less than to be the all-powerful, all-knowing master of the universe. "A sound magician," he says to himself, "is a mighty god."

In turning to magic, Faustus is not repudiating the scholarly passion that enabled him to master a succession of academic disciplines. Rather, he is finding a new, more satisfying outset for that passion. A direct line runs from his earlier response to Aristotle—"Sweet analytics, 'tis thou hast ravished me"—to his embrace of necromancy: "'Tis magic, magic, that hath ravished me."

For many centuries, the expansion of knowledge by and for itself had been a goal, and it led to spectacular achievements in the Middle Ages, including Isidore of Seville's massive *Etymologiae*, a seventh-century encyclopedic compilation of "everything that it is necessary to know," and Vincent of Beauvais's *Speculum maius*, a thirteenth-century compendium of history, natural science, and doctrine totaling more than 3 million words. Faustus shares something of the ambition that motivated these earlier attempts to plumb nature's treasury and assemble all knowledge. He is bursting with questions about the nature of things: "Are there many spheres above the moon?" "Are all celestial bodies but one globe?" "Have they all one motion?" "Why are not conjunctions, oppositions, aspects, eclipses all at one time, but in some years we have more, in some less?" With the aid of his spirits, Faustus says, he will "resolve me of all ambiguities."

But his ultimate purpose is different from that of the old encyclopedists, and that difference marks a key break between the Middle Ages and the Renaissance. As the vision of what magic would enable Faustus to do swells up in him—"How am I glutted with conceit of this!" he cries—his mind races through one enterprise after another:

> I'll have them fly to India for gold,
> Ransack the ocean for orient pearl,
> And search all corners of the new-found world
> For pleasant fruits and princely delicates. (1.1.84–87)

These are not disinterested scientific inquiries; nor are they impossible dreams like raising the wind or rending the clouds. Instead, they are sensual extravagances of the kind in which European monarchs and their wealthiest followers in the sixteenth century were actually indulging themselves. For his models, Marlowe did not have to look across the Channel to Philip II of Spain or François I of France. From his perch in the Ralegh circle, he had a privileged position to observe the heady mix of royal power, lucrative monopolies, nascent colonialism, and vast riches concentrated in a few hands. Only a short time earlier he had been a student cloistered in Corpus Christi College reading heavy tomes of theology; now he had before him the spectacle of his patron Ralegh who wore a sable-trimmed cloak festooned with pearls and whose agents brought him sassafras, maize, pearls, and above all, tobacco from the "new found" land of Virginia. Faustus enacts the dream of linking Marlowe's two worlds, of translating the specialized knowledge of scholarship into the acquisition of limitless luxuries.

The play makes explicit the exploitation that underlies these luxuries. It is precisely such exploitation that Faustus's magic power promises to confer upon him:

> As Indian Moors obey their Spanish lords,
> So shall the subjects of every element
> Be always serviceable. (1.1.123–25)

"Indian Moors"—a phrase that jumbles together the racial and religious others of East and West—denote the native peoples of the Americas who were, as Marlowe knew, being worked to death by the Spanish colonists in silver mines and sugarcane fields. Hovering somewhere in the background is the great Dominican Bartolomé de Las Casas's searing exposé, *A Short Account of the Destruction of the Indies*. Describing in graphic detail the horrors inflicted on people robbed, raped, set upon by dogs, and mutilated, Las Casas likened the *conquistadores* to devils and demanded that the whole vicious enterprise be halted. But the riches flowing into Spanish coffers were irresistibly alluring, and the colonists were licensed to continue their work. Through his knowledge of magic, Faustus intends to make the devils work directly for him.

The power over the human and natural world to which Faustus aspires is the power of European colonists at their most ruthless, the power to make everything and everyone "serviceable." But Faustus himself does not need to wield a sword in order to gain his end. The magician's vision of how his domination will be achieved befits the fact that he is not a soldier but a scholar. It is through study that he will master certain complex instructions or rules—we would now call them algorithms—that will confer upon him a godlike power.

Since there is almost nothing of this vision in the *English Faust Book*, Marlowe's likely inspiration was his friend Harriot's account of how the English could expect to make the peoples they encountered in the New World docile and obedient. "They thought," Harriot had written, that the technological devices we showed them "were rather the works of gods than of men." Faustus echoes this claim: "A sound magician is a mighty god." In *Doctor Faustus*, Marlowe grasped the most radical implication of the activities he witnessed in the Ralegh circle: liberated from all theology-based moral constraints, the pursuit of knowledge is about the pursuit not of virtue but of power. A few years later Francis Bacon would famously write that "knowledge is power," an aphorism repeated in the mid-seventeenth century by Bacon's former secretary Thomas Hobbes. In our own time, the French philosopher Michel Foucault analyzed what he called power/knowledge (*le savoir-pouvoir*).

Marlowe's Faustus is the first great avatar of power/knowledge. For him, knowledge is not something set apart from the effort to control and exploit the human and natural world. It is the key element for the accumulation of power, while at the same time power is the key constitutive agent for the accumulation of more and more knowledge. In Marlowe's imagination, the dream of limitless riches, sensual indulgence, and hidden worldwide networks all come together with the goal of secretly moving others around to one's own advantage, crushing competitors, and manipulating nature.

In an oddly prescient moment in the play, the pregnant Duchess of Vanholt tells her guest Faustus that she is having a craving: "Were it now summer, as it is January and the dead time of the winter, I would desire . . . a dish of ripe grapes." "That's nothing!" Faustus exclaims, as he sends Mephistopheles off to fetch them. When a few moments later the devil enters with grapes, Faustus explains to the astonished duchess that there are two hemispheres in the world: "When it is here winter with us, in the contrary circle it is summer with them." It took only the devil's air travel to satisfy her craving. "Believe me, Master Doctor," she tells him, "they be the best grapes that e'er I tasted in my life before." We are in our familiar world, but it is a world that Marlowe could only imagine as the consequence of a fatal compact with the devil.

Faustus knows perfectly well that what he is doing is strictly forbidden, and if he needs a reminder, the Good Angel keeps warning him not to incur God's wrath. But what is the point of the warning? The two biblical passages that he has placed next to each other, in the manner of the syllogisms beloved of Renaissance schoolmasters, seem to settle the matter: If we sin we die; everyone sins; therefore everyone dies. The principle of *Che sarà, sarà* that for Faustus follows from this conclusion licenses whatever he might choose to do. After all, what lies on the other side of death, salvation or damnation, has nothing to do with moral worth. Practicing virtue will accomplish nothing; practicing magic will change his life and the lives of others. Faustus dreams of travel to distant places, of studying "strange philosophy," of learning the secrets of kings. He imagines himself walling his country with brass; levying troops to "chase the Prince of Parma from our land"; and—as if this too were a grand heroic act—filling "the public schools with silk / Wherewith the students shall be bravely clad." No more puke-colored gowns.

This last ambition brings us back to Marlowe at Cambridge, bristling at all the restrictions and brooding about his future. We know that there came a point when he knew he had no desire or vocation to become a minister and that, if he did, he would be only a "divine in show." We know too that there came a point when he agreed to do something clandestine— exactly what is not clear—in the service of the state. It is this agreement and its consequences that lie at the heart of Marlowe's profound personal investment in the Faustus story.

In Marlowe's play, as in his German source, Faustus initially conjures up a hideous devil whom he peremptorily orders to go away and return in the more agreeable form of Mephistopheles. Mephistopheles tells the conjuror that the incantations in themselves did not actually compel him to appear. "I came now hither of my own accord," he says, drawn by the prospect of getting Faustus's soul. It is not clear whether this claim is true or false; after all, the devil is the master of deceit. In a farcical scene later in the play, Faustus's clownish servant Robin finds his master's book and recites a garbled form of the conjuration: *Polypragmos Belseborams framanto pacostiphos tostu Mephistopheles.* Lo and behold, the angry Mephistopheles appears, complaining that "From Constantinople am I hither come / Only for the pleasure of these damned slaves" (3.2.36–37).

Whatever the force of the magical formulas, there is nothing mechanical or automatic in the encounter between Faustus and Mephistopheles. Instead, the devil has an intense desire to recruit the magician—"O, what will not I do to obtain his soul?"—and the magician feels an equally intense excitement at being recruited: "Had I as many souls as there be stars, / I'd give them all for Mephistopheles." The play brilliantly captures the courtship dance that leads up to the demonic compact—the fraught conversations, the misgivings, the assurances, and the promises, the approach to the fatal moment after which there is no turning back. The scenes are among the most remarkable and psychologically penetrating that Marlowe ever wrote, and with good reason: they are charged with the decision that shaped his life.

Marlowe's recruitment is not likely to have happened all at once, in a single afternoon. He probably had the particular pleasure of being wooed for some time. Whoever conducted the wooing evidently was appealing and persuasive. He must have carried with him an air of worldliness, of having seen and done things far beyond the circumscribed boundaries of the university. He offered the cloistered divinity student an otherwise completely inaccessible whole world of adventure. And he must have made the student feel powerful and important. Marlowe was being singled out from the others and offered something because of his special gifts.

If the scenes in *Doctor Faustus* are any indication, the person who recruited Marlowe to work for the spy service was surprisingly candid. The devil does not pretend to be other than he is. "What are you that live with Lucifer," Faustus asks. "Unhappy spirits," Mephistopheles replies, that "are forever damned with Lucifer." "Where are you damned?" he asks the devil; "In hell," comes the reply. Faustus immediately follows up, as if he has detected a lie: "How comes it then that thou art out of hell?" Mephistopheles's answer is devastating: "Why this is hell, nor am I out of it." Marlowe was famous as the master of the "mighty line"—grand, often exotic words—but these ten simple monosyllables are as powerful as anything he ever wrote.

Such candor, one might think, would defeat the devil's whole purpose, but the effect, as Marlowe depicts it, is exactly the opposite. Faustus becomes ever more determined to sign away his soul. The devil continues with an account of how excruciating it is to lose everlasting bliss, but Faustus responds with a kind of contempt. "What," he asks dismissively, "is great Mephistopheles so passionate / For being deprived of the joys of heaven?" And then, swollen with narcissistic self-congratulation: "Learn thou of Faustus manly fortitude." Egotism here is twisted together with a strange form of denial.

As in certain intimate conversations where the pain of what is being said is too great to handle, Faustus simply refuses to credit what his companion is saying. "Hell hath no limits," Mephistopheles explains; "Where we are is hell, / And where hell is must we ever be," to which Faustus replies, "Come, I think hell's a fable." When Mephistopheles continues to insist—"I am damned and am now in hell"—Faustus shuts the conversation down. If this is hell, he says, "I'll willingly be damned here. What? Walking, disputing, etc.?"

As an MA student, Marlowe would have fully imbibed the dark warnings of Calvinist theology, and nothing in the life he had lived at Cambridge and in London could have given him any assurance that he was one of the elect rather than one of the damned. It is possible that as he completed *Doctor Faustus*, he was gripped, despite all his vaunted skepticism, by a personal fear of damnation. "Cut is the branch that might have grown full straight," intones the chorus, after Faustus has been hauled down to hell, "And burnèd is Apollo's laurel bough / That sometime grew within this learned man." The learned man who wrote these lines might have imagined that the same words could be spoken of him and might have concluded that, like his character, he was doomed. After all, he knew that he was neither willing nor able to abandon the course of life on which he had embarked. The link to the spy service, the skepticism, and the transgressive imagination were essential parts of his identity, all bound together with his poetic genius. Though they might be leading to destruction, he could not turn away from them.

But perhaps Marlowe was not gripped by any such fear. It is at least as possible that he believed that the whole story of hell and damnation was a fantasy, akin to other fantasies he had played with and staged over the course of his career. Hell, he could have told himself, was merely a poetic invention, a fable cunningly designed to terrify the gullible masses into obedience.

Like everyone in his world, Marlowe would have been introduced to the concept of hell at an early age. Generation after generation of impressionable children were treated to tales of horrific punishments in an imagined afterlife: stench, rivers of fire, gnawing worms, swirling sulfur and pitch. Sharp stones rained down like hail on the unprotected bodies of the damned. Adulterers were strung up by their eyebrows and hair; sodomites were covered in blood and filth; unmarried girls who lost their virginity were shackled in flaming chains; women who had had abortions were impaled on flaming spits. Virtuous pagans were nonetheless blinded and placed forever in a deep pit. And, of course, there were innumerable atheists, heretics, Muslims, and Jews, tortured for all eternity by grotesque devils with sharp teeth, flaming eyes, and long claws.

From his immersion in Christian texts, Marlowe knew perfectly well how little of this elaborate demonic underworld actually came from Scripture. The realm of the dead that the Hebrew Bible called *Sheol* was not a place of punishment but simply the darkness of the grave. In the Greek New Testament, Jesus refers multiple times to a place called Gehenna where the wicked will go, but he gives the name, which derives from Hinnom, a sinister valley near Jerusalem, no further substance. The gruesome hell that was depicted in paintings and preached to Marlowe and his contemporaries had been lifted from Virgil and other pagan poets or spun out of the overheated imaginations of medieval artists and writers. Most people credited its literal existence, but a small number of skeptics concluded that it was a fiction, one that had for centuries helped to confer authority and riches on a small number of hypocrites.

Marlowe may not have believed in the existence of a vast underground realm to which the souls of sinners were dragged off to suffer eternal punishments, but he saw clearly that hell was good for theater. His imagination was excited by all that it could do with the idea of hell, just as it had been excited in *Tamburlaine* by all that it could do with the idea of the East. In *Doctor Faustus*, as in innumerable medieval paintings and poems, the Seven Deadly Sins—pride, covetousness, wrath, envy, gluttony, sloth, and lechery—parade across the stage, but the play explicitly terms them a "pastime" or a "show." They are more burlesque than warning. So too, after making fun of Catholics crossing themselves, the play takes gleeful pleasure in depicting "bell, book, and candle," the solemn rite of excommunication, at the climax of which Faustus and Mephistopheles, making themselves invisible, strike the pope and his friars and chase them off the stage with fireworks.

Nonetheless, it wasn't only for purposes of farce that *Doctor Faustus* drew on the vast inheritance of sin, damnation, and hell. Marlowe had clearly decided he could do wonders with the Faust book. He took on its whole mythical apparatus, complete with Lucifer, Beelzebub, the Seven Deadly Sins, incubi and succubi, exorcism, and all the rest, and confronted it with a skeptical intellectual, drawn precisely in his own image: "I think hell's a fable." The confrontation is a weird one, since that same intellectual has called up the spirits from hell in the first place, but it is astonishingly effective.

"Think'st thou that Faustus is so fond"—that is, so foolish—"to imagine / That after this life there is any pain?" Faustus speaks these words to a devil who assures him that there is plenty of pain in the afterlife, far more than he can imagine. But the very fact that the skeptical words are openly spoken before a large audience, and not by a Muslim or a Jew but by a Christian scholar, is a radical act. "These are," Faustus declares, "trifles and mere old wives' tales." Of course, the play proves Faustus wrong. In his diary, the Elizabethan entrepreneur Philip Henslowe inventoried the props that were in storage in the Rose Theater. They included a hellmouth, huge, gaping mechanical jaws, perfect for receiving a skeptic like Faustus at the end of act five.

The genius of Marlowe's play does not depend on the hoary stage device of the hellmouth. Its unique power comes not from dragging the doubter off to eternal punishment in the afterworld but from reimagining what hell is and relocating it in the here and now. Hell is an awareness of how painfully limited life is. Hell is a progressive loss of interest in the books and subjects that had once seemed so endlessly fascinating. Hell is a vast enterprise of global exploitation that merely produces luxuries for wealthy patrons. Hell is a plan to save one's country that shrinks into a set of tricks played on minor adversaries. Hell is a craving for access to secrets that, once revealed, shrivel into ennui: "Well, I am answered." Hell is the despair produced by the Calvinist doctrine of predestination, a despair constantly fueled by pious warnings that cannot possibly be followed and by tantalizing hopes that cannot and will not be fulfilled.

"I'll willingly be damned!" The brilliance of the strategy is to make the recruited one—who is, after all, frankly informed that he is about to ruin his life—actively pursue his own destruction. The arrangement has to be formally concluded: as security, Lucifer demands a deed of gift written in blood. Before it is drawn up, there is one more moment of candor, as if to prove that nothing whatever has been withheld. "What good will my soul do thy lord?" Faustus asks, and the devil replies that misery loves company. "Why," Faustus asks in surprise, "have you any pain that torture others?" "As great as have the souls of men," the devil declares, adding, "But tell me, Faustus, shall I have thy soul?"

The answer, of course, is yes. Faustus stabs his arm to draw blood to write the fatal document. His blood at first congeals, so that he cannot complete the words, but Mephistopheles brings coals to liquify it again. "Now will I make an end immediately," Faustus declares, and, dipping his pen into his blood, he writes that he bequeaths his soul to Lucifer. He signals his completion of the deed of gift by quoting in the Latin of the Vulgate Jesus' last words on the cross: *Consummatum est*, "It is finished." In this demonic context, the words are blasphemous, but they also serve as an acknowledgment, whether conscious or not, that the life Faustus has lived up to this point is decisively over.

Marlowe seems present, body and soul, in this scene, as if he has penned it with his own blood.

The Privy Council's letter that got Marlowe his MA degree is one piece of evidence that at Cambridge he had agreed to work for Walsingham's secret service. The almost unbearable intensity of the contract scene in *Doctor Faustus* is a different kind of evidence, not documentary but emotional, that its author knew what it was to have made a fateful, life-changing choice. Clearly Marlowe was involved directly or indirectly in betraying people whom he knew and who trusted him. These betrayals, as he must have perfectly understood, would have the direst consequences for those on whom he was reporting. Whether it troubled his conscience or whether he even had much of a conscience to trouble, did it occur to Marlowe at the time of his decision that he was making a deal with the devil? And if so, how did he justify or explain it to himself? *Doctor Faustus* provides a tantalizing, if elusive, series of hints.

The recruitment of Marlowe at Cambridge took place at a moment when the Prince of Parma—the Spanish governor of the Netherlands and the commander of the force that the Spanish Armada was to transport to England—was much on everyone's mind. Faustus's intention to "drive the Prince of Parma from our land" was not in the German sources; it is something Marlowe added. The Spanish Armada could not possibly carry enough troops to subdue the entire island by themselves. The invasion of England that the Spanish were planning depended heavily on the assumption that a significant portion of the population would rise up in support of the Roman Catholic cause. Walsingham was not employing his network of spies to ferret out sentimental believers in the old faith; he was concerned about a potential fifth column mobilized by agents in the pay of Spain or the Vatican.

In the event, of course, it was the Protestant wind—the violent storms that drove the Spanish fleet off course—that doomed the Spanish Armada. But that fortuitous outcome lay in the future. At the moment when Marlowe was recruited, he may well have believed (or been told by the recruiters) that he could do something incredibly significant for his country: he could in effect build a wall of brass around it, protecting it from its mortal enemies. It is an all-too-typical fantasy, of the kind that over the centuries has lured innumerable idealistic youths into situations of extreme personal danger as well as morally compromised lives.

Marlowe's motivation need not have been purely altruistic. He may also have dreamed, like Faustus, that he could enrich himself and dress in silks and finery; that he could encounter the princes of the world; that he could satisfy his wildest desires. He would have access to the hidden knowledge that the likes of him, a mere cobbler's son, would never otherwise have had.

By the time he wrote *Doctor Faustus*, he was in a position to look back on the decision he had once made and reflect on the consequences. The play does not depict the outcome as either happy or heroic. Faustus does indeed meet princes and kings, but he does so not as a conqueror but as a glorified court entertainer. Welcoming him as a celebrity notorious for his "knowledge in the black art," the German emperor expresses a particular interest in getting a glimpse of Alexander the Great and his paramour, and Faustus dutifully complies. The magician is someone who can conjure up famous figures long dead—"Both in their right shapes, gesture, and attire / They used to wear during their time of life"—and make them seem alive again. This is, of course, a dramatist's special gift as well, one that Marlowe, a magician of language, had deployed when he brought to life Dido and Aeneas and Tamburlaine. *Doctor Faustus* is not dismissive of this gift, but it is a far cry from the dreams that motivated the scholar's original decision to cross the line into dangerous territory.

Faustus cannot actually bring the dead back to life. The bodies of Alexander and his paramour "long since are consumed to dust," and all he can offer, with the aid of his demon-actors, is an illusion, a lively show to amuse his imperial host. The magician's theatrical performances, like Marlowe's own, are not restricted to aristocratic audiences alone. Later in the play, several humble scholars come to him with a similar request: having debated who among women "was the beautifulest in all the world," they have concluded that it must have been Helen of Troy. Could they see her for themselves? Faustus obliges and has one of his demons appear in the form of "that peerless dame of Greece." The scholars are grateful and go off mumbling the incoherent praises that usually greet such spectacles.

Notwithstanding his contract with the devil, Faustus does not wind up building the wall of brass or dressing his fellow scholars in silk. He can entertain the rich and powerful, outsmart skeptics, and bilk the credulous—all very amusing achievements, though hardly ones for which anyone is likely to sell his soul. His magic skills evidently cannot change the course of history or alter the nature of institutions. He can don a cloak of invisibility and slap the pope, but he cannot bring down the papacy. As if he were still a brilliant university student, he can ask innumerable questions and gain access to knowledge he would not otherwise have had, but the knowledge he obtains leaves him cold. He achieves fame as a conjuror, but he knows that he has made a rotten bargain. After each of his successes, he sinks into a deeper depression: "Despair doth drive distrust into my thoughts."

The alternation of public frolic and inward misery, structuring much of the play, reflects the German narrative, with its discontinuous string of amusing episodes and the magician's periodic bursts of regret. But the structure may reflect something else as well: Marlowe's own experience of alternating states of exhilaration and disenchantment. Neither the thrill nor the misery is once and for all; they continually displace each other, often suddenly and without warning. And always in Faustus, as almost certainly in Marlowe too, there is an ominous sense of a fixed time limit, a final moment of reckoning that is steadily approaching.

In his darkest moments, Faustus can no longer endure what he has done to himself or go on with the knowledge of the impending and inescapable denouement. He contemplates changing his life. But the contract, signed with his own blood, is irrevocable. At any sign that he wishes to annul the contract, the demonic powers to which he has sold his soul immediately threaten to arrest him, as they put it, and tear him to pieces. In terror, he renounces his intention.

It is not fear alone that leads to this renunciation. The devils are masters of distraction as well as menace. As soon as they perceive Faustus to be wavering, they bring out gaudy spectacles, fireworks, entertainments. Mephistopheles offers something more: he dangles before Faustus the tantalizing prospect of satisfying his most extravagant desires. This prospect pulls him back from the suicidal ideation—"swords and knives / Poison, guns, halters, and envenomed steel"—that constantly torments him. He would already, he says, "have done the deed / Had not sweet pleasure conquered deep despair."

The alternating rhythm of despair and pleasure culminates in the opportunity "to glut the longing of my heart's desire," as Faustus puts it, and sleep with Helen of Troy. Once again it is not the real Helen with whom he can have sex; the magician is perfectly aware that she has long since rotted away. It is rather a succubus, a demon in the shape of a female who seduces men and survives by collecting their semen. But the illusion is thrilling, and Faustus is willing to give himself over, body and soul, to it.

The demonic impersonation here plays a sly game with theatrical impersonation: the Elizabethan audience knew that a boy actor was playing the part of the demon who is playing the part of Helen. Marlowe crafts the scene around a passionate kiss: "Sweet Helen, make me immortal with a kiss; / Her lips suck forth my soul, see where it flies!" The words call for an erotic intensity that may have been at least as unsettling to contemporary audiences as the conjuring of devils. Marlowe has the

characters repeat the kiss—"Come, Helen, come, give my soul again"—
and then draws out the moment with some of his most brilliant poetry:

> Here will I dwell, for heaven is in these lips,
> And all is dross that is not Helena ...
> O, thou are fairer than the evening air
> Clad in the beauty of a thousand stars;
> Brighter art thou than flaming Jupiter
> When he appeared to hapless Semele;
> More lovely than the monarch of the sky
> In wanton Arethusa's azure arms;
> And none but thou shalt be my paramour. (5.1.98–112)

These extraordinary verses collapse the distinction between active and passive, god and human, male and female. Faustus and Helen and the demon and the boy who is playing the demon who is playing Helen all merge into the sexual tangle of Jupiter and the monarch of sky and hapless Semele and wanton Arethusa.

For years, angry moralists had been declaring that the Elizabethan public theaters were sinks of vice—"idleness, unthriftiness, whoredom, wantonness, drunkenness, and what not"—and demanding that they be shut down. "Satan hath not a ... fitter school to work and teach his desire to bring men and women into his snare of concupiscence and filthy lusts of wicked whoredom" than theaters, sputtered the minister John Northbrooke, and therefore it is necessary that they "should be forbidden and dissolved and put down by authority." Their very existence, preachers thundered, made London even worse than Sodom and inevitably provoked God's wrath. Why were so many Londoners dying hideous deaths every year in outbreaks of plague? The answer was simple, said the vicar Thomas White: "The cause of plagues is sin, if you look to it well; and the cause of sin are plays; therefore, the cause of plagues are plays."

*Doctor Faustus* is Marlowe's provocative response to these charges. *If you think that the playhouse is the school of Satan and that the players are his servants, I will bring Satan himself on stage and conjure up a host of actual devils to frighten and to entertain you. If you think plays excite lust, I will give you tantalizing glimpses of the most beautiful woman who ever lived. And if you think that the theater has turned London into Sodom, I will give you a beautiful boy, dressed in woman's clothing, and have him kiss a fellow actor so passionately on the lips that he will seem to have sucked forth the soul. Of course, I will mark it all out as unspeakably wicked, just as the preachers say it is.* Faustus, as the play makes clear, is hurtling toward a bad end.

But Marlowe made sure that Helen's kiss—the closest that Elizabethan stage conventions would allow to the representation of sexual intercourse—would be the moment in the play that everyone who saw or read it remembered. It calls forth the play's most ecstatic poetry—"Was this the face that launched a thousand ships / And burnt the topless towers of Ilium?"—and for a moment at least, the loss of Faustus's soul seems a bargain worth making.

♦ ♦ ♦

SOME YEARS AFTER Marlowe's death, *Doctor Faustus* was revised on the occasion of a theatrical revival. Whoever updated the script evidently felt that further clarification was needed and added in the final act a new exchange between the magician and his devil. Mephistopheles gleefully tells Faustus that he has no hope of heaven and urges him to despair. "O thou bewitching fiend," Faustus exclaims, "'twas thy temptation / Hath robbed me of eternal happiness!" "I do confess it," Mephistopheles answers:

> 'Twas I that, when there wert i'the way to heaven,
> Damned up the passage: when thou took'st the book
> To view the scriptures, then I turned the leaves
> And led thine eye. (B text 5.2.59ff)

The revision lamely calls attention to something striking about the play that Marlowe wrote. In his version, as we have seen, the devil did not try to deceive Faustus. To distract him, yes; to allure him with pleasures and promises; to be angry when he threatened to pull away from his contract. But Mephistopheles does not lie or hide any of the risks. He does not conceal that as a fallen spirit, he is himself in agony, and when Faustus declares jauntily, "I think hell's a fable," the devil replies, "Ay, think so still, till experience change thy mind." The demonic truthfulness, the refusal to soften the consequences of the arrangement that Faustus proposes to make, seems to be part of Mephistopheles's allure.

Among the many additions that Marlowe made to the play's literary source, perhaps the most startling was his depiction of a passionate relationship between the magician and the devil. If a homoerotic element is playfully half-concealed in the scene with the boy who played Helen, it is far more open in Faustus's bond with Mephistopheles. "Had I as many souls as there be stars," Faustus declares, "I'd give them all for Mephistopheles!" Faustus is nominally selling his body and soul to Lucifer, but when the time comes to sign the fateful deed with his own blood, it is not Lucifer whom he has in mind: "Lo Mephistophelis, for love of thee / I cut mine arm."

At a moment early in the play, Faustus asks Mephistopheles to fetch him a wife, but despite the agreement to grant all his wishes, the devil refuses: "Tut Faustus, marriage is but a ceremonial toy." "If thou lov'st me," the devil adds, "think no more of it." The subject never arises again. Faustus's relationship with Mephistopheles takes the place of the marriage he had requested. They are inseparable. They travel as a couple, laugh together, question and challenge each other, share plans, trade accusations, argue, reconcile.

Faustus is initially thrilled at what he takes to be his own dominant role. It is he, after all, who has conjured up the devil in the first place and who repeatedly calls upon him to appear: "Come Mephistopheles," he commands, "*Veni, veni, Mephistopheles.*" The devil dutifully appears. "How pliant is this Mephistopheles," Faustus remarks, "Full of obedience and humility: / Such is the force of magic and my spells." With Mephistopheles at his side, Faustus feels stronger, more secure. "When

Mephistopheles shall stand by me," he says to himself, "What God can hurt me? Faustus, thou art safe."

As the exchanges unfold over the course of the play, the positions gradually change. As Faustus grows defensive, anxious, and unstable, Mephistopheles becomes increasingly frank, confident, and in control. The devil continues to appear to obey the magician's commands, but the balance of power has shifted. When Faustus wavers in his fealty and talks of breaking the contract, Mephistopheles, as Lucifer's agent, firmly pulls him back into line by threatening to punish him. Then a moment later, as if nothing has happened, the devil returns to the show of pliant service. Faustus is more and more defined by the demonic marriage he has contracted. He understands that the relationship with Mephistopheles is destructive, that it is literally going to kill him, but he cannot tear himself away. When, in the play's spectacular close, the clock strikes twelve and the demons come for him, the dying Faustus's final words, poised between ecstasy and horror, are "ah Mephistopheles!"

As Marlowe depicted him, Faustus at the beginning of the play is not "in the way to heaven"; on the contrary, he is in the midst of an existential crisis, having reached the "end" of every discipline he has studied. It is he who reviews and rejects each of these disciplines, he who turns the pages of the Bible, he who falls in love with Mephistopheles, and he who proposes to sell his soul to the devil in exchange for twenty-four years of extraordinary power and knowledge.

If Marlowe was bringing to these remarkable scenes his own crucial life decisions—giving up the safe plan to become a divine, for which his studies at Cambridge had prepared him, and instead involving himself in the spy service—he is taking on himself the principal responsibility for what he has done and for what he knew might lie ahead. He understood that there were risks; he was probably even explicitly warned of them. But he dismissed these risks with the insouciance of youth or pushed them somewhere out of his consciousness. And if he sensed that he might in the end be torn apart by what he was choosing to do, he told himself that this end was very far off or even that he longed to be torn apart.

Was there a moment when Marlowe realized that he was trapped? That he had fewer and fewer choices? He had always felt smarter than everyone else, quicker, more agile. He understood that most people believed in grotesque lies, fantasies promoted by those in power in order to exploit the underlings. He saw the world as a cruel, evil farce, but he thought he could stay in front of the tide of evil. He saw that even the exploiters, those on the top, not only promulgated but clung for themselves to absurd lies, lies about God, about the state, about their own motives. He saw that Thomas Harriot and perhaps the Wizard Earl had found a different way to avoid succumbing either to the lies or to despair, through a fascination with mathematics and with the natural world, but he was not a scientist. He was closer in spirit to Ralegh, but Ralegh commanded power and wealth and hence a measure of protection that he, Marlowe, would never possess.

The Marlowe who wrote *Doctor Faustus* was still quite young, but he had lived out in the world and had had the opportunity to witness the sobering fate of many of those who had been drawn into the murky sphere he had entered. He may have tried a few times to get out of what he had let himself in for, but he was always drawn back in—threatened, frightened, cajoled, distracted. The end that had once seemed so distant—a theoretical possibility, not a probable outcome—now seemed to be drawing ever closer. But what, after all, was the alternative, even if he could somehow reach it—the dullness of a small parish somewhere?

Besides, Marlowe could have told himself, the end was going to come anyway, sooner or later. *Che sarà, sarà.* He could in the time left to him at least satisfy his intellectual curiosity and satisfy his desires, though both led him in dangerous directions. And he knew that he possessed a rare gift, the gift of poetry. He could turn the things he most feared into art. At the end of *Doctor Faustus*, conjuring up his character's anguish at the approach of death, Marlowe recalled a line of Latin verse that he loved from Ovid's *Amores: O lente, lente currite noctis equi!* "O gallop slowly, slowly, you horses of the night!" The poet knows that his words will not make time actually slow down, but his art can play with time and turn its cold, inescapable passage into something beautiful:

Stand still, you evermoving spheres of heaven,
That time may cease, and midnight never come!
Fair nature's eye, rise, rise again, and make
Perpetual day, or let this hour be but a year,
A month, a week, a natural day,
That Faustus may repent, and save his soul.
*O lente, lente currite noctis equi!*
The stars move still, time runs, the clock will strike.

CHAPTER 17

# Neptune's Smile

A POWERFUL PLAYWRIGHT MAY draw his blood and infuse it into more than one of his characters. Shakespeare would become the supreme master of this distributed personhood—he was intensely, intimately present in young Hamlet and also in the Ghost of old Hamlet, in Othello and also Iago, in Lear and also Edmund. In *Tamburlaine* and *The Jew of Malta*, Marlowe had a far narrower range of identification: the title characters take up most of the air. But *Doctor Faustus* marked a breakthrough—and one from which Shakespeare probably learned.

Marlowe poured himself into the figure of a scholar, born of poor parents, who turns away from the study of theology and makes a fatal compact with the devil, but he also clearly identified with the devil. Mephistopheles is far more than a stock tempter. He appears when summoned, as if he were a social inferior at the beck and call of his lord, yet he is also strikingly independent and resourceful, with an unexpected complexity and self-awareness. He is an intellectual companion, possessing funds of abstruse knowledge that the learned Faustus craves access to. At the same time, he is an entertainer, gifted at distracting Faustus and lifting his spirits when he falls into a melancholy mood. He is supremely alluring, but his allure depends on a surprising personal candor. Though his goal is to entrap Faustus—"O, what will not I do to obtain his soul!" he declares—he succeeds in doing so not by concealing this goal or by lying about the terrible consequences but by making Faustus desire to be entrapped.

In *Tamburlaine*, Marlowe indulged himself and his audience in a fantasy of boundless power—the power to rise from nothing, the power to conquer, smash, burn, take, the power to kill. In *The Jew of Malta*, he indulged himself (and again, his audience) in a fantasy of boundless cunning—the cunning needed to outsmart enemies, to undermine the existing order of things, to accumulate more and more. The central fantasy in each case is compelling enough to fill the play with an incandescent energy, but neither power nor cunning can last forever. Death waits at the end, in the form of the disease that finally afflicts Tamburlaine and the outsmarting that undoes Barabas. The plays show little or no interest in what of value might be saved from these endings: there is no promise of renewal, no gesture toward a renewed state or family.

*Doctor Faustus* traffics in both supreme power and supreme cunning, but the play insistently asks what lies on the other side of the fantasy. Of course, the answer, as with the other plays, is death, but that is only the formal conclusion. After all, everyone's life has a limit, whether it is the twenty-four years that Faustus bargains for or some other number. Absolute power was only a hopeless fantasy—whatever Marlowe had performed for the secret service showed him that there were limits to his ability to protect his country from its real or imagined enemies. Absolute cunning was equally hopeless—by the time he wrote *Doctor Faustus*, Marlowe had met people like "Sweet Robin" Poley, whose cunning far exceeded his own. That left the dream of absolute knowledge, which is the specific lure of Faustus. A life without religious illusions seemed to hold out the promise of limitless inquiry, with no restrictions on the questions that it was possible to ask and answer. But that dream too is dashed. Marlowe's character bears witness to a sense of emptiness that lies on the other side of forbidden knowledge and to a realization that there will always be mysteries impossible to resolve.

So what has been gained and what is left at the end of the day? For lowborn Marlowe, as for his lowborn character Faustus, social barriers, otherwise rigidly policed, had crumbled and fallen. The author of

*Tamburlaine*, *The Jew of Malta*, and *Doctor Faustus* was "very well known," as Marlowe himself put it, to several of the grandest aristocrats in the realm. He had through his extraordinary poetic skill—the equivalent of his character's sorcery—crossed a line that was strictly closed to almost everyone else. When in one of his sonnets Shakespeare wrote that he envied "this man's art and that man's scope," he might well have been thinking of Marlowe.

But social boundary-crossing was hardly enough to compensate for the limits of power, cunning, and knowledge with which Marlowe was painfully grappling. Neither in *Tamburlaine* nor in *The Jew of Malta* had he fully faced those limits, but in *Doctor Faustus* he seems to have looked unflinchingly at his own life. To judge from the character he created, he found himself confronting anxiety, regrets, a sense of waste, fear, the hectic turning from one goal to another, and a lingering awareness of having done something disastrously wrong.

The question for Marlowe going forward was what could be salvaged from this wreckage. The hint of an answer lies in an emotional element in the tragedy that is not completely emptied out by the failure of Faustus's dreams. Marlowe's plays had successively explored the dangerous desire for power, wealth, and knowledge. In the time that was left to him, Marlowe turned to a form of desire that was even more dangerous to explore in public, in the strange zone where trust and betrayal, pleasure and pain, eros and death are fused.

Before *Doctor Faustus*, Marlowe had not exactly avoided the subject of sexual desire. In *Tamburlaine*, he created the sultan's daughter Zenocrate, but though the conqueror is given to extravagant expressions of devotion to her—"Zenocrate, the loveliest maid alive, / Fairer than rocks and pearl and precious stone"—she is a fantasy figure who bears little or no relation to anything Marlowe was really interested in or able to represent. In *The Jew of Malta*, the Jew's Muslim sidekick Ithamore falls madly in love with the prostitute Bellamira: "What an eye she casts on me! It twinkles like a star." But Marlowe ridicules the whole business. He has the besotted Ithamore, absurdly invoking Dis, the god of the underworld, as "Dis above," quote none other than Marlowe's own "Passionate Shepherd to

His Love": "Thou in those groves, by Dis above, / Shalt live with me and be my love."

After *Doctor Faustus*, Marlowe wrote a play that explores much more explicitly the sexual current that flows just below the surface in the relationship between Faustus and Mephistopheles. Like virtually everything else he wrote, this play was a bold experiment. A few years earlier, as we saw, Marlowe probably collaborated with Shakespeare in writing one or more of the sprawling chronicle plays about the fifteenth-century Wars of the Roses, the vicious dynastic struggles during the reign of Henry VI. The *Henry VI* plays had many vivid moments, but they lacked a powerful, central human focus, as if the sweep of events made it impossible to enter deeply into the lives of any one individual. Marlowe set about to provide such a focus, and in doing so he went beyond chronicles and in effect created the English history play.

In scouring records of the English past, Marlowe came across the relatively obscure king Edward II, who reigned from 1307 until he was deposed and murdered in 1327. According to the chronicler Holinshed, Edward, upon ascending the throne, "began to play diverse wanton and light parts, at the first indeed not outrageously, but by little and little, and that covertly." Holinshed goes on to say that Edward called back to England "his old mate" Piers de Gaveston, who had been exiled in France, and showered him with high honors. The honors would have seemed excessive for anyone, but they were all the more shocking given that their recipient was of relatively humble birth, a fact that enraged the aristocrats around the king. In Gaveston's company, the chronicler continued, Edward was "so corrupted that he burst out into most heinous vices . . . passing his time in voluptuous pleasure and riotous excess." Ordinarily detailed and explicit, in this case Holinshed left the precise nature of the "heinous vices" in the dark. King Edward, he wrote, "gave himself to wantonness." He and Gaveston lived "that kind of life," indulging themselves in "filthy and dishonorable exercises."

In the life of this fourteenth-century king, Marlowe saw a way to stage and to probe an erotic, obsessive, destructive relationship. Holinshed wrote that it was a wonder "that the king should be so enchanted" with

Gaveston and would "so addict himself" to him. Marlowe's *Edward II* is a study in addiction.

The play begins with Gaveston reading aloud a letter sent to him by the newly crowned king: "'My father is deceased; come, Gaveston, / And share the kingdom with thy dearest friend.'" "Sweet prince, I come," Gaveston says;

> these thy amorous lines
> Might have enforced me to have swum from France
> And like Leander gasped upon the sand,
> So thou wouldst smile and take me in thy arms. (1.1.1–9)

Modern historians continue to debate whether Edward and his favorite were lovers. Some point out that the king was married to Isabella of France and fathered four children. They argue that the rage his relationship with Gaveston aroused in the barons had to do only with the honors and riches showered on the lowborn favorite and that the favorite's interests were not sexual but venal.

Marlowe leaves no room for doubt. The king in his play is married and a father, but that hardly precludes an ardent sexual desire for his male favorite. The favorite, for his part, is intensely interested in honors and riches, but that hardly precludes his reciprocating the king's desire. Upon receiving Edward's amorous lines inviting him to return to England, Gaveston immediately indulges in erotic fantasies—he will hasten to his lover's arms—and at the same time begins to calculate how he can use and retain the position he will soon occupy. The favorite knows that the barons and, for that matter, the king's wife will be bitterly hostile to his presence at court. He plans a series of dazzling entertainments that will distract his royal lover from the danger that he will run by ignoring this hostility.

Holinshed mentioned these entertainments. Gaveston, he wrote, furnished the king's court "with companies of jesters, ruffians, flattering parasites, musicians, and other vile and naughty ribalds." But Marlowe transforms them into a seductive phantasmagoria. Knowing the king's tastes, Gaveston arranges for wanton poets and musicians "that with touching of a string / May draw the pliant king which way I please." At night there will be Italian masques and during the day, when the king takes a stroll,

> Like sylvan nymphs my pages shall be clad;
> My men, like satyrs grazing on the lawns,
> Shall with their goat-feet dance the antic hay;
> Sometime a lovely boy in Dian's shape,
> With hair that gilds the water as it glides
> Crownets of pearl about his naked arms,
> And in his sportful hands an olive-tree,
> To hide those parts which men delight to see,
> Shall bathe him in a spring. (1.1.50–64)

*To hide those parts which men delight to see.* Marlowe is on the edge: what parts are these?

The persecution of homosexual behavior, as we have observed, was rare in Elizabethan England: the laws on the books were one thing; the enforcement of those laws quite another. What went on in the dark between same-sex couples who routinely slept together, all through adolescence and often into adulthood, was almost never the object of anxious policing, let alone prosecution. But the social code depended upon a minimum of discretion, something like don't-ask-don't-tell. In *Edward II*, the king and his favorite throw discretion to the winds. The question that the play raises is what happens when the open secret is no longer a secret at all.

The queen and the nobles are shocked by the hold that Gaveston has upon Edward. The powerful Baron Mortimer claims that the issue is not the king's "wanton humour" but the disparity in class: "I scorn that one so basely born / Should by his sovereign's favour grow so pert." But the claim is at most half-true, for the play is saturated with anxiety about the erotic bond between the king and his favorite. "Now my lord and king regards me not," complains the queen to Mortimer,

> But dotes upon the love of Gaveston.
> He claps his cheeks and hangs about his neck,
> Smiles in his face and whispers in his ears,
> And when I come he frowns, as who should say,
> "Go whither thou wilt, seeing I have
>   Gaveston." (1.2.49–54)

The king flaunts his pleasure openly—"Embrace me, Gaveston, as I do thee"—and when the barons insist on the favorite's banishment, he becomes desperate. "My heart is as an anvil unto sorrow," he cries, "And makes me frantic for my Gaveston."

The magic for which Faustus was willing to sell his soul becomes the obsessive, all-consuming pleasure that Edward II takes in his minion, a pleasure for which he is willing to risk his kingdom. The nobles rise up in rebellion and succeed in capturing and killing Gaveston. Edward sets out to avenge his lover's murder, and to make his erotic prerogative clear, he immediately finds another young minion on whom to shower his love and his gifts. "Spencer, sweet Spencer, I adopt thee here," he declares. The love object this time is not baseborn; he is a baron. But the barons, as if to prove that the roots of their hostility lay deeper than class resentment, once again demand that the king give up his favorite. Do rebels now dare, Edward asks, as he embraces Spencer, to appoint for their sovereign "His sports, his pleasures, and his company?"

The answer is yes, or at least they will not allow the particular sports, pleasures, and company that the king—the "unnatural" king, as he is called—craves. Spencer too is executed at the hands of a new rebellion, led this time by Queen Isabella and Mortimer, whom she has taken as her lover. Edward, charged with "looseness" and corruption, is forced to resign the throne and is then imprisoned in a dungeon, into which flows all the filth of the castle's privies. "O Gaveston," the deposed king declares, "it is for thee that I am wronged."

Edward's jailors are surprised that anyone can long survive in these conditions—"I opened but the door to throw him meat," one remarks,

"And I was almost stifled with the savour." Impatient at the king's unexpected endurance, Mortimer hires an assassin named Lightborn—an Anglicized version of Lucifer—to complete the job. A specialist in murders that leave no physical marks, Lightborn boasts such techniques as poisoning flowers, piercing the windpipe with a needle, and blowing poison into the ear. (As he often did, Shakespeare picked up the hint and used it in *Hamlet*.)

The assassin's method in Edward's case seems particularly suited to the homophobic rage that his open relationships with Gaveston and Spencer had aroused. In an eerie scene, a bed is brought onto the stage, and the exhausted Edward, who has been forced for days to stand up to his knees in raw sewage, is urged to lie down and rest. Lightborn, professing a great desire to comfort the king, sits down next to him on the bed, whereupon the king starts in alarm. When Lightborn offers to leave—"If you mistrust me, I'll be gone, my lord"—the king asks him to stay. The little exchange is a miniature courtship, which is immediately followed by the murder. Lightborn calls on his henchmen to bring in a table and press it down upon Edward—"But not too hard, lest that you bruise his body." That directive makes it clear that Edward is not to be pressed to death. Instead, the staging almost certainly follows the chronicler Holinshed, who reported that the murderer thrust a red-hot spit into the anus of the king. The text of the scene does not include stage directions here, but the dialogue makes it clear that the dying Edward issues an incredibly loud scream. "I fear me that this cry will raise the town," one of the henchmen says.

*Edward II* is a tragedy, but the core of the tragedy is difficult to specify. Edward is hardly blameless. He is grossly irresponsible, petulant, petty, foolish, and vengeful. His kingdom must suffer from his indifference to its well-being, but the play never brings the kingdom as a whole into focus. Marlowe's interest is in the violent resentment that his illicit desires arouse in the small ruling elite and above all in the chaos that these desires visit upon the king's own life. Gaveston and Spencer, the objects of his passion, are conniving, greedy, and self-serving; they encourage the worst qualities in their royal lover. The barons are prickly, violent, and inordinately proud. At the play's end, Edward and his two lovers are dead, but so are their enemies. Mortimer, who seemed for a moment to have triumphed, is toppled and executed, and Isabella, suspected of complicity in the king's murder, is sent to the Tower. What are we left with? A vision of all-consuming, hopeless, self-destructive love. In Marlowe's time, there was as yet no name for what in 1894 Lord Alfred Douglas, Oscar Wilde's lover, would call "the love the dares not speak its name." *Homosexual* was a term not yet invented; "sodomy," the crime described in the Tudor law, designated an act and not a sexual orientation. With his characteristic daring, in *Edward II* Marlowe was gesturing toward something new, unheard of, dangerous.

Did Marlowe think that this love was a disgrace or sin and that it always had to end in disaster? A few years after his death, Francis Meres, a churchman and dabbler in literature, jotted down what must have been some gossip that had been circulating about the late poet. "Christopher Marlowe," he wrote, "was stabbed to death by a bawdy servingman, a rival of his in his lewd love." Marlowe had been happy in his muse, remarked another contemporary, but was "unhappy in his life and end." There was no question, thought this anonymous writer, that Marlowe possessed unusual "wit," that is, intelligence. "Pity it is that wit so ill should dwell, / Wit lent from heaven, but vices sent from hell." Neither Meres nor his contemporary specified what they mean by "lewd love" or "vices sent from hell." Perhaps they did not know quite what to call it.

Perhaps too it is in the context of these ugly comments that we should understand the shocking remark that Thomas Kyd claimed Marlowe made. According to Kyd—who penned the words, he said, "with reverence and trembling"—Marlowe "would report St. John to be our Savior Christ's Alexis . . . that is, that Christ did love him with an extraordinary love." There is tantalizing evidence that in the short time between the writing of *Edward II* and his death, Marlowe was rethinking the meaning of an extraordinary love.

✦ ✦ ✦

THE EVIDENCE COMES not in a play but in a poem that Marlowe wrote at a terrible moment when writing for the theater was not possible. In late January 1593, the plague returned to London. The telltale buboes appeared in underarms and groins; people who were fine in the morning were dead by nightfall; houses with the infected were nailed shut, a crudely painted red cross on the door as a warning to passersby to stay away; carts rolled through streets piled high with corpses on the way to hastily dug trenches. By the end of the visitation, one out of every twelve inhabitants of the enormous capital had died.

When the death rates reached a certain number, the playhouses were all shut down, along with most other collective venues apart from the church. Those who could afford to escape the city did so, and Marlowe was one of them. Therefore he was not there when his Cambridge friend John Greenwood—with whom he had shared meals at Corpus Christi College—was hanged at Tyburn for heterodox beliefs. He was not there when the placard threatening to cut the throats of all the foreigners and signed "Tamburlaine" was posted on the Dutch Church wall. He was not there when the government informer reported that Cholmeley had heard Marlowe expound sound reasons for atheism. He was not there when the agents of the Privy Council went looking for him in Norton Folgate, Bishopsgate, and Shoreditch. And he was not there when those same agents seized his erstwhile roommate Thomas Kyd and, after ferreting through his papers, hauled him off to the torture chamber.

Instead, Marlowe was in bucolic Kent at the country house of his wealthy friend Thomas Walsingham. A year older than Marlowe, Thomas was a second cousin of the spymaster Sir Francis Walsingham. As a young man, he too had been recruited into the secret service, probably as a courier; one document places him at the time of the Babington conspiracy accompanying the sinister Robert Poley into Sir Francis's inner sanctum on Seething Lane.

There was a good reason for Thomas Walsingham to have accepted such employment whenever it came his way. The third son of the family, he had little expectation of a substantial inheritance, and indeed in the late 1580s he found himself in prison for debt. But his oldest brother died, and so too, before the debt was settled, did the next oldest. Thomas suddenly found himself the heir to Scadbury, the family estate described in an inventory as including "gardens and orchards enclosed with brick walls and planted with excellent fruit, three barns, three large stables, a granary, pigeon house and fish ponds, a park well impaled [fenced] about, four hundred acres stored with deer and conies [rabbits] and other stock of cattle, timber, trees."

Thomas was now a country gentleman. He had no experience in managing such an extensive property, but he found help from a tough, clever London-based business agent named Ingram Frizer. Frizer was good with money, which is to say that he already had extensive experience in loansharking, extortion, and other dubious business practices in which he generally came out ahead. He had a particular gift for luring improvident young men into ruinous agreements. Frizer did not intend to make Thomas Walsingham one of his victims; on the contrary, he had a vital interest in enhancing his employer's prosperity, for he seems to have used Walsingham's distinguished name to sanitize his shady operations. His devoted service to Walsingham gave him a veneer of respectability, and he evidently left the rougher aspects of the trade to a sidekick, Nicholas Skeres. Skeres, a thoroughly miserable piece of work, had played a bit part for Seething Lane in the entrapment of Babington. It is likely that Thomas Walsingham knew him from that time, as did Marlowe.

With the plague taking its grim toll in London, Frizer and Skeres probably also found it convenient to stay at Scadbury, along with Marlowe. Frizer and Skeres were occupied with business, namely, the swindling of a young man who regarded them as his special friends. The gullible victim left traces of his resulting financial predicaments in a series of legal complaints. Marlowe and Walsingham were at leisure. After the ruthless competitiveness of London theater life and the dangerous episode in the Netherlands, Marlowe must have felt deliciously at ease. This was the existence his friend Watson had constantly angled for but failed to achieve, the pastoral retreat of which Elizabethan writers of limited means always dreamed: not a position as tutor to small children or as secretary to an important official, though those positions were desirable enough, but days and weeks of sweet idleness in a beautiful country house and in the company of a wealthy gentleman who shared an interest in Latin poetry. The whole setting in Scadbury bespoke comfort and security, with the rest of the world kept at bay. The house was even surrounded by a moat, with its entrance by way of a drawbridge.

Marlowe may have brought an account of his new play, *The Massacre at Paris*, set at the time of the St. Bartholomew's Day Massacre in 1572, more than twenty years earlier. The play is saturated with murders, mostly by stabbing but also by shooting, strangling, and poisoning. But with the theaters all shuttered, Marlowe had little incentive to dwell upon it, and besides, Thomas Walsingham's tastes lay elsewhere, in ancient poetry and modern tales of love. Marlowe decided characteristically to try something new—a long narrative in rhyming verse, based on a Latin poem by an obscure sixth-century-CE writer known as Musaeus Grammaticus. Perhaps the host and poet sat down together and read the poem, a retelling of the ancient Greek myth of Hero and Leander.

In Musaeus's account, the chaste Hero, a priestess of the love goddess Venus, lived in a tower on the European side of the Hellespont (in today's Istanbul). The handsome young Leander, who lived in Abydos, on the opposite side of the narrow strait, fell madly in love with her and, after much pleading and wooing, persuaded her to agree to sleep with him. Guided by a light she placed in her tower, he swam nightly across the Hellespont, and they made love. The passionate affair continued through the summer, but with the change in the weather, they sadly agreed to put off seeing each other until the spring. But one winter's night lovesick Leander, seeing the light in Hero's tower, attempted to swim to her across the turbulent waters. The wind extinguishing the light, the lover lost his way and drowned. When his body washed ashore, the distraught Hero threw herself from the tower to her death.

In Marlowe's hands, this tragic tale took on an unexpectedly lighthearted tone. What he wrote—more than eight hundred lines—is almost entirely joyous, playful, ironic, and funny, and it ends not with the two deaths but with the ecstatic consummation of their love. Missing are the notes of bitterness and despair that run through so much of his work. There is mockery of the lovers, but it is largely gentle and forgiving. They fall madly in love because they are beautiful and young and full of life—how else should we expect them to behave? And if they fix their urgent desires on each other with little or no prior knowledge or deliberation, this suddenness too is exactly how it has to be. Falling in love is not a matter of reasoned choice.

This is the same irrational urgency that arose in *Edward II* as well—the play offers no explanation for Edward's love for Gaveston or later for Spencer. But in *Hero and Leander*, Marlowe treats this passion not as a tragic anomaly but as the stuff of comedy. His image for the sudden awakening of interest is the sight of runners undressing before a race. "When two are stripped, long ere the course begin," he writes, "We wish that one should lose, the other win." To the person whose desire is instantly aroused, there is no point in trying to explain it or mull it over:

> The reason no man knows: let it suffice,
> What we behold is censured by our eyes.
> Where both deliberate, the love is slight;
> Who ever loved, that loved not at first sight? (1:173–76)

Shakespeare was struck by the clinching line, and in *As You Like It*, he has one of the characters quote it when she falls in love. Unbeknownst to her, the object of her passion, Ganymede, is actually a young woman dressed as a man. (More accurately, it is a boy actor pretending to be a woman dressed as a man.) But gender fluidity, as Shakespeare clearly understood, is part of Marlowe's meaning. Hero and Leander are a heterosexual pair, but the image of the two runners stripping for a race is implicitly homosexual. The point is that the gender does not matter; desire comes with the same suddenness, intensity, and inevitability in both heterosexual and homosexual forms.

Perhaps it was the pastoral setting; perhaps Marlowe and Thomas Walsingham were having a flirtation or a happy affair. For whatever reason, in *Hero and Leander* the sexual torment and sadism of *Edward*

*II* have dropped away. Marlowe invented an episode, completely absent from his source, to capture the new spirit. When Leander strips naked to swim across the Hellespont, the sea god Neptune thinks that Ganymede, Jove's handsome young cupbearer and lover, must have left heaven and come for a visit. Neptune decides that his lucky day has come.

The waves wind around Leander and pull him down to the ocean floor, "where the ground / Was strewed with pearl, and in low coral groves, / Sweet singing mermaids, sported with their loves." The "lusty god" embraces the young man and releases him only when he realizes that he is not Ganymede. Half-drowned, Leander manages to reach the surface and begs to be allowed to swim to Hero.

Neptune consents, but he is not finished with the swimmer:

> He watched his arms, and as they opened wide
> At every stroke, betwixt them would he slide
> And steal a kiss, and then run out and dance,
> And as he turned, cast many a lustful glance
> And threw him gaudy toys to please his eye,
> And dive into the water, and there pry
> Upon his breast, his thighs, and every limb,
> And up again, and close beside him swim,
> And talk of love. (2:183–91)

There is no more explicit representation of a gay encounter in English Renaissance literature, and Marlowe goes out of his way to play with the spectacle. "You are deceived, I am no woman I," Leander tells the amorous god. "Thereat smiled Neptune."

Neptune's smile marks a new note of amused tolerance in Marlowe. Leander's desire is fixed on Hero, but when he understands that Neptune is not simply making a mistake, he genuinely regrets the pain that his rejection of the god's advances is causing. "In gentle breasts," Marlowe writes, there is always such pity, even for desires that are not shared. "And who have hard hearts," he adds, with a glance at the homophobes of the world, but "vicious, harebrained, and illiterate" boors?

Leander finally reaches the shore, where Hero admits him into her tower. At first the virgin puts up some resistance, but it is neither wholehearted nor serious. "Treason was in her thought, / And cunningly to yield herself she sought." Marlowe's account of the consummation contains a characteristic touch of cruelty, qualified by an awakening into mutual pleasure:

> She trembling strove; this strife of hers (like that
> Which made the world) another world begat
> Of unknown joy. (2:291–93)

Only when these lines are slowed down and reread does the radicalism of Marlowe's vision, slyly signaled in a parenthesis, become clear. Nowhere in Judaism, Christianity, or Islam is the world said to have been created in the "strife" of sexual intercourse. It is as if for this pagan setting, the poet generated an alternative creation story.

This scene of "unknown joy" is as far as Marlowe evidently reached. When, five years after his death, *Hero and Leander* was first printed with a dedication to Thomas Walsingham, the publisher Edward Blount acknowledged that the poem was unfinished and ended it with the Latin tag *Desunt nonnulla*, "Some things are missing." Perhaps Marlowe intended to continue the story to the tragic conclusion it had in its Latin source. Some years later another poet, George Chapman, did just that, in a suitably sober, moralizing vein. But perhaps, as the story came alive in Marlowe's imagination, it took a very different direction from Musaeus's original. The spirit of all he actually wrote seems very far from drowning and suicide, and Marlowe may simply have decided to end it happily.

CHAPTER 18

# Into the Light

On May 18, 1593, Marlowe's idyll came to an abrupt end. A visitor named Henry Maunder knocked on the gate and demanded entrance to Scadbury. Maunder wore the uniform and badge of a state official. He was one of the royal messengers, officers charged with such tasks as delivering urgent and confidential correspondence, serving writs, distributing royal proclamations, making searches, and examining witnesses. Before he was permitted to cross the drawbridge into the manor, he would presumably have been asked to state his business. His answer was that he bore a warrant "to repair to the house of Mr. Thomas Walsingham in Kent, or to any other place where he shall understand Christopher Marlowe to be remaining, and by virtue hereof to apprehend and bring him to the court in his company." The warrant added, "And in case of need to require aid," but there is no evidence that Maunder called in backup. Marlowe was arrested.

Maunder and Marlowe may not have been complete strangers to each other, for they both lived in the same London neighborhood of Norton Folgate. Theirs was a small world, and it is possible too that Maunder and Thomas Walsingham had already met at some time or other. The queen's messenger seems to have stayed overnight at Scadbury, for he did not deliver Marlowe to the court, as he was instructed to do, until May 20, two days later. This means that Marlowe must have had several opportunities to try to slip away and escape, but he did not do so. Perhaps he had no place to go, or perhaps he was still wrapped in a sense of tranquil security. He was not, in any case, being held in strict confinement. When Maunder turned his charge over to the queen's Privy Council, the clerk informed Marlowe that he was not being sent to prison but only "commanded to give his daily attendance on their lordships, until he shall be licensed to the contrary."

Marlowe found himself in a baffling situation. A warrant had been issued to find him and bring him in. Once delivered to the clerk of the council, he had had to post bail. But as yet there were no charges against him and no timetable for the resolution of whatever trouble he was in. It is not at all clear that he was given any further information or that he had any way of knowing how serious the trouble was. He might have thought it was all a minor matter or a mistake. After all, he had not been put into a cell, let alone shown one of the law's instruments of torture. He was free to move about, since the daily attendance to which he was commanded meant only that he had to stay within easy range of the queen and her council so that he could be questioned at their pleasure.

By the time of his arrest on the eighteenth, Marlowe may already have heard something about the menacing placard, signed Tamburlaine, that had been posted on London's Dutch Church wall on May 5. It is possible too that he somehow learned that Kyd had been arrested on the twelfth. But in his rural retreat and then in the custody of the queen's messenger, Marlowe was unlikely to have been informed about the allegedly heretical document found in Kyd's rooms or about whatever it was that Kyd said under torture.

Marlowe was still less likely to have learned that the authorities had somewhat earlier received an anonymous informant's memo entitled "Remembrances of Words & Matter against Ric: Cholmeley." This was the memo that associated Marlowe with a crew of dangerous malcontents and claimed that Marlowe had "read the atheist lecture to Sir Walter Ralegh & others." Some three months after Marlowe was murdered, a shady character named Thomas Drury would write a letter requesting a reward for having "set down" and presented to the authorities "the notablest and vilest articles of atheism that I suppose the like were never known or read of in any age." These "articles of atheism," Drury added, "were delivered to Her Highness, and command given by herself to prosecute it to the full." Drury did not name the memo for which he was hoping to be rewarded; nor did he specify the date when the queen was shown it, but since he was listed in an earlier warrant as Cholmeley's "companion," he was likely referring to the one that implicated Marlowe. It is at least possible then that the order to go after Marlowe on charges of atheism—"prosecute it to the full"—came from the queen herself. But as yet Marlowe would have known nothing.

After Marlowe's arrest on May 18, he might well have expected to be called in for questioning, but days passed with no further clarification of his situation. He could have begun to hope that the whole business had been forgotten, but in fact a case was building up against him. In the wake of Kyd's confession and the Cholmeley memo, the privy councilors were quietly collecting further evidence.

On May 26 the council received a long note from Marlowe's old enemy, Richard Baines. The note, now in the British Library, was preserved among the papers of Sir John Puckering, the tough jurist who may have been in the torture chamber when Kyd blurted out his former roommate's name and who was subsequently the recipient of Kyd's two letters incriminating Marlowe. Puckering himself may have initiated the inquiry into the charges against Marlowe. He or someone in his employ would have contacted an informant, one of those figures indispensable for this kind of police work, who in turn contacted Baines, who claimed to have privileged access to Marlowe's "horrible blasphemies and damnable opinions."

It is not clear whether Marlowe and Baines had seen each other since the time in Flushing, sixteen months earlier, when they had shared a room. That was the occasion on which Baines had gone to the military governor and accused Marlowe of counterfeiting. Marlowe had managed, through his powerful connections, to escape the end for which the accuser had no doubt hoped. But Baines had not dropped the charge. At the end of his note to the Privy Council, he alleged that Marlowe had continued his criminal enterprise and was even justifying it by claiming "that he had as good Right to coin as the Queen of England." According to Baines's report, Marlowe boasted "that he was acquainted with one Poole, a prisoner in Newgate who hath great skill in mixture of metals, and, having learned some things of him, he meant through help of a cunning stamp-maker to coin French crowns, pistolets, and English shillings."

In 1593, as before, the source of Baines's animus toward Marlowe is a mystery. That they shared a great deal—Cambridge education, theological interests, an association with Rheims, recruitment into the spy service, a proclivity to utter wild blasphemies—could conceivably have brought them together as allies and friends, but their commonalities seem in this case to have sharpened the enmity. Baines had already tried once to destroy Marlowe. The report he signed and submitted to the Privy Council suggests that his desire to see Marlowe dead had only intensified.

The things Baines claimed that Marlowe was saying seem purposely designed to shock. Even now many of them are startlingly offensive. In the late sixteenth century, they were almost literally unspeakable, or rather they were speakable only by someone who was insanely reckless. To declare, as Marlowe was said by Baines to have declared, that "Christ was a bastard and his mother dishonest" was to cross a line that, in this period, could not be crossed without the most devastating consequences, but if the document is to be believed, Marlowe was only just beginning.

Possibly Marlowe never said anything of the kind attributed to him and Baines was making it all up. Some of the remarks that the report puts into the mouth of Marlowe strikingly resemble remarks that Baines himself had uttered years before, according to the confession he had written and signed after his arrest and imprisonment in Rheims. They are boilerplate blasphemies, the things that wicked atheists are expected to say.

Puckering was evidently persuaded, however, that Baines's note contained at least some truth, and he had reason to believe it did, for both Kyd's testimony and the informant's report on Cholmeley seemed to offer detailed corroborating evidence. Among his many charges, Baines even reported that "one Ric[hard] Cholmeley hath confessed that he was persuaded by Marlowe's reasons to become an atheist." To be sure, Baines and Cholmeley (and for that matter, the informant who wrote the report on Cholmeley) may have been acquainted and could have plotted together to destroy Marlowe. They all swam in the same polluted water of spying, provocation, and betrayal. But since there is no evidence at all that Baines and Kyd knew each other, let alone that they were in collaboration, the resemblance between their independent accounts of what Marlowe was saying is striking.

What precisely Kyd, when tortured, said about Marlowe is not known, but in the follow-up letters that he wrote to Puckering after Marlowe's murder, he alleged that it had been Marlowe's custom "to jest at the divine scriptures" and "gibe at prayers." Though Baines presented Marlowe's opinions as anything but funny, many of the remarks he assembled and submitted take the form of blasphemous jests and jibes:

- That Christ was the son of a carpenter, and that if the Jews among whom he was born did crucify him, they best knew him and whence he came.
- That Christ was a bastard and his mother dishonest.
- That the angel Gabriel was bawd to the Holy Ghost because he brought the salutation to Mary.
- That Saint John the Evangelist was bedfellow to Christ and leaned always in his bosom; that he used him as the sinners of Sodom.
- That the woman of Samaria and her sister were whores, and that Christ knew them dishonestly.
- That all the apostles were fishermen and base fellows, neither of wit nor worth; that Paul only had wit, but he was a timorous fellow in bidding men to be subject to magistrates against his conscience.
- That if Christ would have instituted the sacrament with more ceremonial reverence, it would have been had in more admiration; that it would have been much better being administered in a tobacco pipe.
- That Christ deserved better to die than Barabbas, and that the Jews made a good choice, though Barabbas were both a thief and a murderer.

- That if there be any God or good religion, then it is in the Papists, because the service of God is performed with more ceremonies, as Elevation of the Mass, organs, singing men, shaven crowns, etc.
- That all Protestants are hypocritical asses.
- That all the New Testament is filthily written.
- That if he were put to write a new religion, he would undertake both a more excellent and admirable method.

In the wake of this mockery, there was not much left to believe in, but Marlowe could offer at least one affirmation: "That all they that love not tobacco and boys are fools."

The defenders of orthodoxy in the sixteenth century may have felt more at ease in writing philosophical refutations than in fending off ridicule. Theologians sharpened their quills against anyone who challenged their doctrines and in response wrote long polemical treatises in Latin. Jests were a different matter: they crossed the boundary between learned and popular, they could be all too easily grasped and passed along, they had the raucous suddenness of a burst of laughter, and they enacted a liberation from very fear that theology was meant to promote.

The provocative wisecracks were not merely Marlowe's private opinions; they were, like subversive scenes on the public stage, liable to infect the masses. Indeed, according to the report, they were designed to be infectious. "Almost into every company he cometh," Marlowe "persuades men to atheism, willing them not to be afeared of bugbears and hobgoblins." The whole purpose of religion—its "first beginning"—"was only to keep men in awe." Laughter is the enemy of awe.

The anonymous informer reported that Richard Cholmeley, supposedly converted to atheism by Marlowe, said that "Moses was a juggler." The Baines note repeats and makes sense of this gibe. According to Baines, Marlowe was claiming "that Moses was but a juggler, and that one Harriot, being Sir Walter Raleigh's man, can do more than he." The link between Moses and Harriot would have enabled contemporaries to grasp the implication, only latent in Harriot's account of his experience in Virginia, that religious faith originated in mistakenly treating as a miracle what was only technological superiority. "It was an easy matter," Baines reported Marlowe saying, "for Moses being brought up in all the arts of the Egyptians to abuse the Jews, being a rude and gross people." Moses, according to Marlowe, was a cunning Machiavellian ruler who manipulated the people's naïve faith:

> Moses made the Jews to travel forty years in the wilderness (which journey might have been done in less than one year) ere they came to the Promised Land, to the intent that those who were privy to most of his subtleties might perish and so an everlasting superstition remain in the hearts of the people.

The "everlasting superstition" referred to here is nothing less than the belief in God on which the three great monotheisms, Judaism, Christianity, and Islam, all rest.

Harriot was rumored to believe that men and women existed in the world before Adam and Eve. Though he was careful never to write such a dangerous notion down, something he said about Virginia, when he discussed it in the privacy of the Ralegh circle, must have confirmed a comparable speculation in Marlowe. For Baines reported that Marlowe was telling his listeners that "the Indians and many authors of antiquity have assuredly written above sixteen thousand years agone whereas Adam is proved to have lived within six thousand years."

Six thousand years was the chronological span that pious Christians, counting the begats in the Bible, had calculated would reach all the way back to the creation of Adam and Eve. The Garden of Eden in Genesis was the definitive beginning of human history. If the record of humanity went back earlier than that, then the Bible's account of the first humans was mistaken, and the whole account of creation was called into question.

Educated Elizabethans knew that some "authors of antiquity," as Marlowe (or Baines) called them, claimed that history extended well beyond the six-thousand-year limit. The so-called "father of history," the ancient

Greek Herodotus, wrote that the Egyptians had written records extending more than sixteen thousand years into the past. But Herodotus had for centuries been dismissed as the "father of lies." Harriot seems to have told Marlowe that "the Indians," his Algonkian informants, had, in their oral legends, confirmed Herodotus.

What Baines attributed to Marlowe, then, was much more than a set of irreverent quips calculated to offend conventional sensibilities. The mix of jokes, theses, aphorisms, blasphemies, and reasoned arguments sketched the rough outline of a radical critique of religion. The informer had assembled traces of the notorious "atheist lecture." Baines wanted to persuade the privy councilors that Marlowe was an apostle of unbelief and therefore a poisonous threat to the whole community of the faithful. "I think all men in Christianity," the report piously concludes, "ought to endeavor that the mouth of so dangerous a member may be stopped."

Nothing in the legal procedures of the time suggests that Marlowe would have been given access to this document or the anonymous report on Richard Cholmeley that also implicated him, or that he even had an inkling that they had been written.

◆ ◆ ◆

NO FORMAL ACCUSATION had been brought against Marlowe yet. More time passed without further notice from the Privy Council. He was in limbo, waiting and waiting to find out what the arrest was all about. Twelve days after Henry Maunder had come to Scadbury to arrest him, he still had no clarification.

This strange threshold state might well have provoked a combination of anxiety and boredom, so when Marlowe received an invitation to spend the day—Wednesday, May 30—with three acquaintances, it may have offered relief or at least distraction. The rendezvous was set for Deptford, only a few miles from Greenwich Palace, where the queen and her councilors met and hence well within the range Marlowe was instructed to observe.

Deptford, now part of greater London, was at the time a bustling port town on a bend in the Thames, south of the river, with docks, tenements, and workshops. It was there in 1580, on returning from his epochal three-year circumnavigation of the globe, that Francis Drake had docked his ship the *Golden Hind* and been knighted in the presence of the queen. Tourists came to gawk at the ship and break off little pieces as souvenirs. Various houses accommodated visitors and prepared meals for guests, and it was to one of these, a house owned by the widow Eleanor Bull, that Marlowe went on the appointed day.

An account published in 1600 and meant to show how God, "the true executioner of divine justice," had brought about "the end of impious atheists," said that Marlowe was invited to the widow Bull's house by "one named Ingram." Whether Ingram Frizer actually issued the invitation is not known, and it is impossible to determine whether Marlowe was casually invited or summoned. The men he met in Deptford were neither fellow poets and playwrights nor former companions from the university nor intellectuals in the circles of Ralegh or Percy. Two of them, the shady businessman Frizer and his accomplice Nicholas Skeres, Marlowe would have known from their recent stay at Scadbury. They had evidently returned to London. The third was Robert Poley.

Poley had very recently arrived England from a mission abroad. According to an official document, he was paid £30 "for carrying letters in post for Her Majesty's special and secret affairs of great importance, from the Court at Croydon the 8th of May 1593 into the Low Countries to the town of the Hague in Holland, and for returning back again with letters of answer to the Court at Nonsuch the 8th of June 1593, being in Her Majesty's service all the aforesaid time." Thirty pieces of silver was a handsome sum, even for a month-long trip to deliver such highly sensitive correspondence. In fact, Poley was back well before the June date mentioned in the document, since he was in Deptford on May 30. Presumably, "being in Her Majesty's service all the aforesaid time," includes the day spent in Marlowe's company.

Almost everything that is known about the events that transpired that day derives from the interpretation of a single official document, the inquest into Marlowe's death, filed on June 1. Marlowe, Frizer, Skeres, and Poley arrived at Eleanor Bull's house in Deptford Strand—the riverfront area of the town, with docks, chandleries, and workshops—at ten in the morning. At that time of day during the workweek, the neighborhood must have been filled with the sounds and smells of industry and commerce. The four men went into a small room, sparsely furnished with a bed and a table with a bench. They were the only occupants of the room, and they talked there quietly until it was time for dinner (the term in this period for what we call lunch). The widow Bull's house was not a proper tavern or inn, but presumably she would have had her servants prepare the food or ordered food to be brought in for her guests. If there was meat, she would have expected them to cut it with the knives that most men in this period carried in sheaths at their waists.

After dinner the four men went outside and walked in the garden. For hours they continued their conversation out of earshot. About six p.m. they entered the small room once again and ordered supper. When they had finished supper, none of them made any immediate move to depart. Marlowe lay down on the bed. The other three sat at the table next to one another on the bench, perhaps playing backgammon.

Then something happened. For more than eight hours there had been only the soft murmurings of the four men talking together. Now suddenly from inside the room, there was loud shouting followed by cries and the noise of a struggle. The noise continued for some time, and then there was silence. When the door was opened, the household witnesses saw one of the men bleeding from cuts on his scalp and another lying dead. The dead man was Christopher Marlowe.

The bailiff was called, and he took the three men, who had made no attempt to flee, into custody. The presiding coroner, William Danby, conducted an inquest and wrote up his findings in Latin in the report he filed on June 1. (Marlowe, who loved Latin, would have been pained by its crude style and might have said that it was "filthily written.") The inquest was conducted in the presence of sixteen named jurors, who swore to its accuracy, as best they could determine. Danby seems not to have inquired what the men had been doing in the house and adjoining garden for the whole day, and the widow Bull probably could not have told him, even if she had been listening at the door, since the report says only that the four men were "quiet."

After dinner, according to the inquest, an argument arose between Marlowe and Frizer about the bill—the coroner's report calls it "le recknynge." The two men uttered malicious words to each other, and the term that the account uses for this exchange—*publicaverunt*—suggests that the words were heard by others outside the room. Marlowe and Frizer were not face to face. Marlowe, the inquest says, was lying on the bed; Frizer, his back turned away from Marlowe, was sitting on the bench between Skeres and Poley. Suddenly—*ex subito*—the enraged Marlowe rose up, reached over, and pulled Frizer's dagger from its sheath, which he wore around his waist. He struck Frizer on the head—presumably with the dagger's hilt and not its blade—and gave him two flesh wounds, each two inches long and a quarter-inch deep.

Hemmed in on the bench and unable to move, Frizer feared for his life. Somehow—the report does not provide any details—he managed to get to his feet, struggle with his assailant, and recover his dagger. He did so, it seems, without cutting his hand on the blade or receiving any further wound. He then drove the dagger—which the report specifies was of the value of twelve pence—just above Marlowe's right eye to the depth of two inches. "From this mortal wound the said Christopher Marlowe then and there instantly died." Modern medical experts have debated whether it is likely that someone could have died instantly from such a wound.

As Marlowe and Watson had done years before after the killing of Bradley, the three men stayed with the corpse until the authorities arrived. They had plenty of time to coordinate their story of what happened. They would have had time, had it been needed, to make the flesh wounds on Frizer's scalp more visible (or to make them in the first place). They clearly agreed to emphasize that Frizer had had no choice. The three were seated, the report states, so tightly together that in no way—*nullo modo*—could Frizer flee from Marlowe's malicious attack. A few sentences later, the same point: Frizer, afraid for his life, was unable to get away from the attack in any way (*aliquo modo*). And yet again, in the defense and saving of his own life, Frizer could not get away from Marlowe by pulling back. The authorities duly found that Frizer had killed Marlowe in self-defense. After briefly remaining in custody, he was issued a full pardon and released.

Marlowe's body was taken for burial in the Church of St. Nicholas, on Deptford Green. In the parish register the vicar carelessly wrote "Christopher Marlow slaine by ffrauncis ffrezer." No grave marker, if ever one was placed on the site where he was buried, survives.

That Marlowe was killed is certain. But everything else about the events at the widow Bull's house on May 30, 1593, is open to question. Contemporaries immediately began to circulate stories, most of them morality tales about the inevitable fate of atheists and none of them remotely reliable. In our own time, historians have pored over every detail and come up with a variety of conflicting theories about what actually happened. In her well-documented 2002 biography, Constance Kuriyama concluded that "the simplest and most probable hypothesis is that Marlowe was not assassinated at all, and that the coroners' report is a reasonably accurate account of what happened." In Kuriyama's scenario, Frizer invited Marlowe to a feast and then demanded that he pay a share of the bill. Short of cash—the closing of the theaters and the wait for the Privy Council's interrogation having exacerbated his perennial penury—the quick-tempered Marlowe was outraged and impulsively reached for Frizer's dagger.

In 2005 another biographer, Park Honan, reviewed the same evidence and pointed the finger at Frizer, who had a financial interest in maintaining the reputation of his employer Thomas Walsingham. "Marlowe, the famous 'atheist,'" Honan writes, "had become an intolerable, ruinous, and deadly burden for anyone who hoped to profit at Scadbury." Frizer was not ordinarily in the business of murder, but his comfort and security depended on getting rid of this burden. And the aftermath seemed to prove the effectiveness of his crime. Prosperous and eminently respectable, Frizer subsequently flourished as the business agent of Walsingham's wife Audrey, and he profited handsomely as the fortunes of his aristocratic master and mistress soared. No rumors of atheism or sodomy, of the kind a prolonged friendship with Marlowe might have generated, tarnished Sir Thomas's reputation. After 1603 the Walsinghams were among the favorites of Queen Elizabeth's successor, King James I, and his queen.

The most sustained inquiry into Marlowe's murder was conducted by the historian Charles Nicholl in his gripping 1992 book *The Reckoning*. Nicholls's detailed investigation reveals, as in an Agatha Christie mystery, that virtually everyone Marlowe encountered, including the widow Bull, had dirty hands or at least a plausible reason to be involved in an assassination. Nicholl finally settles on a complicated plot in which the Earl of Essex had Marlowe killed as part of a maneuver against his rival Sir Walter Ralegh. For others who have examined the surviving evidence, it is Ralegh who is the likeliest mastermind of Marlowe's murder, while still others, including Leslie Hotson, Samuel Tannenbaum, and the novelist Anthony Burgess, argue that Thomas Walsingham, or even Walsingham's soon-to-be wife Audrey, initiated the conspiracy.

The case remains open, and it is exceedingly unlikely that anyone, at this distance of more than four hundred years, will crack it to everyone's satisfaction. Notwithstanding Marlowe's hot temper, a simple argument over the bill seems improbable. What kind of "feast" begins at ten a.m., continues through lunch, takes a break for the long afternoon, and then picks up again for supper? Why these four men, all of whom had connections to the secret service? Why did Poley, though charged with delivering secret messages of great importance, spend an entire day at Deptford? If Frizer was so tightly penned in, how did he suddenly get up, recover his dagger, and deliver a fatal thrust? Why did Poley and Skeres not rise from the bench and restrain Marlowe—or might the evidence suggest rather that they did restrain him, so that Frizer could stab him through the eye socket? And why were Frizer and the others so quickly released?

Closest to my own view is that advanced in David Riggs's 2004 biography, *The World of Christopher Marlowe*. Marlowe, Riggs proposes, was killed because of his atheism. Riggs thinks that the fatal command was given by Elizabeth herself when she urged that it be prosecuted "to the full." An assassination in the backroom of an inn is not what is usually meant by a prosecution. But it is possible that an overly zealous servant of hers could have thought he was carrying out the monarch's wishes. A draft copy of Baines's report survives in the archives, having been drawn up, according to the heading, after Marlowe on "Whitsunday died a sudden and violent death." The copy is endorsed, "As sent to her H." So someone thought Her Highness would be interested.

Marlowe was a genius but a profoundly disturbing one. His plays were themselves provocations. They said things about power, about money, about Jews, about hell, about God, and about sex that had never been said before, at least in public. Above all, they said them with startling frankness and a stupendous, unheard-of eloquence.

> Nature, that framed us of four elements
> Warring within our breasts for regiment,
> Doth teach us all to have aspiring minds.

> Is it not passing brave to be a king,
> And ride in triumph through Persepolis?

> I count religion but a childish toy,
> And hold there is no sin but ignorance.

> And thus methinks should men of judgment frame
> Their means of traffic from the vulgar trade,
> And, as their wealth increaseth, so enclose
> Infinite riches in a little room.

> Fornication? But that was in another country; and besides, the wench is dead.

> My men, like satyrs grazing on the lawns,
> Shall with their goat-feet dance the antic hay.

A few years after Marlowe's murder, the Puritan minister Thomas Beard published a book, *The Theatre of God's Judgments*, in which he collected instructive stories of divine vengeance. One of his prime instances was the fate of Marlowe, "a playmaker and a poet of scurrility." Having made himself notorious for "atheism and impiety," the playmaker found himself in a play of God's making: "In the London streets as he purposed to stab one whom he owed a grudge unto with his dagger, the other party perceiving so avoided the stroke that withal, catching hold of his wrist, he stabbed his own dagger into his own head." In Beard's retelling, the denouement took place not in a private room but in the open, and the fatal weapon was Marlowe's own. The changes make the moral lesson easier to grasp: "The manner of his death being so terrible—for he even cursed and blasphemed to his last gasp, and together with his breath an oath flew out of his mouth—that it was not only a manifest sign of God's judgment but also an horrible and fearful terror to all that beheld him." And lest the reader somehow miss the point, Beard underscored it: "Herein did the justice of God most notably appear, in that He compelled his own hand which had written those blasphemies to be the instrument to punish him, and that in his brain, which had devised the same."

Beard and several other contemporaries celebrated the murder at Deptford as the fate that Marlowe had coming to him. Against their glee is set a small number of appreciations of Marlowe's extraordinary learning and talent. In 1598 the printer Edward Blount brought out the first edition of *Hero and Leander* with a dedicatory letter to Thomas Walsingham. The letter is cautious—it says that Walsingham valued the "parts" of worth in the deceased, implying that there were other parts he did not value—but at least it shows that Marlowe's name was not poison in some circles. Five years after Marlowe's death, Blount wrote, "the impression of the man that hath been dear to us" lived on, making it seem appropriate to publish this unfinished poem, the final "issue of his brain" before "the stroke of death" silenced him.

Had Blount not decided to print *Hero and Leander*, it could easily have been lost forever. And without it, Shakespeare is unlikely to have written his tribute to the contemporary from whom he had learned the most. For the better part of a decade, Shakespeare had studied every move that Marlowe made. He probably read *Hero and Leander* in manuscript in 1593, around the time of Marlowe's death, as he seems to have been inspired by it to write his own long erotic poem, *Venus and Adonis*. But when in 1598 Shakespeare drew on Marlowe's work again, their whole complex relationship seems to have flooded over him, and he did something that he never did anywhere else in his work: he directly quoted a contemporary. "Dead shepherd," one of his characters suddenly says, "now I find your saw of might"—that is, now I find your saying powerful—and then quotes the saying: "Who ever loved that loved not at first sight?"

That Shakespeare does not mention Marlowe by name is entirely in keeping with the pastoral setting of the play; *As You Like It* is a story of shepherds and shepherdesses in the Forest of Arden. But it also captures something of the ambivalence in Shakespeare's relationship with Marlowe, an ambivalence that may have gone back to the first time they met to work together on plays for Henslowe. If Marlowe's powerful influence on Shakespeare is manifest in *Titus Andronicus, The Merchant of Venice, Richard II*, and elsewhere, so too is Shakespeare's resistance to Marlowe.

Without naming names, however, Shakespeare acknowledged his immense debt to the "dead shepherd." The society into which they were born in 1564 was culturally backward. The fourteenth-century Italian poet and humanist Petrarch, who had taken all of Europe by storm, was only just coming into vogue in England, some two hundred years after his death. The work of Machiavelli, who died in 1527, could not be printed, let alone translated into English, and could be spoken about only in whispers. Copernicus was persona non grata at the universities, and the scientific atomism of Lucretius, though it had been returned to circulation on the Continent in 1417, was anathema. New ways of thinking had secretly made it across the Channel and were quietly brewing under the surface, but they were held in check by a state-sponsored repression, constantly reinforced with harsh punishments.

Officially, the medieval worldview was still intact in England, even late in Elizabeth's reign. The earth was at the center of the universe, and the sun and the planets circled around it in their perfect crystalline spheres. The structure of society was ordered in the way it was by God, as were gender roles and sexual positions, and it was folly or worse to call the arrangements into question or to try to rise above one's station or to desire what the church or state told you that you were not allowed to desire. Christianity was the only true religion, and anyone outside the Christian community, whether Jew or Muslim or skeptic, was in the grip of the devil. At the end of days—which could come at any moment—souls and bodies would be reunited and brought before God for the Last Judgment. He would consign the damned to an eternity of torment in Hell, the saved to bliss in Heaven.

For the cultural life of England to move forward, someone had to come along and break through the suffocating carapace of inherited dogma. A cobbler's son from Canterbury, without any elite support or resources or sense of family entitlement, seems an unlikely candidate for this role. And yet perhaps this very unlikelihood was part of what it took: Marlowe had no stake in the system to begin with, nothing to lose, except of course his life. He was reckless, daring, unscrupulous, transgressive. It is tantalizing to imagine what he might have written had he lived a long life, or even survived, as Shakespeare did, into his fifties. But perhaps the wonder is that he existed at all and that he made it to the age of twenty-nine.

❖ ❖ ❖

THROUGH THE FISSURES Marlowe had made, light began to flow. He had made it possible to write in a new way about violence, ambition, greed, and desire. He offered poetic liberation: thanks to his astonishing style, the expressive power of the English language took a great leap forward. Shakespeare did not choose to write in the same way—Marlowe was too reckless, too hyperbolic, too relentlessly destructive. But Shakespeare saw that he could now enter territory into which no one before Marlowe had dared to venture.

Shakespeare was the recipient of Marlowe's gifts of reckless courage and genius, but he did not want to be Marlowe. The cost was too high. It was far too easy to be misunderstood, and the misunderstanding could prove fatal. In the same play in which he violated his own unwritten rule and quoted Marlowe, Shakespeare added another, deeper reference to his fellow playwright. In *As You Like It*, the court jester Touchstone—one of Shakespeare's most intelligent and at the same time least lovable clowns—is flirting with a simple shepherdess. Touchstone makes a punning reference to the exiled Ovid, the ancient poet whose love poems

Marlowe translated at the beginning of his brief career. The shepherdess, of course, does not understand the pun, and Touchstone adds a strange comment. "When a man's verses cannot be understood," the jester says, "it strikes a man more dead than a great reckoning in a little room" (3.3.9–12). For the briefest moment, we are back in the little room in Deptford where Ingram Frizer thrust his knife through Marlowe's eye. And then, scarcely missing a beat, the play goes on.

# ACKNOWLEDGMENTS

In the 1990s the screenwriter Marc Norman came to see me on several occasions to solicit my ideas for a biopic based on the life of Shakespeare. I repeatedly told him to forget Shakespeare and write a movie instead about Christopher Marlowe. Norman ignored my urging and was hardly the worse for it: he teamed up with Tom Stoppard and wrote the screenplay for the hugely successful *Shakespeare in Love*. Still, I do not think that I was far off the mark: Marlowe's life is fascinating. When, a few years ago, I shared this fascination with my beloved agent Jill Kneerim, she immediately asked, "What are you waiting for?" As I had done in earlier projects, I relied not only on her infectious enthusiasm but also on her wisdom, and I grieve that Jill did not live long enough to hold this current book in her hands. In the wake of Jill's death, Zoë Pagnamenta ably assumed responsibility for seeing the project through, and I am immensely grateful to her for her skilled guidance, expert advice, and unfailing support.

Harvard University, where I am privileged to teach, is a wonderfully supportive and stimulating institution. The astonishing resources of its Houghton and Widener libraries and of the Harvard Art Museums are matched by the inexhaustible richness of its human community. I am intensely aware of how fortunate I am in my remarkable students and colleagues. I want to acknowledge a particular debt of gratitude to one aspect of my life at Harvard that may not seem immediately relevant to a book on a sixteenth-century writer: my involvement for the past twenty years in Harvard Scholars at Risk. This project, which provides refuge to scholars and writers threatened by oppressive regimes, has introduced me to an array of remarkably brave individuals and has given me insight into what it is like to live in societies without freedom of expression or the right to privacy. In certain crucial respects, the world of Christopher Marlowe was closer to that of North Korea than North Carolina.

My indebtedness extends to other institutions as well. Pembroke College, Cambridge University, where I am honored to be a fellow, graciously provided accommodation while I spent time pursuing my research. Dr. Alex Devine, the sublibrarian of the Parker Library at Corpus Christi College, where Marlowe was a student, gave me valuable advice and access to crucial materials. For the opportunity to present a segment of my research in a lecture co-hosted by the Centre for Early Modern Studies and the Faculty of English, I am grateful to Merton College, Oxford, and to Professor Lorna Hutson. At Oxford, Professor Richard Ovenden, Bodley's librarian and the director of the Bodleian Library's Centre for the Study of the Book, was thoughtful and generous in his assistance. In London I relied, as I have done for many years, on the fabulous resources of the British Library and the Warburg Institute.

Much of the actual writing of this book was done during residences in Italy at the Villa i Tatti, Harvard's Center for Italian Renaissance Studies. I am deeply grateful to Alina Payne, the director of this remarkable institution, and to its staff and fellows. I extend my sincerest thanks as well to the equally remarkable American Academy in Rome, particularly to its director Aliza Wong and its head librarian Sebastian Hierle.

On numerous occasions, my three beloved sons, Josh, Aaron, and Harry, have patiently heard me out on the subject of Christopher Marlowe and have always buoyed me up. Over the years, designing and teaching courses with Luke Menand and with Joseph Koerner has taught me an enormous amount, and I am grateful for their enduring collaboration and friendship. Robert Pinsky read an early draft of this book and offered valuable advice on it, as on so much else. Rory Loughnane, reader in early

# ACKNOWLEDGMENTS

modern studies and co-director of the Centre for Medieval and Early Modern Studies at the University of Kent, kindly read a later draft and caught several missteps. I am indebted to the intellectual generosity and unfailing kindness of many other friends and colleagues including Paul Audi, Larry Bacow, Homi Bhabha, Daniel Blank, Mark Brayshay, Horst Bredekamp, Kirsten Burke, Jay Cantor, Glenda Carpio, Francis Ford Coppola, Bart van Es, Aubrey Everett, Alan Garber, Henry Louis Gates Jr., Adam Gopnik, Anselm Haverkamp, David Hillman, Petra Hofman, Jeffrey Knapp, Thomas Laqueur, Jill Lepore, Hartmut Liseman, Laurie Maguire, Geoffrey Marsh, Joe Moshenska, Laura Murphy, Alan Nelson, Scott Newstok, Edward Paleit, Elizabeth Propst, Meredith Reiches, Moshe Safdie, Jürgen Schläger, Jason Scott-Warren, Bailey Sincox, Holger Syme, Misha Teramura, and Leah Whittington. My able assistant Daniela Nieva has cheerfully carried out both large and small tasks to get the manuscript to the finish line.

This is the fifth book on which I have had the good fortune to have as my editor Alane Salierno Mason. For all that she has given me—careful readings, exacting criticisms, insightful suggestions, underling trust, and enduring friendship—I am, as ever, immensely grateful.

My profoundest debt—a debt beyond words—is to my wife, Ramie Targoff.

# NOTES

## Texts

Of Marlowe's writings, only the two parts of *Tamburlaine the Great*, published anonymously, appeared during his lifetime; all his other plays, poems, and translations were printed posthumously. The precise chronology of composition is difficult to determine. No literary manuscript in Marlowe's own hand survives, and there is no evidence that he concerned himself with the publication of any of his works. Unlike Shakespeare, whose colleagues produced after his death a carefully edited collection of his plays, no contemporary of Marlowe undertook to produce an edition of his complete works. Moreover, the theater is an inherently collaborative form. Scholars have detected Marlowe's hand in scenes in several plays by Shakespeare and others, and traces of other playwrights' hands have been detected in several of Marlowe's plays. Some plays in the period were clearly authored by multiple playwrights working together, and even plays written by a single author were often altered by others when they were revived for new productions or taken on tour.

The state of Marlowe's texts therefore is complex and contested. The title page of *Dido, Queen of Carthage* lists the authors as Christopher Marlowe and Thomas Nashe, but whether much or even any of the writing was done by Nashe is unclear. In a letter to the "Gentlemen Readers," the printer of the two parts of *Tamburlaine*, Richard Jones, mentions that he "omitted and left out some fond and frivolous gestures," but what exactly he chose to cut is impossible to determine. Marlowe's last play, *The Massacre at Paris*, survives only in an extremely imperfect and incomplete form. Above all, his most celebrated play,

*Doctor Faustus*, exists in two strikingly different forms, the so-called A Text and B Text. I have followed the consensus of modern scholars in regarding the A Text as closer to what Marlowe wrote, but as the authorial manuscript does not survive, doubts will inevitably remain.

All this said, in his tragically brief life Marlowe produced a brilliant body of work, one whose distinctive power was acknowledged with something like awe by his contemporaries and that continues to thrill readers and audiences to this day. Modern literary theory, together with a heightened awareness of the contingencies of print culture, is sometimes said to have led to the disappearance of the author, but in Marlowe's case, the passage of more than 450 years has only served to heighten the sense of his individuality.

All citations of Marlowe's plays are from *The Complete Plays*, ed. Mark Thornton Burnett (Dent, 1999). For Marlowe's poems and translations, I have used the texts edited by Stephen Orgel (Penguin, 1971). Among other editions, I have consulted *The Complete Works of Christopher Marlowe*, ed. Roma Gill et al., 5 vols. (Clarendon Press, 1986–98); the Oxford Drama Library edition (for *Tamburlaine, Parts I and II, Doctor Faustus, A- and B-Texts, The Jew of Malta,* and *Edward II*), ed. David Bevington and Eric Rasmussen (Clarendon Press, 1995); *The Works of Christopher Marlowe*, ed. C. F. Tucker Brooke (Clarendon Press, 1910); *Marlowe's Plays and Poems*, ed. M. R. Ridley (Everyman's Library, 1955); *The Complete Plays of Christopher Marlowe*, ed. Irving Ribner (Odyssey Press, 1963); *Christopher Marlowe: The Complete Plays*, ed. J. B. Steane (Penguin, 1969); *Tamburlaine, Parts I and II*, ed. Anthony B. Dawson (Norton, 1997); *The Jew of Malta*, ed. T. W. Craik (Benn, 1966); *Dr. Faustus*, ed. Roma Gill (A&C Black, 1989); *Doctor Faustus*, ed. David Scott Kastan and Matthew Hunter, 2nd ed. (Norton, 2023); and *Doctor Faustus: The B Text*, ed. Mathew R. Martin (Broadview Press, 2013). A helpful selection of the key sources for Marlowe's plays is *Christopher Marlowe: The Plays and Their Sources*, ed. Vivien Thomas and William Tydeman (1994; reprint Routledge, 2011).

A number of valuable websites are being launched for the study of Marlowe and his texts, including the following (with special thanks to Rory Loughnane of the University of Kent):

### *The Christopher Marlowe Project*
A digital site connected to the *Oxford Marlowe: Collected Works*, with links to ongoing events and related online databases, resources, and forums. https://research.kent.ac.uk/marlowe-works/

## Life

I have drawn throughout this book on a significant number of important biographical studies of Marlowe. Among these are John Bakeless, *Christopher Marlowe: The Man and His Time* (Morrow, 1937) and Bakeless's two-volume *The Tragicall History of Christopher Marlowe* (Harvard University Press, 1942); Frederick Boas, *Christopher Marlowe: A Biographical and Critical Study* (Clarendon Press, 1940); Mark Eccles, *Christopher Marlowe in London* (Harvard University Press, 1934); Park Honan, *Christopher Marlowe: Poet and Spy* (Oxford University Press, 2006); Lisa Hopkins, *Christopher Marlowe: A Literary Life* (Palgrave Macmillan, 2000); Leslie Hotson, *The Death of Christopher Marlowe* (1925; reprint Russell & Russell, 1967); Arata Ide, *Localizing Christopher Marlowe: His Life, Plays, and Mythology, 1575–1593* (Boydell & Brewer, 2023); Constance Kuriyama, *Christopher Marlowe: A Renaissance Life* (Cornell University Press, 2002); Charles Nicholl, *The Reckoning: The Murder of Christopher Marlowe* (1992; rev. ed. Vintage, 2002); David Riggs, *The World of Christopher Marlowe* (Henry Holt, 2005); and William Urry, *Christopher Marlowe and Canterbury*, ed. Andrew Butcher (Faber & Faber, 1988). On Marlowe's literary career, see Patrick Cheney, *Marlowe's Counterfeit Profession: Ovid, Spenser, Counter-Nationhood* (University of Toronto Press, 1997); Cheney, ed., *The Cambridge Companion to Christopher Marlowe* (Cambridge University Press, 2004); and Sarah K. Scott and Michael L. Stapleton, eds., *Christopher Marlowe the Craftsman: Lives, Stage, and Page* (Ashgate, 2010).

In an appendix to her biography, Constance Kuriyama includes transcriptions and translations of many of the key documents that directly relate to Marlowe's life, and I have for the most part drawn on these, though I have modernized the spelling and punctuation. The chronology of Marlowe's works and, to some extent, of the events in his life is unclear and often highly contested. Though it cannot resolve all the key issues, a very helpful guide is Lisa Hopkins, *A Christopher Marlowe Chronology* (Palgrave Macmillan, 2005).

Impressive archival research conducted over the past decades has enabled us to understand Marlowe's life far better than was possible in the 1960s, when my own interest was first aroused, and I have gratefully relied on this research. But Marlowe remains something of an enigma. In part, this is because of the fragmentary and elusive nature of the traces of his life. In May 1592, for example, when *The Jew of Malta* was drawing large crowds to the Rose Theater on the south bank of the Thames, Marlowe was taken before a judge in London and charged with threatening two officials, a constable and a beadle. We know the names of the judge and the officials, and we know that Marlowe pledged to "keep the peace," but we have no clue what it was all about. So too, four months later, Marlowe was arrested on the street in Canterbury and charged with attacking the tailor William Corkine with a stick and dagger. Marlowe responded by charging Corkine with attacking him. A month later the matter was dropped. Once again we do not know what was actually going on. Less than a year later Marlowe was murdered in circumstances that have never been adequately explained.

But it is not simply the gaps in the historical record that make Marlowe so difficult to grasp. Artistic genius is always a mystery. What can explain a Caravaggio or a Beethoven? The recurrent attempts to discover that someone other than Shakespeare wrote Shakespeare's plays is not, in my view, the result of a paucity of proof—there is abundant evidence that the man from Stratford-upon-Avon wrote the works that bear his name—but rather a tribute to the difficulty of understanding how anyone could have accomplished all that he did. Marlowe accomplished far less—seven plays compared to Shakespeare's thirty-seven—but he did so in only a few tumultuous years before his murder at twenty-nine. He managed in that brief time to break through the formidable barriers that had been erected to constrain both creative energy and freedom of thought. How he did it is the subject of this book.

Given the state of the texts and the records of the life, it is not surprising that my account of Marlowe is conspicuously marked by words like *perhaps* and phrases like *may have* and *could have*. There is a great deal of speculation and guesswork in any attempt to make sense of his existence. I admire but have not allowed myself the liberty taken by Anthony Burgess's novel *A Dead Man in Deptford* (Hutchinson, 1993) or the many other fictional recreations of Marlowe's life. At the other extreme, J. A. Downie, reviewing the documented traces of Marlowe's life, has called into question virtually all attempts to construct a coherent biographical account or to place that account in a meaningful relation to his works. Obviously, neither I nor the scholarly biographers listed above agree with Downie, but it seems fair to register his programmatic skepticism: "Marlowe: Facts and Fictions," in *Constructing Christopher Marlowe*, ed. J. A. Downie and J. T. Parnell (Cambridge University Press, 2000), 13–29; and "Reviewing What We Think We Know About Christopher Marlowe," in Scott and Stapleton, *Marlowe the Craftsman*, 33–46.

For Marlowe's contemporaries, I have generally begun with the entries in the invaluable *Oxford Dictionary of National Biography*. Shakespeare is cited from *The Norton Shakespeare* 3rd ed., ed. Stephen Greenblatt et al. (Norton, 2015). Unless otherwise noted, translations of Greek and Latin texts are drawn from the Loeb Library editions. For the theatrical culture of the period, my first point of reference has been the multivolume project Alan H. Nelson, ed., *Records of Early English Drama* (University of Toronto Press, 1989). For Henslowe's diary, I have used the edition edited by R. A. Foakes and R. T. Rickert, 2nd ed.

(Cambridge University Press, 2002). The four volumes of E. K. Chambers, *The Elizabethan Stage* (Clarendon Press, 1923), remain extremely useful.

My own first ventures into Marlowe's life and works date back to "Marlowe and Renaissance Self-Fashioning," in *Two Renaissance Mythmakers: Christopher Marlowe and Ben Jonson*, ed. Alvin B. Kernan (Johns Hopkins University Press, 1977), and "Marlowe, Marx, and Anti-Semitism," *Critical Inquiry* 5, no. 2 (1978): 291–307. I developed and incorporated the former essay in my *Renaissance Self-Fashioning: From More to Shakespeare* (University of Chicago Press, 1980).

CHAPTER 1: **A WORLD APART**

Foreign visitors to England who left a record of their impressions include the anonymous Italian author of *A relation, or rather A true account, of the island of England with sundry particulars of the customs of these people, and of the royal revenues under King Henry the Seventh, about the year 1500*, trans. Charlotte Augusta Sneyd (Camden Society, 1847); "The London Journal of Alessandro Magno 1562," ed. Caroline Barron, Christopher Coleman, and Claire Gobbi, *London Journal* 9, no. 2 (1983): 136–52; Orazio Busino, "Diaries and Despatches [sic] of the Venetian Embassy at the Court of King James I, in the years 1617, 1618," trans. Rawdon Brown, *Quarterly Review* 102, no. 204 (1857): 398–438; Thomas Platter, *Journal of a Younger Brother*, ed. and trans. S. Jennett (F. Muller, 1963); Philip Julius, *Diary of the Journey of Philip Julius, Duke of Stettin-Pomerania, Through England in the Year 1602*, ed. Gottfried von Bülow and Wilfred Powell (Cambridge University Press, 1892); Lupold von Wedel, "Journey Through England and Scotland Made by Lupold von Wedel in the Years 1584 and 1585," trans. Gottfried von Bülow, *Transactions of the Royal Historical Society*, new ser. 9 (1895): 223–70; and Friedrich I, Duke of Würtemberg, *England as Seen by Foreigners in the Days of Elizabeth and James the First*, ed. William Brenchley Rye (Smith, 1865). On the queen's makeup, see Farah Karim-Cooper, *Cosmetics in Shakespearean and Renaissance Drama* (2006; rev. ed. Edinburgh University Press, 2019), 20–21.

For Machyn, see *The Diary of Henry Machyn, Citizen and Merchant-Taylor of London, 1550–1563*, ed. John Gough Nichols (Camden Society, 1848). The visitor whose view of the animal fights I quote is Alessandro Magno. For the French ambassador's account of Elizabeth, see "An Audience with Queen Elizabeth I," 2004, EyewitnesstoHistory.com.

Parts of this chapter appear in "Competitive Consumption," my review of the Metropolitan Museum's exhibition *The Tudors: Art and Majesty in Renaissance England*, in *New York Review of Books*, December 22, 2022.

CHAPTER 2: **HANDWRITING ON THE WALL**

On Kyd's arrest, see Arthur Freeman, "Marlowe, Kyd, and the Dutch Church Libel," in *English Literary Renaissance* 3, no. 1 (1973): 44–52. Freeman's *Thomas Kyd: Facts and Problems* (Clarendon Press, 1967) remains the best source for information about Kyd's life. The *Dictionary of National Biography* entry on Thomas Kyd is by J. R. Mulryne.

As writers who had not attended university, Kyd and Shakespeare were subject to very similar attacks, as observed in Bart van Es, "*'Johannes fac Totum'*? Shakespeare's First Contact with the Acting Companies," *Shakespeare Quarterly* 61, no. 4 (2010): 551–77.

In many ways *Hamlet*, with its vision of friends—schoolmates—recruited by the government into spying on their friends, participating deliberately or inadvertently in murderous schemes, and finally being destroyed as collateral damage, reflects the story of Marlowe's life.

As the queen's sergeant at law, Sir John Puckering had been a prosecutor at the trial of the Babington Plot conspirators (cf. N. G. Jones, "Puckering" in the *Dictionary of National Biography*). In his letter to Puckering, Kyd says that he and Marlowe had been "writing in one chamber" some two years before his arrest, that is, in 1591, but he does not make clear whether they were living together (as I think likely) or were merely sharing a room in which to write. Constance Kuriyama suggests that, despite the bitter end, Kyd and Marlowe had once been friends: "Second Selves: Marlowe's Cambridge and London Friendships," *Medieval and Renaissance Drama in England* 14 (2001): 99.

On plague, see my essay "What Shakespeare Actually Wrote About the Plague," *New Yorker*, May 7, 2020, from which I have adapted several passages. On Huguenot refugees, see Laura Hunt Yungblut, *Strangers Settled Here Amongst Us: Policies, Perceptions, and the Presence of Aliens in Elizabethan England* (Routledge, 1996); Randolph Vigne and Charles Littleton, *From Strangers to Citizens: The Integration of Immigrant Communities in Britain, Ireland, and Colonial America, 1550–1750* (Sussex Academic Press, 2001); and Nigel Goose and Liên Luu, *Immigrants in Tudor and Early Stuart England* (2005; reprint Liverpool University Press, 2013).

On the anti-immigrant placard, see Eric Griffin, "Shakespeare, Marlowe, and the Stranger Crisis of the Early 1590s," in *Shakespeare and Immigration*, ed. Ruben Espinosa and David Ruiter (Routledge, 2014), 13–36. The xenophobia in the period, underlying the placard, is analyzed in C. W. Chitty, "Aliens in England in the Sixteenth Century," *Race* 8, no. 2 (1966): 129–46; and Yungblut, *Strangers Settled Amongst Us*.

The source of the allegedly heretical document discovered in Kyd's room was identified in the early twentieth century by William D. Briggs in "On a

Document Concerning Christopher Marlowe," *Studies in Philology* 20, no. 2 (1923): 153–59. John Proctor was replying to an unidentified contemporary who had espoused Arrianist views but had recanted. See George T. Buckley, "Who Was 'The Late Arrian'?" *Modern Language Notes* 49, no. 8 (1934): 500–3.

CHAPTER 3: **THE GREAT SEPARATION**

The concept of the "Great Separation" (*Loslösung*) comes from Friedrich Nietzsche, *Human, All Too Human*, trans. R. J. Hollingdale (Cambridge University Press, 1986), aphorism 3. Much of the passage seems to me highly relevant to Marlowe:

> The great separation comes suddenly, like the shock of an earthquake: all at once the young soul is devastated, torn loose, torn out—it itself does not know what is happening. An urge, a pressure governs it, mastering the soul like a command: the will and wish awaken to go away, anywhere, at any cost: a violent, dangerous curiosity for an undiscovered world flames up and flickers in all the senses. "Better to die than live *here*," so sounds the imperious and seductive voice. And this "here," this "at home" is everything which it had loved until then! A sudden horror and suspicion of that which it loved; a lightning flash of contempt toward that which was its "obligation"; a rebellious, despotic, volcanically jolting desire to roam abroad, to become alienated, cool, sober, icy: a hatred of love, perhaps a desecratory reaching and glancing *backward*, to where it had until then worshiped and loved; perhaps a blush of shame at its most recent act, and at the same time, jubilation *that* it was done; a drunken, inner, jubilant shudder, which betrays a victory? a victory? over what? over whom?—a puzzling, questioning, questionable victory, but the *first* victory nevertheless: such bad and painful things are part of the history of the great separation. It is also a disease that can destroy man, this first outburst of strength and will to self-determination, self-valorization, this will to *free* will: and how much disease is expressed by the wild attempts and peculiarities with which the freed man, the separated man, now tries to prove his rule over things! He wanders about savagely with an unsatisfied lust; his booty must atone for the dangerous tension of his pride; he rips apart what attracts him. With an evil laugh he overturns what he finds concealed, spared until then by some shame; he investigates how these things look if they are overturned. There is some arbitrariness and pleasure in arbitrariness to it, if he then perhaps directs his favor to that which previously stood in disrepute—if he creeps curiously and enticingly around what is most forbidden. Behind his ranging activity (for he is journeying restlessly and aimlessly, as in a desert) stands the question mark of an ever more dangerous curiosity. "Cannot *all*

values be overturned? And is Good perhaps Evil? And God only an invention, a nicety of the devil? Is everything perhaps ultimately false? And if we are deceived, are we not for that very reason also deceivers? *Must* we not be deceivers, too?"

For philosophical reflections on suddenness, see Karl Heinz Bohrer, *Suddenness: On the Moment of Aesthetic Appearance*, trans. Ruth Crowley (Columbia University Press, 1994).

On the Marlowe household, Honan, *Marlowe: Poet and Spy*, is particularly helpful, along with Urry, *Marlowe and Canterbury*; Riggs, *World*; and Kuriyama, *Renaissance Life*. "At no time in his life" could Christopher Marlowe's father "be found in a moderately satisfactory economic position." Urry, *Marlowe and Canterbury*, 26. See also the interesting reflections in Andrew Butcher, "'Onelye a boye called Christopher Mowle,'" in *Christopher Marlowe and English Renaissance Culture*, ed. Darryll Grantley and Peter Roberts (1996; reprint Routledge, 2020), 1–16.

John and Katherine's daughter Mary was born in May 1562, and their son Christopher in February 1564. After Kit's birth there followed the steady succession of children with whom parents in this period of extremely high mortality attempted to leave behind some living traces of themselves: Margaret, born in 1565; a son who did not live long enough to be christened, in 1568; Jane in 1569; Thomas in 1570; Anne in 1571; Dorothy in 1573; and another Thomas (names were often reused after death) in 1576. The survival rate is fairly typical of the sixteenth and seventeenth centuries. The diarist Elizabeth Walker, granddaughter of Shakespeare's friend John Sadler, bore eleven children, including three stillbirths. Of the eight live births, only two survived to adolescence—a daughter who died at sixteen of smallpox and another daughter who died in childbirth.

At the time of Marlowe's death, not a single printed work bore his name. It was his death—and probably its sudden and shocking character—that seemed to trigger a commercial interest in his work and, more particularly, in featuring his name as author. For a fascinating and provocative account of this printing history, see András Kiséry, "An Author and a Bookshop: Publishing Marlowe's Remains at the Black Bear," *Philological Quarterly* 91, no. 3 (2021): 361–92. On Marlowe's reputation, see C. F. Tucker Brooke, "The Reputation of Christopher Marlowe," *Transactions of the Connecticut Academy of Arts and Sciences* 25 (1922): 307–408.

On late sixteenth-century Canterbury, Urry, *Marlowe and Canterbury*, is indispensable. James Felle is described on 45; Bale on 13; the headmaster's payment on 19; Graddell on 37. The inventory of the father's possessions was drawn up in 1605, but most of the items in it are described as old—hence they are likely to have been the ones with which Christopher and his siblings grew up. The absence of tools in the inventory suggests that John Marlowe, close to seventy years old, must have retired and sold them off. Also see John Brent, *Canterbury in the Olden Time*, 2nd ed. (Marshall Simpkin & Co., 1879).

On the dismantling of the shrine to Thomas à Becket and the broader attacks on Catholic ritual sites, see Eamon Duffy, *The Stripping of the Altars: Traditional Religion in England, 1400–1580* (Yale University Press, 2022). Protestant iconoclasm is analyzed in Joseph Koerner, *The Reformation of the Image* (University of Chicago Press, 2008), and in James Simpson, *Under the Hammer: Iconoclasm in the Anglo-American Tradition* (Oxford University Press, 2011). Simpson draws out a parallel with the Chinese Cultural Revolution in *Reform and Cultural Revolution* (Oxford University Press, 2002). Protestant attacks on the Catholic ritual calendar are chronicled in Ronald Hutton, *The Rise and Fall of Merry England: The Ritual Year, 1400–1700* (Oxford University Press, 1994). On Bale in Canterbury, see E. J. Baskerville, "A Religious Disturbance in Canterbury, June 1561: John Bale's Unpublished Account," *Historical Research: Bulletin of the Institute of Historical Research* 65, no. 158 (1992): 340–48. Maid Marion without breeches comes from *REED* (Kent) 1:xcii; the payment to the man in the devil's clothes from *REED* (Kent) 1:lxxv; John Johnson and his paper labels from Urry, *Marlowe and Canterbury*, 9; Grindal's letter from *REED* (Kent) 1:xcii–xciii.

The attempt to suppress popular culture met with predictable resistance. That is, after all, why Morris dancers were still dancing against the law outside the mayor's house. In 1561 the ever-vigilant John Bale tried to put a stop to the customary lighting of bonfires on Midsummer Eve, the vigil of Saint John the Baptist's nativity, "doubtless," Bale thought, "in contempt of the Christian religion." But "foulmouthed Bale" had an adversary in the person of Richard Borowes, alias "railing Dick." Borowes—whom Bale memorably described as a "smellfeast," a sponger with a nose for a free meal—got a drum and used it to gather a troupe of more than a hundred boys. Together they went to the bull stake and, in defiance of Bale and the church authorities, lit a great bonfire. They marched around it, the outraged Bale wrote, "as in procession, with birch boughs in their hands, singing most filthy songs of bawdry," and were tremendously pleased with themselves.

Riggs, *World*, gives a richly detailed account of the structure and curriculum of the King's School, Canterbury. Riggs notes that "twelve of the seventy-eight Scholars on the two lists of Marlowe's contemporaries pursued university degrees; all but one went to Cambridge" (54). The teacher whose goal was "to make those purest authors our own" was Richard Brinsley (51). Latin learning as "the labour-intensive alternative to indigenous youth culture" is on 41. A more detailed account of Elizabethan schooling is T. W. Baldwin, *William*

*Shakspere's Petty School* (University of Illinois Press, 1943) and Baldwin, *William Shakspere's Small Latine and Lesse Greeke*, 2 vols. (University of Illinois Press, 1956). See also Lynn Enterline, *Shakespeare's Schoolroom: Rhetoric, Discipline, Emotion* (University of Pennsylvania Press, 2012).

The headmaster during the years preceding Marlowe's enrollment was paid something extra for "setting forth of tragedies, comedies, and interludes." The tradition of student acting must have continued during Marlowe's time, and it evidently turned up some talent. In 1592 two professional actors were taken to court for having lured several King's School students to "go abroad in the country to play plays contrary to law and good order." The students expressed fear that they would lose their scholarships and be expelled, but the tempters, like the scoundrels in *Pinocchio*, told the boys that they would make just as much money if they performed in public and "hanged out a shoe or a pot to beg." In court, the two players confessed and said that they would reform. They do not seem to have been severely punished, and indeed the authorities generally winked at the practice of luring or even kidnapping talented students to perform professionally.

CHAPTER 4: **THE MASTER'S BOOKS**

Augustine on despoiling the Egyptians is from *De doctrina christiana*, chap. 40.

Peter Clark, *English Provincial Society from the Reformation to the Revolution: Religion, Politics, and Society in Kent, 1500–1640* (Harvester Press, 1977), notes that "in the 1560s fewer than one in ten of the Canterbury inventories referred to a book.... By the 1580s Canterbury book ownership had risen so steeply that well over one in four of the inventories referred to a book, and the next decade saw a further rise, with over a third listing a volume or more" (98). Most of the books in question were Bibles and liturgical books.

Of the students at the King's School Canterbury, Clark notes that 40 percent were boarders; the per capita charge for fees and boarding was a substantial £12 per annum. The master earned a relatively high £20 per annum, plus extra funds for special tutoring.

For Archbishop Cranmer's eloquent argument that education should not be limited to the elite, see *The Works of Thomas Cranmer*, ed. John Edmund Cox (Parker Society, 1844): "To exclude the ploughman's son and the poor man's son from the benefit of learning, as though they were unworthy to have the gifts of the Holy Ghost bestowed on them, as well as on others, is as much to say, as that Almighty God should not be at liberty to bestow his great gifts of grace on any person, nor no where else but as we and other men shall appoint them to be employed, according to our fancy, and not according to his most godly will and pleasure; who giveth his gifts, both of learning and other perfections in all sciences, to all kinds and states of people indifferently" (16:398–99).

On what he calls "the Renaissance debate" in Elizabethan education, see Kenneth Charlton, *Education in Renaissance England* (Routledge & Kegan Paul, 1965). Thomas Healy remarks on the inner "contradiction in Elizabethan education," in Healy, "Marlowe's Biography," in *Marlowe in Context*, ed. Emily C. Bartels and Emma Smith (Cambridge University Press, 2013), 339.

I have quoted Ascham from Roger Ascham, *The Scholemaster*, ed. R. J. Schoeck (J.M. Dent, 1966). For Ascham's life, see Lawrence Ryan, *Roger Ascham* (Stanford University Press, 1963) and the *Dictionary of National Biography* article by Rosemary O'Day. William Thomas's *The History of Italy* (1549) has been edited by George B. Parks (Cornell University Press, 1963).

In the first printed edition of *Dido, Queen of Carthage* (1594), Nashe's name, in much smaller print, is on the title page after Marlowe's. On the basis of stylometric analysis, Thomas Merriam, "Marlowe and Nashe in *Dido Queen of Carthage*," *Notes and Queries* 47, no. 4 (December 2000): 425–28, argues that Marlowe was principally responsible for the first two acts and Nashe for the last three. But Darren Freebury-Jones and Marcus Dahl reviewed the findings and found no substantial evidence of Nashe, in "Searching for Thomas Nashe in *Dido, Queen of Carthage*," *Digital Scholarship in the Humanities* 35, no. 2 (2020): 296–306.

CHAPTER 5: **BRIGHT COLLEGE YEARS**

On the Cambridge University course of study that Marlowe followed, Riggs, *World*, has a particularly illuminating account on which I have drawn. He lists the debate topics on 91. Riggs thinks the course of study consumed "every waking hour" (78). Joel Altman, *The Tudor Play of Mind: Rhetorical Inquiry and the Development of Elizabethan Drama* (University of California Press, 1978), is a valuable guide to the kinds of questions that university students in this period were trained to address. Peter Mack, *Elizabethan Rhetoric: Theory and Practice* (Cambridge University Press, 2002); Lisa Jardine, "Humanism and the Sixteenth Century Cambridge Arts Course," *Journal of the History of Education Society* 4, no. 1 (1975): 16–31; and Anthony Grafton and Lisa Jardine, *From Humanism to the Humanities: Education and the Liberal Arts in Fifteenth- and Sixteenth-Century Europe* (Harvard University Press, 1986) are also highly useful. For the complaint that lectures were being delivered to empty halls, see Mark H. Curtis, *Oxford and Cambridge in Transition, 1558–1642: An Essay on Changing Relations Between the English Universities and English Society* (Clarendon Press, 1959), 96–97. The praise of Marlowe's command of Latin is cited in Boas, *Marlowe: Biographical and Critical*, 19.

In Marlowe's time, Corpus Christi College was also known as Bene't College, after the adjoining St. Bene't Church. See Robert Masters and John Lamb, *History of the College of Corpus Christi and the Blessed Virgin Mary in the University of Cambridge* (Cambridge, 1831). The master of Corpus, Robert Norgate, drew up a schedule for the undergraduates, quoted in Richard Hardin, "Marlowe and the Fruits of Scholarism," *Philological Quarterly* 63, no. 3 (1984): 387–88. The statute regarding the duties of tutors is drawn from Curtis, *Oxford and Cambridge in Transition*, 79.

On the training in disputations that was meant to culminate in the triumphant *Sic probo*—"Thus I prove"—see the advice of James Duport, a tutor in Trinity College: "When you dispute, think it not enough barely to pronounce and propound your arguments, but press them, and then urge them home, and call upon your adversary for an answer, and leave him not till you have one." Cited from Curtis, *Oxford and Cambridge in Transition*, 116. A character in Marlowe's *Doctor Faustus* wonders "what's become of Faustus, that was wont to make our schools ring with *sic probo*" (1.2.1–2). The answer lies in Faustus's disillusionment with the whole system: "Is to dispute well logic's chiefest end? / Affords this art no greater miracle?" (1.1.8–9).

On Matthew Parker, see V. J. K. Brook, *A Life of Archbishop Parker* (Clarendon Press, 1962); on the Parker Library, see Bruce Dickins, "The Making of the Parker Library," *Transactions of the Cambridge Bibliographical Society* 6, no. 1 (1972): 19–34.

The regulations at Cambridge were a small part of a much larger concern to mark class and status differences by dress. By the Elizabethan statute of 1574, no one was permitted to wear in his apparel "any silk of the color of purple, cloth of gold tissued, nor fur of sables, but only the King, Queen, King's mother, children, brethren, and sisters, uncles and aunts; and except dukes, marquises, and earls, who may wear the same in doublets, jerkins, linings of cloaks, gowns, and hose." No one could wear "caps, hats, hatbands, capbands, garters, or boothose trimmed with gold or silver or pearl; silk netherstocks; enameled chains, buttons, aglets: except men of the degrees above mentioned, the gentlemen attending upon the Queen's person in her highness's Privy chamber or in the office of cupbearer, carver, sewer [server], esquire for the body, gentlemen ushers, or esquires of the stable." On and on the statutes go, not neglecting the damascene ornamentation on swords and daggers or the trappings of horses and carefully making certain no doubt important exceptions: "Note that her majesty's meaning is not, by this order, to forbid in any person the wearing of silk buttons." Curtis, *Oxford and Cambridge in Transition*, 55.

A recent Marlowe biographer, Arate Ide, has argued that, by the time Marlowe arrived at Cambridge, Thexton had already moved to a nearby chamber in Corpus and that his place in Marlowe's dormitory room was taken by Samuel Beadle, the son of a Canterbury carpenter. Ide, *Localizing Marlowe*, 73.

On Francis Kett, see Dewey Wallace, Jr., "From Eschatology to Arian Heresy: The Case of Francis Kett (d. 1589)," *Harvard Theological Review* 67, no. 4 (1974): 459–73.

On Bruno in England, see Hilary Gatti, *The Renaissance Drama of Knowledge: Giordano Bruno in England* (1989; reprint Routledge, 2013); Ernan McMullin, "Giordano Bruno at Oxford," *Isis* 77, no. 1 (1986): 85–94; and Andrew D. Weiner, "Expelling the Beast: Bruno's Adventures in England," *Modern Philology* 78, no. 1 (1980): 1–13. On disputes in England over Copernicus, see John Russell, "The Copernican System in Great Britain," in *The Reception of Copernicus' Heliocentric Theory*, ed. Jerzy Dobrzycki (Springer, 1973), 189–239. For a more skeptical view of Bruno's account of his experience at Oxford, see Mordechai Feingold, "Giordano Bruno in England Revisited," *Huntington Library Quarterly* 67, no. 3 (2004): 329–46. Feingold claims that Bruno's abrasive personality, far more than his cosmology, accounted for his hostile reception. For a still controversial claim that Bruno was involved in spying on his hosts in the Italian embassy, see John Bossy, *Giordano Bruno and the Embassy Affair* (Yale University Press, 1991). The richest and most persuasive exploration of Bruno's relation to Marlowe is Rosanna Camerlingo, *Teatro e teologia: Marlowe, Bruno e i puritani* (Liguori, 1999).

Alan H. Nelson, ed., *Records of Early English Drama: Cambridge*, 2 vols. (University of Toronto Press, 1989), hereinafter cited as *REED*, is the crucial resource for theatrical activity in and around the university. For the prohibition of attendance at bullbaitings, etc., see *REED* 1:146; for the vice-chancellor's complaint, 1:291. For students advertising their plays, see John Harington, *Letters and Epigrams of Sir John Harington*, ed. Norman Egbert McClure (1814), cited in Peter Roberts, "The Studious Artizan: Christopher Marlowe, Canterbury and Cambridge," in *Christopher Marlowe and English Renaissance Culture*, ed. Darryll Grantley and Peter Roberts (Scolar Press, 1996), 35. For the disrupted performances, see Andrew J. Power, "Marlowe's Chamber Fellow and a Dramatic Disturbance at Cambridge in 1582," *Notes and Queries* 56, no. 1 (2009): 39–40. See also Daniel Blank, "Actors, Orators, and the Boundaries of Drama in Elizabethan Universities," *Renaissance Quarterly* 70, no. 2 (2017): 517–24. For Rainolds's attack on plays, see *Overthrow of Stage Plays* at https://quod.lib.umich.edu/e/eebo/A10335.0001.001?view=toc.

Students were not the only ones involved in writing plays; the master of Caius College, Thomas Legge, wrote an elaborate trilogy, *Richardus Tertius*, which he had performed in 1578–79 in the hall of St. John's.

Among the many important recent studies of homosexuality in early modern England, notable are Alan Bray, "Homosexuality and the Signs of Male Friendship in Elizabethan England," *History Workshop Journal* 29, no. 1 (1990): 1–19; Bray, *Homosexuality in Renaissance England* (Columbia University Press, 1995); Jonathan Goldberg, *Queering the Renaissance* (Duke University Press, 1993); Goldberg, *Sodometries: Renaissance Texts, Modern Sexualities* (Fordham University Press, 2010); David M. Halperin, *How to Do the History of*

*Homosexuality* (University of Chicago Press, 2002); and Bruce R. Smith, *Homosexual Desire in Shakespeare's England: A Cultural Poetics* (University of Chicago Press, 1991).

The investigation of a robbery at Eton College in 1541 brought to light a sexual relationship between the headmaster Nicholas Udall and two of his students. Udall confessed and was convicted, but he had powerful friends and was released after imprisonment for just under a year. Well-known as a writer, translator, playwright, and educator (with a reputation for mercilessly beating his students), he went on to be appointed headmaster of the prestigious Westminster School. This appointment did not imply approval of pederasty, but it does indicate that the general attitude toward homosexual relations in this period was far more indifferent than the ferocity of the statute suggests. The courts generally turned a blind eye to anything short of the forcible anal rape of an underage boy, while in painting and poetry the culture featured many expressions of same-sex intimacy.

CHAPTER 6: **Gold Buttons**

On late sixteenth-century universities, I have found particularly useful Curtis, *Oxford and Cambridge in Transition*; H. C. Porter, *Reformation and Reaction in Tudor Cambridge* (1958; reprint Cambridge University Press, 2015); and Lawrence Stone, "The Educational Revolution in England, 1580–1640," *Past and Present* 28, no. 1 (1964): 41–80. On the children of the elite invading the universities, Curtis quotes J. E. Neale, *Elizabethan House of Commons* (Cape, 1949): "In the fifteenth and early sixteenth century, most of the male children of the aristocracy and the landed gentry were educated at home by tutors. But by the latter half of the sixteenth century the situation changed. There was, as one historian put it, a 'cultural revolution' that is the inverse of our own" (63). "Invasion" is Curtis's term (65). The phenomenon was noted and lamented in 1577 by William Harrison, *Description of England*, quoted in Curtis (70). Burghley's order restricting career paths is quoted in Riggs, *World*, 71.

For Gabriel Harvey, see Virginia F. Stern, *Gabriel Harvey, His Life, Marginalia, and Library* (Clarendon Press, 1979). A brilliant essay by Lisa Jardine and Anthony Grafton, "Studied for Action: How Gabriel Harvey Read His Livy," *Past and Present* 129, no. 1 (1990): 30–78, illuminates Harvey's reading practices and those of the period more generally. On Harvey's age, see Mark Eccles, "Brief Lives: Tudor and Stuart Authors," *Studies in Philology* 79, no. 4 (1982): 62. On Harvey and Spenser sharing a bed, see Andrew Hadfield, *Edmund Spenser: A Life* (Oxford University Press, 2012).

In 1579 Spenser paid tribute to Harvey in his first published work, *The Shepherd's Calendar*. Harvey's observation that "good fellows" were reading Machiavelli is quoted in Curtis, *Oxford and Cambridge in Transition*, 119. "Almost all great men," he jotted to himself, "were outstanding orators either by nature or by art." Stern, *Gabriel Harvey*, 153. "A perfect orator," Harvey wrote in the margins of one of his books, is "a most excellent pleader and singular discourser in any civil court, or otherwise; not a bare professor of any one certain faculty." Jardine and Grafton, "Studied for Action," 43.

On Thomas Nashe, see Charles Nicholl, *A Cup of News: The Life of Thomas Nashe* (Routledge & Kegan Paul, 1984); Jonathan Crewe, *Unredeemed Rhetoric: Thomas Nashe and the Scandal of Authorship* (Johns Hopkins University Press, 1982); and Andrew Hadfield, "Marlowe and Nashe," *English Literary Renaissance* 51, no, 2 (2021): 190–216. Nashe's resentment of excessive sobriety is from "Christs Teares," in *Works*, ed. Ronald B. McKerrow, 3 vols. (Sidgwick & Jackson, 1910), 2.122–23. For Nashe's obsessive attacks on Harvey, see Nicholl, *Cup of News*, 32–35; Nashe, *The Unfortunate Traveller and Other Works* (1594), ed. J. B. Steane (Penguin Classics, 1972), 292–93.

On Ramus and rhetoric in the English universities, see Wilbur Howell, *Logic and Rhetoric in England, 1500–1700* (1961; reprint Princeton University Press, 1966). There is a brilliant account of Marlowe's staging of Ramus's murder in John Guillory, "Marlowe, Ramus, and the Reformation of Philosophy," *English Literary History* 81, no. 3 (2014): 693–732.

On Marlowe's encounter with Ortelius, see David Keck, "Marlowe and Ortelius' Map," *Notes and Queries* 52, no. 2 (2005): 189–90; Emrys Jones, "'A World of Ground': Terrestrial Space in Marlowe's 'Tamburlaine' Plays," *Yearbook of English Studies* 38, no. 1/2 (2008): 168–82; and especially Ethel Seaton, "Marlowe's Map," *Essays and Studies* 10 (1924): 13–35. Ortelius based the map of Central Asia, as he acknowledged, on one drawn by an English merchant, Anthony Jenkinson, who had gone to Moscow in the late 1550s, met with Ivan the Terrible, and then, with the tsar's letters of safe conduct, traveled overland through Tartar lands to Bukhara. (The turbaned ruler in the tent, as the label on the map explains, is an image of "Ioannes Basilius Magnus Imperator," that is, Tsar Ivan.)

For skepticism that the Corpus portrait can be securely connected with Marlowe, see Stephen Orgel, "Tobacco and Boys: How Queer Was Marlowe?" *GLQ: A Journal of Lesbian and Gay Studies* 6, no. 4 (2000): 555–76; and Lukas Erne, "Biography, Mythography, and Criticism: The Life and Works of Christopher Marlowe," *Modern Philology* 103, no. 1 (2005): 28–50. Against Erne's skepticism ("The lavish costume bespeaks considerable wealth" [29]), I cite the argument of A. D. Wraight, *Christopher Marlowe and Edward Alleyn* (Adam Hart, 1993), 68–69.

CHAPTER 7: **RECRUITMENT**

The widow Katherine Benchkin was the mother of John Benchkin, a fellow student at Corpus and presumably one of his friends. For a detailed description of Mrs. Benchkin's possessions, see Kuriyama, "Second Selves," 90.

On religious polemics in the period, see Alexandra Walsham, *Charitable Hatred: Tolerance and Intolerance in England, 1500–1700* (Manchester University Press, 2006). Pole's comment and the other examples of sectarian hatred are taken from Walsham. See also Rainer Forst, *Toleration in Conflict: Past and Present* (Cambridge University Press, 2013); Ole Peter Grell and Bob Scribner, eds., *Tolerance and Intolerance in the European Reformation* (Cambridge University Press, 1996); Benjamin J. Kaplan, *Divided by Faith: Religious Conflict and the Practice of Toleration in Early Modern Europe* (Belknap Press of Harvard University Press, 2007); Joseph Lecler, *Toleration and the Reformation*, trans. T. L. Westow (Association Press, 1960); James Simpson, *Burning to Read: English Fundamentalism and its Reformation Opponents* (Belknap Press of Harvard University Press, 2010). For Marmaduke Pickering, see Porter, *Reformation and Reaction*, 146. The estimate of the number of students coming monthly to Rheims is from Eccles, *Marlowe in London*, 28. The list of items seized from Caius's rooms is drawn from Hadfield, *Spenser*, 54.

On the spy service, see Conyers Read, *Mr. Secretary Walsingham and the Policy of Queen Elizabeth*, 3 vols. (Clarendon Press, 1925). Camden's description of Walsingham is from 1:340; the account of David Jones from 3:321–22; Nicholas Berden is from 2:331–33. See also Stephen Budiansky, *Her Majesty's Spymaster: Elizabeth I, Sir Francis Walsingham, and the Birth of Modern Espionage* (Penguin, 2005); Austin K. Gray, "Some Observations on Christopher Marlowe, Government Agent," *PMLA* 43, no. 3 (1928): 682–700; and Stephen Alford, "Some Elizabethan Spies in the Office of Sir Francis Walsingham," in *Diplomacy and Early Modern Culture*, ed. Robyn Adams and Rosanna Cox (Palgrave Macmillan, 2011): 46–62.

The hotter Protestants were grimly certain that the pope—not only Sixtus V but any pope— was the Antichrist. In a remarkable letter to Walsingham in December 1586, the double agent Maliverey Catilyn boasted about the work he had been doing while serving time in Newgate prison for his supposed Catholic sympathies. Catilyn befriended Catholic prisoners there and relayed whatever intelligence he could winkle out of them. He described accompanying several Catholic women to the roof of the prison to witness as the remains of those who had been hanged, drawn, and quartered were hoisted on poles. On the rooftop, he no doubt echoed the expressions of grief that the prisoners must have uttered at the spectacle of those whom they regarded as holy martyrs, but to Walsingham, Catilyn, alluding to Satan's temptation of Christ, makes a wry, gospel-inflected joke: "For a special favor they carried me up to the top of a pinnacle and showed me all the quarters of the traitors standing on that place, wishing me to fall down and worship them; but offered me no kingdom" (cf. Alford, "Some Elizabethan Spies," p. 56).

Among Walsingham's agents who could have been sent to instruct Marlowe was Gilbert Gifford, who was at the English College in Rheims for two years, from 1583 to 1585. Some four years older than Marlowe, Gifford had been studying for the priesthood first in Douai, then in Rome, and latterly in Rheims. Though he had been a troubled and irregular student, in October 1585 he was admitted to the deaconate, one step below Catholic priest. Shortly thereafter he began to turn up in Walsingham's records as a critically important figure in the plot to catch Mary, Queen of Scots. Gifford is perhaps the supreme example of the uncertain space occupied by many of the double agents. As soon as the trap he had so carefully helped to lay for Babington and the others was sprung, he vanished. He returned to Rheims where in March 1587 he was ordained a priest, and then later that same year, he was arrested in a brothel in bed with a man and a woman. The French authorities did not know what to do with him. They considered expelling him from the country, but then, thinking better of it and finding incriminating ciphers in his rooms, they put him on trial and condemned him to prison for twenty years for betraying the Catholic cause. When in 1590 the Protestant army of Henri IV besieged Paris, Gifford died, probably from starvation, in his prison cell.

On Baines, see Roy Kendall, *Christopher Marlowe and Richard Baines: Journeys Through the Elizabethan Underground* (Fairleigh Dickinson University Press, 2003). The description of William Allen is Baines's; Kendall, *Marlowe and Baines*, 8. On Poley, see Eugénie de Kalb, "Robert Poley's Movements as a Messenger of the Court, 1588–1601," *Review of English Studies* 9, no. 13 (1933): 13–18; Ethel Seaton, "Marlowe, Robert Poley, and the Tippings," *Review of English Studies* 5, no. 19 (1929): 273–87; and Seaton, "Robert Poley's Ciphers," *Review of English Studies* 7, no. 26 (1931): 137–50. Nicholl, *Reckoning*, is particularly good on the types of people drawn into the spy service in this period and the motives that drew them. The pervasive anxiety that encouraged the development of multiple spy networks is described in Lacy Baldwin Smith, *Treason in Tudor England: Politics and Paranoia* (Princeton University Press, 1986).

CHAPTER 8: **IN THE LIBERTIES**

On Norton Folgate, I am indebted to the extraordinary generosity of Geoffrey Marsh, who knows every inch of that neighborhood, past and present, and who introduced me to many of Marlowe's neighbors. See also Marsh's remarkable social history, *Living with Shakespeare: Saint Helen's Parish, London, 1593–1598* (Edinburgh University Press, 2021). The statutes against vagabondage are quoted from Chambers, *Elizabethan Stage*, 4:260, 270; the actors' petition to Leicester and the license are also from Chambers, 2:86, 87.

Among Marlowe's sources for *Tamburlaine*, in addition to Ortelius and the translation of Pedro Mexia's *Silva*, there is a description in English of Tamburlaine in Andreas Cambinus's *On the Origin of the Turkish and Ottoman Empire*. Marlowe would have encountered many more accounts in Latin, including Poggio Bracciolini's *The Vicissitudes of Fortune*, Petrus Perondinus's *Life of Tamburlaine the Great*, Paolo Giovio's *Notable Men and Women of Our Time*, and Battista Fregoso's *On Memorable Deeds and Words*.

For Ibn Khaldun's encounter, see *Ibn Khaldun and Tamerlane: Their Historic Meeting in Damascus, 1401*, ed. and trans. Walter J. Fischel (University of California Press, 1952): 29–47; emended version in "The Scholar and the Sultan: A Translation of the Historic Encounter between Ibn Khaldun and Timur," Ballandus, August 30, 2014, at https://ballandalus.wordpress.com/2014/08/30/the-scholar-and-the-sultana-translation-of-the-historic-encounter-between-ibn-khaldun-and-timur/.

On John Lyly, see G. K. Hunter, *John Lyly: The Humanist as Courtier* (Harvard University Press, 1962). On the Children's Companies, see Edel Lamb, *Performing Childhood in the Early Modern Theatre: The Children's Playing Companies (1599–1613)* (Palgrave Macmillan, 2009). On Robert Greene, see Richard Helgerson, *The Elizabethan Prodigals* (University of California Press, 1976). Greene's irregular work habits are described by Nashe in the letter to the reader in *Strange Newes* (1592). The underworld slang is adapted from Thomas Harman, *A Caveat for Common Cursitors* (1566), in *Cony-Catchers and Bawdy Baskets: An Anthology of Elizabethan Low Life*, ed. Gamini Salgado (Penguin, 1972), 150.

On the size of the military, see Charles Cruickshank, *Elizabeth's Army* (Clarendon Press, 1966). On discharged soldiers in London, see Nicholas Utzig, "Our Wars Are Done: Returning from War in the Drama of Shakespeare and His Contemporaries," PhD dissertation, Harvard University, 2022. The fate of the weaver White and of many others is recounted in F. G. Emmison, *Elizabethan Life: Disorder* (Essex County Council, 1970), 63–64.

On the "liberties" of London, see Stephen Mullaney, *The Place of the Stage: License, Play, and Power in Renaissance England* (University of Chicago Press, 1988).

Thanks to the detailed account book that he kept, noting income and expenses, Philip Henslowe is the key figure in any attempt to understand the development of the commercial theater in London: Henslowe, *Henslowe's Diary*, ed. Foakes and Rickert, and Carol Chillington Rutter, *Documents of the Rose Playhouse* (Manchester University Press, 1984). The momentous emergence of professional playing companies and the building of freestanding playhouses in London have been the objects of scholarly investigation since the 1923 publication of the four volumes of Chambers, *Elizabethan Stage*. Among the many distinguished studies are William Ingram, *The Business of Playing: The Beginnings of the Adult Professional Theater in Elizabethan London* (Cornell University Press, 1992); Glynne Wickham, *English Professional Theatre, 1530–1660* (Cambridge University Press, 2000); Roslyn Lander Knutson, *Playing Companies and Commerce in Shakespeare's Time* (Cambridge University Press, 2001); and Helen Ostovich, Holger Schott Syme, and Andrew Griffin, *Locating the Queen's Men, 1583–1603: Material Practices and Conditions of Playing* (Ashgate, 2009). Holger Schott Syme, in "The Meaning of Success: Stories of 1594 and Its Aftermath," *Shakespeare Quarterly* 61 (2010): 490–525, has significantly revised our understanding of commercial strategies in a highly competitive marketplace. Repertory scholars argue that most people went to see a "Strange's Men play" or "Queen's Men play," rather than one by Kyd or Marlowe or Greene.

CHAPTER 9: **THE CONQUEST OF LONDON**

Beside Ortelius, on whom he relied for geographical references, Marlowe found much of what he needed in a popular work by the Spanish humanist Pedro Mexia that had been translated into English and published in 1571 under the title *The Forest, or Collection of Histories No Less Profitable than Pleasant and Necessary*. For contemporary reactions to Marlowe's *Tamburlaine*, see Richard Levin, "The Contemporary Perception of Marlowe's *Tamburlaine*," *Medieval and Renaissance Drama in England* (1987); and Charles Whitney, *Early Responses to Renaissance Drama* (Cambridge University Press, 2006).

Holger Syme has challenged the widespread belief that *Tamburlaine* was an extraordinary innovation; see Syme, "Marlowe in His Moment," in *Christopher Marlowe in Context*, ed. Emily C. Bartels and Emma Smith (Cambridge University Press, 2013), 275–84. Syme argues that we simply do not know enough about the whole range of theatrical performances in the period to be confident that it was a radical departure. Its power over the imagination of contemporaries may be gauged, however, by the rapid diffusion of blank verse as the chosen medium for most poetic drama and by the surprising number of children who were christened Tamburlaine in the wake of Marlowe's success. See Rick Bowers, "Tamburlaine in Ludlow," *Notes and Queries* 45 (1998): 361–63; and Misha Teramura, "Tamburlaine in Ludlow, Again: Onomastic Evidence Reconsidered," *Notes and Queries* 63, no. 3 (2016): 464–66.

That the censor did not interfere with Marlowe's play, despite its disturbing implications, is perhaps explained as the consequence of the exotic setting and of the spectacle, welcome to all good Christians, of the defeat of the Turks. In *Localizing Marlowe*, Ide argues that for this reason Tamburlaine was regarded in the late sixteenth century as something of a hero.

On Edward Alleyn, see the *Dictionary of National Biography* entry by S. P. Cerasano; Cerasano, "Edward Alleyn, the New Model Actor, and the Rise of the Celebrity in the 1590s," *Medieval and Renaissance Drama in England* 18 (2005): 47–58; Cerasano, "Alleyn and Henslowe"; and Wraight, *Marlowe and Alleyn*.

On the risks entailed by accusations of atheism, see Michael Hunter, "The Problem of 'Atheism' in Early Modern England," *Transactions of the Royal Historical Society* 35 (1985): 135–57; and Michael Hunter and David Wootton, eds., *Atheism from the Reformation to the Enlightenment* (Clarendon Press, 1992). The execution of Aikenhead, urged on by the Scottish clerics, was the last under the Blasphemy Act, but the act remained in force. As late as the 1920s, people were convicted, fined, and imprisoned for calling into question or mocking the state-sanctioned religion.

CHAPTER 10: **Secret Sharers**

On Marlowe's probable hand in the *Henry VI* plays, see Gary Taylor and Gabriel Egan, *The New Oxford Shakespeare: Authorship Companion* (Oxford University Press, 2017). "Provocative agent" is the phrase of Nicholas Brooke, "Marlowe as Provocative Agent in Shakespeare's Early Plays," *Shakespeare Survey* 14 (2007): 34–44. There is a brilliant account of Shakespeare's relationship with Marlowe in James Shapiro, *Rival Playwrights: Marlowe, Jonson, Shakespeare* (Columbia University Press, 1991). I discuss Shakespeare's financial calculations and his social anxiety in *Will in the World: How Shakespeare Became Shakespeare* (Norton, 2004).

Donne's lines on singing at doors for meat are from *Satire 2*: "Sir; though (I thank God for it) I do hate." On patronage in this period, see Guy Fitch Lytle and Stephen Orgel, eds., *Patronage in the Renaissance* (Princeton University Press, 2014). On the Tudors' taste in clothing and jewels, see Elizabeth A. H. Cleland and Adam Eaker, eds., *The Tudors: Art and Majesty in Renaissance England* (Metropolitan Museum of Art, 2022), and my review of the exhibition, "Competitive Consumption," *New York Review of Books* 69 (2022), on which I have drawn for this account. Churchyard's complaint is from Edwin Haviland Miller, *The Professional Writer in Elizabethan England: A Study of Nondramatic Literature* (1959; reprint Harvard University Press, 2014), 119. Richard Robinson's happier outcome is cited in Gerald Eades Bentley, *The Professions of Dramatist and Player in Shakespeare's Time, 1590–1642* (1972; reprint Princeton University Press, 2015), 90. For Nashe's threats, see "Pierce Penniless and His Supplication to the Devil" (1592), in *The Unfortunate Traveller and Other Works*, ed. J. B. Steane (Penguin, 1972), 49–145.

CHAPTER 11: **Hog Lane**

Montaigne's reflections on his friendship with Étienne de la Boétie are in his great essay "On Friendship." For the Renaissance cult of friendship, see Reginald Hyatte, *The Arts of Friendship: The Idealization of Friendship in Medieval and Early Renaissance Literature* (Brill, 1994); Ullrich Langer, *Perfect Friendship: Studies in Literature and Moral Philosophy from Boccaccio to Corneille* (Droz, 1994); Alan Bray, *The Friend* (University of Chicago Press, 2003); Peter Burke, "Humanism and Friendship in Sixteenth-Century Europe," in *Friendship in Medieval Europe*, ed. Julian P. Haseldine (Stroud, 1999), 262–72; and Barry Weller, "The Rhetoric of Friendship in Montaigne's *Essais*," *New Literary History* 9, no. 3 (1978): 503–23.

For Watson's poetry, see Thomas Watson, *The Complete Works (1556–1592)*, ed. Dana Sutton, 2 vols. (Edward Mellen Press, 1997). On Watson's life, see the *Dictionary of National Biography* entry by Albert Chatterley; Chatterley, "Thomas Watson: Works, Contemporary References and Reprints," *Notes and Queries* 48, no. 3 (2001): 239–49; Eccles, "Brief Lives"; and the discussions in Nicholl, *Reckoning*; Riggs, *World*; Kuriyama, *Renaissance Life*; and Honan, *Marlowe: Poet and Spy*. The remark about the Watson's "knavery" was made by William Cornwallis, whose elder daughter was evidently the object of one of Watson's scams. Watson's offer to be Philip Howard's Ganymede is in Latin: *Inde satis foelix, dicar tuus esse Poeta, / Et famulus fieri cum Ganymede Iouis*. On the vogue for pastoral, see Paul J. Alpers, *What Is Pastoral?* (University of Chicago Press, 1996).

On the passionate shepherd, see R. S. Forsythe, "The Passionate Shepherd and English Poetry," in *PMLA* 40, no. 3 (1925): 692–742; Bakeless, *Tragicall History*, 2:149–60; Susanne Woods, "'The Passionate Sheepheard' and 'The Nimphs Reply': A Study of Transmission," *Huntington Library Quarterly* 34, no. 1 (1970): 25–33; and Douglas Bruster, "'Come to the Tent Again': 'The Passionate Shepherd,' Dramatic Rape and Lyric Time," *English Renaissance Literature* 33, no. 1 (1991): 49–72. For some examples of replies, see "Replies and Parodies," Come Live with Me, https://comelivewithmeballad.com/replies-parodies/.

CHAPTER 12: **The Counterfeiters**

The account of Baines's "confession," with its eerie relation to the charges he later leveled at Marlowe, is from Kendall, *Marlowe and Baines*, quotations on 513 and 521. Marlowe's boast that he learned to counterfeit from Poole is taken from the note that Baines wrote to the Privy Council the next year (Kuriyama, *Christopher Marlowe*, 220), but it is consistent with the account of the accusation in Robert Sidney's letter.

CHAPTER 13: **STRANGE COMPANY**

On the Stanley family, see Barry Coward, *The Stanleys, Lords Stanley and Earls of Derby, 1385–1672: The Origins, Wealth, and Power of a Landowning Family* (Manchester University Press, 1983).

On Ferdinando Stanley's involvement in the theater, see Lawrence Manley and Sally-Beth MacLean, *Lord Strange's Men and Their Plays* (Yale University Press, 2014). Alleyn, who was the central figure in many of the plays performed by the company, must have had a prodigious memory: "This pace of production meant that in less than a year, between 19 February 1591/92 and 1 February 1592/93, Edward Alleyn had to recall or learn at least twenty-nine major roles, many of them hundreds of lines long, in fact among the longest roles created in the period" (71). For Sir Edward Stanley's expedition to Malta, see Lisa Hopkins, "'Malta of Gold': Marlowe, *The Jew of Malta*, and the Siege of 1565," *(Re)Soundings* 1, no. 2 (1997).

On the reception and uses of Machiavelli, see Irving Ribner, "Marlowe and Machiavelli," *Comparative Literature* 6, no. 4 (1954): 348–56; N. W. Bawcutt, "Machiavelli and Marlowe's *The Jew of Malta*," *Renaissance Drama* 3 (1970): 3–49; Alessandro Arienzo and Alessandra Petrina, *Machiavellian Encounters in Tudor and Stuart England: Literary and Political Influences from the Reformation to the Restoration* (Routledge, 2013); and Cristiano Ragni, "Marlowe's 'Damnable Opinions': Bruno, Machiavelli, and Gentili in *The Massacre at Paris*," *InVerbis: Lingue Letterature Culture* 6, no. 2 (2016): 35–53. It was not only at university that Machiavelli's works were being secretly read. *The Prince* was quickly translated into Latin—Latin being more widely understood in England than Italian—and then into English. The whole book was laboriously copied by hand—one of the surviving manuscripts appears to have been written out by Thomas Kyd—and secretly circulated. For the anti-Jewish theological context in which Machiavelli makes his appearance in Marlowe's play, see G. K. Hunter, "The Theology of Christopher Marlowe's *Jew of Malta*," in Hunter, *Dramatic Identities and Cultural Tradition: Studies in Shakespeare and His Contemporaries* (Liverpool University Press, 1978).

On the death of Ferdinando Stanley, see William Jeffcoate, "Why Did the 5th Earl of Derby Die?" *Lancet* 357, no. 9271 (2001): 1876–79; and Judith Bonzol, "The Death of the Fifth Earl of Derby: Cunning Folk and Medicine in Early Modern England," *Renaissance and Reformation* 33, no. 4 (2010): 73–100.

CHAPTER 14: **DANGEROUS ACQUAINTANCES**

The revised (2022) *Dictionary of National Biography* entry on Sir Walter Ralegh, by Mark Nicholls and Penry Williams, is unusually full and helpful. Philip

Edwards, *Sir Walter Ralegh* (Longmans, Green, 1953), remains informative. On Ralegh's theatrical sense of life, which may have attracted him to Marlowe, see my *Sir Walter Ralegh: The Renaissance Man and His Roles* (Yale University Press, 1973). The charges of atheism against Ralegh are weighed in Ernest Strathmann, *Sir Walter Ralegh: A Study in Elizabethan Skepticism* (Columbia University Press, 1951). Persons's charge about the "school of atheism" appears in Robert Persons, *An Advertisement Written to a Secretary of my Lord Treasurers of England, by an English Intelligencer as He Passed Through Germany Towards Italy* (1592), 18.

Marlowe might have been introduced to Ralegh by the learned poet and playwright George Chapman, who maintained a long-term relationship with them both. In later years, he wrote a continuation of the poem *Hero and Leander* that Marlowe left unfinished when he was murdered in 1593, and he likewise wrote a long poem celebrating Ralegh's "discovery" of Guiana in 1595 and urging Queen Elizabeth to support his patron's plans for Guiana's colonization.

On Thomas Harriot, see John W. Shirley, *Thomas Harriot: A Biography* (Clarendon Press, 1983); Robert Fox, ed., *Thomas Harriot: Science and Discovery in the English Renaissance* (Routledge, 2023); and Susanne S. Webb, "Raleigh, Hariot, and Atheism in Elizabethan and Early Stuart England," *Albion* 1, no. 1 (1969): 10–18. Harriot knew that the defenders of orthodoxy were always watching and hoping for him to make a fatal blunder. He did his best to keep his Epicurean views to himself or to share them only in private with trusted friends.

On the Algonkians brought to London and the impression they made, see Alden Vaughan, "Ralegh's Indian Interpreters, 1584–1618," *William and Mary Quarterly* 3rd ser., 59, no. 2 (2002): 341–76. A German visitor to London at the time got a glimpse of them and reported that though they were now clad in brown taffeta, "their usual habit was a mantle of rudely tanned skins of wild animals, no shirts, and a pelt before their privy parts." "No one was able to understand them," he added, "and they made a most childish and silly figure." But Ralegh understood that his guests—who seem not to have been kidnapped, as so many other Natives were, but to have made the long voyage willingly—could be something more than an exotic curiosity. Hence his eagerness to have Harriot learn their language and travel to Virginia to observe the disposition of the inhabitants.

I explore the subversive implications of Harriot's *Brief and True Report* in my *Shakespearean Negotiations: The Circulation of Social Energy in Renaissance England* (University of California Press, 1988), 21–65.

On Marlowe's relation to the printers and their stalls in St. Paul's Churchyard and elsewhere, see Kiséry, "Author and Bookshop." Kiséry's focus is on the posthumous publication of Marlowe's work, but he suggests as well that the printers may have known and discussed some of these works while the author was still alive.

CHAPTER 15: **WIZARDRY**

On Henry Percy, the 9th Earl of Northumberland, see Gordon Batho, "The Wizard Earl of Northumberland: An Elizabethan Scholar-Nobleman," *Historian* 75 (2002): 19–23; Batho, "The Library of the 'Wizard' Earl: Henry Percy, Ninth Earl of Northumberland (1564–1632," *Library* 15, no. 4 (1960): 246–61; Batho, *Thomas Harriot and the Northumberland Household* (Oriel College, 1992); Mark Nicholls, "The 'Wizard Earl' in Star Chamber: The Trial of the Earl of Northumberland, June 1606," *Historical Journal* 30, no. 1 (1987): 173–89; Robert Kargon, "Thomas Hariot, the Northumberland Circle and Early Atomism in England," *Journal of the History of Ideas* 27, no. 1 (1966): 128–36; and Stephen Clucas, "'Noble Virtue in Extremes': Henry Percy, Ninth Earl of Northumberland, Patronage and the Politics of Stoic Consolation," *Renaissance Studies* 9, no. 3 (1995): 267–91. (For Percy's awakening interest in science, see esp. 269–70). Misha Teramura has edited "Against Friendship: An Essay by the 'Wizard' Earl of Northumberland," *English Literary Renaissance* 47, no. 3 (2017): 380–411.

On Simon Forman, see Louis Adrian Montrose, "'Shaping Fantasies': Figurations of Gender and Power in Elizabethan Culture," in *Representations* 2 (1983): 61–94; Barbara Howard Traister, *The Notorious Astrological Physician of London: Works and Days of Simon Forman* (University of Chicago Press, 2000); Lauren Kassell, *Medicine and Magic in Elizabethan London: Simon Forman, Astrologer, Alchemist, and Physician* (Clarendon Press, 2005); and Per Sivefors, "Sex and the Self: Simon Forman, Subjectivity and Erotic Dreams in Early Modern England," in *Pangs of Love and Longing: Configurations of Desire in Premodern Literature*, ed. Anders Cullhed et al. (Cambridge Scholars, 2013). On Forman's theater-world clients, see Susan P. Cerasano, "Philip Henslowe, Simon Forman, and the Theatrical Community of the 1590s," *Shakespeare Quarterly* 44, no. 2 (1993): 145–58.

On John Dee, see Peter J. French, *John Dee: The World of an Elizabethan Magus* (Routledge & Kegan Paul, 1972); Glyn Parry, *The Arch-Conjuror of England: John Dee* (Yale University Press, 2011); Mordechai Feingold, "A Conjurer and a Quack? The Lives of John Dee and Simon Forman," *Huntington Library Quarterly* 68, no. 3 (2005): 545–59; and R. Julian Roberts and Andrew G. Watson, *John Dee's Library Catalogue* (Bibliographical Society, 1990). R. Julian Roberts is the author of the substantial entry in the *Dictionary of National Biography*. See also David Collins, "Learned Magic," in Collins, ed., *The Cambridge History of Magic and Witchcraft in the West* (Cambridge University Press, 2015), 332–60.

For the cracking in the theater during a performance of *Doctor Faustus*, see T.M., *The Black Book* (1604): "like one of my Devells in Dr. Faustus when the old Theater cracks and frighted the audience," in *Christopher Marlowe's Doctor Faustus: A 1604-Version Edition*, ed. Michael Keefer (Broadview Press, 1991), lv. For the extra devil, see William Prynne, *Histrio-Mastix* (1633): "The visible apparition of the devil on the stage at the Bel Savage playhouse in Queen Elizabeth's days (to the great amazement both of the actors and spectators), whiles they were there profanely playing the *History of Faustus*, the truth of which I have heard from many now alive who well remember it, there being some distracted with that fearful sight," in *English Professional Theatre, 1530–1660*, ed. Glynne Wickham, Herbert Berry, and William Ingram (Cambridge, 2000), 303; and G. J. R., quoted in Chambers, *Elizabethan Stage*, 3:424. See also Genevieve Guenther, "Why Devils Came When Faustus Called Them," *Modern Philology* 109, no. 1 (2011): 46–70.

## CHAPTER 16: THE FAUSTIAN BARGAIN

A sampling of the vast critical literature on *Doctor Faustus* may be found in David Scott Kastan, ed., *Doctor Faustus: A Two-Text Edition*, 2nd ed. (Norton, 2023). On the comparably vast scholarly literature on the historical Faust, see the texts collected and translated in Philip M. Palmer and Robert P. More, *The Sources of the Faust Tradition: From Simon Magus to Lessing* (Oxford University Press, 1936). A lively and richly informative recent account is by Anthony Grafton, *Magus: The Art of Magic from Faustus to Agrippa* (Belknap Press of Harvard University Press, 2023).

Among the many fine essays on Marlowe's play, I have found particularly resonant Edward Snow, "Marlowe's *Doctor Faustus* and the Ends of Desire," in *Two Renaissance Mythmakers: Christopher Marlowe and Ben Jonson*, ed. Alvin B. Kernan (Johns Hopkins University Press, 1977), 70–110; and C. L. Barber, "The Form of Faustus' Fortunes Good or Bad," *Tulane Drama Review* 8, no. 4 (1964): 92–119. Snow brilliantly analyzes the uses of the word "end" in Marlowe's play. Calvin's grim words are from *Institutes of the Christian Religion*, 3:23. On Faustus and the desire to know everything, see Leonard F. Doster, "The Man Who Wanted to Know Everything," 1980 Bithell Memorial Lecture (University of London, 1981). On the failure of Faustus's knowledge, see Katherine Eggert, *Disknowledge: Literature, Alchemy, and the End of Humanism in Renaissance England* (University of Pennsylvania Press, 2015), 134–43; and Andrew Duxfield, *Christopher Marlowe and the Failure to Unify* (Ashgate, 2015), 65–87. Pope John Paul II named Isidore of Seville patron saint of the internet.

The earliest printed texts of *Doctor Faustus* conclude with a very peculiar Latin tag: *Terminat hora diem, terminat Author opus*, "The hour ends the day; the author ends his work." These words are not spoken by anyone in the play; they are presumably meant to be the author's words penned at the moment he brought his work to its end. The phrase, tying together the magician doomed at the day's end and the author at his play's conclusion, confirms what has all along been implied: Faustus and Marlowe are inseparably linked.

For the attacks on the theater, see Chambers, *Elizabethan Stage*, 4:197 (Thomas White), 4:198 (John Northbrooke), and 4:222 ("idleness," Phillip Stubbes).

CHAPTER 17: **NEPTUNE'S SMILE**

On *Edward II*, see Roslyn L. Knutson, "Marlowe, Company Ownership, and the Role of Edward II," *Medieval and Renaissance Drama in England* 18 (2006): 37–46; Graham Hammill, *Sexuality and Form: Caravaggio, Marlowe, and Bacon* (University of Chicago Press, 2000); and the works on homosexuality cited for Chapter 5.

On the close of *Hero and Leander*, see Marion Campbell, "'Desunt Nonnulla': The Construction of Marlowe's *Hero and Leander* as an Unfinished Poem," *English Literary History* 51, no. 2 (1984): 241–68; and Gordon Braden, "Hero and Leander in Bed (and the Morning After)," *English Literary Renaissance* 45, no. 2 (2015): 205–30.

CHAPTER 18: **INTO THE LIGHT**

The inventory to Scadbury is quoted in Honan, *Marlowe: Poet and Spy*, 329. On Henry Maunder, see Mark Brayshay, "Messengers, Pursuivants and Couriers: Agents of the English State, c.1512–c.1640," in *Postal History: Multidisciplinary and Diachronic Perspectives*, ed. Bruno Crevato-Selvaggi and Raffaella Gerola (Quaderni di storia postale, 2020). I am grateful to Geoffrey Marsh for information about Maunder. Marlowe's death was the object of much moralizing by contemporaries; see Brooke, "Reputation of Marlowe."

In 1923–24 the twenty-six-year-old Leslie Hotson made his spectacular find of the records of the inquest into Marlowe's murder: Hotson, *Death of Marlowe*. Since then there has been a flood of scholarly and popular speculation. Nicholl, *Reckoning*, provides the richest details, but Nicholl's theory that Marlowe was murdered as a pawn in the factional struggle between Ralegh and Essex has not been widely accepted. The claim that the invitation to Deptford came from Frizer was made by William Vaughan, *The Golden Grove* (1600); see Nicholl, *Reckoning*, 77. Nicholl argues that in most details Vaughan is reliable.

Nicholl notes that, of the twenty-six disbursements to Poley extant in the official records for the years from 1588 to 1601, the 1593 payment is the only one to contain the phrase "being in Her Majesty's service all the aforesaid time." Therefore, "technically speaking," Nicholl writes, "Poley was on government business" on the day he joined Marlowe, Frizer, and Skeres in Deptford. One wonders if the thirty pieces of silver also paid for whatever role he played in the events that transpired on May 30. The document recording payment to Poley is in Nicholl, *Reckoning*, 32. See also Alford, "Some Elizabethan Spies," 52.

Paul E. J. Hammer, "A Reckoning Reframed: The 'Murder' of Christopher Marlowe Revisited," *English Literary Renaissance* 26, no. 2 (1996): 225–42, argues that Marlowe's death is more likely to have been "a momentary blunder" than a planned killing. That view is shared by John Bossy, "Trust the Coroner," *London Review of Books* 28, no. 24 (2006): 14; by Kuriyama, *Renaissance Life*, 136; and most recently by Ide, *Localizing Marlowe*. Honan, *Marlowe: Poet and Spy*, 342, places the blame on Thomas Walsingham.

# INDEX

Page numbers in *italics* refer to illustrations.

*Abduction of Helen, The* (Watson), 210
Act of Uniformity, 229
actors, 146–48, 300; *see also* theater companies
*Aeneid* (Virgil), 44–45, 49
*Aesop's Fables*, 48
Aguecheek, Sir Andrew, 58
Aikenhead, Thomas, 140, 310
Alexander the Great, 244
Algonkian language, 201, 202
Algonkians, 206, 275, 313
Allen, Cardinal William, 93, 94, 95, 98, 99, 103, 188
Alleyn, Edward "Ned," 137–39, *138*, 147, 177, 183, 216, 312
Alleyn, Joan Henslowe, 137, 139
*Alphonsus, King of Aragon* (Greene), 140
*Amores* (Ovid), 70, 71–72, 251
*Amyntae Gaudia* (Watson), 168–69
*Amyntas* (Watson), 161, 164
ancient poetry, 43–45

anti-Catholic plays, 34
*Antigone* translation (Watson), 160
antiquities, study of, 38–52
antisemitism, 183–84
antitheatrical movement, 66; *see also* moralists
Aquinas, Thomas, 30
Archbishop of Canterbury, *see* Whitgift, John, Archbishop of Canterbury
*argumentum in utramque partem*, 67–68
Ariosto, Ludovico, 6
aristocracy, 76, 77, 88, 122, 147, 149–50
Aristophanes, 48
Aristotle, 40, 63, 69, 78, 82, 88, 224, 231, 234
Arthur, Katherine, 24; *see also* Marlowe, Katherine Arthur
Arthur, Thomas, 25
Arthur, Ursula, 25
arts, training in, 78

*As You Like It* (Shakespeare), 265, 283, 284–85
Ascham, Roger, 41–43
  *The Scholemaster*, 41–42, 48
atheism, 93, 94, 204–5, 279, 280–81, 310
atomism, 200
Augustine, Saint, 39–40, 44, 224

Babington, Anthony, 106–12, *109*, 165, 307
Bacon, Francis, 7, 236
Baines, Richard, 98–101, 103–4, 107, 110, 172–73, 175, 186, 270–73, 280, 311
Baldock, Robert, 178–79
Bale, John, 33, 34–35, 299
Ball, Cutting, 119
Ball, Em, 119
Ballard, John, 106–7, 109
Barnfield, Richard, 151
Barrow, Henry, 58, 59–60
Beard, Thomas, 283
  *The Theatre of God's Judgments*, 280–81
Bede, *Sermons*, 48
Belgium, refugees from, 10–11
Benchkin, Katherine, 90, 306
Berden, Nicholas, 111; *see also* Rogers, Thomas
betrayal, threat of, 165
Bible, 42, 43, 70, 231, 232, 233, 241
Billingford Hutch, 69
Bishop of London, 72
Bishop of Winchester, 119
Black Mass, 229
blank verse, 134, 135, 137
Blasphemy Act, 310
Blount, Edward, 31, 282

Boccaccio, 42
Boleyn, Anne, 3, 191
book burnings, 72
book-buying public, 118
Borrowes, Richard, 299
Boswell, James, 199
Bosworth Field, battle of, 178
Botticelli, Sandro, 6
Bradley, William, 167, 170, 278
Brahe, Tycho, 211
Bridewell prison, 17, 18, 104
*Brief and True Report* (Harriot), 202–4, 206–7
Browne, Leonard, 27
Browne, Robert, 58
Brownists, 58
Bruno, Giordano, 60–61, 140, 158, 211, 302
Bucer, Martin, 54
Buckle Book, 63
Buggery Act, 73–74, 75
Bull, Eleanor, 276, 277, 279, 280
Bull, the, 113
Burgess, Anthony, 280
Burghley, Lord; *see* Cecil, William, Lord Burghley
Burnell, Anne, 165, 166
Burnell family, 166
Buttery Books, 58, 59, 89–90, 111
Byng, Andrew, 93–94

Caesar, Julius, 41
Caius, John, 93–94, 98
Calvin, John, 96, 114, 232–33
Calvinism, 240
Calvinists, 100
Cambridge University, 3, 36, 51, 119, 175–76, 182, 199, 209, 227, 229, 238, 240, 243–44, 250, 271
  attendance as class distinction, 76

College of Corpus Christi and the
   Blessed Virgin Mary, 53–75,
   59, 77–87, 89–90, 95–96,
   111, 153, 229, 235, 262
 commencement ceremony at, 64
 course of study at, 62–63, 67–68
 dress code at, 55–56, 302
 Elizabeth I visits, 79
 examinations at, 88
 Gonville and Caius College, 65,
   66, 107
 Greco-Roman tradition taught at,
   62–63
 influx of wealthy to, 81
 King's College, 66
 Latin used at chapel of Corpus,
   95–96
 Marlowe at, 53–75, 77–87
 peculiarity of, 57–58
 Pembroke College (Hall), 80
 Peterhouse College, 58
 recruitment at, 88–112
 schedule at, 62–64
 St. John's College, 66
 student life at, 63–65
 theatrical entertainment at, 64–65
 Trinity College, 66
Camden, William, 96
Campanella, Tommaso, 223
Canterbury, England, 32–34, 53–54,
   57, 81, 100, 111, 117, 154, 176,
   228, 284
 Marlowe's youth in, 23–28
 reformers in, 34–35
 Roman Catholicism and, 33–34
*Canterbury Tales* (Chaucer), 34
Carthage, 44
Castellio, Sebastian, 47
Catholic Church; *see* Roman Catholic Church

Catholic Humanists, 62
Catholic rebels, 197
Catholic sympathizers, 114, 171
Catholic terrorists, 222
Catholicism; *see* Roman Catholicism
Catilyn, Malivery, 306–7
Cawking, Mrs., 111
Cecil, Robert, 192
Cecil, William, Lord Burghley, 55,
   56, 77, 93–94, 96, 159, 171, 175,
   190
Chapman, George, 267, 313
Chappell, William, 56
Charles V, Holy Roman Emperor,
   220
Chaucer, Geoffrey, 48
 *Canterbury Tales*, 34
Cholmeley, John, 119–20
Cholmeley, Richard, 205–7, 215–16,
   262, 269–70, 272–73, 274
Christianity, 38–41, 42, 57, 58,
   283–84; *see also* Judeo-
   Christian tradition; Protestant-
   ism; Roman Catholicism
Church of England, 4, 33–34, 57,
   58, 69, 76, 89, 94–96, 165, 187,
   189, 233
Church of St. Nicholas, 279
Churchyard, Thomas, 150, 151
Chytraeus, David, 47
Cicero ("Tully"), 41, 42, 47, 63, 69
class, universities and, 76–87
clergy, as only professional option for
   university graduates, 77
Clink, the, 119
Coligny, Admiral Gaspard II de, 96
Colonna, Vittoria, 6
*Compleat Angler, The* (Walsingham),
   194
Condell, Henry, 155

conquistadores, 236
Conrad, Joseph, 154
Copernican theory, 60–61
Copernicus, Nicolaus, 283
Cortés, Hernán, 198
counterfeiting, 170–75, 184
Cranmer, Thomas, 26, 48, 300
criminality, fascination with, 23
Croydon, 276
Cruickshank, G. C., 123
Cuffe, Henry, 179
curriculum, shift from theology-based to classics-based, 77
Curtain, the, 113, 120
*Cymbeline* (Shakespeare), 219

Dalton, Mr., 165
Danby, William, 277–78
Dare, Virginia, 201
Davies, Sir John, 72
de la Boétie, Étienne, 158
de Vere, Edward, Earl of Oxford, 161
dead, speaking with the, 46
dedications, 150–51, 160, 161, 168–69
Dee, John, 212, 220, 226
Della Porta, Giovanni, 210
Deptford, England, 275–76, 277, 279, 280, 285
Devereux, Robert, 2nd Earl of Essex, 96, 150, 171, 280
di San Giuseppe, Sebastiano, 197
Digges, Anne, 166
disputations, 63, 302
dissidents, 91–95, 102
*Doctor Faustus* (Marlowe), 51, 68, 82–83, 85, 224, 226–52, 227, 253–55, 259, 292, 302, 315
genesis of, 213–16, 217–19, 220–22, 226, 227–28

Latin in, 228, 315
literary sources of, 213–16, 217–19, 226
Marlowe's personal investment in Faustus story and, 238, 245–46, 315
power/knowledge in, 236–37
as response to moralists' attack on theater, 247–48
sources of, 238
Donne, John, 149
"The Bait," 163
daughter of, 139
Douai, France, 159
double translation, task of, 46
Douglas, Lord Alfred, 261
Dover, England, 24, 176
Drake, Sir Francis, 165, 201, 276
Drayton, Michael, 32
dress, as marker of social ambition, 85, 302
Drury, Thomas, 269–70
Dudley, Robert, Earl of Leicester, 122, 150
Dulwich College, 139
Durham House, 195–96, 201, 207, 216
Dutch Church, 10, 11, 262, 269
libel of, 10–16, 18, 19
Dutch Protestants, 170

Earl of Essex, *see* Devereux, Robert, 2nd Earl of Essex
Earl of Essex's Men, 154
Earl of Leicester, *see* Dudley, Robert, Earl of Leicester
Earl of Leicester's Men, 122, 154
Earl of Oxford's Men, 154
Earl of Southampton, *see* Wriothesley, Henry
Earl of Sussex's Men, 154

Earldom of Derby, 175, 176–92
education, 38, 41, 50–51, 76–77
Edward II, 256–61, 265
*Edward II* (Marlowe), 31, 85, 86, 156, 178, 256–61, 265–66
Edward VI, 4, 146
Egypt, 39
Eliot, T. S., 184
Elizabeth I, Queen of England, *xii*, 4, 66, 91, 146, 159, 178, 187, 188, 201, 220, 280
  aging of, 191
  assassination plots and, 92–93, 95, 99, 103, 104, 107–12, 171
  Catholic uprising against, 209
  court of, 5–6
  death of, 114
  education of, 41
  excommunication of, 94–95, 103
  issue of succession and, 8
  levies of troops under, 123–24
  Ralegh and, 197–98
  social mobility under, 77
  theatrical entertainment and, 121–23, 124
  threats to, 100
  tracks gift giving, 149–50
  visits Cambridge, 79
Elizabethan culture, 73, 149
Elizabethan drama
  condemnation of, 13, 73, 121, 122–23, 125, 247
  language and form of, 125
  stage conventions and, 248
  subsidized by authorities, 65–66, 73
  *see also specific authors and works*
Elmley, John, 36
Elyot, Thomas, 47
encyclopedists, 234
England, Spanish plot to invade, 244
English Book of Common Prayer, 95

English College, Rheims, 92, 93, 95, 97–100, 103, 104, 159, 172, 284
*English Faust Book*, 213–16, 217–19, 226, 236
English language, 3
English Renaissance, 7, 23, 40–42, 48, 139, 235
  celebration of friendship in, 164–65
  Renaissance humanism, 40–42
Erasmus, 43, 47, 48, 62
espionage, 91–98, 100–112, 114, 116–17, 171, 172, 243
*Etymologiae* (Isidore of Seville), 234
Evaunce, Thomas, 63
*Everyman*, 125
executions, 3, 4–5, 9, 35, 59–60, 109–10, 140, 262

*Fall of the Late Arrian, The* (Proctor), 18, 51, 57
Faunt, Nicholas, 100–101, 104
Faust, Johann Georg, 213–16
Felle, James, 33
festive rituals, banned, 34–36, 124–25
fiction, vs. truth, 42, 43
First Folio of 1623, 143, 155
Fitzalan Henry, 12th Earl of Arundel, 160
Flushing, England, 170–73
forgery, 170–75; *see also* counterfeiting
Forman, Simon, 218–29
Fortescue, Captain (pseudonym), 106–7
Foucault, Michel, 236
France, 96, 123, 158
  Catholic exiles in, 91–93
  refugees from, 10
Fraunce, Abraham, 161

freedom of thought, 23
French poetic models, 3
friendship, Renaissance celebration of, 164–65
Frisius Gemma, 48
Frizer, Ingram, 263, 276–77, 278–79, 280, 285
Frogmorton, Master, 4

Gaveston, Piers de, 256–61
Gent., P.F., 213–16, 236
gentry, 83, 88, 149
Gerard, John, 188–89
Gifford, Gilbert, 174, 307
gift exchange, 149–50
*Golden Hind*, 276
Golding, Arthur, 70–71
Googe, Barnabe, 6
*Gort a Ghearradh* ("The Field of Cutting"), 197
Gospels, 42, 92
Gosson, Stephen, 47
Graddell, Dorothy Marlowe, 24
Graddell, Thomas, 24
Gray, Arthur, Lord Deputy of Ireland, 80, 197, 198
Greco-Roman tradition, 62–63, 164
vs. Judeo-Christian tradition, 38–41
Greek language, 50, 52, 160
Greene, Fortunatus, 119
Greene, Robert, 14, 76–77, 78, 118–20, 136–37, 140
*Alphonsus, King of Aragon*, 140
Greenwich Palace, 275
Greenwood, John, 58, 59–60, 262
Gresshop, John, 46–48, 49, 50–51, 69, 70, 100
Grey, Lady Jane, 4
Grimald, Nicholas, 6
Guiana, 225
Gunpowder Plot, 222

Hague, the, 276
*Hamlet* (Shakespeare), 13, 155, 166, 253, 260, 296
Hare, Robert, 114
Harriot, Thomas, 199–200, 201, 202–3, 204–5, 212, 220, 222, 223, 236, 251, 273–74, 313
*Brief and True Report*, 202–4, 206–7
Harris, Thomas, 56
Harrison, William, 76
Harvey, Gabriel, 78–80, 83, 182, 305
*Hekatompathia, The, or, Passionate Century of Love* (Watson), 161
hell, concept of, 240–42
Heminges, John, 155
*Henry IV* (Shakespeare), 156
Henry VI, King of England, 142
*Henry VI* trilogy (Shakespeare), 143–46, 151, 179, 256
Henry VII, King of England (Henry Tudor), 178
Henry VIII, King of England, 3, 73, 77, 95, 146, 147, 178, 186
break with Rome, 3–4, 5, 33, 34, 186
Catholic uprising against, 209
executions ordered by, 3
King's School and, 26
makes himself Supreme Head of Church, 4
Henslowe, Philip, 119–20, 122, 125–26, 127, 137, 139, 141, 143, 148, 177, 218, 242, 283, 308
heresy, 2, 5, 16–17, 19, 57, 58–62, 93, 95, 96, 97, 99, 107, 134, 140, 173, 189, 204, 212, 241, 262, 269, 308
*Hero and Leander* (Marlowe), 31, 156, 264–66, 282

Herodotus, 275
Herrick, Robert, 163–64
Hesketh, Richard, 189–91, 192
heterodoxy, 212, 262; *see also* heresy
Hilliard, Nicholas, 6, 210, *211*
*History of the Damnable Life and Deserved Death of Doctor John Faustus, The*, 213–16, 217–19, 226, 236
*History of the World, The* (Ralegh), 223–24
Hobbes, Thomas, 236
Hog Lane, 158–69
Holbein, Hans the Younger, 6
Holinshed, Raphael, 256–61
Homer, 63
homosexuality, 73–75, 154, 258–59, 261, 265, 266
Honan, Park, 279
Hotson, Leslie, 280, 316
Howard, Henry, Earl of Surrey, 3, 51, 160
Howard, Philip, 13th Earl of Arundel, 160
Howard family, 160, 161
Huddleston, Sir Edmund, 114
Hues, Robert, 212, 223
Huguenots, 23, 96, 102, 111
humanities, 83
Hurault, André, Sieur de Maisse, 5
hypocrisy, 66–67

iambic pentameter, 134
*Introduction of the Eight Parts of Speech, An* (Lily), 29
Ipswich, England, 115
Ireland, 123, 197
Isidore of Seville, *Etymologiae*, 234
Isocrates, 48

Italian poetic models, 3
Italy, 43, 158, 197
 travel to, 41, 42
 universities in, 3

James I, King of England, 114, 222, 279
James VI, King of Scotland, 192
Jenkinson, Anthony, 305
Jesuits, 171
*Jew of Malta, The* (Marlowe), 15–16, 31, 103, 148, 156, 190, 203, 212, 216, 229, 253, 255
 antisemitism in, 183–84
 class outsider as hero in, 229–30
 as fantasy of boundless cunning, 254
 Machiavelli and, 181, 182, 184–86, 212, 312
 as message to Lord Strange, 187–88, 221
 plot of, 180–81
 religious skepticism in, 203
 success of, 180–81, 292
Jews, 9, 10, 15, 184
Johnson, John, 35
Johnson, Samuel, 116, 199
Johnson, William, 116
joint-stock companies, 154
Jones, David, 111
Jones, Hugh, 27
Jonson, Ben, 129, 155, 223
Judeo-Christian tradition, vs. Greco-Roman tradition, 38–41
Justinian, 30

Kelley, Edward, 220
Kent, England, 262
Kepler, Johannes, 200, 211
Kett, Francis, 56–57
*King Lear* (Shakespeare), 253

King's School, Canterbury, 26–27,
    30–31, 32, 35–36, 53, 70, 100,
    117, 185, 229, 300
  instruction in Greek at, 52
  instruction in Latin at, 28–31, 36,
    41, 49, 51
  schedule at, 36
  study of Greco-Roman culture at,
    38, 41, 43–52
Kuriyama, Constance, 279
Kyd, Thomas, 22, 51, 61, 142, 177,
    189, 261, 262, 269, 270, 272
  arrest of, 11–16, 17–19
  death of, 21
  heretical text and, 16–18
  implicates Marlowe, 19–21, 51, 75
  letter to Puckering, 173, 270, 272,
    296
  penmanship of, 12–13
  *The Spanish Tragedy*, 14, 15, 17, 18
  torture of, 17–19, 57

*Lamentable Tragedy, Mixed Full of
    Pleasant Mirth, Containing the
    Life of Cambyses, King of Persia,
    A*, 125
Las Casas, Bartolomé de, *A Short
    Account of the Destruction of the
    Indies*, 236
Latin language, 3, 33, 36–37, 50, 52,
    67, 71, 73, 95–96, 102, 161
  in *Doctor Faustus*, 228, 315
  instruction in, 28–31, 36, 41, 49,
    51
  in Mass, 229
law, 77, 78
Leonardo da Vinci, 6
Lewgar, Thomas, 57, 60
Liberties, the, 120–22
Lily, William, 29, 52
Linacre, Thomas, 47

Locke (Lok), Anne, 113
Lodge, Thomas, 14, 177
London, England, 113–26
  City of, 11
  conquest of, 127–40
  plague in, 15, 151, 168, 247, 262,
    263
  theater life in, 263
  unemployment in, 8
Lord Admiral's Men, 154, 177
Lord Strange's Men, 154, 176–92
Low Countries, 170, 276
loyalties, ambivalent, 110
Lucian, 43, 50, 51
Lucretius, 43, 283
Lyly, John, 47, 117–18, 119, 120

*Macbeth* (Shakespeare), 219
Machiavelli, Niccolò, 15, 186, 202,
    203–4, 224, 283, 312
  influence on Marlowe's *Jew of
    Malta*, 181, 182, 184–86, 212
  Machiavellian hypotheses, 283
  *The Prince*, 79, 181–85, 312
Machyn, Henry, 4–5
*Mad* magazine, 164
*Mankind*, 125
Manteo, 201, 202, 313
Marlowe, Anne, 24
Marlowe, Christopher, 7, 12, 14–15,
    24, 165, 180
  accused of converting Cholmeley
    to atheism, 273–74
  accused of threatening officials, 293
  arrested for attacking Corkine,
    294
  arrested for counterfeiting,
    174–75
  arrested on charges of "atheism,"
    268–69, 270
  as artistic genius, 294

"atheist lecture" delivered by, 205–7, 215–16, 262
Baines's accusations against, 272–75
biographers of, 48, 293
breaking into London theater scene, 116–26
burial of, 279
at Cambridge, 51, 53–75, 77–87, 88–112, 153, 199, 209, 227, 229, 238, 240, 243–44, 250, 262, 271
chronology of compositions difficult to determine, 291
collaborative playwriting and, 141–57, 257, 291
critics of, 136–37
death of, 18, 19, 156, 223, 277–78, 280–81, 282
desire to be known, 153–54
earns bachelor's degree, 85, 88
education of, 43–52, 53–75, 70, 77–87, 88–89, 90–92, 115, 116, 146, 148, 209, 240, 243–44
effectively declares intention to enter priesthood, 89
*English Faust Book* and, 213–16, 217–19, 226
as an enigma, 292
espionage and, 53–54, 88–112, 114, 116–17, 238–39, 243
Faustian bargain of, 226–52
"great separation" and, 22–37, 297–98
Greco-Roman tradition and, 43–52
heresy and, 61–62, 189
homosexuality and, 75
imprisonment for Bradley's murder, 168, 170
inquest into his death, 276–77, 316
at King's School, 26–37, 38, 41, 43–52, 53, 70, 100, 185, 229
Kyd implicates, 19–21
Kyd's characterization of, 22
in London, 113–26
Lord Strange and, 176–92
Lord Strange's Men and, 154, 177
Lucian's influence on, 51
master's degree studies, 85, 88–89, 90–92, 115, 116, 209, 240, 243, 243–44
in Netherlands, 170–73, 263
Percy and, 208–13, 224
personal investment in Faustus story, 238, 245–46, 315
personal readings at Cambridge, 69–70
possible portrait of, 85–87, 86
as "provocative agent," 156–57
Ralegh and, 193–207, 224
recruited for spy service, 243–44
religious skepticism and, 83, 133, 140, 141, 205–7, 215–16, 262
scholarship held by, 68, 82–83, 88, 89, 90
Shakespeare and, 143–46, 152–57
siblings, birth of, 298
social status of, 148, 178
spelling of his name, 89–90
suddenness of, 22, 23
sword fight with Bradley, 167–68
unexplained absences from Cambridge, 90–91
Walsingham and, 100–106
Watson and, 158–69
youth of and family of, 23–26
*see also* Marlowe, Christopher, works of

Marlowe, Christopher, works of
  collaboration on *Henry VI*,
    143–46, 257
  *Doctor Faustus*, 51, 68, 82–83, 85,
    220–21, 224, 226–52, 227,
    253–55, 259, 292, 302, 315
  *Edward II*, 31, 85, 86, 156, 178,
    256–61, 265–66
  *Hero and Leander*, 31, 156,
    264–66, 282
  *The Jew of Malta*, 15–16, 31, 103,
    148, 156, 180–81, 183–88,
    190, 203, 212, 216, 221–22,
    229–30, 253, 254, 255, 292
  *The Massacre at Paris*, 15–16,
    81–82, 264, 291
  "The Passionate Shepherd to His
    Love," 162–63, 164, 255–56
  *Tamburlaine the Great*, 84–85, 126,
    127–37, 138, 139–40, 141–44,
    142, 148, 155–56, 177–78,
    180, 194–96, 203, 212, 229–
    30, 234, 241, 253–55, 291
  *Tamburlaine the Great, Part 2*,
    131–34, 156, 291
  *The Tragedy of Dido, Queen of Car-
    thage*, 31, 45, 49–50, 115–16,
    118, 291
  translation of Ovid, 70, 71–72
Marlowe, Dorothy, 24
Marlowe, Jane, 24
Marlowe, John, 23, 24–25, 26, 27,
    31–32, 298–99
Marlowe, Katherine Arthur, 24, 26,
    31, 32
Marlowe, Margaret, 24
Marlowe, Mary, 25
Marlowe, Thomas, 25
Marlowe family, 23–26, 30, 31–32,
    298; *see also specific family members*
Marprelate, Martin, 10

Marshalsea prison, 104, 105
Mary, Queen of Scots, 4, 42, 92,
    95, 102, 160, 165, 179, 186–87,
    209, 307
  cipher used to communicate with
    Babington, *109*
  consents to assassination plot, 108
  execution of, 20
  imprisonment of, 103, 106–12
Mary I, Queen of England and Scot-
  land (Mary Tudor), 51, 114, 146
Mass, 229
*Massacre at Paris, The* (Marlowe),
    15–16, 81–82, 264, 291
Maunder, Henry, 268, 269, 275
*Mayflower* (ship), 60
Menippus, 50–51
*Merchant of Venice, The* (Shake-
  speare), 150, 156, 283
Merchant Taylor's School, 13, 14
Meres, Francis, 261
*Metamorphoses* (Ovid), 41, 47, 48,
    70–71
Michelangelo, 6
monasteries, 77
monastic libraries, 53–54
Montaigne, Michel de, 158, 164
moralists, 13, 34–36, 75, 121, 122,
    125, 182, 229, 247; *see also*
    Puritans
More, Thomas, 3, 43, 48–49, 56
Morgan, Thomas, 107–8
Morris dances, 34, 35, 299
Moses, Miles, 65
Mudd, Thomas, 65
Musaeus Grammaticus, 264

Nashe, Thomas, 14, 31, 45, 76, 78,
    80, 115–16, 119, 123–24, 143,
    150, 151, 153
Native Americans, 201–4

necromancy, 192, 214, 219, 226, 227–28, 234
Netherlands, 10–11, 100, 123, 170–72, 171, 175, 243–44, 263, 276
*New Oxford Shakespeare, The: Authorship Companion* 143
New Testament, 47, 48, 231, 241
New World, 7, 236
Newfoundland, 212
Newgate prison, 9, 174
Nicholl, Charles, 280, 316
Nicolò de' Tudeschi (Panormitanus), 48
Nietzsche, Friedrich, 22, 297–98
Norfolk, England, 57
Norgate, Robert, 62, 63, 90
Norton Folgate neighborhood, 113–15, 159–60, 165, 167
Norwich, England, 115
Norwich Castle, 57
"Nymph's Reply, The" (Ralegh), 193–94, 224

"Old Alleynians," 139
*On Waters and Fountains* (Watson), 210
Ortelius, Abraham, 83, 84, 115, 305
Ospringe, England, 24
*Othello* (Shakespeare), 253
otherness, obsession with, 23
Overbury, Thomas, 219
Ovid, 30, 43, 44
  *Amores*, 70, 71–72, 251
  exile of, 72
  *Metamorphoses*, 41, 47, 48, 70–71
  translation of, 70–71
Ovington, Thomas, 27
Oxford University, 3, 36, 54, 55, 89, 93, 117, 119, 158, 175
  attendance as class distinction, 76
  Bruno at, 60–61
  course of study at, 67–68
  influx of wealthy to, 81
  Merton College, 64
  peculiarity of, 57–58

pagan culture and religion, 38–52, 204
Paris massacre, 11, 15
Parker, Dorothy, 164
Parker, John, 68–69
Parker, Matthew, 53–54, 68, 89
Parker scholarship, 53–54, 68–69, 89, 101, 112
Parliament, 10
  Buggery Act, 73–74, 75
Parma, Prince of, 243–44
Pashley, Christopher, 57, 60, 82, 83
pastoral poetry, 161–65
patronage, competition for, 150–51, 152, 154–55
Paul, Saint, epistles of, 42, 43, 231
Peele, George, 177
Penry, John, 58, 59–60
Percy, Henry, 9th Earl of Northumberland, 175, 193, 208–13, 211, 216–18, 220, 251, 276
  charged with complicity in Gunpowder Plot, 222
  as model for Faustus, 221–22, 226
  in Tower of London for sixteen years, 222–24, 225
Percy, Thomas, 209, 222
Persons, Robert, 95, 204, 205
Petrarch, 42, 48, 167, 283
Philip II, King of Spain, 97, 98, 165, 166, 187
*Philip of Spain, The* (ship), 165
philosophy, 40
Pickering, Marmaduke, 96
Pilgrimage of Grace, 186, 209

Pius V, Pope, 94, 103
Pizarro, Francisco, 198
plague, 6, 8–9, 15, 25, 65, 151, 168, 247, 262, 263
Plato, 40
Plautus, 30, 41
playhouses, 120–23, 124, 125, 148, 151, 229, 247, 308
   design of, 124–25
   Elizabeth I's interest in protecting, 122–23
   moralists' attacks on, 13
   the plague and, 6, 9, 262
   see also specific theaters
playwrights, source of income, 148–49
playwriting, collaborative, 141–57
Poley, Robert "Robin," 104–9, 110, 111, 165, 254, 262, 276–77, 278, 280, 316
political radicalism, 56
Poole, John, 170, 171, 174, 312
*Portrait of a Young Gentleman (said to be Christopher Marlowe)*, 85–87, 86
Portugal, 123
Potter, William, 82–83, 83
*Prince, The* (Machiavelli), 79, 181–85, 312
Privy Council, 11–12, 15, 19, 91–93, 100, 110, 143, 165–66, 171, 243, 262, 269–70, 270, 275, 279
Proctor, John, *The Fall of the Late Arrian*, 18, 51, 57
Protestant radicalism, 59, 60, 61; see also specific sects
Protestant Reformation, 2, 3, 9–10, 28–29, 53–54, 58
Protestantism, 3–5, 8, 17, 28–29, 34, 41–42, 61, 171, 186–87, 189–90

Protestants, 9–10, 10–11, 23, 26, 102, 111, 161, 182, 306; see also specific sects
public spectacles, 35; see also executions; theatrical entertainment
publishers, commercial, 118
Puckering, Sir John, 19, 20–21, 173, 270, 272, 296
Punter, 66
Puritans, 9, 10, 34, 58, 58–60, 66, 67, 146, 165, 229

Queen's Men, 122, 154
Quintilian, 69

Rainolds, John, 66–67
Ralegh, Sir Walter, 119, 150, 193–207, 195, 208, 210, 212, 220, 224, 251, 269, 273, 276, 280, 313
   circle of, 194, 235, 236
   in Guiana, 225
   hatred of Catholicism, 216
   *The History of the World*, 223–24
   as model for Faustus, 216, 217–18, 221–22, 226
   "The Nymph's Reply," 193, 194, 224
   at Rose, 194–95
   spectacular rise of, 197–207
   in Tower of London, 222–24, 225
Ramée, Pierre de la, 78; see also Ramus, Peter
Ramus, Peter, 78, 81–82
*Rape of Lucrece, The* (Shakespeare), 151
Raphael, 6
reformers, 34–36
religious conflicts, 3–5, 9–10, 41–42; see also specific conflicts

religious dogma, 17, 18, 57, 58–61, 273
religious regimes, changing, 17; *see also specific regimes*
religious skepticism, 133–34, 134, 140, 141, 186, 204
revenge plays, 14, 15
Rheims, France, 91, 92, 93, 95, 97–100, 101, 103, 107, 114, 159, 172, 173, 271
*Richard II* (Shakespeare), 156, 219
Richard III, King of England, 178
*Richard III* (Shakespeare), 178, 179–80
Riggs, David, 67, 280–81
Roanoke Island, 201, 202
Robinson, Richard, 150–51
Rogers, Thomas, 111
Roman Catholic Church, 160
Roman Catholicism, 3, 5, 8, 17, 41–42, 58–62, 92, 94, 159, 160, 171, 244
  Canterbury and, 33–34
  Index of Prohibited Books, 181
  in Low Countries, 170
  Stanley family and, 186–87, 189–90
Roman Catholics, 9–10, 160, 161, 165, 175, 209, 210–11, 306–7
  Elizabeth I and, 94–95
  recruited by Walsingham, 104–6
Roman Inquisition, 60, 61, 223
Rome, 44, 244
*Romeo and Juliet* (Shakespeare), 145
Rose Theater, 125–26, 138, 139, 177, 178, 180, 194–95, 242, 292
Rudolf II, Holy Roman Emperor, 220

Sadoleto, Jacopo, 47
St. Augustine's Abbey, Canterbury, 33
St. Bartholomew's Day Massacre, 10, 96, 264
St. Bene't's Church, 58

St. Botolph, Bishopsgate, 114
St. George's Church, 27
St. George's Parish, 25
St. Mary Spital, 113
Samarkand, 115
Savage, John, 107, 109
Scadbury, 263, 264, 269, 275, 276, 279
scholarship system, 77
Scholasticism, 62, 98
*Scholemaster, The* (Ascham), 41–42, 48
"school of atheism," 206
Scotland, 100
  rebellion in, 103
Seething Lane, 96–98, 100–106, 107, 165, 171–72, 262, 263
Seneca, 191
Separatists, 60
*Sermons* (Bede), 48
Shakespeare, William, 36–37, 75, 135, 136, 137, 142, 226, 255, 279, 282–83
  acquires status of gentleman, 148
  collaborative playwriting and, 143–44, 257
  dedications and, 151
  financial success of, 147–48, 155
  identification with his own characters, 253–54
  imitation and parody of Marlowe, 155–57
  income of, 147–48
  Lord Strange and, 177, 178, 179, 180, 187
  Marlowe and, 143–46, 152–57, 283, 284
  multiple roles of, 147–48
  as shareholder in playing company and part-owner of playhouse, 147–48
  *see also* Shakespeare, William, works of

Shakespeare, William, works of
  As You Like It, 265, 283, 284–85
  Cymbeline, 219
  Hamlet, 13, 155, 166, 253, 260, 296
  Henry IV, 156
  Henry VI trilogy, 143–46, 151, 179, 256
  King Lear, 253
  Macbeth, 219
  The Merchant of Venice, 150, 156, 283
  Othello, 253
  The Rape of Lucrece, 151
  Richard II, 156, 219
  Richard III, 178, 179–80
  Romeo and Juliet, 145
  sonnets of, 152–53
  Titus Andronicus, 155–56, 283
  Troilus and Cressida, 145
  Twelfth Night, 58
  Venus and Adonis, 151, 156, 282
  The Winter's Tale, 219
Shaw, Michael, 27
Shoemakers' Company, 24
Shoreditch, 6, 221, 262
Short Account of the Destruction of the Indies, A (Las Casas), 236
Sidney, Mary, Countess of Pembroke, 168–69
Sidney, Robert, 170, 174–75, 209, 217
Sidney, Sir Philip, 151, 170
Skeres, Nicholas, 263, 276–77, 278, 280
Smerwick, Ireland, 197
  massacre in, 198
Smithfield, 4
social ambition, 76–87
  dress as marker of, 85, 302
  stymied, 81–83

social hierarchy, 149
sodomy, 261, 279
Solinus, 47
sonnet, the, 3
Sophocles, 48
Southwark, 104
Spain, 93, 114, 123, 165, 197, 244
Spanish Armada, 8, 165, 188, 243–44
Spanish army, 10, 170
Spanish Inquisition, 10
Spanish Tragedy, The (Kyd), 14, 15, 17, 18
Speculum maius (Vincent of Beauvais), 234
Spencers of Althorp, 81
Spenser, Edmund, 78–79, 80–81, 305
Stanley, Ferdinando, Lord Strange, 19, 175, 176–92, 193, 221
Stanley, Sir William, 171, 188
Stanley, Thomas, 178, 186–87
Stanley family, 176–92
Strange, Lord, see Stanley, Ferdinando, Lord Strange
Stratford-upon-Avon, England, 143, 145, 148, 155, 176–77, 178
succession, issue of, 8, 190–91
Sweeting, William, 27
Syme, Holger Schott, 309

Tamburlaine the Great (Marlowe), 84–85, 126, *138*, *142*, 155–56, 178, 180, 194–95, 196, 234, 241, 253, 255, 291, 309
  class outsider as hero in, 229–30
  fantasy of boundless power in, 254
  religious skepticism in, 133, 140, 141, 203, 212
  success of, 127–37, 139–40, 141–44, 148, 177, 308

*Tamburlaine the Great, Part 2* (Marlowe), 131–34, 156, 291
Tannenbaum, Samuel, 280
Tasso, Torquato, 6
Terence, 30, 41, 148, 185
theater companies, 14, 122, 124–25, 147, 154, 308; *see also specific companies*
theater of cruelty, 23
theaters, *see* playhouses
Theatre, The 6, 113, 120
*Theatre of God's Judgments, The* (Beard), 280–81
theatrical entertainment, 149
  at Cambridge University, 64–65, 300
  condemnation of, 13, 73, 121, 122–23, 125, 247
  subsidized by authorities, 65–66, 73
  *see also* playhouses
theology, 77
Theophilus of Antioch, 48
Thexton, Robert, 57, 60, 65, 83, 302
Thirty-Nine Articles, 58, 233
Thomas à Becket, St., 23
  shrine of, 34
Timur the Lame (Tamburlaine), 115–16
*Titus Andronicus* (Shakespeare), 155–56, 283
Topcliffe, Richard, 103
Torporley, Nathaniel, 212, 223
torture, 17, 104, 114, 172, 269, 272
*Tottel's Miscellany*, 51
Tower of London, 160, 209, 222–24, 225
*Tragedy of Dido, Queen of Carthage, The* (Marlowe and Nash), 31, 45, 49–50, 115–16, 118, 291
translation, 3
  of Ovid, 70–71, 72
  task of double, 46
  *see also specific works*
*Troilus and Cressida* (Shakespeare), 145
truth, vs. fiction, 42, 43
Tudor dynasty, 175, 178, 190; *see also specific monarchs*
Tusser, Thomas, 6
12th Earl of Arundel, *see* Henry Fitzalan, 12th Earl of Arundel
*Twelfth Night* (Shakespeare), 58
Tyburn, gallows at, 9, 59–60, 262

Udall, Nicholas, 304
Unitarianism, 17
universities
  attendance as class distinction, 76, 304
  cabals at, 96
  course of study at, 62–63, 67–68, 302
  curriculum of, 77
  divisions in, 93
  dress codes at, 55–56, 84–85, 302
  English vs. Italian, 3
  homosexuality at, 73–75
  monastic origins of, 56
  organization of, 55
  peculiarity of, 57–58
  secret Catholicism at, 93–94
  separation enabled by, 54–55
  shift from theology-based to classics-based curriculum, 77
  social distinctions at, 55–56, 76–87
  surveillance of students at, 97–98
  theater and acting at, 300
  *see also* Cambridge University; Oxford University

university graduates
  alienation of, 81–83
  ordained as priests, 83

Valla, Lorenzo, 43
Vatican, 244
Vaughan, Jane, 114
Vaughan, Stephen, 113–14
Venice, 43
*Venus and Adonis* (Shakespeare), 151, 156, 282
Vincent of Beauvais, *Speculum maius*, 234
violence, fascination with, 23
Virgil, 1, 21, 41, 44
  *Aeneid*, 44–45, 49
Virginia, 201, 202, 203, 235
Vlissingen, Netherlands, 170

Walsham, Alexandra, 92
Walsingham, Audrey, 279, 280
Walsingham, Frances, 107
Walsingham, Sir Francis, 96–97, 97, 98, 100–106, 106–12, 110, 159, 165, 171–72, 175, 184, 190, 243, 262, 279, 307
Walsingham, Thomas, 159, 262–63, 264, 268, 280, 282
Walton, Izaak, 194
Wanchese, 201, 202, 313
Warner, Walter, 212

Wars of Religion, 10
Wars of the Roses, 141, 177, 256
Watson, Thomas, 158–69, 210, 263, 278, 311
  *The Abduction of Helen*, 210
  *Amyntae Gaudia*, 168–69
  *Amyntas*, 161, 164
  *Antigone* translation, 160
  death of, 168–69
  *The Hekatompathia, or, Passionate Century of Love*, 161
  imprisonment for Bradley's murder, 168
  sword fight with Bradley, 167–68
  *On Waters and Fountains*, 210
White, Thomas, 247
Whitehall, royal residence of, 1
Whitgift, John, Archbishop of Canterbury, 72
Wilde, Oscar, 261
*Winter's Tale, The* (Shakespeare), 219
witchcraft, 35, 192, 220; *see also* necromancy
Woodall, Master, 4
Wriothesley, Henry, Earl of Southampton, 145, 151, 152
Wyatt, Thomas, 3, 51, 191–92

Yeomans, Joan, 105
Yeomans, Mr., 105
Young, Justice, 111